Lost Leaves

Lost Leaves

Women Writers of Meiji Japan

Rebecca L. Copeland

University of Hawai'i Press
Honolulu

*Publication of this book has been assisted by
a grant from the Japan Foundation.*

00 01 02 03 04 05   5 4 3 2 1

Library of Congress Cataloging-in-Publication Data
Copeland, Rebecca L., 1956–
Lost leaves : women writers of Meiji Japan /
Rebecca L. Copeland
p. cm.
Includes bibliographical references and index.
ISBN 0–8248–2229–3 (cloth : alk. paper)
— ISBN 0–8248–2291–9 (pbk. : alk. paper)
1. Japanese literature—Meiji period,
1868–1912—History and criticism.
2. Japanese literature—Woman authors
—History and criticism.
3. Women authors, Japanese—Meiji period,
1868–1912. I. Title.
PL726.6.C64   2000
895.6'099287'09034—dc21   99–058864

Designed by Janette Thompson (Jansom)
Printed by The Maple-Vail Book Manufacturing Group

For Rick

Contents

Illustrations

Preface

I suppose the seed for this study was planted while I was in graduate school, although I was not aware of it then. At the time I was completing my dissertation on the writer Uno Chiyo (1897–1996), a woman whose career spanned the Taishō–Heisei reign years. When attempting to chart the genealogy of literary women who had preceded her, I blissfully accepted the standard interpretation: the Heian period (794–1185), with its great flowering of female talent, was followed by two hundred years of utter silence—broken briefly by Higuchi Ichiyō in the Meiji era but not finally shattered until the 1920s when women writers began to emerge in overwhelming numbers. I counted Uno Chiyo in this force—a veritable army of women writers that included Nogami Yaeko, Miyamoto Yuriko, Hirabayashi Taiko, Hayashi Fumiko, and many others less renowned.

Because Higuchi Ichiyō was presented in the standard literary histories not only as a "single leaf" in a forest of male writers, but as such a tragically bright and vulnerable talent, it was easy to believe that she had been an anomalous burst of song in a history of silence. I assumed, therefore, that if there had been a catalyst for this great resurgence of writing by women in the 1920s, it would be located in the journal *Seitō* (1911–1916). Uno had referred to it in several of her autobiographical essays, commenting on the way Hiratsuka Raichō's inaugural essay had roused her spirit. Moreover, many of the women who emerged as writers in the 1920s had been contributors to its pages. Having successfully defended and published my dissertation on Uno Chiyo, I determined that my next project would be to explore the source of this great revival of female writers.

My preliminary study of *Seitō* produced two offspring. First it culminated in an entry on Hiratsuka Raichō, the driving force behind the journal, in *Japanese Women Writers: A Bio-Critical Sourcebook*, edited by Chieko Mulhern; but perhaps more important, it led me to *Jogaku zasshi*. All the while that I was reading studies of *Seitō*, I had the nagging suspicion that the journal had not simply sprung intact from the black hole of a two-hundred-year silence. There must have been a catalyst to this catalyst. And the more I read the more I found myself being led to *Jogaku zasshi*, to Meiji Women's School, and to Iwamoto Yoshiharu.

I conducted my research on *Seitō* over two summers spent on the campus of International Christian University in Tokyo, where I had access to the university library. While browsing through the stacks, I discovered to my delight that the library contained a complete set of *Jogaku zasshi*. The journal issues, tucked neatly in faded lavender boxes, were clearly not often exhumed. I felt I had stumbled upon an unexplored treasure. Each time I opened one of those dusty boxes and pulled out the issues for that year—bound together with soft white string—I had a new and wonderful encounter with a Meiji woman writer. Here in the very age when Higuchi Ichiyō, aided by the sympathy and encouragement of generous Meiji men, had lit her thin and flickering candle, I found a veritable chandelier of female authorship. The more I explored, the more I came to find a wealth of women writers in the Meiji period. (And had I dug deeper I might have found that the resounding "darkness" of the Tokugawa had not been that dark after all.) Each woman was accompanied by an intriguing story of her own. Indeed, just being a woman writer in the Meiji period necessitated a story. My challenge, then, was not to find enough to write about but to limit myself to a focus manageable in a single study. To that end I elected to look at three women. And I selected women who were loosely tied to one another through their affiliation with *Jogaku zasshi* and Meiji Women's School: Miyake Kaho, Wakamatsu Shizuko, and Shimizu Shikin. This study is just a beginning.

Acknowledgments

I am indebted to numerous people, organizations, and grants. Washington University, my present employer, supplied me with a Grimm Traveling Fellowship for research in East Asia. This grant, buttressed by an AAS–NEAC short-term travel grant, permitted me to begin my original inquiry into *Seitō*, an inquiry that led me to *Jogaku zasshi* and a host of Meiji women writers. The Midwest Japan Seminar generously invited me to speak to its members in March 1993, providing me with an opportunity to present my fledgling work on women and journalism in Meiji–Taishō Japan. The encouragement I received at that forum persuaded me to continue my research. My determination was further bolstered by Eiji Sekine of Purdue University, who invited me to contribute a paper to the volume of *Review of Japanese Culture and Society* that he was editing for Josai University. When I told Eiji that I wanted to write on Shimizu Shikin but still had precious little material, he contacted Professor Sachie Kitada, presently of Josai University, and she sent me copies of what seemed to be every article ever published on Shimizu Shikin. There were surprisingly more than a few and, moreover, from a diversity of journals. Inspired by these many kindnesses, I published my first article on a Meiji woman writer: "Shimizu Shikin's 'The Broken Ring': A Narrative of Female Awakening." Sections of this article are reprinted with revisions in Chapter Four.

Kokugakuin University in Tokyo was next to lend assistance when it offered me a guest researcher position in the spring of 1995. The research that I was able to conduct was invaluable, and the faculty and staff members I met during my stay at the university were accommodating and cordial. In this capacity I am especially grateful to Mr. Nobukatsu Shimoyama of the International Exchange Program. My research there contributed to a paper that I read at the 1995 Association for Asian Studies in Washington, D.C., "Meiji Journals and the Construction of the 'Woman Writer.'" Eventually I was to publish a revised and expanded version of this paper in the *Harvard Journal of Asiatic Studies,* a privilege for which I am indebted to Professor Howard Hibbett, editor of the journal, and to the anonymous readers of my manuscript. Portions of the Introduction and the Conclusion to this present study are taken from that article; permission to reprint this material is gratefully acknowledged.

Ultimately it was a six-month research grant from the Japan Foundation in 1997 that provided me with the means to finalize my research and begin transforming all the materials into readable drafts. During this period I once again benefited from the kindness of Kokugakuin University, where it was my great pleasure to work once again with Professor Yasuyuki Ogikubo. Despite his hectic schedule, Professor Ogikubo met with me weekly to read through the obscure and difficult Meiji-era texts that I would bring to him. Carefully and patiently he would explain each detail of the texts, giving me mini–history lessons along the way, searching for books with illustrations of the coiffures or garments—now long forgotten—that appeared in the stories we read. It goes without saying that this study would not have been possible without him. I am also grateful to Ms. Kazuko Nakayama of Ferris Women's College, who helped me sort my way through the library's holdings on Wakamatsu Shizuko.

This book has been a long time in the making. Along the way I have been buttressed and guided by sympathetic friends, patient family members, and generous colleagues—more than I can acknowledge here. My colleagues at Washington University have been inexpressibly helpful. Sally Hastings of Purdue University has been ever generous with her time and wisdom. The two anonymous reviewers provided insightful suggestions for improvements. Edward Seidensticker and Donald Keene have been constant sources of inspiration and support. Sharon Yamamoto, my editor at University of Hawai'i Press, has been incredibly patient and reassuring. My sister Judy not only read my drafts but carefully edited my *HJAS* article (and other less successful journal submissions). My parents were a trusted refuge. My husband, Rick Ruby, has provided that ever important space for play—an invaluable haven away from the rigors of academe. And he preserves this space for me while I'm off on my research jaunts in Tokyo, taking special care of Naya, Taru, and Lance.

Introduction

Recovering Lost Leaves

This emergence of a woman author is symbolic of the period but we will not
deal with this aspect.

—Kōsaka Masaaki, *Japanese Thought in
the Meiji Era,* 1958

Re-vision—the act of looking back, of seeing with fresh eyes, of entering an
old text from a new critical direction—is for women more than a chapter in
cultural history: it is an act of survival. Until we can understand the assumptions in which we are drenched we cannot know ourselves.

—Adrienne Rich, "When We Dead Awaken:
Writing as Re-Vision," 1979

Mention women writers of the Meiji period (1868–1912), and most enthusi-
asts of Japanese literature immediately call to mind Higuchi Ichiyō
(1872–1896), the promising young author who died at the age of twenty-
four.[1] Although most studies seek to establish alliances between Ichiyō and
her Heian-era (794–1185) foremothers, Murasaki Shikibu and Sei
Shōnagon,[2] few acknowledge her association with her female contemporaries. Rather, Ichiyō is presented, much as her pen name implies, as a "single leaf" among male authors.[3] Literary historians, both inside and outside
Japan, dutifully describe her exchanges with her male counterparts, her association with the male literary coterie known as the Bungakukai (Literary
World), and the admiration male critics expressed for her talent, which they
believed transcended gender. "Conceal the author's name," says one contemporary of Ichiyō's work, "and [a reader] would probably never guess it was
written by a woman."[4] In his biographical study of the author, Robert Danly

1

quotes another critic: "She had as much talent as any man."[5] Consequently, Danly situates Ichiyō among her male peers to the near exclusion of her female contemporaries. But to suggest that Ichiyō be considered "as talented as any man" implies that being as talented as any woman is not quite talented enough. This kind of criticism renders women's work not only secondary but peripheral. The only way a woman can earn recognition as a significant writer, therefore, is to transcend her sex. Higuchi Ichiyō must be transformed into an honorary man before she can be accepted for serious study.

But there were other women writing during Ichiyō's lifetime—more than most scholars of Japanese literature today realize. By the time Ichiyō died in 1896, more than twenty women were writing for publication in major periodicals and over one hundred works by female authors had been published. The better known among this group were Nakajima Shōen (1863–1901), Miyake Kaho (1868–1944), Koganei Kimiko (1871–1956), Wakamatsu Shizuko (1864–1896), Shimizu Shikin (or Shigin, 1868–1933), Tazawa Inafune (or Inabune, 1874–1896), and Kitada Usurai (1876–1900). Why have these women been so summarily dismissed from literary histories?[6]

Miyake Kaho is commonly described as the first woman writer in the modern era.[7] Indeed, she is presented as "the female Tsubouchi Shōyō." While Shōyō is not regarded as an important writer today, he is credited for his significant contributions to the literary field through his incisive essay on fiction, *Shōsetsu shinzui* (The Essence of the Novel, 1885). Why has his female counterpart been ignored? If Kaho is mentioned at all, she and her female contemporaries are generally described as negative foils by which to measure Ichiyō's superior accomplishments. Kaho is dismissed as an imitator and hardly a serious writer.[8] Wakamatsu Shizuko is brushed aside as a mere translator, an imitator of another sort. And Shimizu Shikin has been discredited as frivolous because she allowed marriage to silence her.

In summarily removing all female competition from their presentations of Ichiyō, conventional literary histories fail to consider her contemporary reputation. Like Kaho, Shizuko, and Shikin she was categorized as a woman writer, or *keishū sakka*,[9] and she was evaluated—as were they—according to gender-coded criteria. To ignore the cultural milieu within which Ichiyō worked desexualizes her writing in a way that is anachronistic, neutralizes her accomplishments, and accords to her a singularity that is unwarranted. Moreover, removing Ichiyō from the context of her female peers consigns an entire generation of writers—indeed, the first generation of modern Japanese women writers—to obscurity.

In this study I restore this lost generation of women writers by recovering the female literary tradition that Ichiyō's canonization has erased. My intent is not to minimize Ichiyō's accomplishments. Rather, I seek to recover her context by exploring the attitudes toward women and women's writing that prevailed in Meiji Japan. How was it that women came to write in the Meiji period? What connection did their newfound literary activity have with that of the past? How did they negotiate their way through a literary environment that was now so decidedly male? An examination of the way women writers were received and presented at the end of the nineteenth century will contribute to our understanding of the way women are received and presented at the end of the twentieth century. Furthermore, a discussion of the kind of gender-inflected expectation and prejudice that women confronted in the Meiji period is certain to deepen our understanding of their accomplishments.

Considerable strides have already been made in defining Japanese women's writing as a discrete field of inquiry. Translators and biographers have turned their attention to women writers with greater frequency.[10] Scholars of Japanese literature are now calling for a more analytical conceptualization of Japanese women's writing. In keeping with this call, more textual and archival groundwork is required. My study, therefore, positions Miyake Kaho, Wakamatsu Shizuko, and Shimizu Shikin as "literary predecessors." And in analyzing the conditions under which they worked, lived, and wrote, we can establish historical precedents for their successors. This project, therefore, is a step in the direction of the larger enterprise of defining a modern female literary tradition.

Whenever a nation undergoes a shift in traditional paradigms, a stratum of people previously submerged rises to the surface—where they find themselves confronted with possibilities and opportunities heretofore unimagined. In the Meiji period, with its immense changes in culture, society, and politics, members of society who had once stood on the periphery of power scrambled to make their way to the top. Certain members of the underclass were able to climb upward. Young men from rural regions found positions within the central government. And women, discovering a chink in the wall that had shielded them from view, were able to step out into the public light. Chapter One offers a brief overview of the Meiji period and the changes it precipitated that are pertinent to this discussion. Among the issues I consider are education for women, employment for women, and the way the "Woman Question" was used by male intellectuals of the day as a metaphor for Japan as a nation. Throughout I will focus on *Jogaku zasshi* (Woman's Education Magazine), the first mass-circulated journal to address women and women's concerns.

Iwamoto Yoshiharu (1863–1942), one of the founders of this journal, suggested in an early essay that writing was an appropriate employment for women because they could pursue it between the bedroom and the kitchen. In Chapter One I discuss essays by Iwamoto in which he endeavors to define the woman writer's unique role in society and thus elucidates many of the contradictory expectations that attended the female author of the Meiji period. Ironically, while Iwamoto was trying to promote women's writing he was at the same time institutionalizing a program for women's texts which subordinated them to those by men and to male expectations of female authorship. Within this program women writers were beset by a barrage of conflicting assumptions. Held to rigid moral standards that precluded a wide range of expression, their works were criticized nonetheless as unrealistic and unimaginative. Encouraged to explore and refine their "female essence," they were reprimanded when their expression of that essence ran counter to received notions of femininity. Pushed and pulled at every turn, the Meiji woman writer had to devise various strategies if she meant her voice to be heard. Chapter One discusses the ironies implicit in a situation wherein male mentors are in charge of defining the "female voice."

One of the first women writers to brave this literary environment was Miyake Kaho—Iwamoto Yoshiharu's student and a frequent contributor to his journal. When she wrote *Warbler in the Grove (Yabu no uguisu)* in 1888, she did not model herself after the many illustrious female authors of earlier centuries. Rather, she chose models from among her male contemporaries, notably Tsubouchi Shōyō. *Warbler in the Grove* is said to be the female version of Shōyō's *Character of Modern-Day Students (Tōsei shosei katagi)*. Her indebtedness to Shōyō was deepened by the fact that he helped publish her work—editing her draft and contributing a preface.

Many of the first attempts at prose fiction by women in the Meiji period are said to be little more than imitations of men's writing. Indeed, women are often identified according to the man they most resemble. Kaho was "the female Shōyō"; Kitada Usurai, "the female Ozaki Kōyō"; and Tazawa Inafune, "the female Yamada Bimyō." This kind of criticism situates the woman's work as secondary to the male model and raises two interesting points concerning the evaluation of women's writing. First, when women began to reemerge as writers in the modern period after "centuries of silence," there was already a concept of what was good and proper for writing women. This concept distinguished the critical evaluation of their works from that of their male counterparts. And second, this concept of women's writing was directly related to characteristics that had distinguished writing by women in earlier centuries. But whereas the women writers of the tenth and eleventh centuries were acknowledged as superior writers, they were also confined to a tradition that made them inaccessible or inappropriate to a modern literature. Women's writing of the earlier era was limited by its elegance. It was too "effeminate"— too interested in its own subjectivity to engage the broad concerns of a modern society. Meiji women writers who wrote "like women," therefore, removed themselves from any engagement with issues of modernity. They faced a dilemma. If they attempted to move beyond the parameters of women's writing, they were rebuked for imitating men. If they conformed to those parameters, they were ignored for being feminine and thereby insignificant.

Chapter Two continues my discussion of what defined "women's writing" by focusing on Miyake Kaho and her debut piece, *Warbler in the Grove.* If Kaho is ignored today as a trivial writer, it is because she corresponded too closely to Meiji expectations of a woman writer. What was a woman writer to do? Many persisted in their "imitation." Others tried to find a language that answered demands for the feminine while engaging contemporary issues. For some of these writers, translation was the solution. Translations of Western works mark an important transition in early Meiji literature. Translations provided Japanese writers—both male and female—a conduit between seemingly moribund Japanese traditions and the prized Western novel. For women writers, translation offered a way to circumvent the demands of "feminine" writing. Although women writers were expected to limit their expression to the elegant and the private, female translators were apparently under no such obligation.

Wakamatsu Shizuko, the subject of Chapter Three, was the most prominent female translator of the Meiji period. Shizuko struggled to create a language suitable for her translations. Traditional Japanese, to which most women writers confined themselves, was too archaic, and the colloquial style their male contemporaries advocated was too prosaic and at times vulgar. Shizuko invented her own modern Japanese. Although her contribution is now overlooked, she had a direct impact on the development of a modern written language for Japanese prose fiction. Moreover, the works she translated—most of them serialized in *Jogaku zasshi*—influenced the writers of her day. Her translations of Adelaide Anne Procter's poetry, for example, offered a direct-address, first-person narrative that led her contemporaries to similar narrative experiments. Her rendition of Tennyson's *Enoch Arden* and similar poems provided early examples of romantic love—a concept that was to have a profound impact on the way Meiji writers came to regard relations between the sexes. Additionally, her translation of Frances Burnett's *Little Lord Fauntleroy* (1890–1892) introduced readers to the possibility of a child narrator and to the importance of literature for children. Many critics believe this work influenced Higuchi Ichiyō to write her masterpiece, "Growing Up" (Takekurabe, 1896). In Chapter Three I examine Shizuko's translation of *Little Lord Fauntleroy*, compare the Japanese rendition to the English original, and analyze the reception both met in their respective environments.

Of the three women writers I discuss in this study, Shimizu Shikin is the most interesting and the most tragic. She made her debut in the pages of

Jogaku zasshi with a short story, "The Broken Ring" (Koware yubiwa, 1891). A bold work, written in colloquial language, "The Broken Ring" argues for a woman's right to happiness. Shikin's first-person narrator is an outspoken feminist aware of the inequities around her and determined not to play the role of silent victim. Although this work received favorable reviews from prominent critics of the day, Shikin failed to continue writing in this vein. In successive works she returned to the classical idiom and to age-old plots delineating female self-sacrifice. Are these later works a complete denial of the vision she presented in her debut piece? Or, in reverting to the safety of "feminine discourse," is she subtly suggesting the importance of that vision? In Chapter Four I read her later works against the promise of "The Broken Ring" and suggest the difficulties a woman faced when writing contrary to what was deemed appropriate to her sex. Shikin's last work, "Imin gakuen" (A School for Émigrés, 1899), concerns a woman of outcast (*eta*) status. Many have suggested that this work influenced Shimizaki Tōson's *Broken Commandment* (*Hakai*, 1906). While considering this influence, I read Shikin's work allegorically, much as Tōson's has been read. What were the implications for a woman writer who aligned herself with an outcast?

Any "re-visioning" of Meiji literary history for women must necessarily consider Higuchi Ichiyō. She, after all, is the measure against which we must evaluate her contemporaries. In conclusion, then, I situate these early women writers vis-à-vis Higuchi Ichiyō to explore the ramifications of Ichiyō's canonization at the expense of their erasure. And in summarizing the critical assumptions that Meiji women writers encountered, I describe the way these assumptions have influenced (and in some cases still influence) the ensuing female literary tradition.

Chapter One

Educating the Modern Murasaki
Jogaku Zasshi *and the Woman Writer*

Where is the Modern Murasaki hiding? Where the Meiji Shōnagon? Eagerly
I await your appearance. Nay, even more than I, our very society longs for
your arrival.

—Shimizu Shikin, 1890

The men of new Japan, to whom the opinions and customs of the western
world are becoming daily more familiar, while they shrink aghast, in many
cases, at the thought that their women may ever become like the forward,
self-assertive, half-masculine women of the West, show a growing tendency
to dissatisfaction with the smallness and narrowness of the lives of their
wives and daughters—a growing belief that better-educated women would
make better homes, and that the ideal home of Europe and America is the
product of a more advanced civilization than that of Japan.

—Alice Mabel Bacon,
Japanese Girls and Women, 1902

Miyake Kaho's literary debut in 1888 was the catalyst that roused aspiring
women authors from their "centuries of silence."[1] After Kaho opened the
gates, works by women trickled out yearly: eleven in 1889; thirteen in 1891;
and finally, in a relative deluge of activity, twenty-four in 1895.[2] Most notable
among these early writers were, in addition to Kaho, Wakamatsu Shizuko,
Nakajima Shōen, Shimizu Shikin, Koganei Kimiko, Kitada Usurai, and, of
course, Higuchi Ichiyō. As diverse as these women were—hailing from different classes, regions, and economic situations—almost all, with the exception
of Usurai and Ichiyō, shared one thing in common. Either they had attended
Christian schools or they had associated with *Jogaku zasshi* (Woman's
Education Magazine).

Education, most literary historians agree, particularly Western-flavored mission-sponsored education, was the single most important factor leading to the renewal of writing by women in the modern era.[3] To understand the reemergence of women as writers, therefore, one must consider their educational opportunities. Since education for women in the Meiji period (1868–1912) is entwined with social, religious, political, and economic concerns, it is difficult to speak of one without engaging all the others. It is also impossible, as well as distracting, to address all these concerns in a study that proposes to discuss female literary franchise.[4] To explore the various checks and balances that simultaneously inspired and constrained the Meiji woman writer, I will use *Jogaku zasshi* as the stage upon which to present my study. This journal, founded and managed by men, was intensely devoted to raising the level of a woman's education and incorporated over the course of its twenty-year history a wealth of essays and articles concerning female literacy, education, and social roles. Inaugurated in 1885, a highly significant year in Japanese history for a variety of reasons,[5] *Jogaku zasshi* employed literature and literary-minded individuals in its efforts to encourage women to participate more actively in society. Equally responsible for fostering literary ambitions among its female readers, the journal provides a rich environment for an exploration of this emergence of women's writing in Meiji Japan.

Sōma Kokkō (1876–1955), an avid *Jogaku zasshi* fan, offers one of the more incisive histories of the journal and the social climate that produced it in her autobiographical account *Mokui—Meiji, Taishō bungakushi kaisō* (Silent Changes: Literary Reminiscences of the Meiji and Taishō Periods, 1961). Kokkō charts her own coming-of-age as a Meiji woman, and aspiring writer, alongside the developments in the journal and thus provides a rare window into the world of the *Jogaku* reader. She indicates that the journal was required reading among enlightened Meiji youth—both male and female.[6] She has described how, as a girl, she managed to acquire nearly every issue, though she lived a great distance from Tokyo where *Jogaku* was published. Some issues she received secondhand from friends and some from her aunt, Sasaki Toyosu (1853–1901, also known as Toyoju or Toyoshi), an outspoken member of the Tokyo Women's Reform Society, who brought copies to the city of Sendai whenever she paid her niece a visit. *Jogaku zasshi* offered the young Kokkō example after vibrant example of intelligent and active women. Journal entries included biographies of pioneering women from both Japan and the West as well as interviews with and articles about contemporary female leaders such as Atomi Kakei (1840–1926), founder of one of the first academies of higher learning for women, or Ogino Gin (1851–1913), Japan's first licensed female physician. But more significant for Kokkō were the contributions written by the many outstanding women of her day: there were essays by the eloquent women's rights activist Nakajima Shōen (née Kishida Toshiko), translations from English literature by the brilliant Wakamatsu Shizuko, and short stories by Shimizu Shikin and Miyake Kaho. Kokkō, like many young women of her age and class, longed to travel to Tokyo, work for *Jogaku zasshi*, and enter the Meiji Women's School, which was administered by the journal's editor Iwamoto Yoshiharu (1863–1942).[7]

More than just an enlightenment journal, *Jogaku zasshi* offered its impressionable young readers an alternative to passive obedience. The magazine spoke of female strength, of innate female intelligence and abilities, and of female independence. For nearly two decades the journal afforded women an important outlet for self-expression and an invaluable conduit for information on current events, Western culture and society, new trends in social attitudes, and opportunities in employment and education. Yet despite the significance of this journal, scant attention has been paid to it in English-language studies.[8] Japanese scholarship has paid greater heed to *Jogaku zasshi*, but the focus has been largely on the contributions the journal made to the founding of *Bungakukai* (Literary World, 1893–1898) and the fostering of romanticism in Japanese literature. Inoue Teruko, for example, says that "the greatest service *Jogaku zasshi* performed . . . was to give birth to Hoshino Tenchi (1862–1950), Kitamura Tōkoku (1868–1894), and the other men responsible for the early romantic movement in literature."[9] Although *Jogaku zasshi*'s role in this regard is certainly significant, the eagerness with which certain scholars have linked the journal to this male enterprise has minimized its impact as a component of Meiji women's cultural history. For the journal also gave birth to Wakamatsu Shizuko and Shimizu Shikin and provided space for Koganei Kimiko's poetry, Nakajima Shōen's essays, and Miyake Kaho's stories as well as literary encouragement to countless other writers.

The importance of this encouragement cannot be overemphasized. Even had *Jogaku zasshi* never produced a single woman writer, the journal would have contributed to the resuscitation of women's writing in modern Japan simply by creating a climate in which female literary expression was deemed possible and desirable. During the Meiji and Taishō periods, and to some extent even today, writers were defined by the coterie, school, journal, or mentor with which they associated. For reasons that will be explained, women did not have easy access to these conveniences. Women could not attend the universities, where many of these literary alliances were made, nor did they have the wherewithal to produce the variety of journals that would be decisive in determining an author's literary voice.[10] In the beginning, they needed male mentorship—such as that provided by *Jogaku zasshi*. By opening a space for female self-expression, however, the journal was also responsible for creating and maintaining the boundaries of that space. *Jogaku zasshi* was equally significant for defining what was appropriate to female authorship and the reception thereof.

Attitudes in Early Meiji

The original editors of *Jogaku zasshi*, the three men Iwamoto Yoshiharu, Kondō Kenzō (d. 1886), and Ōba Sōkichi,[11] did not envision a literary magazine. As the journal's title implies, they inaugurated *Jogaku zasshi* in 1885 in order to improve educational opportunities for elite young Japanese women and encourage their aspirations. The editors note in their founding proclamation:

> Deploring the fact that our mothers, our sisters, and our wives are treated as inferiors in this world, we . . . now have established *Jogaku zasshi* with the purpose of improving women's condition by providing them with a model of ideal womanhood that combines both the Western concept of women's rights and the traditional virtues of our own country. [*JZ* 1 (July 20,1885):3]

The editors were interested in producing, through their dissemination of "*jogaku,*" or studies for and about women, educated and responsible female leaders who would dedicate themselves to improving the social, political, and cultural status of women in Japan—thus contributing to the modernization of the nation overall. The founding statement continues:

> Western scholars contend that you can judge the level of a nation's civilization by the status of its women. When we look at the women in Japan today, can we conclude that our nation is civilized?

The answer was obvious. So too was the question. Discussions of women's issues and women's education had not by any means originated with *Jogaku zasshi*. In the early 1870s the status of women had become a central concern for many of the young progressive thinkers of the age. Concubinage, prostitution, patriarchal marriage customs, and education for women were conspicuous topics among the articles published in the *Meiroku zasshi* (Meiji Six Journal, 1874–1875), a short-lived but influential periodical supported by Fukuzawa Yukichi (1835–1901), Nakamura Masanao (1832–1891), and Mori Arinori (1847–1889), among others. As Sharon Sievers notes in her study of early feminist consciousness in the Meiji, "the arguments were full of contradictions, and the debate itself, carried in growing numbers of newspapers and periodicals, often lapsed into silliness and superficiality."[12] Nevertheless, most discussants seemed to agree that higher education for women was an essential component of a strong and civilized nation. The Emperor Meiji himself had remarked in 1871 that female education was indispensable to the health and advancement of the nation.[13] The impact of this attention to female education was felt in 1872 when the compulsory education edict made elementary schooling mandatory for both boys and girls. Yet as Ann Harrington has noted, whereas elementary education was expected of girls, higher education was not.[14] And there remained a noticeable lack of institutions for women— a situation deplored by intellectuals like Mori and Fukuzawa. Without an advanced education, these men argued, women would never be able to plumb their true potential, thus depriving the nation of an invaluable resource.

To a large extent, the Woman Question *(fujin mondai)* became the focal point for reformers' efforts to "civilize" Japan. "Woman" was positioned as a metaphor for all that was backward and shameful in Japan. From an Orientalist regard, Woman signified Japan itself: a weak nation amidst superior Western powers. Because these reformers believed that a nation's civilization could be measured by the status of its women, a belief Sharon Sievers has termed "one of the favored patriarchal myths of the nineteenth-century West,"[15] they judged the condition of womanhood in Japan alongside the condition of Japan in the (Western) world at large. By improving the status of Woman, these men assumed, they could improve the status of the nation. And in order to improve Woman/Nation, men needed to improve her education. But what educational opportunities were available to women in 1885? According to Chieko Mulhern there were "nationwide . . . nine women's schools at the secondary level with a total of 600 students."[16] These, she contends, were little more than finishing schools for upper-class women. Additionally, there were three non-Christian private academies, such as the Atomi School for Women founded in 1875. But the bulk of education for women beyond the elementary stage was conducted by British and North American Christian missionaries.

Although edicts against Christianity (vestiges of the Tokugawa era) had remained in place until 1873, when the government quietly rescinded them, the first Christian institution for women, "Miss Kidder's School" (later Ferris Seminary), was founded in Yokohama in 1870 and was shortly followed by a host of similar institutions throughout the nation.[17] By 1890 there were forty-three Christian boarding schools for girls, accommodating 3,083 students; fifty-six day schools with 3,426 students; and six schools for "Bible Women" with total enrollments of 126.[18] Missionaries were adamant in their zeal to educate young women. True evangelism, they believed, could not take place until women had been converted to Christianity—and, more important perhaps, had been educated to what these missionaries perceived as the nation's immorality, namely sexual promiscuity, prostitution, and concubinage. In order to reach these women, Protestant missions dispatched single women like Mary Kidder to the field. In 1888 there were 150 missionary couples in Japan and 124 unmarried female missionaries. By way of contrast, there were, at the same time, only 27 unmarried missionary men. Native Japanese women were recruited to serve as "Bible Women," as well, charged with proselytizing among their own sex and kind.[19]

While the mission schools made great strides in advancing the cause of women's rights in Japan—providing education where little alternative was to be found and lambasting the sexual abuse of women—they were shortly to be criticized for emphasizing subjects inappropriate to Japanese womanhood. In many schools, English was the only language of instruction and Western history, literature, and philosophy the only topics. While rendering students fluent in English, this curriculum left them unschooled in the niceties of Japanese social intercourse. Sōma Kokkō describes the curriculum at her mission school in Sendai, the Miyagi Women's School, as being completely Americanized, with only a smattering of Japanese and classical Chinese studies: "We had been encouraged only in English, and as we faced graduation, we had been equipped with no skill that would aid us as Japanese women."[20] Perhaps Kokkō and her peers had been too well trained in the manner of "the forward, self-assertive, half-masculine women of the West," for five of her classmates went "on strike" against the American administration in 1892 and demanded curricular changes. They were dismissed.

The 1880s, as Carol Gluck has pointed out, saw a reaction against the "materialistic civilization" of the West and a renewed insistence on "indigenous customs and manners" (fūzoku shūkan) and morality (tokugi).[21] For women this meant that emphasis shifted from Western studies and the sciences to Confucian ethics and native poetry. Ikebukuro Kiyokaze (1847–1900), a teacher of traditional Japanese studies in the women's division of Dōshisha (a mission-sponsored Christian school in Kyoto), an early contributor to Jogaku zasshi, and also a waka poet, attacked the state of mission-school education for women:

> Maybe they can read Kant's philosophy or Milton's poetry, but they can't manage a simple letter in Japanese. So how will they ever impress the world with their writing?
>
> Of course, a few may travel to the United States, dabble in studies there, and return with a specialty. But not every woman can do this. That is why I tell these American teachers to add at least a smattering of Japanese and Chinese studies. [JZ 159 (April 27, 1889):6]

As Naruse Jinzō (1858–1919), founder of Japan Women's College, put it several years later, missionaries erred when they tried to make "European or

American women out of our daughters, and their educational efforts tended to produce undiscriminating westernization, which our society does not want."[22] Statements from graduates of mission schools seem to bear him out. When Sōma Kokkō entered the Miyagi Women's School, her foreign teacher exclaimed proudly, "I will make you girls into wonderful American ladies."[23]

To a certain extent the efforts of such educators were successful. When Wakamatsu Shizuko graduated from Ferris Seminary in 1882, the headmaster boasted of her: "She is not only versed in the English idiom but has an Anglo-Saxon way of thinking and perceiving things."[24] Shizuko's education was apparently not the "handicap" that Ikebukuro Kiyokaze and Naruse Jinzō imagined. She became a prominent contributor to *Jogaku zasshi*, writing in both English and Japanese, and an important translator of English literature. Despite Iwamoto's respect for Shizuko's abilities (he was to marry her in 1889), he was not himself a fan of mission-school education for women. Riding the tide of the anti-Westernism backlash and the insistence on moral education that had begun to swell in the mid-1880s, Iwamoto found himself speaking out against the Western-style furnishings and facilities that mission schools allowed—particularly the central heating.[25] Such luxuries, he believed, were simply ill founded. Meiji Women's School, opened in 1885 by Japanese Christians in reaction to the Americanization of Christian education offered by the missionaries, was spartan by comparison and purposely so.

But more than the luxuries afforded by the mission schools, Iwamoto and the founders of the Meiji Women's School resented the fact that American missionaries seemed to think they had territorial rights to both Christianity and education. These Japanese men insisted that one did not need to be American or Americanized to be Christian; nor did one have to first westernize before advancing the cause of Japanese women. Iwamoto particularly regretted that the missionaries appeared to ignore—or, worse, debase—what he regarded as traditional feminine virtues. Unlike Ikebukuro Kiyokaze, however, Iwamoto was less concerned with training in *waka* and Confucian ethics than he was with the personal and physical characteristics of "gentleness and sweetness." When he and his colleagues founded *Jogaku zasshi*, they pledged to improve women's condition by combining the Western ideals of the emancipated woman with native ideals of feminine grace—thereby "creating a perfect woman." This "perfect woman" was envisioned as the necessary companion to the "enlightened Meiji man." Before turning to the women that Iwamoto guided on their way to professional authorship, however, we must consider the social context that produced men like Iwamoto. Knowing what kind of world awaited the Meiji woman writer will help us to understand the choices she made in her literary career.

Iwamoto: The Woman Writer's Benefactor

Sōma Kokkō, eventually a student at Meiji Women's School, describes her teacher, Iwamoto Yoshiharu, as follows:

> As I remember him, Iwamoto Sensei . . . possessed all the attributes of male beauty—a splendid beard and full red lips. Those who came to hear him could not take their eyes off him, and he met their gaze with his own strong eyes, never wavering. . . . We all eagerly awaited his lectures, and when we left the hall after his class, our eyes glittered with excitement. We felt thrilled to be alive. We were in complete awe of his genius.[26]

Christian educator and evangelist, journalist, women's rights advocator and sometime agitator, Iwamoto Yoshiharu enthralled and inspired impressionable young women like Sōma Kokkō for two decades (1885–1905). As a leading administrator of the Meiji Women's School, Iwamoto was directly responsible for the education of many of Japan's progressive women. His academy also provided employment for these women, as well as for many of the young men who would become the brightest lights in the early Japanese romantic literary movement: Tenchi, Tōson, and Tōkoku. In his roles as editor and educator, Iwamoto nurtured the fledgling efforts of several women writers. As a result, literary historians have dubbed Iwamoto the woman writer's benefactor: her *onjin*.

Raised in samurai traditions and trained by Nakamura Masanao (or Keiu, 1832–1891) and Tsuda Sen (1837–1901), both influential Meiji Christian educators, Iwamoto soon found himself called to work for the improvement of the nation.[27] Like his contemporary Tokutomi Sohō (1863–1957), Iwamoto turned not to government service but to the medium of the press.[28] The press, as James Huffman has shown in his study of Fukuchi Gen'ichirō (1841–1906), was an appropriate avenue at this time for "enlightening the masses" and rendering social change. Editor of Tokyo's first daily newspaper the *Nichi Nichi*, founded in 1872, Fukuchi believed the press functioned as a tool for "shaping the thinking of the day and controlling the fundamental political thought of the public. . . . 'Newspapers are the eyes and ears of the world, the movers of mankind.'"[29]

Iwamoto was no stranger to print media. He had begun his work to "move mankind" in 1881 when he joined the staff of Tsuda Sen's *Nōgyō zasshi* (Journal of Agriculture), a journal meant less to disseminate information about improved farming methods than to dispense ideas on nutrition, healthful eating habits, and socially responsible attitudes toward nature—human and otherwise. In October 1884, Iwamoto began to contribute to *Shōgaku zasshi* (Journal of Elementary Education). Earlier that year he had begun to assist Kondō Kenzō, a fellow member of Tsuda's agricultural academy, in his enterprise *Jogaku shinshi* (New Magazine for Women's Education). Fundamentally dedicated to reforming the nation through educational journalism, regardless of the subject, Iwamoto began to gravitate from the improvement of carrots and eggplants toward the improvement of women.

The Founding of *Jogaku zasshi*

Jogaku shinshi, the precursor to *Jogaku zasshi*, lasted only a few months, though why it failed is uncertain. Kondō Kenzō, its chief editor, disbanded the enterprise in May 1885. In July, he and Iwamoto joined forces to establish the bimonthly *Jogaku zasshi*. Kondō is largely credited with coining the term *"jogaku."* In issue 111 of *Jogaku zasshi*, May 26, 1888, the term is given in English as "the study of women." But in issue 143, January 5, 1889, Iwamoto explains the term to mean: "to teach women the spirit of charity, education, nursing, and evangelism. . . . In short, *jogaku* acknowledges a woman as a member of society and directs her on the path to advancement."

"Advancement" for both Iwamoto and Kondō meant self-cultivation for the betterment of the state. Women too were candidates for *"risshin shusse"* (self-establishment and public advancement), but such success was not possible unless women were properly educated, and properly enlightened to their own unique role, or "mission," in the family, the nation, and the world. Both men believed this role was necessarily separate from that for men. Just as indiscriminate attempts to "westernize" Japanese women were misguided, so too were attempts to "masculinize" them. Giving women an education that put them on a par with men was a waste of time—not because women were incapable of excelling in their lessons in "Kant and Milton" but because these lessons not only did women no good, they rendered them useless, contributed to their unhappiness, and ultimately led to the destruction of the home (and nation). Again, in the words of the poet and educator Ikebukuro Kiyokaze:

> Male and female students possess the same innate ability to learn. . . . But no matter how extensive a woman's training, she cannot stand before the world and lecture on her ideas; . . . she cannot join government service or become an assemblyman. She cannot do significant work in agriculture or industry. . . . Her territory is narrow. . . . While men put their knowledge to use and earn the respect of the world, advancing their names throughout the public realm, no one ever hears of these women. Their scholarship molders. Thus their learning is a handicap. [*JZ* 158 (April 20, 1889):6]

To educate a woman for a man's role was meaningless. But this did not mean women had no need of an education. The editors of *Jogaku* believed that women had a special mission in life—one they could perform as women and within the boundaries of their "domestic realm." True service to the nation, and to its women, could not occur while women occupied themselves with entering male domains. "We advocate women's education before women's rights," Iwamoto was quick to declare.[30] Women could not satisfactorily answer their own goals in life if they were kept ignorant.

Jogaku zasshi, therefore, had two aims. It meant to encourage women to strive for an education appropriate to their role in society. But just as important, the journal meant to awaken men to the injustices women had long endured. Iwamoto and Kondō took pains to dispel abusive attitudes—such as *danson johi* (revere men/despise women)—and to lash out against customs and habits that were deemed harmful and demeaning to women. Of particular concern were prostitution, concubinage, and the patriarchal marriage institution, which denied women (among other rights) the right to marital choice, the right to custody of their own children, and the right to property. True education, the editors believed, could not take place until pernicious attitudes about female inferiority had been eradicated. In other words, the purpose of the journal was not only to educate women but to educate the men who were charged with their protection and direction. Consequently, *Jogaku* readers were evenly divided between men and women.

Even though education had been made compulsory for girls, fewer than 50 percent of young women attended school.[31] The nation's educational system was failing women because the nation's families did not value education for their daughters. By far the majority still viewed education for women as a detriment to their character and to their future potential as wives. Iwamoto and his editorial staff, in turn, regarded parents as a detriment to a woman's education. In an English-language announcement describing the founding of an Orphan Girls' School, for example, readers learn:

> The schoolmaster intends to live with the orphan children and bring them up according to his own standard of education. In this task he will be entirely free from the hampering influence of parents, which, according to the *Jogaku*, is the principal obstacle to modern female education in Japan. [JZ 303 (February 6, 1892):1]

For girls with parents, however, the desire for advanced education against the family's wishes could have disastrous results. Otis Cary, quoting from Naruse Jinzō's biography of Paul Sawayama, *A Modern Paul in Japan* (1893), relays the following tragic anecdote:

Four girls who were eager to obtain an education resolved that they would either do this or die in the attempt. They took a solemn oath by which each promised to commit suicide unless she could induce her family to send her to school. One of them wrote a letter to a principal of an academy, and the reply fell into the hands of her parents, who severely rebuked her, saying that women did not need an education. After listening in silence to their reproofs, she went to her own room and there committed suicide. The brother of another of these girls was a student in the Tokyo Imperial University. After his graduation she begged him to take her with him to Tokyo and put her in a girls' school. He showed no sympathy with her desires, and she also took her own life. The third girl became a Christian. This led to her being so severely persecuted by her parents that she was driven into insanity. The fourth of the band, more fortunate than the others, was allowed to enter the normal school at Niigata.[32]

To avoid similar tragedies, *Jōgaku zasshi* was charged not only with providing information and encouragement to the women who were already sufficiently educated to read its pages, but also to transform the attitudes of Japanese parents, brothers, and husbands.

The Ideal Female Reader

The first issue of *Jōgaku zasshi*, dated July 20, 1885, was edited by Kondō Kenzō and published by Manshundō. It was printed on small octavo sheets, roughly twenty pages in all, and cost four sen. For one sen more the editors would send the journal by mail. Subscribers were promised a small discount. The first issue opened with an illustration of legendary Empress Jingū (201–269) presiding over her war camp as she prepares for battle in Korea.[33] On the next page appeared a roster of all the women serving at the imperial court as of July 15, 1885. Although there was little explanation to accompany the roster, the implication seemed to be that these were women to emulate. Following the opening proclamation for the journal came announcements for the different ladies' clubs, such as the Rōmaji Club, the Women's Association of Western Coiffures, and the Ladies' Etiquette Club. While these sodalities would seem fairly innocuous today, each addressed topics that challenged contemporary notions of femininity. The Rōmaji Club, for example, advocated the adoption of romanized script in lieu of traditional Japanese letters. Since women were often regarded as the perpetuators of traditional Japanese poetry, indeed of traditions in general, the suggestion that they should also dabble in foreign script was somewhat progressive. Even more so was the advocating of foreign coiffures. As Sievers has pointed out, men were encouraged to cut their hair in favor of Western styles but women were legally

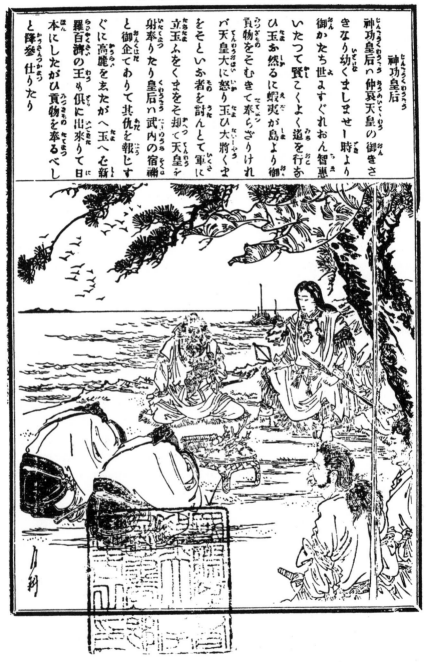

神功皇后

神功皇后ハ仲哀天皇の御きさ
きなり幼くましませ一時より
御かたち世ょすぐれおん智惠
いたつて賢くよく道を行ふ
ひ玉ふ然るに蝦夷が島より御
貢物をそむきて奉らざりけれ
バ天皇大に怒り玉ひ大將く王
をそとといふ者を討んとて軍に
立玉ふをくさをそ却て天皇や
射奉りたり皇后ハ武內の宿禰
と御企てありて其仇を報じす
ぐに高麗を玉たがへ玉へ心新
羅百濟の王も俱に出來りて日
本にしたがひ貢物を奉るべし
と降參仕りたり

Figure 1　Empress Jingū presiding over her war camp as she prepares for battle in Korea. *Jogaku zasshi* 1 (July 20, 1885). (Courtesy of Nihon Kindai Bungakkan)

banned from similarly changing theirs. The implications behind a woman bobbing her hair were apparently profound. Certainly hair had long been associated with a woman's sexual identity.[34] This refusal to allow her to change her coiffure was a not-so-subtle attempt to deny women self-expression and keep them bound to traditional sexuality. Or, as Sievers notes, women were expected to "become repositories of the past rather than pioneers, with men, of some unknown future."[35]

While it seemed the journal was trying to encourage women to assume a more progressive stance, it also incorporated articles that reminded them of their importance as "repositories of the past." The first issue of the journal, for example, offered articles on poetic conventions, verse in the *waka* form, and a discussion of traditional koto music. There were tips on self-improvement—how to whiten skin, how to fashion a perfume pouch, how to apply makeup—as well as the requisite household advice—how to stop a lamp from smoking, how to heat cold rice. Of additional interest was an article comparing marriage customs around the world. Subsequent issues continued in a similar vein. Each introduced and explained a literary term, generally from classical poetry. Each contained biographies of "outstanding women," as well, most more legendary than actual, such as the classical poet Ono no Komachi (fl. 800s) or the sword-wielding Tokiko who avenged her husband's death. Moreover, each issue defined popular phrases, such as *"hako iri musume"* (daughters kept in boxes),[36] and instructed on the proper usage of terms like *"sama"* (mister/madam) and *"dono"* (sir). Some issues ran question/answer columns, with readers writing in to answer such queries as "Where does the term *'umazume'* [barren, lit. stone woman] originate?" One respondent suggested that the term referred to Empress Jingū, who had put a stone on her stomach to prevent the start of labor at an inconvenient time. The intended audience of the magazine can be discerned by the inclusion of such articles as "How a Lady Should Address Her Maid."

Of much amusement today are articles introducing aspects of Western culture to curious readers. The second issue, for example, carried a chart comparing Western and Japanese women in such categories as hair, nose, and even bodily functions.[37] The comparison seemed to suggest that even though women around the world are anatomically similar there are crucial differences—an implication that underscored the editors' determination to avoid, in their construction of the perfect Japanese woman, outright adulation and imitation of the West. Although the editors advocated the practice of English, the simplification of the difficult Japanese script, improvement in physical education for girls, and modification of hairstyles and fashions in favor of those more practical and comfortable, they did not see the West as the absolute model. They were astute enough to realize that Westerners were not them-

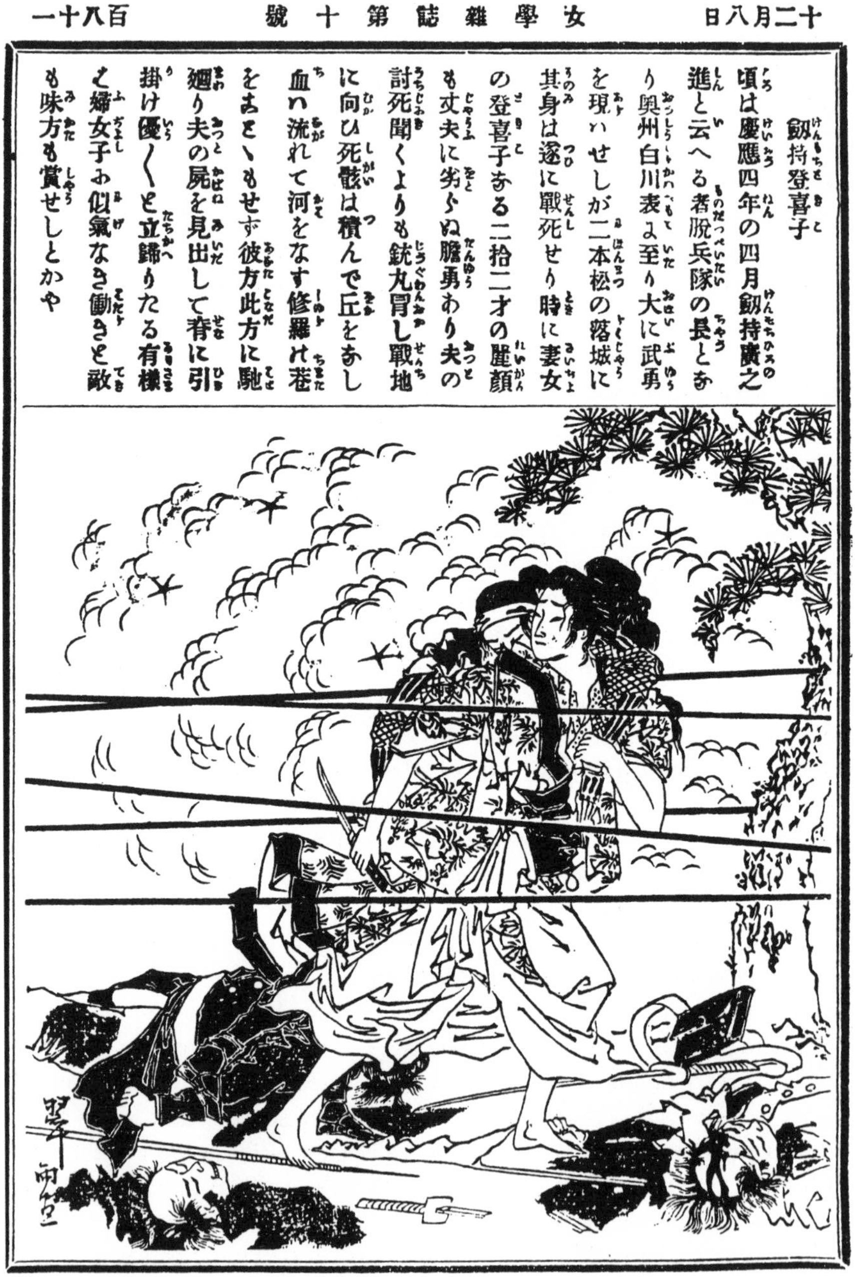
十二月八日　女學雜誌第十號　百八十一
劒持登喜子
頃は慶應四年の四月劒持廣之
進と云へる者脱兵隊の長とな
り奥州白川表に至り大に武勇
を現はせしが二本松の落城に
其身は遂に戰死せり時に妻女
の登喜子なる二拾二才の麗顔
も丈夫に劣らぬ膽勇あり夫の
討死聞くよりも銃丸冒し戰地
に向ひ死骸は積んで丘をなし
血は流れて河をなす修羅の巷
をなとゝもせず彼方此方に馳
廻り夫の屍を見出して脊に引
掛け優〳〵と立歸りたる有様
は婦女子に似氣なき働きと敵
も味方も賞せしとかや

Figure 2 Tokiko retrieves her husband's body from the battlefield in 1869. *Jogaku zasshi* 10 (December 8, 1885). (Courtesy of Nihon Kindai Bungakkan)

The Women's Magazine
(JOGAKU ZASSHI.)

No. 34.　　　　　第 參 拾 四 號

* * *
!!!!!!!!!
@ @
○

* This *
is a woman's
natural waist
which corset never yet
disgraced. Inside it is
a mine of health. Outside
of charms it has wealth.
It is a thing of beauty true,
and a sweet joy forever
new. It needs no art-
ful padding vile
or bustle big
to give it "style."
It's strong and solid
plump and sound, and
hard to get one arm around.
Alas, if women only knew the
mischief that these corsets
do, they'd let Dame Nature
have her way, and never
try her "waist" to "stay."

大きもの
地もさんらざりけり
をし丸るめ虚空をぐつと呑けれバ須彌も天ん

小きもの
けし粒の中くりあけて堂建て〻一間かあふ
て手習をせん

!!!!!!!!!
○

* This *
is the
shape of
a woman's waist
on which a corset tight
is laced. The ribs deform-
ed by being squeezed, press
on the lungs till they are
diseased. The heart
is jammed and
cannot pump.
The liver
is a
tor-
pid lump.
The stomach
crushed cannot
digest, and in a mess
are all compressed. Therefore this silly woman grows to
be a fearful mass of woes. but
thinks she has a lovely shape tho'
hideous as a crippled ape.

Figure 3　Table of Contents page from *Jogaku zasshi* 34 (September 5, 1886). The bottom section—generally reserved for "*Calendar Events*," "*Special Announcements*," or "*Pearls of Wisdom*"—features a clever illustration protesting corsets. (Courtesy of Nihon Kindai Bungakkan) selves always content with Western ways. In Western journalism at this time, much attention was being given to dress reform, for example. Articles in *Jogaku* reflected these concerns. There was no reason to cast off the kimono in favor of Western apparel, such as the corset, that warped the woman's body.

This critique of Western fashion is not to suggest that *Jogaku* advocated a strictly Japanese world. Rather, the journal called for moderation and cautioned against unbridled enthusiasm for all things foreign. By the end of the 1880s, the period of intense westernization had passed and Japanese intellectuals throughout the nation were now going about the business of adapting what had been adopted. While certain features of westernization were being reviled—such as the corset and the "ladies first" brand of chivalry—others were being heralded. The constant appearance of articles debating the merits of the West made *Jogaku* immediately attractive and seemingly progressive for its day. In addition to mixing Western-inspired content with articles on native traditions, from August 15, 1886 (issue 32), the table of contents and frequently the title page and the calendar of events as well were rendered in a mixture of English and Japanese, giving the journal a decidedly cosmopolitan flair while at the same time appealing to mission school students and their foreign teachers.

Figure 4   The front cover of *Jogaku zasshi*. On the right is the cover to the first issue; on the left, the cover to the hundredth issue. The cover design changed periodically and at one point was written in English. (Courtesy of Nihon Kindai Bungakkan)

Jogaku zasshi's response to women was as schizophrenic as its bilingual title page. On the one hand, it honored women who had transgressed the boundaries of customary femininity—women who were impressively strong, passionate, and courageous. Empress Jingū and Tokiko campaigned upon the battlefield. Ono no Komachi, renowned for her passionate poetry, was a rebel of another kind, as was a contemporary example, Nakajima Shōen, originator of the term "daughters kept in boxes." Shōen's earlier appearance on the Freedom and Popular Rights *(Jiyū minken undō)* lecture circuit had propelled her into the political arena, well beyond the security of the home. Even the Western women presented in the journal—Joan of Arc, Florence Nightingale, George Eliot—were those who subverted standard notions of female domesticity. But if the journal beguiled its female readers with images of aggressive, self-certain women, it reminded them on the other hand that a woman's place was in the home and the measure of her value was her ability to procreate. The "ideal woman," as construed by the editors, belonged to the elite. She had the time and inclination to concern herself with poetry and to worry over hairstyles and comparative anatomy. Thanks to the "education" proffered by *Jogaku zasshi*, she would be able to manage her household resourcefully, heating cold rice and not letting her lamp smoke. Well groomed (from

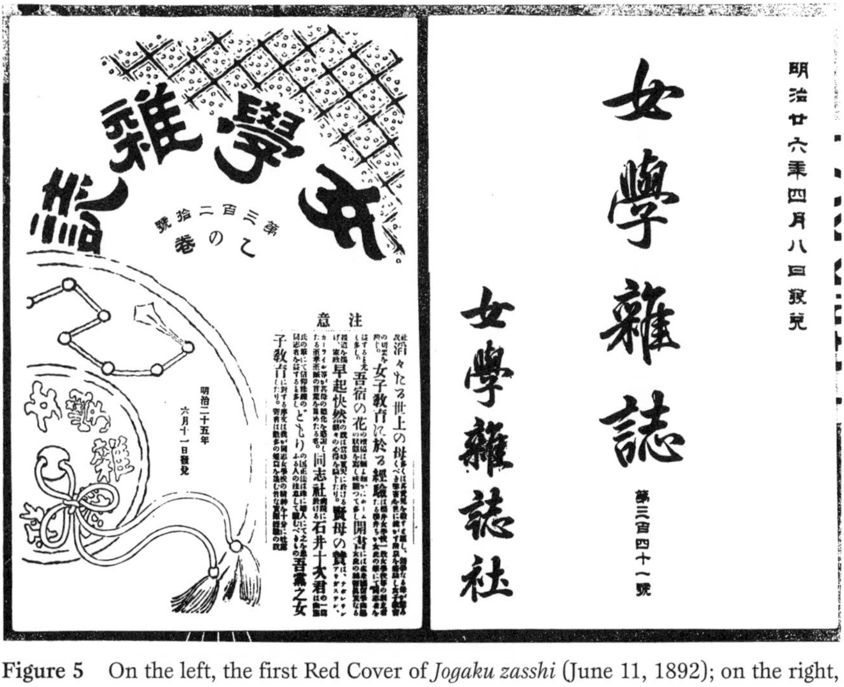

Figure 5   On the left, the first Red Cover of *Jogaku zasshi* (June 11, 1892); on the right, the last Red Cover (April 8, 1893). (Courtesy of Nihon Kindai Bungakkan)

face powder to perfumed pouches), adept at Japanese literary traditions, she should be content to dream of powerful heroines.

This ideal woman underwent a transformation after May 24, 1886, when Kondō Kenzō died suddenly, leaving Iwamoto as the sole editor. Under Iwamoto's control, *Jogaku zasshi* became a provocative forum for discussion of some of the more controversial issues facing women in the Meiji period, from prostitution to dress reform. The journal's ideal changed from a cultured but sheltered lady to an informed and socially active woman. During this new phase of its existence, transcriptions of political speeches began to appear along with summaries of sermons by Uchimura Kenzō (1861–1930), Uemura Masahisa (1857–1925), and other Christian leaders who advocated religious freedom, charity, and love-based marriages. Scholars recently returned from overseas offered reports on the social and political climates abroad, particularly those concerning women (issue 152, March 9, 1889). Articles arguing the pros and cons of female suffrage in Britain (issue 32, August 15, 1886) or describing the temperance movement in America (issue 107, April 28, 1888) cropped up regularly. Statistics as to the salaries for female factory workers abroad and the numbers of women employed as nurses or teachers in Japan were equally common (issue 60, April 16, 1887).

Each issue opened with an editorial essay. Whether written by Iwamoto (often under the guise of one of his pen names) or left unsigned, most editorials after 1886 were of his authorship. These editorials dealt with topics from the common to the controversial: women and motherhood, women and art, women and Christ, women and politics. In the sixty-fifth issue (May 21, 1887), Iwamoto printed the editorial "Kan'in no kūki" (An Atmosphere of Adultery), the English title rendered as "Adultery of the Nation." In this essay Iwamoto castigated those who made it a practice to attend the costume balls and dance parties that had become the fashion. Iwamoto did not consider dance itself immoral. In fact, *Jogaku zasshi* encouraged Western-style social intercourse between men and women. But Iwamoto regretted that the atmosphere surrounding these parties led to rumor, scandal, and the implication that adultery was an acceptable social practice. "People have grown immune to such [behavior]. Scandals involving proper ladies are now commonplace. Divorce has grown common. It is frightening. Shocking! But we close our eyes and pretend not to see" (p. 18).

Although Iwamoto framed his diatribe in terms of the general, the catalyst for his editorial was a particular scandal that had occurred at a fancy dance ball *(fuanshi bōru)* hosted by Prime Minister Itō Hirobumi (1841–1909) on April 20, 1887. The four hundred guests at Itō's official residence sashayed and cavorted through the night in outlandish masquerade. The prime minister dressed as a Venetian nobleman, his wife as a Spanish princess. Japanese dignitaries costumed themselves as samurai, mountain priests, or legendary heroes, while their wives and daughters dressed the part of romantic heroines from Japanese legend. As George Sansom describes the event, these elegantly arrayed Japanese women were ardently pursued by the young foreign gentlemen in attendance at the party, many of whom "appeared in Japanese dress."[38] During the midst of the festivities, Itō accosted Prince Iwakura's daughter, a married woman. Iwamoto's description of the outrage was discreet: "At a certain celebration, a married woman was 'pressured' and 'pursued.' And later money was sent to her husband. And these are high society people. Such stories are not unusual today" (p. 18). No names were named, but the background for the piece was obvious and perhaps Iwamoto's ire—now directed at the bureaucratic elite instead of at nameless prostitutes and abstract concepts—hit too close to home. The journal was penalized with a two-month ban. Issue 66 did not appear until July 9, 1887.[39]

Iwamoto did not let government pressure shake his resolve to combat what he saw as the nation's adulterous atmosphere. He was adamant in his zeal to eliminate prostitution and concubinage. But Iwamoto believed these evils touched everyone's life, not just the unfortunate woman entangled in the sordid business. Good women, young women, married women, old women— all women were vicitmized by a system that condoned the sale of human bodies. In order to eliminate prostitution, however, reformers would have to do more than draft new laws. There was a sickness at the heart of society that would have to be treated—else the symptoms would persist. To that end, while Iwamoto carried articles in his journal that passionately attacked prostitution and concubinage, he also helped the Tokyo Women's Reform Society, founded in 1886, in its campaign to push for moral reform. He served as the tutelary editor of the society's magazine, he participated in various lecture tours across the nation, and he opened the doors of Meiji Women's School to the society's meetings and conferences. But social agitation was only one approach to moral reform. Iwamoto also believed that education was an essential weapon in helping women battle the injustices that they faced.

One of the reasons why men persisted in their immoral behavior, he believed, was that their wives had no leverage in the household. A man could install a concubine in his home or spend his money on prostitutes, and his wife was helpless to stop him. If the wife were educated, however, she could engage her husband in rational discussion. They could converse as equals— as friends—and she could counsel him to forgo his wrongful behavior (issue 65, May 21, 1887). Or, should this tactic fail, she could leave the man if she were able to assume dignified employment outside the home. Iwamoto admired Yajima Kajiko (1832–1922), controversial founder of the Tokyo Women's Reform Society, because she had divorced her alcoholic husband rather than submitting to his abusive treatment.[40]

But what sort of employment opportunities were available to women in the 1880s? Of course, women in the agricultural sector had always worked—either in the fields or at "by-employments such as silkworm raising, spinning, weaving, and straw sandal-making."[41] With the onset of industrialization, many of these rural women found employment, frequently under slavelike conditions, in textile mills and mines. Lower-class women in the cities survived by taking in piecework such as: "matchbox assembly, shaving toothpicks, sewing sandal straps, painting blackboards, making Japanese-style socks, stretching tobacco, carving fan spokes, polishing metal wares, and sorting scrap paper."[42] Other occupations available to these women included menial work as domestics, street vendors, hairdressers, laundresses, or operators of small-scale businesses such as tea stalls or boarding houses. Women of higher class took employment as teachers of dance, tea, and flower arrangement. After the Meiji Restoration these women could also teach in public or private schools or they might find positions in nursing, private tutoring, printing, or telegraph operations. But as Wakamatsu Shizuko observed in her essay on the condition of women in Japan: "Even the best occupations open to women have been, however, considered rather short of honorable, and she has followed them mostly from necessity."[43] Poor women worked; wealthy women volunteered.

Under ordinary circumstances, therefore, Iwamoto did not encourage women to seek outside employment:

> If women work freely alongside men outside the home, then the home will become little more than a hotel for the married couple, and husbands and wives will become competitors. No, I feel women should keep the house and have jurisdiction over it. [JZ 80 (October 15, 1887):182]

Inspired by Victorian notions of "true womanhood," Iwamoto believed the female sex to be intrinsically purer than their male counterpart. He therefore charged women with protecting the cultural and moral centers of society. A woman was to be "guardian of the interior" and "queen of the home" (hōmu no joō). Her mission in life was to make a nurturing shelter for her children and a blissful refuge for her husband, a sanctuary where he might come to escape the violent challenges of the outside world (issue 102, March 24, 1888).

Although Iwamoto's vision of femininity did not differ significantly from that of the traditional Confucian model—such as that portrayed in the eighteenth-century handbook Onna daigaku (Greater Learning for Women) —it was distinct nonetheless. In stressing a woman's moral superiority (a notion antithetical to Confucianism, which warned of her five vices: disobedience, quick temperedness, a tendency toward slander, envy, silliness), Iwamoto advocated her dominion over the domestic realm. The home was to be hers—her haven, the vehicle of her self-expression. Iwamoto's idea of separate spheres, as restrictive as it may seem today, was nevertheless liberating for women who had never had a social space of their own. Raised to accept a position in life that was defined according to her relationship to a man— father, husband, or son—a woman had no "identity" of her own. As a familiar proverb stated: she had "no home in three worlds."[44] Iwamoto's vision elevated women from essential "homelessness" to a position of authority over her own social realm. No longer was she to be a servant in her husband's house, disenfranchised before her husband's family. Rather the wife and the husband—an integral pair obedient to one another and not to an extended family—were to exercise equal authority over their own respective spheres.

To assist a woman in maintaining her authority, Iwamoto included articles in *Jogaku zasshi* that exalted her moral purity while at the same time instructing her how to apply herself to housekeeping. In 1888 he instituted a "household science and physics" column in the journal:

> Subjects taught a woman are to help in her practical understanding. Science helps her in building a fire; chemistry, in cooking; geography, in setting up house; and astronomy, in determining the weather. Women are not to be locked up inside the house, nor forced to venture out. They are to make their homes a bright and clean place. [*JZ* 102 (March 24, 1888):3]

Like most of his male contemporaries, Iwamoto was explicitly interested in producing "good wives and wise mothers."[45] His science, physics, and other "new" subjects, therefore, were intended to prepare women not for careers outside the home but for a more active domesticity. To that end, he introduced his "science" articles with titles of the following variety: "How to Distinguish Beef from Horse Flesh" or "Eggs Cannot be Boiled on Top of a High Mountain" (issue 246, January 1, 1891).[46]

Iwamoto's favoring of domestic roles for women did not mean that they should be relieved of social responsibilities. Rather, the *Jogaku* reader, through her capacity as "queen of the home," was expected to do what she could to improve society. She started by educating her children and advising her husband. She was urged to join volunteer organizations, such as the Tokyo Women's Reform Society, antiprostitution leagues, and charities. If she must work, she was advised to enter the teaching and nursing professions because they employed her innate gifts. She was also encouraged to write.

Bungaku as Jogaku : A Literature for Female Education

Women had long been acknowledged as the most avid readers of prose fiction (*shōsetsu*), and certain categories of fiction had long been used as a tool for educating them.[47] It is hardly surprising, therefore, that Iwamoto would latch onto prose fiction as a means of reaching especially those women not already being served by new institutions like the Meiji Women's School. But there were problems with this approach. For fiction, in general, was not fit for female readers, or so Iwamoto believed.

Indeed, from the point of view of most former samurai, the *shōsetsu* was hardly fit for any reader. Many Meiji intellectuals of samurai descent still clung to the notion that fiction writing was a frivolous enterprise pursued by unsavory hacks and read surreptitiously by men (or women) of questionable integrity. Much of Tokugawa and early Meiji fiction had indeed appealed to the reader's voyeuristic interest in the licensed quarters. Christian minister Uchimura Kanzō lamented that "'men of letters *(bunjin)* and 'men of plea-sures' *(suijin)* had become synonymous" and fiction writing was too closely associated with the brothels to be considered a dignified occupation.[48] Iwamoto agreed. Reprints of older works, such as the "playful compositions" *(gesaku)* of the Edo period (1600–1868), offered only lust and lewdness as far as Iwamoto was concerned. Female characters were admired for selling themselves into prostitution—largely to support worthless men. Such works could hardly be entertained by an educator at pains to abolish the sexual exploitation of women.[49]

Indulging in fiction of this variety was not only unproductive. It could in fact prove harmful, as it could lead the gullible and naive to unrealistic flights of fancy—or, worse, if Nakamura Masanao was to be believed, to adultery, burglary, and murder.[50] Fiction, in short, was subsumed under the subversive label of falsehood: a Buddhist sin of speech; a Confucian breach of ethics.[51] Meiji intellectuals were understandably taken aback to discover that prose fiction—in the form of the novel—was accorded respect in the West. Not only were novels popular among the Western elite, but prominently placed men had themselves written them. Progressive Japanese began to reexamine their own prose traditions and determined that a native version of the novel might prove beneficial to their nation as well—provided certain reforms were carried out. Fiction, therefore, joined the long list of items to be reformed in order to render Japan a modern (Western) nation. One way former samurai could accept fiction writing was by making it utilitarian: placing it in service to the state. If used properly, certain Meiji defenders of fiction argued, the novel "was unsurpassed as a teacher and ideal as a mechanism for bringing about social reform and enlightenment of the populace."[52]

Iwamoto, too, believed that literature had a purpose. It should be used as a tool to "inspire readers with high moral principles" (JZ 27 [June 25, 1886]:243) In a sense, he was an advocate of a modernized version of the didactic dictum *"kanzen choaku"* or "reward virtue/chastise vice."[53] He there-fore made every effort to ensure that the literary works he published in his journal met his agenda. His agenda, of course, was to educate women—and accordingly he felt that most contemporary works, though they might appeal to men, were not suitable for women. The latest works by Tsubouchi Shōyō, for example, featured either male heroes no woman could possibly hope to emulate or else female protagonists who were too morally suspect, too old fashioned, or too vapid to interest educated and elite young women. The character Osei, in Futabatei Shimei's *Ukigumo* (Drifting Cloud, 1887), was far too shallow-minded for Iwamoto's imagined female reader. True, Tōkai Sanshi's *Kajin no kigū* (Strange Encounters with Beautiful Women, 1885–1897) did feature two intelligent heroines from Spain and Ireland. But the style was, in Iwamoto's eyes, so pedantic that only the crustiest Chinese scholar could appreciate it, thus rendering the work incomprehensible to most female readers.

Not all of Iwamoto's contemporaries agreed with his insistence that fiction serve an educational mission. Ishibashi Ningetsu (1865–1926) observed of this moral criterion: "Iwamoto loved literature; he just misunderstood it."[54] Tsubouchi Shōyō most notably took exception to the notion that art should be made subservient to political or educational agendas. Whereas he agreed that the novel should seek to reveal "truth,"[55] and do so in a realistic manner, he argued against the didactic as well as fantastic legacy left by the Tokugawa *gesaku* tradition. In his groundbreaking manifesto on the art of fiction, *The Essence of the Novel* (*Shōsetsu shinzui*, 1885), he urged writers to adopt Western mimetic strategies. As James Fujii notes, "Shōyō's tract emphatically stresses two imperatives—to portray human emotions skillfully and to develop a written language adequate to the task of presenting these feelings in a realistic manner."[56]

Iwamoto was not only aware of Shōyō's regard of fiction but even responded to it in *Jogaku* essays. Though he tried to accommodate a variety of literary views in his journal, he could not himself move beyond the notion of literature with a higher purpose. Even so, struck by the literary fever that was sweeping the nation, Iwamoto allowed his journal to serve as a forum for a variety of literary positions. From the outset Iwamoto had given literature a place in the journal, though by and large he had focused either on the native poetic traditions or on introductions to Western classics such as Shakespeare's dramas, Tennyson's poems, or Scott's novels. In 1886, he began to include essays debating such controversial issues in contemporary Japanese literary theory as the appropriateness of colloquial narratives *(genbun itchi)* or the virtues of didacticism *(kanzen chōaku)*. He also allowed space for reviews of contemporary works, serializations of translated works, and publication of original stories. Consequently, contributions by well-known or newly rising male writers and critics increased. Meiji Japan's first professional literary critic, Ishibashi Ningetsu, started contributing to the journal in 1887; the promising young writer Yamada Bimyō (1868–1910) commenced submitting works in June 1888, soon to be followed by contributions from Uchida Roan (also known as Fuchian, 1868–1929) and Hoshino Tenchi.

By the late 1880s, Iwamoto became conscious of the fact that the very subjects of his efforts were being denied a voice in their own representation. In the first decade of the Meiji period, the women's movement had been largely established and conducted by men. By the early 1880s, several women had appeared on the lecture circuit, speaking as members of the Freedom and Popular Rights Movement. But the government did what it could to curtail female expression of this variety, revising the police security regulations so that women were excluded from participating in politics at any level.[57] The only other venues were women's clubs, reading groups, and school journals, which kept the female voice insular and denied public outreach. Even *Jogaku zasshi*, this self-described journal for women, was largely a male enterprise founded not by women but for women.

Women were hardly in a position to launch or even control their own journal. They lacked the network, or the fraternal bonds, that would tie them to a periodical. Furthermore, they were denied the authority to produce and control a journal of their own due to state-mandated press regulations *(shin-bunshi jōrei)* that excluded them from editorship. Iwamoto Yoshiharu deplored this state of affairs.[58] In an editorial dated October 15, 1887, he observed that although female reporters and columnists were not unheard of in the West, Japan did not have even one. Women's status, he argued, could not possibly improve if women were barred from the debate.

> We need women journalists to write about women's issues. Men have viewed women as slaves for the past thousand years. It is not likely that they will undergo a transformation in two or three years and start writing for women's rights. [*JZ* 80 (October 15, 1887):182]

For men to write on women's issues, Iwamoto continued, was "like putting makeup over the face of *danson johi* [revere men/despise women]." Women must represent themselves. "Isn't there anyone among my sisters who will energetically, and of her own accord, rise to the task?" (p. 184).

If Iwamoto was eager to see women establish themselves as writers, he was equally insistent that their writing conform to the literary standards that he found meaningful. As the woman writer's benefactor, Iwamoto sought to guide her, instruct her, and mold her to suit his own masculine aims. These aims were just as much directed at benefiting the newly emerging nation-state in Japan as they were at fostering female literary expression. For reformers like Iwamoto, self-expression—male or female—was always subordinate to a larger, absolute good. Thus while Iwamoto and other male reformers encouraged women's self-expression and self-reliance, they did so with the overall objective of using that expression and reliance to build a stronger and richer nation. As Brett de Bary has pointed out in her recent study of gender and imperialism in Japan, "the production of a modern system of sexual difference in Japan cannot be separated from the consolidation of the nation-state, conceived of as a sovereignty."[59] Iwamoto's articulation of appropriate writing by and for women was imbricated with the definition of women's roles in the emerging imperium. Writing by women, therefore, was evaluated according to this imbrication.

While Iwamoto and other like-minded educators and reformers struggled to define a space for women in the literary realm, male writers at the time were similarly struggling to identify their own role and potential as writers. Answers were not obvious. Debates raged. Some argued for didactic aims, others argued against them. Some repudiated the past, others venerated it. Some advocated entertainment, most preferred to focus on the seriousness of writing as a means for exploring "truth." The male literary agenda was by no means stable or straightforward. To a large extent the literary space for women waxed and waned with every shift in dominant male attitudes toward the production and aim of fiction. Women, as we have seen, were not themselves capable of staking their own literary terrain at the time. Men were in charge of the discourse governing both their own literary aims and those for women.

Women as Writers

Since Iwamoto's call for women writers preceded the actual debut of female authors in the modern period, the rationale behind his early articles on women and literature was, first, to establish a need for works by women and, second, to present women as capable of meeting this need. But while Iwamoto was encouraging women to regard writing as a worthy endeavor, he was also reminding men that women had a contribution to make. Iwamoto argued that since contemporary literature was entirely inappropriate for the female reader, women were obliged either to campaign against the lewdness of male-authored works or else take up the brush themselves and write their own morally pure pieces:

> I believe writing is an appropriate employment for women. And I entrust this to them. The books we have nowadays are not good for female readers. And so it is that I hope women will emerge as excellent authors—to rectify this wrong. [*JZ* 32 (August 15, 1886):23–24]

Iwamoto elaborated on what he considered good literature in the essay "Nyoshi to shōsetsu" (Women and Prose Fiction), which appeared in three installments from June 25 to August 15, 1886, in *Jogaku zasshi*.[60] The success of the novel *(shōsetsu)*, Iwamoto stated in an argument clearly indebted to Tsubouchi Shōyō, turned on how skillfully it mastered realism. And the measure of realism was to be found in the novel's ability to move the reader. A good writer, therefore, possessed three essential skills: observation (to perceive truth), sensitivity (to appreciate the emotion of truth), and creative vision (to recreate truth in a believable narrative). Women, he then asserted, were inherently gifted with all three of these skills. Iwamoto's contention was not so obvious as it sounded. Although women had been successful writers in the Japanese classical period, this new emphasis on a literature "informed by Western imperatives . . . to signify modernity, truth, seriousness, the West, and even wholeness as a nation,"[61] consigned the earlier female-dominated tradition to the realm of the frivolous and effeminate. Thus Iwamoto felt compelled to defend the validity of female authorship point by point. And he did so by appealing to what he considered "universal" assumptions concerning the value of prose fiction overall and women's intrinsic abilities therein.

If observation is one of the three essential skills for a writer, then a woman must be expected to excel in this regard because she is "given to trivial detail . . . with a glance, she can take in a person's appearance from head to toe" (*JZ* 32 [August 15, 1886]:22). As for creative vision, Iwamoto admits that men surpass women in this achievement but only because women's education is inferior. With improved education, Iwamoto contends, women would outdo men in their powers of imagination as well (*JZ* 29 [July 15, 1886]:275). Not surprisingly, it is with respect to sensitivity that women are most accomplished:

> In the West it is said that women are the ones most easily moved; and in our country it is women who are the more sympathetic. Because of this it is argued that men see the logic of things . . . while women, listening to their findings, bring the word to others. . . . They feel pity for the poor and sympathize with their suffering, thus they devise ways to rescue them. They feel sorrow for the sick and sympathize with their loneliness, thus they nurse them. All these charitable acts are the work of women. This is a woman's forte, and not to be surpassed by men. [*JZ* 32 (August 15, 1886):23]

In concluding this series of essays, Iwamoto encourages women to take up the writing brush once again. To authorize his challenge he lists, in addition to the Western models of George Eliot, Mrs. Browning, Mrs. Beecher Stowe,

Mrs. Oliphant, and Hannah More, the "late greats" of the Japanese tradition: Murasaki, Sei, Ise (whom Iwamoto identifies as the author of *The Tales of Ise*), and the nun Abutsu.

From this introductory essay on women and prose fiction one can see that Iwamoto already regarded women's writing as not only a separate category but one that appealed to characteristics which he believed distinguished the female sex. Women had the potential to surpass men as writers because, *as females*, they were inherently more sensitive, emotional, observant, and creative. These critical ingredients were discernible in female-authored literature both in the West and in the Japanese literary tradition, he argued. It is unclear how much of either tradition Iwamoto had actually read. Marleigh Ryan questions Tsubouchi Shōyō's familiarity with *The Tale of Genji* by noting that "little sophisticated literary scholarship had been done on [it] by then and it is an excruciatingly difficult novel to read let alone fully comprehend."[62] The same could be said of other works of the Heian period and of other Meiji intellectuals. It is probable, therefore, that Iwamoto relied on other critics for studies and criticism of these works. For the Japanese classics, particularly the *Genji*, it is likely that Iwamoto deferred to Motoori Norinaga (1730–1801) and similar scholars of native studies. Motoori's well-known commentary on the *Genji* affirmed the work's validity as an example of *mono no aware* (courtly sensitivity) and in so doing, as Marianne Harrison points out, "inadvertently prioritized qualities considered 'feminine' by western standards."[63]

In his effort to distinguish Japanese traditions from what he saw as the overwhelming invasion of the Chinese, Motoori Norinaga had turned to the age-old dichotomy of Japanese heart versus Chinese intellect. Consequently, he had raised the *mono no aware* of classical literature—particularly that of *The Tale of Genji*—as the single most significant literary value in the Japanese tradition. He recognized the aesthetic concepts of poetic sensitivity, private emotion, and quiet spirituality as distinctly native traits, prized by all Japanese writers, male and female. Furthermore, he singled out these traits as being inherently "Japanese" (and thereby superior) by comparing them to those which he associated with China—namely, public action, intellect, cold logic, and calculation. His purpose in doing so was not to separate women's writing from men's but to distinguish Japanese from Chinese. As Harrison notes:

> Although Motoori makes a distinction between male and female nature, the perception of *mono no aware,* or "possessing a heart," is understood as a positive trait in human beings regardless of sex. What is clearly expressed as the enemy of *mono no aware* . . . is the heavy reliance on the Chinese style of writing that is too superficially clever and argumentative for his taste.

. . . Thus, in his conceptualization of the Yamato [native Japanese] spirit, Motoori posits a relationship between China and Japan that is similar to the opposition between intellect and emotions that characterize gender distinctions in the West.[64]

The influx of Western ideas during the early part of the Meiji period exposed Japanese intellectuals to Victorian notions of femininity in which male and female natures were defined according to binaries of intellect and emotion. Because of the imbricated relationship between imperialism and sexism, the characteristics that had once marked Japan superior vis-à-vis the Chinese Other were now reversed by these intellectuals and used to render Japan inferior vis-à-vis the West. Reforms, therefore, of traditional dress, hairstyles, and customs for Japanese men were largely geared toward making the "feminized" Japanese male more "masculine" in the eyes of the (male) West.[65] Significantly, at the same time that the Japanese male was struggling to masculinize himself along Western standards, the Western male—at least in England—was struggling to define himself against the feminizing standards of Victorian culture. As Ann Ardis notes in her study of feminisms and new modernisms in the West, "the ideological power stuggle between middle-class men and middle-class women took a new form in the 1860s and 1870s. Constituting itself in opposition to . . . female culture, a new male elite emphasized separation from women rather than appropriation of their virtues, while also valorizing 'manliness,' defined as 'anti-effeminacy, stiff-upper-lippery, and physical hardness.'"[66] In Japan, therefore, reforms of fiction along Western lines, necessarily influenced by exposure to Victorian images of the writer as a "man of letters,"[67] also sought to "masculinize" while "modernizing" the heretofore old-fashioned and effeminate Japanese prose form. Thus when Tsubouchi Shōyō looked back to the Heian tradition, he inflected Motoori's earlier reading of *mono no aware* with a gendered nuance, and in so doing found the classical style "too soft and feminine to serve as an instrument for the expression of modern life."[68]

When Meiji men endeavored to instill the literary arts with prestige and worth, they did so by, among other things, investing the *shōsetsu* with a seriousness of purpose: a mission to uncover the "truth" of society and thereby contribute to its reform. As Saganoya Omuro (1863–1947) reveals in his article "Mission of a Novelist" (Shōsetsuka no sekinin, 1889):

A *shōsetsu* writer is . . . a pursuer of truth, an acquirer of truth, a student of mankind, a master of human beings, a leader of men, an observer of society, a master of society, a social reformer. . . . Only philosophers and *shōsetsu* writers reveal the ultimate and the road to progress.[69]

By entitling the modern *shōsetsu* writer with a social mission of this dimension—a mission that rendered him a "leader of men, . . . a master of society, a social reformer"—Meiji critics assigned the role of writing to the male gender. This did not mean that women were expected to "break their brushes." Rather women were charged with complementing this male mission with one of their own—one that was appropriately "feminine." Just what the "feminine" entailed we shall see shortly. But one obvious characteristic was that genuinely feminine writing adhered to the classical conventions established in the Heian period. Harrison notes that since Japanese intellectuals, such as Shōyō, equated logocentric Western ideals of intellect, reason, and realism with male privilege, it followed that native "emotion" would be subordinated to the female position.[70] Murasaki Shikibu's emphasis in *The Tale of Genji* on *mono no aware*—heretofore a defining aspect of all Japanese literature and gender neutral—thus was requalified as feminine.

The native literary traditions were relinquished to women, those "repositories of the past," and "Murasaki Shikibu was gradually transformed from a mainstream writer to the primogenitor of the 'female literary tradition.'"[71] The male writer was free to assume a masculine prerogative, while at the same time resting assured that the native arts were protected and perpetuated by women.

A Step Backward

Now that literature occupied a visibly social position, literary roles for women, once at the center of the tradition, shifted to its periphery. Iwamoto, in what literary historian Wada Shigejirō has termed a "reversal" of his earlier position on women's writing as an "appropriate employment,"[72] advised that since woman belonged in the home, so too did the woman writer. In "Joshi to bunpitsu no gyō" (Women and the Literary Profession), a two-part essay serialized in 1887, Iwamoto noted:

> A woman becomes a wife and assists her husband; she becomes a mother and educates her children. It is not possible for her to work for the government as well, or to become a judge, an admiral, a governor, a school board member, a doctor, an operator, or a postal clerk. But if there is a job that is appropriate for her, it is writing. She can keep a brush and inkstone in a corner of the kitchen or bedroom and when she has a free moment, transfer her thoughts to paper. [*JZ* 79 (October 8, 1887):162]

Iwamoto, the "benefactor" of women writers, having earlier credited women with the potential talent to rival men as writers, now refines his argument to suggest that women will not become writers like men, because they will not pursue writing as a profession. In so doing he anticipates what will become the standard attitude toward writing by women. Women's writing was acceptable so long as it was considered a hobby or leisure activity conducted somewhere between the bedroom and the kitchen. Two years later, in an 1889 article in the journal *Bunmei no haha* (Mother of Civilization), the anonymous author of "What We Expect of Women Writers" (Joryū shōsetsuka ni nozomu) cautioned that if a woman should shun her "natural calling" of mothering and housekeeping, and "aspire to fame [such as that brought by literature], then we will laugh at her foolishness with gusto and reprove her mistaken beliefs with a thunderous roar!"[73]

Writing as a primary occupation or as a path to "fame" was to be a male activity. As Ikebukuro Kiyokaze had intimated of scholarship, fame in the public (male) realm was not for women (*JZ* 158 [April 20,1889]:6). But if a woman chose to write for her own diversion—"when she has a free moment"—for the edification of her sex, or as an expression of charity, then her activity was admirable and worthy of encouragement. The *Bunmei no haha* critic went so far as to summarize a program for such writers to follow: be feminine, be chaste, be mature. Since an understanding of the implications behind these directives is crucial to our subsequent evaluation of women's writing during the Meiji period, I want to use this critic's "program" as a framework in which to set forth my own analysis of contemporary attitudes toward women writers and the responses they provoked. I begin with his second point; his first I will divide into two sections for greater elucidation. The third point—the maturity of the woman writer—I will address in the concluding chapter of this study.

Chastity: Announcing the New Murasaki

Meiji women were expected not only to write in a language and style that reflected classical tastes but also to lead lives that were as exemplary as those of their Heian counterparts.[74] When Kitada Usurai made her debut at seventeen, for example, she was heralded as the next Murasaki Shikibu. But the criteria for this evaluation seemed to rely less on her actual writing—which was closer to Ozaki Kōyō than Murasaki—than on the public perception of her personality:

> As for her character, she is quiet and reserved, preferring to remain tucked away in her room, with brush and inkstone as friends. An admirable young lady, she steadfastly avoids being stained by the dust of this floating world. . . . For those who have sought the Murasaki Shikibu of the Meiji period— who but she can be the one?[75]

Staying indoors away from the "dust of this floating world" was a central requirement for the Meiji woman writer. She had no need to strive to be "a leader of men" or a "master of society." This she could leave to men. She— even more so than her male counterpart—faced a moral imperative. Since prose fiction still bore the taint of the Tokugawa past, it was her responsibility to ensure that her activities were beyond reproach. As she was believed to be the purer of the sexes, it was her duty to raise the standards of literature and thereby to improve the world for her sisters and daughters. Both Iwamoto and the *Bunmei no haha* critic echoed sentiments regarding the construction of gender that had prevailed in the Victorian West as well as in Late Imperial China. Since women were inherently docile and sweet, they softened the coarseness of men, mollified their violence, soothed their barbarism. Many women writers accepted this vision of female gentleness and purity. Wakamatsu Shizuko indicated that it was a woman's duty to "cleanse the filthy air" of contemporary society with her writing.[76]

Affluent and privileged, the Meiji woman writer was not typical of women in the general population, if writers ever are. Nakajima Shōen, for example, had been raised in a wealthy merchant family in Kyoto. After briefly serving the Meiji empress as a lady-in-waiting and literary tutor, she took a position as a speaker for the Freedom and Popular Rights Movement, where she dazzled audiences with her spirit and eloquence. When women were banned from public speaking, Shōen turned to writing and translating. Eventually she married a politician who was to become the first president of the Lower House.

Like Shōen, most of the women writing at the time shared unusual life stories. Often their fathers, elder brothers, or husbands held important positions as educators or bureaucrats. Many of these women had received the best education then available to their sex. The very term that was used to designate these writers, *"keishū sakka,"* reflects their privileged status. Literally "talents of the inner chambers," the term *keishū (guixiu)* was derived from China, where it had denoted exceptional women of the "female quarters" or "inner palace."[77] In the early Meiji period, the term was used interchangeably with *"joryū"* (woman's style) to indicate works of female authorship.[78] By the end of the Meiji period, *joryū* had replaced *keishū* except when critics referred retrospectively to the women writers of the earlier age. This usage suggests that *keishū* was not simply a gender designation but incorporated qualities pertaining to social class that were no longer present in the women writing after the Meiji.

Because of their privileged backgrounds, therefore, the *keishū sakka* were expected to write not simply as women but as exemplars of their sex. Judgment was harsh for any who strayed beyond what was considered proper and womanly. Miyake Kaho, daughter of a prominent statesman, discovered

how offended critics could be by female-authored works when reviews of
Warbler in the Grove (Yabu no uguisu) appeared in 1888. The story, which we
shall discuss in detail in the next chapter, seems innocuous enough today. If
anything it appears that Kaho took pains to strike the appropriate moral
chords. But she erred when she included conversations among servants. A
critic for *Kokumin no tomo* (The Nation's Friend) took her to task in August
1888. He strongly advised her to avoid any reference to the lower classes in
the future. How could it possibly be that an innocent girl was able to describe
the lower classes so skillfully? His answer, of course, was that she could not.
Either she was not an "innocent" girl or she had had someone else write the
"dirty" parts. The critic cautioned Kaho to "emulate the Murasaki Shikibu of
old and not," as he described women writers of lesser integrity, "the Shikibu
of the back alleys."[79]

By confining women writers to upper-class subject matter and classical
diction, male critics rendered the ideal of a modern Murasaki forever unat-
tainable. That is to say, critics effectively barred women from the modern
movement that tended toward "realism" and fitted them into a fossilized image
of a femininity that most likely had never existed. Moreover, as Susan Gubar
and Sandra Gilbert have suggested of the reception that similarly met British
women writers, by limiting women to this "antique authority" male critics and
writers precluded any "threat of contemporary competition."[80] This is not to
suggest that the *keishū sakka* themselves had no complicity in these restrictions.
Consciously or not, most tried to conform to this ideal of the writing woman.
Koganei Kimiko, known for her graceful translations of English literature into
classical Japanese, declared: "It has been suggested that the trend toward
extreme realism *(kyokujitsuha)* is not appropriate for women, and I tend to
agree. I sincerely hope that if one must write of unpleasant matters *(iyashiki
koto)*, one will not lose sight of one's high-mindedness *(takaki kokoro)*."[81]

At the same time that female authors were asked to withdraw within the
elegant enclosures of the Heian myth, they were told that they had a right, in
fact a moral obligation, to engage society. Through her writing, Iwamoto
declared in "Bunshō no risō" (Ideal Literature), a woman could change the
world. And she could do this without even leaving her home:

> With her tears, a woman can refresh Japan; with her brush, she can move
> the nation. Even if she does not become a teacher, she can teach. Even if she
> does not have the power to vote, she can control future legislation. [JZ
> 152(March 9, 1889):248]

Encouraged by Iwamoto, several women wrote pieces for *Jogaku zasshi* that
advocated social change and a woman's right to pursue happiness. For exam-

ple, the heroine of "Koware yubiwa" (The Broken Ring, 1891) by Shimizu Shikin reflects: "Misfortune and sorrow, it was argued, were not by any means a woman's inherent state. . . . I began to believe that Japanese women, too, had a right to happiness."[82] Shikin's protagonist refuses to assume the mantle of "tragic heroine." Instead she resists her "fate." After extricating herself from an unhappy marriage, she vows to spend the rest of her life working for the good of her sisters so that they not fall into the same trap that had caught her. Shikin's story, which warned readers of the abuses inherent in the current marriage system, exemplified the kind of writing Wakamatsu Shizuko had suggested for women in an 1890 article: "Ideally, I would weave into my stories that which I have learned and discovered in my own meager education, thereby providing, I hope, some measure of benefit to my younger sisters—my readers."[83]

Inspired perhaps by the kind of rhetoric *Jogaku zasshi* offered, Usurai, who just one year earlier had made her debut as the "New Murasaki," took up her brush to move the nation. In her essay "Wretched Sights" (Asamashi no sugata), published by the literary journal *Bungei kurabu* (Literary Arts Club) in March 1895, she described scenes she had witnessed during a visit to the licensed quarters on an annual festival day:

> In front of one of the establishments—I cannot remember the name of the house now—a gang of touts was swarming around a large man in his forties who looked to be a shopkeeper of sorts. . . . Even when they tugged at him, he did not lose his temper. In fact, he smiled at them and, looking somewhat baffled, seemed to be offering his apologies when, just at that moment, the glass shoji slid open and a prostitute in a long outer robe stepped out. She whispered what must have been words of encouragement in his ear for quite some time and, refusing to take no for an answer, led him inside. Surely, he has a wife and child awaiting him at home. If they hear of what has taken place here, how they will weep.
>
> Prostitution is just a trade like any other, I have heard it said. But another with such horrible consequences is hard to imagine.[84]

In the next issue of *Bungei kurabu* an anonymous critic took venomous exception to Usurai's essay, implying that her wanton display of "superficial" knowledge made her little better than a prostitute herself. To counter Usurai's position as a proper woman observing the activities of the Yoshiwara district, the critic assumed the persona of a prostitute:

> That's right, I was sold into the business when I was seven. And since the time I was a courtesan's apprentice I've mastered . . . koto, samisen, incense,

flower arts, tea, . . . fancy words, and love talk, too, until here I am now in my "long outer robe." And you! "The New Murasaki of Japan"! You've learned all you know from reading *Jogaku zasshi, Miyako no hana,* and all those other new publications. How glad I am that my education differs so from that of a disgusting writer like you![85]

Not only had a young lady, who should have remained tucked away in her inner rooms with no knowledge of this world, written of matters beyond her ken; she had done so in a haughty and dogmatic fashion. Here was a mere girl, barely twenty, lecturing men. Usurai's anonymous detractor, it would seem, was not as upset by her topic as by the self-righteous anger that coursed through her essay:

Pulling in customers is the tout's handicraft, as making lace is yours. Whether he draws a customer in or not has nothing to do with you. Don't worry about it. And don't overstep your bounds as a woman. If you have the leisure to criticize us with that fancy writing brush of yours, then your time would be better served sewing dust cloths. That's what we think![86]

What Dolores Palomo has observed of the criticism leveled at eighteenth-century Western women novelists may be applied to Meiji writers like Usurai as well: "Women writers [were] allowed to be cloyingly moralistic but never outspoken, libertine or freethinking."[87] Usurai had made too much of herself and of her own ideas. Like most *keishū sakka,* she was an elite young woman, pampered by her father, soon to be protected by her husband.[88] It was unseemly for such women to take themselves so seriously. Their writing was to be regarded as "housewife art" *(okusama gei),* as it was termed by five men who coauthored a 1908 article in the literary journal *Shinchō* (New Tide): "It is half for self-amusement that women write fiction *(shōsetsu).* But men labor over each page of their manuscript while they write. Women write for entertainment; men suffer."[89]

Iwamoto, as well, believed that the female literary sphere was to remain separate from that of men—replicating the separate social spheres. If a woman were true to her female nature *(josui),* a nature that was distinct from but complementary to a man's, her works would have illimitable value.

With Tears for Water, Blood for Ink

Although Iwamoto never defined female essence *(josui)* per se, critics of his generation referred to it time and again—assuming that the very notion of a female essence would be obvious to others. Here I wish to explore various aspects of this "essence" as represented in the criticism lodged against those women writers who betrayed it, denied it, or simply never recognized it.

The primary characteristic of *josui* has already been noted: a woman should not be outspoken in declaiming her ideas or too ambitious in her approach to writing. Such activity, many believed, was unnatural to women, as the female sex was assumed to be biologically incapable of sophisticated intellectual inquiry. Iwamoto and others argued that this incapacity was not due to any inherent mental lack but was the result of limited educational opportunities compounded by the fact that a woman, busy as she was between bedroom and kitchen, did not have time for sustained thought. A man, however, said Iwamoto, could meditate on a wall for nine years and come up with groundbreaking revelations.[90]

Instead of trying to do what they could not possibly do well, women were advised to express what men could not. In the same *Shinchō* article that proposed the term "housewife art," the authors called for the revival of sentimentalism in fiction, which they felt had been needlessly displaced by naturalism. "We want stories that will make readers cry," they said, "and we want these from women."[91] If "thinking"—that is to say, presenting one's ideas in a forthright and declarative manner—was the province of men, then "emoting" was a woman's forte. According to a critic for *Teikoku bungaku* (Literature of the Empire): "A woman philosopher, a woman logician—now these are contradictions in terms. . . . So why is it that we find women succeeding as novelists *(shōsetsuka)?* There is no reason other than heart *(hāto)*."[92] Iwamoto encouraged the *keishū sakka* to use "her tears for water and her blood for ink as she gave vent to her pure feelings" (*JZ* 152 [March 9, 1889]:247).

In an era when native traditions were quickly being eroded, or so it was believed, the woman writer's work was to offer a brief respite, a return to quieter, simpler values. As Iwamoto and others argued, her works were to be beautiful. They were to bring pleasure, to entertain, and to do so in an elegant *(yūga)* though modest *(onjun)* fashion. Although a woman's writing should be instructive, it should not tire her readers with sophisticated ideas; nor should she aim to offend, startle, or titillate. Indeed, the writing she produced should be seen as a partner to male texts, just as her gentle and sweet nature was thought to balance a man's strength and boldness.

But If They Copy Men . . .

Women who resisted gentility and elegance in their writing and modeled themselves after their male contemporaries drew the ire of critics like Iwamoto. By the time he published his next significant essay on women and writing, "Joryū shōsetsuka no honshoku" (The True Color of Women Writers) in March 1889, a number of women writers had emerged. In 1887, Nakajima Shōen published "Zen'aku no chimata" (The Crossroads of Good and Evil), her adaptation of Bulwer-Lytton's *Eugene Aram*, in *Jogaku zasshi*. In 1889 she contributed an original work, *Sankan no meika* (The Noble Flower of the Valley), a "political novel" based on her own experiences, to the literary journal *Miyako no hana* (Flower of the Capital). Miyake Kaho had made her debut with *Warbler in the Grove* in 1888; Kimura Akebono (1872–1890), then only seventeen years old, published "Fujo no kagami" (Mirror of Womanhood) in the daily *Yomiuri Newspaper* in 1889.[93] Even Iwamoto's younger sister serialized a story in *Miyako no hana* from November 4 to December 16, 1888.

Shōen's works, Iwamoto thought, were too political. Kaho's piece was imitative. Akebono's story involved unrealistic flights of fantasy. None of these texts had the feel of women's writing, at least not as the category had been reinscribed by Iwamoto and others of his generation. Nor did they seem to mesh with the works of their Western counterparts. In "The True Color of Women Writers," therefore, Iwamoto complained that these works lacked "female essence" *(josui)*. The authors were too "captivated by current trends," too imitative of contemporary offerings by men. If only women would apply themselves to that which men do not understand and cannot approach, Iwamoto grumbled:

> There are so many things that male writers overlook. And this is what superior female writers should explore. First of all, someone needs to protest the sorrow facing today's women. Who will complain of the prisoner's miseries, the child's suffering? Who will sing of the beauties of Mount Fuji and Lake Biwa. . . ? Women should make these the focus of their art. Thus, their emotions will be effortlessly fulfilled, their writing most natural.
>
> But if they copy men's behavior—men's baser behavior—they warp their emotions and think impure thoughts. Their writing will then be warped and impure. [*JZ* 153 (March 16, 1889):272]

Iwamoto's exhortation for women writers returned him to his earlier argument. A woman is naturally sympathetic and sensitive. Her creative vision, therefore, must remain focused on that which she sees best. Leave the rest to men.

Curiously, Iwamoto and his peers did not suggest that women were incapable of writing like men. Indeed, as Iwamoto had earlier delineated in his three-part essay "Women and Prose Fiction," women certainly had the potential to rival men because they possessed the three essential requirements for a writer: creativity, observation, and sensitivity. They could write as well as men if they were trained to do so. Iwamoto's contemporary Ikebukuro Kiyokaze noted in his discussion of women's education that a woman could learn as well as a man. But what was the point in her doing so, since she could not use her learning "like a man"? Similarly, women were capable of writing as well as any man. But why should they, since they were not men? A woman was to write "like a woman"—to meet the demands of women's writing.

The essence of the novel, as Tsubouchi Shōyō would have it, was love *(ninjō)*—specifically sexual love. But as we shall see in the following chapters, the portrayal of sexual love was beyond the periphery of most women writers. Morally chaste, the *keishū* writer did not have access to the experiences her male counterparts enjoyed. Nor was the manner in which love had been depicted in the literary traditions of the *gesaku*-era *ninjōbon* or on the kabuki stage accessible to her. Although not all women were interested in singing the praises of Mount Fuji and Lake Biwa, those who attempted to write of the brothels (as did Kitada Usurai) or of lower-class love affairs (Miyake Kaho) were castigated for their presumptuousness and imitativeness. This confining of the woman writer as an author of gentle emotions, coupled with the injunction not to "lose sight of the ideal," meant that women could safely write only about a bland, unsatisfied kind of love, a vague—though certainly not sexual—kind of yearning.

In other words, the "love" a *keishū* writer portrayed was to be confined to marriage. By the mid-Meiji period, particularly following the promulgation of the Constitution, which undercut any hopes women might have had for independence either inside or outside of marriage,[94] most female-authored works were limited to marriage plots. That is, they concerned a young woman's (reluctant) preparation for marriage; her disappointment in the marital union or else her disappointment in her inability to marry the man of her choice or to marry at all; her unfair treatment at the hands of her in-laws once she did marry; and her suicide (or at the very least self-sacrifice) as the result of any or all of these scenarios. That the married state, as presented in these female-authored works, is almost always one of sorrow suggests a subtle protest against the inequitable and outdated marriage system.

Although women had been encouraged to create a literary expression parallel to men's, they were not to think of the two spheres as equal. Reason and logic, engagement in social issues (or issues outside the marital home, more specifically, issues of the brothels), and broad narrative vision—all seen as inherent in male writers—came to be valued above the so-called feminine sensibilities of emotion.[95] Critic Akiyama Shun suggests that this prioritizing of the cerebral and the restriction of women from it was less the expression of an inherent feudalistic misogyny than a calculated effort on the part of the "Meiji (male) elitist . . . to monopolize Western intellectual work."[96] Akiyama's observation further supports the argument that Meiji (male) writers and critics deliberately limited female authors to an "antique authority" in an effort to exclude them from competition in the modern/Western/intellectual realms.

Not only was thinking more important than emoting, but a woman's heart, it would seem, was itself a male construct. When Ichiyō began writing under Nakarai Tōsui's tutelage, for example, he criticized her language as too rough *(arappoi)* for a woman. He compared her carelessness to that of the kabuki female impersonator *(onnagata)* who, afraid of being upstaged by a superior male-role actor, allows his gestures and speech to become vulgar. "Women writers are like this too," Tōsui continued. "They forget that they are women, and their language grows rough. The language a woman uses in everyday conversation may not strike you as coarse when you hear it, but it will when written."[97] Ichiyō had to rewrite her submissions until they struck Tōsui as appropriately feminine.

Almost all the *keishū sakka*, like Ichiyō, reached their readership through the agency of a male mentor. Kaho was advised and assisted by Tsubouchi Shōyō; Usurai by Ozaki Kōyō—in each case, the association was arranged by the woman's father. Shizuko found her voice through Iwamoto; Inafune, through Yamada Bimyō, the editor of *Iratsume* (The Maiden)—both women married their mentors. Koganei Kimiko was assisted by her older brother, the writer Mori Ōgai. To a certain extent these men determined what and where their protégées would publish and, more important, how they would write. This kind of meddlesome mentoring was inherent to the Japanese publishing system, in which a protégé, male or female, depended on an established writer's largesse for access to print.[98] But for male writers, gender was not part of the hierarchical equation. Much of the advice male mentors gave their female protégés was premised on received notions of what constituted "female essence." Women soon learned that they could not write about themselves or about collective female experiences without resorting to codified notions of the feminine. Otherwise, their portraits would be, as Tōsui cautioned, jarring. Ichiyō and the other *keishū sakka* had to learn, like the female impersonator, to represent women as they had been portrayed by men for centuries. Their efforts compelled Yosano Akiko to remark in 1909 that the female characters women writers produced were "lies" *(uso no onna)*— meant to seduce a male reader.[99]

According to Tazawa Inafune (1874–1896), who began her writing career in 1894, a woman who gave vent to her true feelings and really wrote with tears and blood, as Iwamoto had counseled, was accused of being unfeminine. In her posthumously published story "Godaidō" (The Five Great Halls, 1896), her male character (a writer) muses:

These women writers are certainly pitiful creatures. Whenever they allow themselves to describe even a little of their own thoughts, they are immediately derided as hussies *(otenba)*. Fearing just this sort of reaction, they avoid writing what they really want to, all the while hoping to be praised as feminine.[100]

Separate Spheres: The Red and the White

If women were going to write the way Iwamoto thought they should, they needed a forum. Although the literary journal *Miyako no hana*, inaugurated in 1888, *Bungei kurabu* and *Taiyō* (The Sun), both founded in 1895,[101] and the daily newspapers occasionally published women's work, these inclusions were sporadic. Moreover, since women writers were thought to "brighten" particularly those literary journals devoted to the somber offerings by men, their contributions were regarded as little more than window dressing. Consequently, the addition of a woman's work in such a journal was often described as "a clump of budding flowers amidst a forest of beards"[102] or a "splash of red against the green."[103] Women writers were generally regarded, therefore, as decoration and not as legitimate members of any given literary coterie. They had few assurances that their literary efforts would be accepted with the regularity that their male peers enjoyed. Women lacked the network of fraternal bonds and were denied the authority to produce and control a journal of their own—hence the importance of *Jogaku zasshi* to female literary efforts. Although not strictly a female enterprise, it was the closest to offer women a certain measure of journalistic space. And small though the measure was, women could be assured of inclusion—if, that is, their contributions were attuned to editorial expectations.

By 1892, however, *Jogaku zasshi* was threatening to become a venue for young male writers. The journal had begun to showcase some of the brightest male literary talents in Japan, many of whom first achieved attention in its pages. Yamaji Aizan (1864–1917), historian and literary critic, made his debut when his translation of *The Courtship of Miles Standish* was serialized in *Jogaku zasshi* in 1891 and 1892. In February 1892 the young poet Kitamura Tōkoku (1868–1894), an occasional contributor to the journal, published his seminal essay "Ensei shika to josei" (The Pessimistic Poet and Women), which electrified a generation of young readers and opened the door to the romantic movement in modern Japanese literature. Inspired by Tōkoku, Shimazaki Tōson (1872–1943) began contributing to the journal in 1892. Other male writers were soon to follow.

These young men were eager to redirect *Jogaku zasshi* along more purely literary lines. Influenced by literary journals such as *Miyako no hana*, *Shigarami zōshi* (The Weir), and *Waseda bungaku* (Waseda University

Literary Journal), they resented Iwamoto's insistence on didacticism.[104] Writers like Tōkoku and Tōson, who would have preferred to focus exclusively on belles lettres, nevertheless were compelled to offer essays on Milton's wife and Martin Luther's mother and interviews with Frances Willard, the leader of the Women's Christian Temperance Union. Other members of the journal staff, both male and female, urged Iwamoto to include more decidedly political articles.[105] Not surprisingly, Iwamoto felt the journal was being pulled in too many directions. Although he had named women to the staff in 1890, only five contributed to the journal with any regularity.[106] And even though he had instituted numerous policies to encourage female readership—in particular he had simplified the journal's language and added *furigana* "spellings" for all Chinese characters[107]—it seemed that women and women's issues were being supplanted by matters that seemingly had little to do with *jogaku*. Iwamoto realized he would have to take significant measures if his journal was to stay on track.

His solution was unprecedented. After surveying his readership, Iwamoto decided to divide *Jogaku zasshi* into "White Cover" and "Red Cover" issues. From June 1892 to April 1893 he published White Covers on the first and third week of each month and Red Covers on the second and fourth. White Covers were devoted to social reform pieces, literary criticism, poems, and stories for enlightened young men and women. Red Covers, by contrast, were to address women seeking adult education, members of women's associations, and housewives. Accordingly, Red Covers articles dealt with household management and children.

White Covers conveniently allowed Tenchi, Tōson, Tōkoku, and other contributors a forum for articles with pronounced literary and political content. Tōson offered essays on Saigyō's poetry and George Eliot's heroines, for example, while Tōkoku contributed essays on *Crime and Punishment*, democracy, and parliamentary law. With articles ranging across such a wide spectrum, the White Covers issues of *Jogaku zasshi* began to resemble a *sōgō zasshi*, a "composite" or general-interest magazine, of which there were already several popular alternatives, *Kokumin no tomo* foremost among them.[108]

The Red Covers issues, however, now appealed exclusively to women. Readers were entertained with, for example, biographies of such "notable" women as Christopher Columbus' wife and the "wise mothers" of Shakespeare, Carlyle, Napoleon, and St. Augustine. Under the household column (with titles still duly rendered in English), readers could study up on personal hygiene and housekeeping. Additional articles reported on marriage practices in Japan and abroad, on graduation exercises at national girls' schools, and on interviews with girl students. Red Covers did not shun literature by any means but included prose fiction, children's stories, and articles on *The Tale of Genji* (issue 323), the Nun Abutsu's poetry (issue 321), and similarly appropriate classics.

Just as White Covers were now in direct competition with other *sōgō zasshi*, Red Covers had little to distinguish them from the many *fujin zasshi* (women's magazines) now flooding the market. According to an article in an earlier issue of *Jogaku zasshi*, there were by this time more than thirteen journals devoted exclusively to women's education, in addition to the many general-interest women's magazines. Among some of the more notable magazines in the latter variety were *Katei zasshi* (Home Journal), founded by Tokutomi Sohō in 1892 to reach the readers not already served by his *sōgō zasshi (Kokumin no tomo)*. *Iratsume* (The Maiden, 1887–1891), edited by Yamada Bimyō, was devoted to the feminine literary arts, primarily poetry. *Kijo no tomo* (Her Ladyship's Friend, 1887), *Nihon shinfujin* (The New Japanese Lady, 1888), and *Bunmei no haha* (The Mother of Civilization, 1888) were all founded on the principle of *ryōsai kenbo*—that is, on inculcating women's roles as "good wives and wise mothers."

Generally, the staff of White Covers did not overlap with that of its red counterpart. White Covers were, roughly speaking, an all-male enterprise, whereas Red Covers, run by Shimizu Shikin and Wakamatsu Shizuko, were all-female. (Red Covers, therefore, represent the first female-managed, mass-produced journal in Japan.) There were exceptions. Shizuko appeared in White Covers when she contributed translations of English-language works. On two occasions, Kaho had works of prose fiction published in White Covers; Shikin, once. Conversely, Tōson sometimes appeared in Red Covers. Although the division of the journal into White and Red gave women writers more authority over their half, it also subordinated women's literary efforts to those of men. It marginalized women's writing by limiting it primarily to the home and the practical, while men's efforts were held to be critical, cerebral, high art. Woman's position as writer, therefore, explicitly replicated her place in society. Like Iwamoto's "queen of the home," she had jurisdiction over her literary space. But it was a space defined, contained, and conscribed by men.

Surely Iwamoto intended his program to restore women to literary prominence—to give them the voice that attitudes such as *danson/johi* had silenced. Yet in defining this program for women writers, he also tied them to it. Iwamoto's male protégés were able to break away from him and form their own journal, *Bungakukai*. But such alternatives were not available to the women under his guidance, since they lacked the network and the authority to strike out on their own. Despite Iwamoto's yearnings for "excellent women authors," therefore, he helped to construct the attitudes that treated women writers as little more than literary daughters confined in boxes. He confined them to his Red Covers—to the space between the bedroom and the kitchen.[109]

The division of *Jogaku zasshi* into the explicitly male and female spheres of White and Red was significant to the codification of "women's literature"—that is, a literature both for and by women.[110] Articles on certain literary classics—the Nun Abutsu but not the Priest Saigyō—were thought to be more suitable for a female audience. Essays on foreign literature were deemed more fitting for male readership, even when those essays treated female subject matter, such as George Eliot's heroines. This is not to say that foreign topics were unacceptable reading material for women. Handled selectively, examples from the West could prove instructive. Thus biographies of Western women, even when written by men, were held to benefit the Red Covers readership. Moreover, the very qualities that made these works appropriate for women marked them as inappropriate for men and thereby gendered female.

This division did not mean that women were completely excluded from the White sphere or men from the Red. When women wrote or translated creative fiction on topics not represented as "female content," their contributions were published in White Covers and intended for a primarily male audience or for an audience gendered male. As a result, these submissions were considered universal and the women who wrote them were accorded status as provisional members of the White camp. When these same women wrote for an exclusively female audience, however, or wrote of issues limited primarily to female experience, their works were no longer "universal" and were thereby gendered female. "Female" works were occasionally allowed space in the White sphere. But to be so included these works had to represent what were considered feminine values. That is, they were to meet the three literary skills that Iwamoto had enumerated earlier: be attentive to detail (but not imitative), be properly sentimental (but never intellectual), and be imaginative (but not presumptuous). In other words, to enter the White sphere of literature women either had to degender their voices and speak from the neutral position of the universal or else they had to femininize their voices so as to appear appropriately as the female exemplar.

Men could participate in the female sphere. But unlike the neutralizing required of women who wrote "universally," those men who ventured into the female sphere did not have to crossdress or emasculate themselves. Rather, they had to "dress down"—that is, bring the register of their voices down an octave or two to make it more suitable for a female audience. Hence when the twenty-year-old Tōson wrote biographies of Columbus' mother or essays on *The Tale of Genji* for the Red Covers, he was expected to take steps to speak down to his audience (largely middle-aged women) by sounding appropriately fatherly and instructive.

In April 1893, *Jogaku zasshi* reverted to its original format with publication twice monthly. The division of the journal into White and Red had robbed it of its vitality by denying its versatility. Moreover, the marketing of *Jogaku zasshi* as both a general-interest magazine *(sōgō zasshi)* and a women's magazine *(fujin zasshi)* had placed it in direct competition with established journals in those categories, thus diluting its readership. Even after the two covers were reunited, the scars remained. Now the journal was in direct competition with *Bungakukai,*[111] which had siphoned away a large portion of *Jogaku zasshi*'s male genius as well as its readership, both male and female. The Red camp, it would seem, had been overwhelmed by the White.

Iwamoto felt betrayed by Tenchi, Tōkoku, and the other young men he had helped to establish.[112] He was also growing alienated from his earlier stance as a Christian: Christians were increasingly coming under attack for what was perceived as their lack of patriotism.[113] With the proclamation of the Imperial Rescript on Education in 1890, mission schools were forced to forgo public display of Christian ritual. Other Christian schools, such as Meiji Women's School, were attacked as hotbeds of sexual promiscuity. Conservative elements in the government purposely misunderstood Iwamoto's call for reform of the family system and turned his argument on its head by accusing him and his school of corrupting the virtues of Japanese women by inundating them with selfish ideas about love, marriage, and individual freedom. In the wake of the Sino-Japanese War and the upswing in nationalism that it provoked, many schools for women, private and public, began to fold. Of the thirty-one public schools in 1890, fewer than ten were left by 1894.[114]

On February 5, 1896, the Meiji Women's School burned to the ground. Five days later, Iwamoto's wife Wakamatsu Shizuko died. Iwamoto reopened the school at another location, and he continued his work with *Jogaku zasshi*. But both journal and school had lost their spirit. Disenchanted with his idealism and Christian faith, left behind by the young men he had fostered, and abandoned by the loss of a wife, Iwamoto fell into a tailspin of despair from which he would never fully recover.

Modern Murasaki

Jogaku zasshi began, as Michael Brownstein notes, in "an age dominated by two conflicting impulses in Japanese society: the desire to be recognized by the West as a civilized nation and the fear of losing essential Japanese characterizations in the process of achieving that recognition through Westernization."[115] The anxiety this conflict produced had a direct impact on women's roles in the emerging nation-state. While on the one hand Meiji intellectuals were eager to prove that Japanese women (and the nation itself) were as "civilized" as their Western counterparts, on the other they were just as eager to protect in women the quintessential Japanese features that they themselves felt forced to abandon. For women writers this meant an adherence to the classical style, now gendered "female" by the modern dynamic.

Clearly women were not actively discouraged from writing. Male reformers recognized a need for a revival of female authors—as Iwamoto's many essays suggest. But it was the definition of this need that proved confining. Before women had even begun to write in the modern period, male-constructed notions regarding the direction, purpose, and shape of their efforts were in force. Just as a woman's domestic role required that she offer a quiet retreat from the workaday world of masculinity, so her literary role demanded that she create a refuge from the intellectually challenging, morally dubious, westernized realm of the male text. Indeed, the woman writer was there to clean up the filth of contemporary literature with her "own pure hand."

Western feminist literary critics have contended that the lack of a female tradition in Western letters impeded attempts by modern women writers to authorize their literary efforts. In Japan, the opposite could perhaps be argued. The appearance of a glorious literary heritage of female authorship threatened to frustrate the early efforts of modern Japanese women writers. In the first place, modern women were expected to adhere to the styles and concerns of women who had written centuries earlier and who had been redefined in the Meiji period as not only paragons of literary talent but paragons of "femininity." Moreover, the female-dominated literary activity of the past became a foil by which to measure the "modernity" of the male-dominated literary activity of the present. Contemporary works by men were "modern" because they were not classical. Contemporary works by women were "feminine" because they were not modern. Thus while Meiji women were being encouraged on the one hand to join the modern literary sphere of prose fiction along with their male counterparts, they were being reminded on the other that as women they were expected to adhere to the feminine models established by their Heian foremothers. When women experimented with colloquial language, contemporary problems, and the personal subject— essential ingredients for what was deemed modern in a literature now aspiring to the realism of the nineteenth-century Western novel—they removed themselves from those elegant enclosures of the classical, marked "feminine," and invited charges of immodesty, vulgarity, and other unladylike traits. Yet when they resisted the modern impulse and confined themselves to the classical, they were often rendered invisible for their antiquated "femininity."

Political changes conspired against women as well. Although women had been encouraged to remain within the domestic sphere, early Meiji reforms had led them to expect a degree of latitude in their roles there. By the end of the Meiji period, however, particularly with the enactment of the Civil Code in 1898, the promise of greater participation in society at large, or even of authority within the home, had been nullified. The Civil Code remanded women to the demeaning confines of the *ie* (family) system and "attempted to convert all of Japan into a single Tokugawa samurai model, one of the most repressive, from the standpoint of women, in Japanese history."[116] As Sievers describes the implication of this code, "it made it impossible for women to be thought of as anything but commodities in a continuing patriarchal, patrilineal market. . . . *Danson johi*, that attitude of contempt for women that Meiji feminists had struggled against for three decades, was now reemphasized, with official approval."[117]

As Shimizu Shikin ruefully observed in her essay "Jobungakusha nanzo ideru to no osokiya" (Why Are Female Literati So Slow to Appear?, 1890), women now had the education and the abilities to rejoin the modern literary world, but they allowed their talents to waste away because they still clung to misguided modesty. "Do not confuse humility with cowardice," she warned her sisters sharply.[118] But full participation in a modern literary enterprise so decisively male would require extraordinary courage and inventive narrative strategies. In the chapters that follow, I describe three representative women writers and the three different approaches they took to ensuring their access to print.

Chapter Two

Through Thickets of Imitation

Miyake Kaho and the First Song of Spring

She didn't write it.
She wrote it, but she shouldn't have.
She wrote it, but look what she wrote about.
She wrote it, but "she" isn't really an artist and "it" isn't really serious,
of the right genre—i.e., really art.
She wrote it, but she wrote only one of it.
She wrote it, but it's only interesting/included in the canon for one,
limited reason.
She wrote it, but there are very few of her.
                           —Joanna Russ, *How to Suppress Women's Writing,* 1983

To suggest that women are discouraged from writing is too simple. Thus Joanna Russ argues in her humorous though revealing look at the role literary criticism has played in silencing, obscuring, and ignoring female authors. They are not discouraged—not directly. But by holding them to gender-determined criteria that set them apart from the mainstream, women are subtly shelved or silenced.[1]

In many respects, Miyake Kaho has received such treatment. Some contemporary critics believed her debut piece *Warbler in the Grove* was covertly written by Tsubouchi Shōyō. More recent critics have charged that Shōyō, though not actually authoring the work, heavily edited it. (She didn't write it.) If Kaho did indeed write the work, then contemporary critics took her to task for including vulgar subject matter—conversations between menservants and the machinations of a fallen woman. (She wrote it, but she shouldn't have.) Then there were those who minimized the importance of her accomplishment by reading *Warbler* as a female version of Shōyō's *The Character of Modern-Day Students*—a mere imitation and hardly worthy of serious review. (She wrote it . . . but it isn't really art.) Finally, Kaho has been castigated for writing about subjects only women would (or should) enjoy—fancy dress balls, a girls' school, and marriage. (She wrote it, but look what she wrote about.)

Miyake Kaho has long been associated with "women's writing" or *joryū bungaku*. She is acknowledged as the first woman to have written in the modern period. And it is for this reason and this reason alone that her name is recorded in literary histories. (She wrote it, but it's only included in the canon for one, limited reason.) Few scholars bother actually to read her work—so convinced are they by previous criticism that it is not worth the effort—and therefore dismiss her with a summary footnote or two. Since Kaho is deemed unworthy of serious consideration, she often receives no consideration at all. Much of the information available on her is largely secondhand and the product of speculation. That is to say, one critic or literary historian will repeat what another has said without investigating whether or

Figure 6   Miyake Kaho in Western attire. (Courtesy of Nihon Kindai Bungakkan)

not the previous assertion is valid. These speculations have become cited so often that they have made their way into the literary record as undisputed fact. Most of the references to Kaho cite her motivation for writing, her privileged upbringing, and the effect it had on opening doors for her in the publishing world. These descriptions generally situate Kaho alongside her famous contemporary, Higuchi Ichiyō. Kaho is commended for having introduced Ichiyō to the people who would help launch her career. But then she is positioned as representive of everything that Ichiyō was not—thus making Ichiyō's debut and short career all the more poignant and spectacular. Ichiyō was not privileged. She had to push and pull at the doors of the publishing world with her own frail hands, and she died just as she was discovering her true abilities. While the comparison between these women romanticizes Ichiyō, it denigrates Kaho . . . and unfairly so.

Kaho was a vibrant and imaginative writer—attributes that reflect her own character and personality. Though certainly inspired by Tsubouchi Shōyō's *The Character of Modern-Day Students*, her *Warbler in the Grove* is not a mere imitation. It is delightfully inventive, humorous as well as socially engaging, and has a surprisingly fresh and modern feel despite the classical style of the narrative. In this chapter I elucidate my findings by examining *Warbler in the Grove* against the background of contemporary Meiji literature. Because the text is generally unavailable to modern readers of Japanese and completely inaccessible to readers of English, I will summarize it fairly extensively. I will then explicate Kaho's work as a female success story and compare it to the career of her male contemporary, Tsubouchi Shōyō.

Let us begin, then, by examining Kaho's early life and family background, her motivation for writing, and the circumstances that led to her debut. Unfortunately information on Kaho today is sparse at best and biased at worst. Here I rely on the studies by Wada Shigejirō and Shioda Ryōhei, bearing in mind that although these works tend to be the most thorough and unbiased, they are based almost entirely on Kaho's own essay, written shortly before her death at seventy-six, in which she recounts her childhood and early career as a writer: "Watashi no ayunde kita michi—Omoide no hito-bito" (The Path I Took—The People I Remember, 1939). I, too, will defer to Kaho's memory—trying as I do so to keep in perspective the circumstances under which she wrote.

Born to a World of Dust and Smoke

The chrysanthemum blooms and blooms,
While the hollyhock withers;
And to the west the jangle of bits and bridles.

Kaho suggests that this lyric, popular in the years immediately prior to the Meiji Restoration of 1868, aptly describes the world into which she was born.[2] It was a world of chaos, change, uncertainty, and (for most) optimism. The hollyhock of the Tokugawa family was dying, while the chrysanthemum, symbol of the imperial family, bloomed—protected by the horse-riding warriors of the west. For Kaho's family, supporters of the soon-to-be-vanquished Tokugawa regime, the return to imperial rule was met with guarded resistance. Kaho was born nearly a year after the Shōgitai battle in Ueno—a last-ditch effort on the part of retainers still loyal to the shogun to resist the restoration. Kaho thus entered the world, as she recalls, "amidst the dust and smoke of the collapsing Tokugawa shogunate."[3] All was confusion. Even the precise date of Kaho's birth is uncertain—though the reason for the confusion was personal and not political. Kaho's birth date was originally given in the family registry as October 5, 1868, but she believes her actual birth to have been December 23.[4] It seems one of her father's concubines had given birth to a daughter shortly before Kaho's arrival. Since Kaho's father apparently felt it would be inappropriate for a concubine's child to have seniority over the legal wife's offspring, he made certain that Kaho's birthday was listed as the earlier of the two. "Of course, it really makes no difference what month or day I was born," Kaho would declare. "I was born into a world bathed in the grit and dust of the collapsing Tokugawa, and that [more than a calendar date] is what most profoundly determined my own character."[5]

Kaho's name at birth was Tanabe Tatsu. The Tanabes were high-ranking samurai. Originally from Echigo, they served the Tokugawa shogunate in Edo for several generations as police guards (yoriki). Kaho's paternal grandfather, Shinjirō, was "adopted" into the Tanabe family through marriage. A highly regarded scholar of Chinese learning (kangaku), he wrote more than thirty volumes of critical analyses, historical biographies, and Chinese poetry and counted more than one hundred men among his disciples. Shinjirō's second son Ta'ichi (1831–1916), Kaho's father, proved himself to be equally well suited to scholarship. At the age of thirteen he entered Shōheikō, a prestigious academy for Confucian studies and the official Tokugawa college. Upon graduation he became a teacher himself, inheriting his father's pupils and earning more of his own.

Once the Western powers began to make their presence felt in Japan—following the entrance of Commodore Perry's Black Ships in 1853—Ta'ichi set his sights on studying English. His prowess in languages led to his appointment in the newly formed foreign affairs bureau of the Tokugawa government. While others in this bureau agitated for the expulsion of the foreign presence, Ta'ichi advocated an open-door policy—a position that earned him no friends among either the shogun's counselors or the emperor's loyalists.

Nevertheless, he was dispatched on two official missions to France: one in 1863 and another in 1867. It was upon his return voyage from the latter that he learned of the shogun's resignation and the restoration of imperial rule. Discouraged with the shogun's reluctance to resist the imperial authority, and disgusted with the arrogance of the rustic samurai from Satsuma and Chōshū who were the prime movers behind the restoration, Ta'ichi withdrew from bureaucratic service and worked briefly as an import merchant in Yokohama and then as a teacher in Shinagawa. In 1869 the newly formed Meiji government, unable to resist a man of Ta'ichi's talents, invited him to take a position in the foreign ministry *(gaimushō)*. Despite his aversion for the restorationists, the opportunity was too good to turn down.

Kaho's mother, formerly Arai Kimiko, was the daughter of the chief magistrate of Ishikawa in the province of Kai (present-day Yamanashi prefecture). Although Kimiko was eager to see Kaho advance in her studies, she herself had had no appreciable education beyond training in Confucian ethics and Japanese poetry. Her older brother, however, became a high-ranking officer in the Tokugawa navy, and because he studied the Chinese classics under Tanabe Ta'ichi's tutelage, Ta'ichi frequented the Arai house. Here he became acquainted with Kimiko. They married in 1863.

Ta'ichi was handsomely compensated for his work with the Meiji government, and his family lived in luxury. The first nine years of Kaho's life were spent on a large estate in Ikenohata, Tokyo. Her family consisted of an elder brother Jirōichi, her paternal grandmother Shizuko, the widow of her father's elder brother Fukiko and her two children, and her grandmother's elder sister, Nasuko. In addition to sumptuous living quarters for the immediate family, the Ikenohata estate maintained accommodations for the five or six retainers who lived on the grounds with their wives and children. The estate was managed by a bevy of servants. There were livery men in matching blue kimono jackets, four maids to work the kitchen, and five others to serve in the house.[6]

Not surprisingly, Ta'ichi was epicurean in his tastes and given to the Western trends then sweeping the Meiji state. He participated in the 1872 Iwakura Mission to the United States and Europe and upon his return in 1873 set about "westernizing" the furnishings of the Ikenohata mansion. Kaho recalls being outfitted in European dresses when she was three or four, sleeping in beds, and being carted about Tokyo in a two-horse carriage.

In 1877 Ta'ichi moved the family to a magnificent estate on several acres of land near the British Legation in Kōjimachi. The mansion, which had been transported to Tokyo from Shizuoka, boasted special cedar paneling on the ceilings and a veranda fashioned of black persimmon and cherry wood. Here Ta'ichi, a devotee of Edo culture in addition to Chinese and Western, entertained Ichikawa Danjurō IX (1838–1903), Onoe Kikugorō V (1844–1903), and other famous kabuki actors, along with the well-known story-teller San'yūtei Enchō (1830–1900).

From Jesus Schools to Saturday Dances

Ta'ichi's social standing and wealth afforded Kaho a privileged education. She began her schooling at the Kōjimachi Elementary School but was withdrawn after only three months because Ta'ichi decided she would be better served by the newly opened Atomi School for Women. This academy, founded by Atomi Kakei in 1875, catered to wealthy and aristocratic young women, many from the nobility. Ta'ichi wanted Kaho to have an education fit for a princess.

Largely designed as a "finishing school" for feminine accomplishments, the academy offered classes in calligraphy, arithmetic, art, needlework, koto music, flower arranging, poetry, and native studies, as well as Chinese studies. What Kaho most remembered about the school, however, was the atmosphere of freedom and liveliness the headmistress instilled. She describes how Kakei would occasionally invite her into her office for tea, sweets, and sundry conversation. After classes, the girls were allowed to entertain themselves by staging plays. They stitched together makeshift curtains and acted out the scenes then popular on the Tokyo stage.[7] Kaho's fondness for the Atomi headmistress is evidenced by the fact that when she chose her pen name—Kaho—she selected the same character *"ka"* (flower) that Kakei used in her own name.[8]

Kaho's studies at the Atomi School did not last. Her parents removed her from the school when she was thirteen, apparently due to financial considerations. The idyllic life at the luxurious Kōjimachi estate was also short-lived. The mansion was beyond Ta'ichi's means. As a prominent statesman he received a large salary but spent his money as fast as he made it. As Kaho recalls, her father was fond of saying that "money is best viewed on its way out the door."[9] And out the door it went. Not only did Ta'ichi squander the money on frivolous extravagances—lavish parties for his favorite kabuki actors, for example, and grand estates—but, more particularly, he wasted his money in the licensed quarters. Ta'ichi was well known for his debauchery. He was rarely home—despite the luxuriousness of his surroundings—preferring to divide his time between his prostitutes and concubines. Though Kaho found her father's behavior distressing, she of course was powerless to stop him. Nevertheless, the vulnerability and frustration she felt as she watched him squander the family's fortune—and sully its good name—can be found in her later fiction, where she frequently writes of women from good families forced to suffer the affront of concubinage in order to survive. Not only does Kaho write from the concubine's point of view but she also deals with the humiliation the wife endures as her husband replaces her with other women. Kaho's mother, she recalls, bore her husband's heartlessness with stoic silence: sitting ever vigilant before her sewing box. Kaho did not agree with her mother's submissiveness, but she nevertheless admired her fortitude and self-control.[10]

Perhaps in an effort to understand (and excuse) her father's behavior, Kaho explained in later memoirs that his debauchery was a direct result of his disappointment over the Meiji Restoration. She suggests that before the restoration he had been a serious scholar and an industrious statesman (at least from what she had been told). But following the restoration, Ta'ichi had had to humble himself before men from Chōshū and Satsuma, whom he regarded as country bumpkins and far beneath someone of his education. The experience left a bitterness in his heart—a bitterness he tried to dispel by frolicking with prostitutes and actors.[11] As this behavior would have been unseemly for a former samurai, Kaho is not far off the mark in suggesting that it was motivated by Ta'ichi's guilt over having capitulated to the enemy. Ironically, however, the only ones Ta'ichi really harmed with his "protest" were the members of his own family.

Unable to pay his debts, Ta'ichi was forced to yield his magnificent Kōjimachi estate to creditors. Consequently, he moved the family to a much smaller house in Motozonochō. After Kaho withdrew from the Atomi School, she continued her education at home for several years. The family brought in tutors for Chinese as well as native studies. Her mother told Kaho that she would have no need to study sewing—she could always leave that to her maids—but should learn to play the samisen and koto. Kaho began her musical training when she was seven and continued it as long as she lived at home. Her parents tutored her in *waka,* but they also sent her to Nakajima Utako's *waka* academy, the Haginoya.[12] This is where Kaho would eventually meet Higuchi Ichiyō.

When Kaho was fifteen, her mother decided that she should study English, asserting that everyone—even women—needed to know English if they were to succeed in life. Kimiko's desires for her daughter's intellectual development stand in stark contrast to those of Higuchi Ichiyō's mother, who thought that such education was wasted on women. Although Mrs. Higuchi's resistance to education for women was motivated as much by monetary and class considerations as by moral qualms, her attitude represented the norm at the time. Kimiko's constant support of her daughter's intellectual and social advancement was unusual even among the higher classes and would prove instrumental to Kaho's later accomplishments.

To fulfill her aims, Kimiko sent her daughter to the Sakurai Women's School (later known as Joshi Gakuen), where she was taught by Yajima Kajiko (1839–1922).[13] In December, four months after Kaho's matriculation, Kajiko, who was a Christian, instructed the students to bring Christmas presents to school. When Kimiko learned of this she was furious. "We pay our tuition promptly every month and more. There is no call to request these excessive gifts! This is why I hate these Jesus schools!"[14] Kimiko withdrew Kaho immediately. Perhaps the vehemence of her reaction was a reflection of the financial straits the family now faced.

Kaho entered another "Jesus school" three years later. This time her educational journey brought her to Meiji Women's School. Actually, it was family connections that led her to the school. Kimura Kumaji, then the headmaster, had been one of her father's students; and Iwamoto Yoshiharu, a prominent teacher at the school, had attended the Dōninsha with Kaho's brother. As Kaho recalls, she was scheduled to enter the school on the third of March but did not arrive until the fourth. Kimura took her to task for her tardiness. "Were you at home setting out your Doll Festival display?" he charged. "Do you and your family worship idols?"[15] Kimura associated the Doll Festival (Hina Matsuri, observed on the third day of the third month) with Shinto ritual—practices that were anathema to devout Christians in the early Meiji period. When so queried, Kaho's reaction was to wonder half in jest if girls at the school were forbidden to play with dolls.[16]

Kaho's goal in attending Meiji Women's School was to learn English. In exchange for her English lessons, she taught calligraphy as Nakajima Utako's proxy. Kaho also attended other classes and claims to have been especially impressed with Iwamoto Yoshiharu's pedagogical style. For one thing, he had the students practice debate. Young women were not used to expressing their opinions publicly at the time or even speaking in front of others. Since traditional morality had considered women incapable of even *having* intellectually informed opinions, it had deemed silence in women a virtue. The experience, therefore, of speaking to an audience was invigorating and challenging, if not intimidating. Kaho, apparently, was not intimidated, though she was not particularly successful as a debater either. She recounts how once Iwamoto instructed her to argue the pros and cons of the concept of "loyalty" (*chūgi*). Kaho thought about it for a few minutes and then responded: "Loyalty is just loyalty—and no matter how you view it, it causes trouble (*mendō*)." Iwamoto could only laugh.[17]

Although Kaho seemed to enjoy Meiji Women's School, her studies there lasted barely a month. She was forced to withdraw in April when her elder brother died. Jirōichi, the family heir, had been its hope for success. Gifted in scholarship like his father, he had studied English under the direction of

Nakamura Masanao, foreign affairs in Hong Kong, and business at Hitotsubashi University. When he was nineteen he was sent to London as the branch manager for the Mitsui Corporation and was responsible for overseeing thirty to forty employees. He fell ill while in London, however, and was forced to return to Japan where he died en route. He was twenty-two. Kaho states that his death sealed the fate of the Tanabe family.[18] Her father, all hope lost now for revenging himself on the Meiji goverment by creating a successful heir, indulged even more in licentiousness; and Kaho indulged in literature. As Jirōichi's death is generally considered the catalyst that propelled Kaho into a literary career, we shall return to it later. But first we must see Kaho's educational record through to its end.

Kaho found it difficult to sit idly at home, and in the fall of 1886 a close friend told her of the Government Normal School for Women (Kanritsu Joshi Shihan Gakkō, founded in 1874) in Hitotsubashi—presently known as Ochanomizu Women's University. Kaho decided to attend classes there, and once again family connections helped pave the way. The headmaster had been a colleague of Ta'ichi's in the earlier regime and was also one of Ta'ichi's disciples. Kaho was allowed to enter the third-year level and to select whatever courses interested her. Her English course proved to be problematic. Hatoyama Haruko, the instructor to whom she was assigned, thought Kaho was too advanced for the class and assigned her to the "postgraduate" course, which was taught by a foreign woman, Mrs. Prince. Although this class was too accelerated, this did not seem to stop Kaho from participating enthusiastically. Kaho relates how in one lesson, when Mrs. Prince asked for a volunteer to spell "daughter" on the blackboard, Kaho (perhaps still under the influence of Iwamoto Yoshiharu's "assertiveness training") confidently marched forward and wrote "dota." She was met by howls of laughter. Chagrined at her mistake, Kaho began to receive tutorials in "English rhetoric" from one of Ta'ichi's colleagues. Kaho claims that her performance in English class improved so dramatically that the other students began coming to her house after school for help with their assignments.[19]

Kaho's three years at Ochanomizu were profoundly influential. She entered the school during the height of its "Europeanization" when Japan was awash in Western trends. The extent of the Western impact on Japan at the time is best represented by the construction of the Rokumeikan, or "Deer Cry Pavilion." This lavish structure, built in 1883 in Kōjimachi, was the site of gala parties and fancy costume balls. Here Japanese dignitaries hoped to impress their foreign guests with the cultured worldliness of Japanese society. Aristocratic Japanese women, encouraged by their husbands, fathers, and brothers, made their appearance at these functions. Attired in elegant Parisienne fashions, they would sashay through the night on the arms of

Western men while their male relatives looked on in admiration—if not envy.[20] This is the age Iwamoto castigated for its "atmosphere of adultery."

Ochanomizu students—the quintessential "girl student" (*jogakusei*) of the Meiji period—trained assiduously for these Rokumeikan soirees. In order to distinguish themselves as sufficiently modern, they wore their hair loose, ornamented with Western bows and baubles and flowing over their shoulders. Their typical school uniform consisted of the latest European fashions—or a variation thereof—some wearing button-top leather boots with their kimono and *hakama* (divided skirt). On Saturdays the school held socials, or *karaku-kai* (peace and harmony meets), where these young women were instructed in the fundamentals of socializing "Western" style—that is to say, with men. For Kaho, these dances were the highlight of her education at Ochanomizu. As she describes it, on Saturday mornings the girls would rush to the beauty parlors to have their faces painted and their hair dressed. Then they would parade back to the campus in their gorgeous Western gowns—much to the curiosity and sometimes censorial gaze of neighboring residents. The young women would be joined by university men—students as well as instructors—and by members of the Imperial Navy, who arrived in full dress uniform, their swords strapped to their sides.[21]

Figure 7   Woodcut of a dance party at the Rokumeikan. (Courtesy of Nihon Kindai Bungakkan)

The socials were intended to foster better communication skills between men and women, since women at the time were unaccustomed to interacting with men outside their immediate family. But for the most part, the general public was opposed to this kind of dance party—for them it represented not social advancement but moral decay—and the *karaku-kai* was a short-lived event, much to Kaho's disappointment.

Aspirations and Motivations

Given Ta'ichi's training in Chinese studies, it comes as no surprise that literature had always been an important activity in the Tanabe household. As a child Kaho recalls her father reading to her from the Chinese classics. Proud though he was of his intellectual inheritance as a Chinese scholar, he did not discourage Kaho from exploring the "lowbrow" riches of the Japanese tradition. He also read to Kaho from Takizawa Bakin's *Biographies of Eight Dogs* (*Hakkenden*, 1814–1841), Tamenaga Shunsui's *Plum Calendar for Spring Love* (*Shunshoku umegoyomi*, 1832), and Jippensha Ikku's *Shank's Mare* (*Hizakurige*, 1802–1822). Whenever he acquired a Western-language magazine, Ta'ichi would read aloud from it, translating the stories for Kaho as he went. Kaho claims that when her father was not reading to her, she read feverishly on her own: whatever the student-apprentice would bring back from the local lending library, newspapers, even the lettering on the rice bags.[22] She loved the written word—the mere look of print on a page, the lettering on a box or sign—wherever and whatever. She also loved to write.

Kaho began studying *waka* when she was ten. She was diligent with her assignments, often staying up late into the night penning verses. When not practicing *waka,* she entertained herself by writing vignettes and sketches—sometimes for hours at a time. In fact, she has said that once she started on a story, she could not set her pen aside until she had reached a conclusion. She describes herself as being in a near delirious state. She would feel a sense of release, she has said, when she had finally written all she could write and therefore did not like to go back and edit her stories or polish her style.[23] And this is just the way she describes her writing of *Warbler in the Grove.*

Although Kaho's claims to artistic inspiration are certainly reasonable, they also sound like a modest denial of conscious intent or even effort. This description of her literary practices is in keeping with attitudes toward women writers expressed during her lifetime. As noted in Chapter One, women were expected to write for diversion. Writing was to be an emotional burst of energy—an intuitive moment—not a seriously considered and measured activity. Kaho's disavowal of her own intellectual involvement in her creative work minimizes the importance of what she accomplished—and in so doing protects her from charges of presumptuousness. Since this depiction of her artistic process was written in 1934, nearly half a century after the work in question, Kaho's memory of her own activity may have been abetted by the critical assessment her work received.

Kaho's description of her motivation for writing *Warbler in the Grove* is colored by a similar retrospection. In her 1939 memoir, she indicates that she had taken ill in the spring of 1887 and was unable to attend school. She spent her days in bed reading and writing poetry. The family retainer, who was partial to modern literature, brought Kaho stories to read in an effort to keep her entertained. One afternoon he brought her a copy of Tsubouchi Shōyō's first novel, *The Character of Modern-Day Students*, which had been published in book form one year earlier. Shōyō's work, an attempt "to encompass within its pages the whole spectrum of student life in the early 1880s,"[24] is long and intricately woven with plot complications that take the heroes into the pleasure quarters and back to the Ueno War of 1868. Kaho found the story mesmerizing. It seemed to portray the lives of "modern-day students" just as they would have been lived. The dialogue particularly had the flavor of immediacy. Impressed by the "naturalness" of the narrative, Kaho concurred that if this is what a *"shōsetsu"* was—a mere record of one's experiences and observations—then she too could write one.[25]

As Kaho relates in "The Path I Took—The People I Remember," it was while she was recuperating at home, reading books and dreaming of writing her own, that she overheard her mother lamenting the fact that the family had no money to hold a memorial service for the first anniversary of her brother's death. Thus, Kaho has stated, she struck upon the idea of writing a *shōsetsu:* "Not much earlier, I had written a poem card—at Mrs. Nakajima's request—and had been paid seventy-five sen for my effort. . . . I knew then that I could earn money by writing."[26]

Kaho was familiar with the new trend in literature to stress the everyday, the observed, the "truth." It is very likely that someone as well read as Kaho—and as inquisitive—had perused Shōyō's treatise *The Essence of the Novel* (*Shōsetsu shinzui*, 1885–1886). If not, she was certainly aware of Iwamoto Yoshiharu's reiteration of that treatise as it had appeared in *Jogaku zasshi* in 1886 and knew of his encouragement of women writers.[27] When Kaho sat down to write *Warbler in the Grove*, therefore, she was determined to imbue it with a feel of naturalness, immediacy, social content, and "feminine" sensitivity. But, according to Wada, Kaho recognized her limitations: "There was much of life she did not know—the condition of the common folk, for example—and so she consulted the house servants and wrote down what they told her."[28] Apparently the servants reported their conversations to Kaho's parents, because soon the whole family knew what she was up to.

In her foreword to *Warbler*, Kaho indicates that her parents thought her indulgence in prose fiction was a waste of time *(tsumaranu koto)*. But they saw no harm in it. In fact, they encouraged her in her efforts. If she were to write at all, they felt, she should do the best she could.[29]

Once Kaho had finished her manuscript, the resident student-apprentice, who was acquainted with Tsubouchi Shōyō, offered to show him her work. Kaho's parents agreed that this was the thing to do, but only after Kaho had drafted a clean copy. Kimiko offered to copy out a clean draft.[30] With this task accomplished, the student-apprentice carried the work to Shōyō, who read it enthusiastically. He returned the manuscript, which he had edited, with a letter praising Kaho's talents and advising her to pursue publication.

An unknown woman writer, Shioda Ryōhei observes, was not likely to find her way into publication based on talent alone. And here is where Kaho benefited from her father's connections.[31] Heeding Shōyō's recommendation, Ta'ichi saw that the story was brought out as a single volume by Kinkōdō, the company also responsible for publishing the literary journal *Miyako no hana* (Flower of the Capital). Nakane Toshi, the Kinkōdō editor, had been a former colleague of Ta'ichi's from their earlier Tokugawa days—hence the relative ease with which Kaho found her way into print. Ta'ichi also arranged to have Fukuchi Gen'ichirō—the prominent editor of the *Tokyo nichi nichi shinbun* (Tokyo Daily News) and yet another of Ta'ichi's disciples—write a preface to the work. Nakajima Utako, the headmistress of the Haginoya where Kaho studied *waka,* contributed a postscript. And most important, Shōyō allowed the letter he had written Kaho to be published as a preface. Moreover, he permitted his name to appear on the cover of the book as testimony to the quality of the contents. Kaho's debut, largely a family affair, was well feted. And it earned her thirty-three yen and twenty sen—a generous sum, considering the average monthly salary at the time was twenty-five yen.[32]

Wada Shigejirō has misgivings about Kaho's assertion that she wrote the book for money—or, more particularly, that she wrote to raise money for her brother's first memorial service.[33] Wada's concerns turn primarily on a matter of arithmetic. Jirōichi died in April 1886. His first memorial service would have been held the following spring. Kaho dates her foreword to *Warbler* March 1888 and Shōyō's letter is dated February 15. The book was published in June of that year. If the money she earned provided for a memorial service, it would have been for the third anniversary of her brother's death, not the first.

To add to Wada's suspicions about the veracity of Kaho's claims, he notes that she made no mention of her brother's death or indeed of her hope to raise money in her original foreword to the work. She stated rather that she had been motivated by Shōyō's *The Character of Modern-Day Students* and had determined that she would try her hand at a *shōsetsu*. It was much later in her career that she mentioned her mother's distress at being unable to provide her brother a first-anniversary memorial service. Wada has not been the only one to question Kaho's "poverty." In an interview with Kaho carried in *Kokugo to kokubungaku* (National Language and National Literature, 1934), she cites a preface that Kōda Rohan wrote for an Ichiyō collection in which he argued that a daughter of such a wealthy family [as the Tanabes] could not possibly have written for money.[34] Kaho rebuts his assertion in the same interview. "I wrote for money because my father squandered all we had on his own pleasure."[35]

The image of Kaho as an impoverished writer, eager to earn money for her brother's memorial service, is certainly well established and is now part and parcel of the Miyake Kaho biography.[36] Nevertheless, as Wada concludes, poverty is relative. Regardless of Ta'ichi's irresponsibility and debauchery, it is inconceivable that a family of the Tanabes' standing would not have been able to manage a service for the family heir. Thus the kind of poverty Kaho alludes to in her retrospective essays is surely overstated. Kaho clearly did not have to endure the soul-crushing destitution of Higuchi Ichiyō. After all, her family was served by retainers and student-apprentices; and Kaho herself admitted to being so distant from the "common people" that she had to consult the "hired help" for advice—hardly a problem that Ichiyō would have encountered. Still, for a family that at one time had lived in a splendid estate with livery men in matching coats, a maid for every room, and five or six retainers in residence, the shrinkage to a staff of a single retainer and a student-apprentice would have seemed severe indeed. Kaho's mother, therefore, must have been aggrieved not because she could hold no service but because she could not provide her son with the kind of service the Tanabe heir deserved.

What is curious, however, is that Kaho felt compelled to portray herself as an impoverished writer. Later in her life, after she had married Miyake Setsurei (1860–1945), she stated that the income she earned from writing was often what she used to buy new kimonos and other necessities for her children.[37] Even so, the Miyake family was not destitute. Perhaps she found the notion of writing for money dramatic—if not romantic.[38] Kaho may have decided to "remember" her early motivation in this light in order to align herself with Higuchi Ichiyō who was by the 1930s much admired—idolized even—for her perseverance as an impoverished artist. I suspect that Kaho's claim to poverty was motivated by an impulse similar to the one that had her describing her creative process as spontaneous and fever-driven. Kaho presents herself as a writer who is a good daughter and a responsible family member. She wrote to preserve the family name, to honor her brother, to please her mother, and to shield her father—not to satisfy her own interests.

Shioda Ryōhei concludes that this self-portrayal was mere posturing. Kaho loved literature. "Her real motivation for writing *Warbler in the Grove*," he says, "was nothing less than the inability to withstand her own creative desires."[39] Kaho cannot admit to as much. In her 1939 description of her decision to write, nowhere does she say that she wrote for herself or out of some effort to fulfill whatever undisclosed need she might have felt. Rather she downplays her own love of writing (even while revealing in this same essay her very devotion to it). She presents her literary activity in a filial light and thereby obviates any possible charge of unladylike aspirations or intentions. The problem with Kaho's cover-up is that it was so convincing. Her presentation of herself as a now-impoverished-spoiled-little-rich-girl writing to earn money—but for a noble cause—led critics to discount her sincerity as a "real" writer and by extension her resulting work. If *Warbler in the Grove* is just the product of an overprivileged author, temporarily down on her luck, who was not terribly serious about her writing in the first place but merely imitated a "real" writer either for fun or for funds, why bother reading it?

Warbler in the Grove: A Summary

Should one bother to read *Warbler in the Grove*, one might find a surprisingly thoughtful and charmingly humorous work. Divided into twelve sections and covering less than fifty pages in its modern print edition, *Warbler in the Grove* describes the pending marriage between a young couple and the problems and unanticipated solutions the proposed union incurs. More than just a lighthearted romance, however, the narrative is imbued with a moral tone as Kaho projects her own regard of westernization, female education, and social responsibility through her characters' acts, words, and ultimate fates.

Man: "Ah-ha-ha-ha-ha! You *tsuu redeesu* [two ladies] already have your *paatonaa* [partner(s)] picked out. I suppose I don't stand a chance!"

Woman A: "That's not true, not true at all. It's not that we don't want to dance with you. It's just that when we do you whirl about so it makes our eyes spin. This is why we turn you down."

Man: "Well, if you haven't decided on a partner for the *warutsu* [waltz] yet, please allow me."

He duly presents his ornamented *puroguremu* [program] and enters her name. "Until then," he nods, and turns toward the dance floor. A group of young ladies closes in after him, leaving the two behind.[40]

These two ladies, we soon learn, are Hattori Namiko and Shinohara Hamako. The latter is expected to wed Tsutomu—the young man her father adopted into the family with the intention of making him his heir and son-in-law. Tsutomu is just finishing his studies in Europe and is due to return in the summer. Hamako is not looking forward to his arrival. She would much prefer to dance at such soirees as this Rokumeikan New Years Ball. The opening paragraph thus establishes an aura of lively (sexy) exuberance. Even the visual image of katakana-inscribed English words (*tsuu redeesu* and the like) among the traditional print suggests to the reader the dizzying swirl of the Rokumeikan era—where Japanese women whirled through the night in Western gowns and frequently on Western arms. Having thus set the stage, Kaho continues with her introductions. Miss Hattori is described as follows:

> One of the young ladies, barely sixteen, is fair of face. Her eyes are large, her red lips small and tightly pursed. Her cheeks glow with a natural charm, and she has a manner that attracts the admiration of others. The flower decorating her coiled coiffure holds nothing over her own natural beauty. Her waist is not particularly trim and the way she wears her Western dress reveals a familiar comfort. She keeps her gaze downward, her shoulders slightly stooped. But this only adds to her remarkable charm. The gown she wears is pink and of a fine fabric. From time to time she flutters a fan with red tassels against her breast. [Ibid.]

In contrast to Namiko's naturalness and innate feminine modesty, Shinohara Hamako is shrill and flamboyant:

> The young lady beside her appears to be two years her senior. Her nose is high, her brow lovely, and her eyes rather narrow. She has secretly used the very powder she earlier cautioned the maid to avoid, telling her its lead base would damage her health—and as a result her skin is shockingly white. Her hair, twisted high atop her head, ends in a whack of bangs. Crimped in curls across her forehead, it has a reddish tint. Her straw-colored gown, designed overseas, is bedecked with beads. And though she looks a tad uncomfortable, she has cinched her waist so tightly one fears she might snap in two. She stands proudly upright, her lower lip drooping slightly. "Because of her fondness for chatter," the groom has chided behind her back. All in all, she is passably attractive. But nothing like the other young miss. [Ibid.]

Parallel pairing—a common device in traditional Japanese narrative—is one of the strategies Kaho employs in developing the portraits of her characters. She juxtaposes the presentation of a negatively drawn character against that of a positive one. The minute readers are told that Hamako resorts to potentially health-impairing artifice to improve her looks (lead-based powder and tight corsets—symbols of excessive female vanity), we know that she is "bad." Our negative reaction is exacerbated by Namiko—and eventually by the character-ization of Hideko, who serves as a model of modern feminine virtue. A second way Kaho reveals her characters' personal qualities is through the conversa-tions they conduct with one another—a strategy often employed in Tokugawa and early Meiji narrative, as we shall see later in this chapter. Once Kaho has introduced Hattori Namiko and Shinohara Hamako, for instance, she rein-forces the reader's first impression of them through the following exchange:

Woman B:　"Miss Shinohara, your elder brother [fiancé] should be returning soon, shouldn't he?"

Shinohara:　"Yes, he has said he'll be back in the summer. But I'm not look-ing forward to his return. It'll spoil everything!"

Woman B:　"Why on earth? You should be happy. After all, you'll be able to ask him to help you with your schoolwork, will you not?"

Shino:　"Don't be silly! I'm not going to school anymore, not since my father began having his stomach ailment. And you know my mother can't manage a thing. I'm now busy directing the household."

Figure 8　Frontispiece for *Warbler in the Grove*. Hamako is at left, Hideko at right, and Namiko in the lower center. (Courtesy of Nihon Kindai Bungakkan)

B: "Oh? And what about your English lessons? Have you given up on them? But then I suppose that's fine for someone as talented as you are in English *conbaruzeishon* [conversation]."

Shino: "Why? I fully intend to study English. Lately I've been taking lessons with—well, you must know him—Mr. Yamanaka? He's very fluent, you see. Oh, I've been just so busy. Every day—day in and day out—I study English. I'm frightfully busy with household matters as well but . . . I'm never too busy to attend a dance!"

B: "Even with your father ill? My parents always push me to socialize, but I still find it so uncomfortable. I just can't bring myself to dance with foreigners. Besides, I'm so busy with schoolwork that I hardly have time to come to these parties. And then I don't even have a dance partner."

Shino: "Why are you such a stick in the mud? No matter how lethargic I may be at home, the minute I arrive here I suddenly feel *akuchibu* [active]. In the West they call people who do not dance *uoorufurawaa* [wallflower] *(kabe no hana)*, you know. I'm afraid we'll have to count you among their ranks! Oh, look, there's Mr. Miyazaki. It's been ages since he's come to one of these parties. He certainly is an accomplished gentleman. I hear he excels at most anything. Good looks and good natured. Now that's a find, don't you think? I wonder who his partner is? She's so short. And look how horribly she wears her Western dress! Japanese people are just too short to be anything but pathetic in Western attire. And the way they dance! Just like herons plodding around in a muddy marsh. If their clothes don't fit properly, it's all the worse. I normally wear Western dresses all the time. My mother scolds me because the hem of my skirt catches on things on the floor, knocking them over. But I tell her that in the West people are not in the habit of leaving things scattered all over the floor like they do here [in Japanese-style rooms]. The fault lies with her. We're constantly arguing about this."

B: "You look very nice in Western attire. Mr. Miyazaki's younger sister does as well. She looks just like a European lady. At school she's praised as having the best style of all."

Shino: "Oh really? Well, doesn't his *shisutaa* [sister] have such uncommonly large eyes that she looks frightful? Is she very accomplished?"[41] [Ibid.]

Kaho uses dialogue not only to further character development but also to propel the plot forward. In her opening paragraphs, she thus introduces, through a combination of descriptive narrative and dialogue, all but one of the major players in her story: Hattori Namiko ("Woman B"), the neutral, level-headed interlocutor, whom many critics regard as Kaho's alter ego; Shinohara Hamako, the garish, superficial "playgirl"; and Tsutomu, her fiancé. Kaho also alludes here to the entanglement that will ensue. Hamako does not want to marry her intended because she is infatuated with her English tutor, Yamanaka.

With the second section the scene shifts to Yamanaka's room where we learn that he is an orphan whose father died alongside Saigō Takamori. Normally orphans are treated to a sympathetic regard in early Meiji stories and often represent the quintessential self-made success. Kaho includes in her story a number of orphans—men and women—who have pulled themselves up by their proverbial bootstraps and have done so without the help of a doting parent. Indeed, Yamanaka appears to fit the "self-made" mold at first. Through the intercession of his benefactor, a kindly merchant now deceased, Yamanaka has secured a position with Count Shinohara and, as he is clever in English, teaches the count's daughter, Hamako. But rather than being grateful for his good fortune and using this opportunity to benefit the nation—perhaps by rehabilitating Hamako—Yamanaka is revealed to be greedy and deceitful. Involved with a widow named Osada, he in fact despises Hamako. "What a little hussy that one is! . . . Her love of the West is disgusting. Whenever she sidles up next to me I find that she even smells like a filthy foreign beast [ketōjin]!" (p. 127).

In the third section, Kaho introduces us to Hamako's father in a lengthy descriptive passage. We learn, among other things, that he is largely responsible for Hamako's obsession with the West. In the old days, before the restoration, he was quick to cry for the expulsion of foreigners—joining in the "revere the emperor; expel the barbarian" fervor. But he distinguished himself during the restoration and has now been elevated to the status of a count. In keeping with the new trend sweeping the nation, this very same samurai who once called westerners crafty barbarians is now eager to ape their ways. He has in fact visited Europe and as a result of this experience has begun transforming his magnificent estate into a foreign citadel. Kaho continues:

> Believing native foods to endanger one's health, he now insists on Western meals. His house is built of stone with windows of glass. His clothes are fashioned of wool with sleeves as straight and tight as pipes. His maids and menservants are not allowed to dress in native garb but must wear garments of the West. Indeed, all matters great and small are in keeping with the West. . . . This is Miss Hamako Shinohara's father, Michikata. He is fifty years old.

He has no son—only this daughter, Hamako, and he dotes on her—seeing to her training himself. In all things, if it is Western it must therefore be good. Having thus been instructed that young ladies in the West give themselves over to socializing, Hamako has busied herself with a smattering of this and that—afternoons at the theater, evenings at soirees and dance parties. And as for schooling, she concentrates on two subjects only: piano and violin.

In any other family the mother would be responsible for her daughter's training in household matters. But not so in this case. Mrs. Shinohara is countrybred and unaccustomed to reading and writing. Hamako despises her. Should she ever try to counsel Hamako on this or that, Hamako refuses to listen, retorting that she has nothing to learn from an uneducated woman. And so it is that in the Shinohara family, Hamako rules the roost. [P. 129]

The narrative voice here is playfully critical. Count Shinohara, like his daughter, is hardly a character but a stereotype. And like Hamako he is faulted not merely for his excessive westernization but for the superficiality of his appreciation of the other culture. The acerbic tone here goes beyond Shinohara, of course, and implicitly challenges other leaders of the restoration who were able to switch so easily from their pre-Meiji antiforeign fanaticism to their postrestoration adoration of all things Western. Since Kaho's father made no secret of the abhorrence he felt for the early restorationists, perhaps her portrayal of Shinohara was biased. Yet Shinohara's fickleness and love of fashion could also be read as a caricature of Tanabe Ta'ichi's debauchery. In many respects the relationship between the count and his countrybred wife reflects that between Ta'ichi and Kimiko, though one assumes Kaho is not reading herself into the daughter's character.

As the section continues, the scene shifts to a conversation between two maids:

Chambermaid: "Ohhh, what are you doing! The young mistress has not yet returned home. You've got no business sleeping!"

Scullery Maid: "Why? It's already past midnight, is it not? Even men don't stay out so late. And how many nights is it now?"

Chambermaid: "Are you going to start that again? If the master hears you, you'll be in for a scolding. In that place they call the West, having parties that last until the break of day is a regular event, it seems, and the young ladies don't get up before eleven or twelve in the morning. It's the way they do things, he's told you. He wants Japan to hurry up and do the same."

Scullery Maid: "Well, if every household here did the same, it would be just fine with me. We could sleep all day for all I care. But

Chambermaid: the neighbors next door and those across the street get up in the morning and we've got to, too. I'm always sleepy!"

Chambermaid: "Yes, I know. But we're not the only ones to suffer. The mistress is really unhappy with this Western style. Once she told me she wanted Japanese pickles [*takuwan*][42] with her meal, and I gave her some. But the houseboy must have overheard, because he ran around telling everyone she was cuckolding the master with Priest Pickle as her paramour! Ha, ha, ha! But back to the young mistress. . . . Once she comes home she won't go straight to bed. First she has to go on and on about who she saw and what they said and always she ends up turning the conversation to Mr. Yamanaka and making me listen to her latest romantic adventures. It's more than I can bear!"

Scullery Maid: "And to think of the young master off on his travels. He's to be the young mistress' husband, is he not? The master arranged it long ago. And there she goes carrying on like that!"

Chambermaid: "That's *enlightenment*, you dunce! You mustn't cling to your old-fashioned ideas. There is nothing the least bit harmful in a man and woman associating with one another. That's the only way to advance, or so the master always says." [Ibid.]

Dialogue conducted between two lower-class characters about someone of the upper class is yet another method Kaho employs in fleshing out her character portrayals. The narrative structure of section three—following an "upstairs/downstairs" pattern—is remarkably coherent. Having described the aristocrats in all their misguided splendor, Kaho's conversation between servants recasts the foregoing description in a new and devastating light. In a topsy-turvy turn, the maid is forced to defend the count's Western tastes. Although she means to explain the master's expectations to her underling, the fact that she even has to justify his preferences highlights not only their foreign but also their ludicrous nature. In the end, it is the less sophisticated maid who seems to represent the voice of reason. "Well, if every household here did the same, it would be just fine with me." That the unschooled, uncouth servant is more savvy (and logical) than the noble count renders his behavior all the more absurd.

The fourth section transports readers to a lane in Kudanzaka, where several middle school students are returning from their classes. They chat amiably about the difficult assignments, their *geta* sandals clattering over the street while the clever katakana-transcribed English words that they use at various intervals clatter over the text: *resson* (lesson), *defuhigaruto* (difficult), *burazaa* (brother), and *guudobai* (good-bye). In the dialogue that ensues the boys discuss Matsushima Ashio, a classmate and a participant in the conversation, who is being raised by his older sister, Hideko, and therefore lacks some of the advantages the other boys enjoy. Nevertheless, he works hard and excels in his studies. The other boys remark that he is fortunate indeed to have such a helpful and generous sister.

Ashio parts company with the boys and returns to the tiny flat he shares with Hideko. In the dialogue here and in the fifth section, readers are apprised of their situation. The Matsushima siblings are orphans. Although their father left them a small inheritance before he died, Hideko is afraid the money would soon be spent if she allowed herself to continue her schooling at Shimoda Utako's academy.[43] She quits and takes in sewing to supplement their income and keep her brother in school. At first Ashio is ashamed of his sister's employment. But when he hears his landlord, Mr. Miyazaki, who is coincidentally a close friend of Tsutomu (Hamako's intended), commenting on how admirable [*erai*] she is, he begins to see her in a new light and now feels guilty that Hideko has had to abandon her own studies for him. By way of comfort, she tells him that if he feels sorry for her, he should study all the harder and become a fine man. Meanwhile, Ashio goes over his lessons with his sister every day after school. She benefits from the knowledge he brings home (even while correcting his mistakes) and thus receives an education without attending school.

Section six, praised by Tsubouchi Shōyō as the best of the twelve,[44] introduces readers to several girls who can afford to attend school. The scene, set in a dormitory room, is carefully described—establishing both the femininity of the room and its curious blend of West and East:

> Wedged into the Japanese-style alcove, beside the bedding cupboard, are a bookcase and chest-of-drawers—bearing traces here and there of ink spills. A tin washbasin—with several towels folded neatly inside it—sits in front of the chest-of-drawers. Scattered alongside the basin are two or three long-handled combs and a wide-toothed one. Otherwise, the room is neat and tidy—with nothing out of place.
>
> A student sits before the window holding a package the maid has just delivered. She has run her fingers busily through her bangs, tousling them haphazardly over the lovely widow's peak at her hairline. She gazes distractedly at the letter in her lap, forming the words with her lips as she reads, her brow slightly furrowed—perhaps in imitation of Seishi, the frowning Chinese beauty. [P. 132]

The student is Hattori Namiko, whom we met earlier in the first section. She has received a box of treats from home, which she shares with the others in the dormitory, among them Miss Miyazaki, the younger sister of Ashio Matsushima's landlord, introduced in the previous section. Miss Miyazaki (identified at first simply as "Woman") bounds into the room, to borrow Namiko's English-Japanese dictionary, and is invited to partake of some of the goodies.

Woman: "Thanks, I'll call Miss Saitō." She stands in the doorway calling, "Miss Saitō!"

Saitō: "Whaat? Ohh, I'm so terribly sleepy today. Why, I was so tired I fell asleep at the eight o'clock lecture this evening and Miss Aizawa had to shake me awake. Startled, I came back to my room and crawled into bed without even changing clothes! Ohhh."

And while letting out a big yawn, she steps into the room, leaving the sliding door agape despite her attempt to close it.

Woman: "Why Miss Saitō! You must have been raised in a barn!"

Saitō: "Not I. I merely thought it too stuffy in here and am releasing some of your 'hot air'!"

Woman: "Well, you're never at a loss for words!"

Saitō: "My mouth may not want for words, but my stomach wants for food! I'm starving, and I'll thank you for a treat."

Woman: "That's why we invited you."

Saitō: "You deigned to invite me; I deign to dine. Now where is it? Here? You received this from home? Well, let's have a look. Oh my, *kasuteira* [castella] cake from the Fugetsudō Confectionery, a packet of peanuts—I'd say these must have cost at least five sen—and what have we here inside this lacquered box? Ooh, all kinds of delicacies and white fish, too. A homemade specialty no doubt, from the kitchen of the elegant wife of the Honorable Mr. Councillor. How kind of your mother to have sent this to you, Nami. 'Truly a parent's love is deeper than the sea!'"

Woman: "Miss Saitō, while you're jabbering away, I'll just help myself to it all!" [P. 133]

The girls continue their banter as they cut pieces of cake with a letter opener *(pen naifu)*. Again, their conversation is generously punctuated with English words. When one of the girls bounds out of the room on an errand, she is described as being a person of *"kuikki mooshyon,"* the English words "quick motion" inserted parenthetically. When another is offered a slice of the castella, she replies "*menee menee. sankyuu. howa. yuuwa. kaindo*" [Many, many thank you. How you are kind . . .] As one might expect from such a gathering, once the food has been consumed the conversation turns to men and marriage. Namiko reveals that Hamako's "brother" has just returned:

M[iyazaki]: "Oh, isn't he her 'H' *(etchi)*?"[45]

H[attori]: "Well, yes. But they're just engaged right now. Anyway, Hamako refers to him as her older brother."

M: "Can she really expect to marry—I mean, after the way she has misbehaved?"

H: "How can you say such a thing? They are both two very educated people. They haven't done anything untoward. You've been listening to gossip. All of us are now doing what we can so as not to be overlooked by the civilized nations. We apply ourselves tirelessly to those soirees. Of course you and I have no idea what it is really like in the West. But to judge something as wrong simply because we do not understand it is absolutely offensive." [P. 133]

When Kaho wrote *Warbler in the Grove*, the first blush of liberation for women in Japan had faded and attitudes were taking a conservative turn. Here she expresses the changing current by introducing a variety of female characters with a variety of attitudes and aspirations. Most critics assume her own regard of modern tastes and trends is voiced by Hattori Namiko, the character who has the longest soliloquy. In the following exchange, the young women discuss their future intentions and the relevance of education for women:

H: "Female students are just not as relaxed about their studies as males. They rarely skip classes. And even if they are not encouraged to study hard, they do. They study according to their own abilities. But of late, education for women has been so overemphasized that it is becoming a great problem. If women push themselves to such extremes in their studies, as Miss Aizawa does, they weaken their mental health and, as a result, will produce weak children."

A[izawa]: "What a very silly thing to say. I have no intention of marrying."

M[iyazaki]: "Don't say such things, Miss Aizawa. It's better to marry—even if you do become a teacher."

A: "Impossible! What teacher would bend her knee to serve and wait on a man?"

H: "Now you see, that is why scholars of late are saying that women should not be given an education. They argue that it is better to keep women ignorant and unlettered because if you give a girl even a smattering of learning she'll become a teacher, and then she'll have no man as her master. Our nation will not propagate as a result, and so, they conclude, educating women is unpatriotic. I have heard that in the fifth and sixth years of Meiji [1872–1873] women behaved in an altogether outrageous manner. They strutted about in high-waisted *hakama*, their shoulders squared, spouting the most self-righteous nonsense. It must have been absolutely scandalous. I think things have improved considerably now. But then when I hear how women are still treated to an absurd degree of respect in the West, I fear we may revert to the earlier behavior once again. Women today are faced with great responsibility. . . . They say that Napoleon carried out his reform of France on account of his noble mother. Thus if women are not given an education, it is very unlikely that they will become noble mothers. But when they are educated, they turn into offensive women. No, a certain person has said that a woman should select one subject and study it thoroughly, but in such a way that she avoids becoming overly proud. She must continue to respect modest feminine virtue if she is to produce brilliant children and grandchildren. In this way she can create a new nation that can stand proudly among all the other civilized nations of the world."

Saitō: "Oh, I do not agree. Every time I hear these arguments, I feel terribly annoyed. No matter how hard a woman studies, once she marries, she finds it much too demanding to work as well. Not me. I shall remain single and become an artist. A painter. Painting is the 'King' of art. Or perhaps I should use the *fuemi-nin* [feminine] here? It is the 'Queen' of art. I shall definitely become a painter." [Pp. 134–135]

In many respects, Hattori Namiko's attitudes toward marriage, education, and female roles reflect the opinions Iwamoto Yoshiharu presented in the pages of *Jogaku zasshi*—leading one to wonder if perhaps he is the "certain person" to whom she refers. Her attitude toward women of the 1870s was fairly widespread among educators and intellectuals in the late 1880s. The 1870s was seen as a decade of unhealthy extremes: excessive adulation of the West by everyone and excessive imitation of men by women. The year 1872 saw the introduction of compulsory education for both boys and girls, and for a brief period young women who aspired to an education beyond this level dressed and comported themselves like male students—having no other model to follow. Their behavior so scandalized the general populace that a number of newspapers published articles castigating them.[46] By the 1880s educators and politicians alike, concerned by the effects of Anglo-American liberalism and egalitarianism, began to advocate a more "ethical education" based on Confucian texts and modeled on European elitism.[47] Steps were taken to ensure that Japanese women would emulate a more conservative and "feminine" ideal. Women's schools began to emphasize the teaching of Confucian ethics and a greater focus on elegant Japanese traditions—particularly the study of *waka,* tea, and koto—all at the expense of training in the sciences and Western learning.

Section seven returns us to the Shinohara estate. Tsutomu has finally returned, and the house is in turmoil with preparations for his homecoming celebration. Unable to bear the tumult and tension any longer, Tsutomu steps out into the garden, taking care to avoid Hamako's quarters, where she is deep in conversation with Yamanaka. Tsutomu suspects the relationship between the two may be more than it should be; but unable to confirm the truth, he is left with a feeling of nervous unease. While strolling past the carriage house he overhears the groom speaking with the rickshaw puller. In a scene reminiscent of kabuki, Tsutomu steps back into the shadows and eavesdrops:

Rickshaw Puller:	"Hey, the other day I got caught up in some really bad business!"
Groom:	"Why? What happened?"
Puller:	"What happened? That! That vixen of a mistress you have! She had me take her over to the widow's [Osada's] house. That's where Yamanaka—the fellow who's with her now—stays, you know. She invited him to go sneaking off with her to Mukōjima. Blossom viewing being over, the streets weren't crowded. Before I knew it that rascal Yamanaka leaped out of my rickshaw and into hers and off they went together like that. I had nobody to haul around after that and wanted to go on home but had to tag along behind them just the same. I felt plenty stupid, let me tell you. They got out at the Uehan Japanese Restaurant where they stayed for lunch and then some, I imagine. After all that, I figured I'd get at least a one-yen piece. But here she came after a bit, as clever as you please, and handed me fifty sen. Not but half a yen, and with all I'd put up with. I was so mad I couldn't stand it!"
Groom:	"Well, that explains why she went out in Japanese dress the other day—which she never does."

Puller: "So does the fiancé know?"
Groom: "Not a chance of that. We've been paid right and left to
                 keep our mouths shut! It's a secret." [P. 136]

Again, Kaho uses conversations between servants to reveal the untoward behavior of their employers. The servants' honesty and resentment intensify the unsavory antics of the aristocrats. As the rickshaw puller says toward the end of the conversation: "This is an age of pleasure seeking. Flirting with ladies is the Western method; keeping a concubine is the old-fashioned way . . . Either way, you gotta have money. Not much pleasure-seeking for us, huh? Ha, ha, ha" (ibid.). The servant's comment highlights the fact that Hamako's relationship with Yamanaka is not representative of "modern love" but is still inextricably tied to the sordidness of the *gesaku* love-tale *(ninjōbon)*. The very nature of Hamako's tryst with Yamanaka returns her to the traditions of Saikaku and the later *ninjōbon*. Significantly Hamako—this icon of Western modernity—changes into a Japanese kimono for her illicit encounter. Furthermore, she entertains her lover at a Japanese restaurant and presumably in one of those Japanese rooms she professed to abhor in an earlier scene. As Iwamoto concluded in "Adultery of the Nation," behaving immorally at fancy costume balls was no different than keeping a concubine. Where is the progress? Hamako's modernity, we are given to understand, is a mere facade and easily exchanged for yesterday's fashion.

In the eighth section Kaho continues her description of Tsutomu. It is mid-June and hot. Wearing a light flannel suit, a panama hat, and carrying a slender walking stick, he has gone to a boathouse to meet his old friends for a pleasure-boat ride. He is tall and fair. His mouth may be somewhat pinched, but this defect is concealed by his neat inverted "v" of a moustache. In Tsutomu, Kaho depicts her ideal Meiji man. He is conversant with the West—comfortable in his Western attire even in a traditionally Japanese setting. But unlike Shinohara, his foster father, he is not besotted with Western gadgets and gimmicks. Kaho reveals Tsutomu's integrity and "goodness"—and in turn underscores Shinohara's lack of such qualities—in the following soliloquy:

It was disillusioning to see up close [in the West] everything that I had only imagined before from my readings. But it brought me to the conclusion that a proper sense of morality is what is most significant to humanity. . . . Then I returned to my father and found him still as obsessed with the West as before. All he could think to ask me about my five years abroad was, "What kind of coiffure is fashionable now in Paris? What kind of clothing?" I am interested in Western knowledge and technical skill. I have absolutely no interest in social customs. And I don't think this notion of men and women dancing together is altogether wholesome. . . . It is a remnant of heathen behavior. . . .

Moreover, these corsets women feel obliged to cinch about their waists with no thought to their health—all in an earnest effort to follow popular taste! In China they bind feet to keep them small. What's the difference? . . . Once you start in on such things, there are a thousand examples. That is why I do not like the Western concept of morality. While I was sitting at my father's bedside the other day, he began speaking to me of Western customs. Before I knew it I had begun to criticize dance parties. He countered that it was a good way for young people to socialize. Not wishing to contradict a sick man, I fell silent. And this is when Hamako piped in, snorting with contempt, "Sending Tsutomu abroad has been to no avail at all. He still clings to such moldy old Chinese-inspired notions as the one that insists boys and girls should be schooled separately from the age of seven." [Pp. 137–138]

The topic under discussion soon turns to the meaning of success. Tsutomu suggests that the only reason Shinohara wishes him to marry Hamako is because he believes the young man is on his way up the bureaucratic ladder to success. All agree that this kind of social climbing is distasteful.

Tsutomu's opinions echo those of Miyazaki and other "good" male characters in the story who castigate the self-centered and money-grubbing ways of the government officials they see around them—the obvious examples being the count and Yamanaka. In section five, for example, Miyazaki's mother commends Matsushima Ashio, the orphaned schoolboy, for his diligence at his lessons, telling him that if he studies hard he will become a fine bureaucrat someday. This comment launches Miyazaki into a long harangue on the purpose of scholarship and the misguided selfishness of bureaucrats:

Mother, you shouldn't say such things to a boy. You sow the seeds of misjudgment. Ashio, you do not go to school just to become a bureaucrat and draw a salary. You do so to become a man who can contribute to society. Students who graduate from the political science and law courses of the university become bureaucrats, but even so there are many among them whose scholarship pales in comparison to those who have graduated in literature or engineering. Don't you agree, Saitō? Well, as they say, the miller only draws water to his own mill. And that is why, Ashio, you should get the idea of becoming a bureaucrat out of your head and set your heart instead on doing something to benefit the world. [P. 132]

In Kaho's reflective essay "The Path I Took—The People I Remember," she recounts how her elder brother made a similar observation when he was just a boy. While out floating boats with their cousin, Sakurō, the boys began to discuss their dreams for the future. Sakurō declared that he would become a famous engineer so that he could build public works for Japan. Jirōichi decided that he would become a prominent businessman so that he could make Japan rich.[48] In *Warbler in the Grove*, Kaho has her male characters reiterate these aspirations. *Risshin shusse* (self-establishment and public success) was not to be merely a desire for self-success. It was "as much a public as a private activity for the youth of Meiji Japan; it was widely regarded, indeed, as almost a patriotic duty."[49] In her diatribe against the self-centered bureaucrat, Kaho raises the importance of the scholar—those who learn for the sake of learning rather than merely to advance their careers and line their pockets. Although Kaho's portrayal of the count might reflect a subtle criticism of her own father—who dressed her in Western garments and had her attend the finest finishing schools for young ladies—her defense of the scholar redeems her father somewhat, as he, like Tsutomu, was as learned in Western traditions as in Asian.

Having discussed their image of the successful man, conversation next turns to the ideal woman. Tsutomu has revealed that he does not wish to marry Hamako. In response a friend reminds him that Hamako is, after all, accomplished in Western social graces. She has studied piano and violin, and she is particularly adept at dancing. To this Tsutomu snaps: "I have no interest in a wife who can converse with others. The wife I want won't be illiterate either, but she will practice wifely virtues. . . . I much prefer a wife who can knit to one who can dance. The former can contribute to the household" (p. 138). It dawns on readers, of course, that Tsutomu has just described Hideko, the selfless young woman who is industrious and intelligent.

Section eight, like most of the sections in the story, is ingeniously crafted. The opening scene is described with theatrical nuance. Having set the stage, the narrator invites the characters to make their entrances; their behavior and mood are calculated to harmonize with the setting. In earlier sections we were introduced to a Rokumeikan ballroom, a Western-style mansion, a woman's dormitory. In this section we find ourselves on a pleasure boat bound for Mukōjima. Our heroes drink sake and nibble on snacks while they drift along the Sumida River. This is largely a man's realm—an entertainment off limits to proper ladies. But Kaho nicely captures the camaraderie between friends who have not seen one another for five years. Normally one would expect gentlemen on such an outing to regale one another with friendly banter and sake-induced repartee. But our heroes, perhaps suggestive of the Meiji intellectual ideal, engage one another in the serious discussion of statesmanship. Curiously, though appropriately given the Sumida River setting, their discussion is framed by talk of women. When the pleasure journey begins, Hamako is the topic of choice—and Tsutomu's disillusionment with her is the catalyst that initiates the flow of ideas. Once the boat reaches its destination, Tsutomu's conversation too has reached its goal. A conversation that began with the westernized Hamako ends with the female ideal. As the pleasure boat docks, readers realize that the narrative is on its way to its romantic climax.

Section nine, therefore, is necessarily hurried—as if Kaho herself cannot quite wait for the promised encounter between Tsutomu and Hideko. But first she has some business to attend to. Count Shinohara dies, Tsutomu succeeds to his title, and just when it seems he will have to set a date for his marriage, he reveals to Mrs. Shinohara that Hamako is involved with Yamanaka. Since Hamako is not interested in honoring the marriage agreement, Tsutomu is able to end their relationship without damaging his ties to the Shinohara household. He remains the heir to the estate and magnanimously sees to it that Hamako marries Yamanaka in a proper ceremony. He sets her up in a lovely house, with maids aplenty, and places a large portion of the Shinohara inheritance at her disposal. As the section closes, Yamanaka is found in a house of assignation *(machiai)* plotting with Osada a way to free himself of Hamako without freeing himself of her money.

The consequences of Yamanaka's deceit are brought out in part ten, another short section. Osada visits Hamako, where she finds her engrossed in an issue of *Jogaku zasshi*. When Osada tries to push Hamako out of the house, declaring that *she* is Yamanaka's true wife, an explosive shouting match ensues. Osada eventually leaves—and so does Yamanaka, having completely squandered Hamako's money.

By the time we reach section eleven, it is autumn and Tsutomu is out with friends enjoying the fall colors at a teahouse. A member of his party informs Tsutomu that Hamako has moved to Yokohama where she has become a Christian, dispensing with all her lavish finery. Tsutomu begins to admire a poem card left behind in the teahouse. He and his friends discuss the virtues of Japanese poetry—its depth and subtlety—and their regret that Western tastes in literature have grown so overwhelming that even in women's schools the Japanese traditions are being eroded. When Tsutomu questions the teashop owner about the card, she indicates that it was written by a young woman who lives alone with her fifteen-year-old brother. Could it be? Suddenly Hideko happens along with Ashio. As Miyazaki, the Matsushimas' landlord, is present, he invites the two to join them, thereby introducing Tsutomu to Hideko. Tsutomu realizes what readers have known all along: Hideko is the woman for him.

Not surprisingly, then, as section twelve opens they are in the midst of their wedding ceremony, which is held in tasteful Japanese style at the

Kōyōkan in Shiba Park. Had Count Shinohara still been alive, he would have insisted that they conduct the event at the Rokumeikan. But his wife—like Hideko and Tsutomu—prefers the native traditions. Thus the narrative has come full circle. Opening on New Year's night in the Rokumeikan—site of Western excess—the story concludes in a Japanese restaurant at year's end. The narrative journey brings the surviving characters away from superficiality and back to sincerity; away from flirtatious infidelity and into marriage. Even Hamako makes the journey in her own way, moving from social scandal into marriage to the Christian church.

As the story ends we are told that Matsushima Ashio, Hideko's younger brother, advanced to university and upon graduation became a famous engineer building important public works for the good of the nation. He has married Miyazaki's younger sister. Namiko's dormitory friends, Misses Saitō and Aizawa, entered the Higher Normal School for Women, where they distinguished themselves and have since become scholars. They have not married, not yet, but who knows what the future will bring? Yamanaka and Osada have dropped out of sight; it seems they have met with misfortune. And Namiko has married Miyazaki.

A Female Success Story

Overall, *Warbler in the Grove* appeals to readers as a lighthearted romance. Characters are drawn in black and white. They are good, or they are bad. The good find happiness and success; the bad disappear to unknown but surely unhappy fates. Embedded in the frivolity and fun of the romance, however, one finds the expression of certain concerns that are generally assumed to project the author's own opinions and experiences. These ideas involve three social issues that were popular topics of discussion during this era: westernization, women's education, and individual responsibility.

Kaho paints those who advocate blind adoration of the "West" with boldly unflattering strokes. This is particularly true of Count Shinohara and his daughter Hamako. Greed and self-motivated success also come in for attack. The ideal man, as Kaho portrays him, is intelligent, sensitive, and eager to work for the improvement of the nation. Women, too, have social responsibilities, in Kaho's scheme, and are candidates for *risshin shusse*. In many respects *Warbler in the Grove* may be read as a female success story. During the course of the narrative, Kaho depicts the variety of ways women might establish themselves as significant individuals and members of society. With the exception of the two unmarried women who become female scholars, however, Kaho measures a woman's success through the success of the men with whom she associates. If men distinguish themselves as statesmen, scholars, engineers, and entrepreneurs —or if they denigrate themselves as liars, toadies, and thieves—women distinguish (or denigrate) themselves as their daughters, sisters, wives, and mothers.

It is easy to read *Warbler*, therefore, in a regressive light and many critics have done so. With the exception of Wada Shigejirō, most modern critics see Kaho's work as a transparently didactic disavowal of westernization and a jingoistic idealization of Japanese traditions. Many of these critics support their assertions by referring to the fact that Kaho married Miyake Setsurei in 1892. Because Setsurei was a prominent nationalist and editor of *Nihonjin* (The Japanese), a fervently patriotic journal, critics conclude that Kaho was herself expressing nationalistic tendencies when she wrote *Warbler*. Even though this reading of Kaho's work is clearly anachronistic, her marriage to Setsurei has been viewed as the culmination of her career—as if it were the true conclusion to *Warbler in the Grove*. Yanagida Izumi, writing in 1938, goes so far as to suggest that Kaho's choice of Setsurei as a husband was the most brilliant stroke of her career: "Naturally she would have had plenty of offers for marriage, but of all the bourgeois suitors, she held out for an unkempt philosopher like Setsurei, a man with nearly hermitlike propensities. . . . She chose brilliantly, and this discernment alone is her greatest masterpiece, I believe."[50]

A cursory look at Namiko's speech in section six, as well as the overall plot of the story, lead one to accept these critics' evaluation of *Warbler in the Grove* (and of Kaho herself) as a conservative-minded trumpeter of Japanese traditions. After all, Kaho reserves the greatest success in the story for the women who demonstrate the most traditionally (Japanese) "feminine" attributes. Hamako, the westernized shrew, is punished; Hideko, the *waka*-writing, needle-plying gentlewoman, is rewarded (assuming that marriage to Tsutomu is indeed a reward). Wada Shigejirō suggests, however, that Kaho does not criticize westernization or education for women per se. What she takes to task is the superficiality of both.[51] Namiko reviles those women of an earlier age, not because they agitated for equal rights, but because they did so at the expense of their innate femininity—dressing in masculine garb and behaving "unnaturally." Hamako, as well, is not criticized for being a "new woman." Indeed, Wada suggests she is more "traditional" in her helplessness than the other women in the story. Hamako is taken to task for being fickle and irresponsible. Namiko (Kaho's alter ego, after all) represents the positive outcome for women who are allowed to pursue education and Western styles but who at the same time retain their own "natural" native femininity.

Of course, Hideko is generally believed to embody traditional femininity writ large. Yet curiously, she is also the most independent woman in the story. She supports herself and her younger brother with her own selfless industry and ingenuity. The implication is that even after marriage she will do the same. Tsutomu, it will be recalled, lists resourcefulness as one of his criteria for the perfect wife. When the story concludes, therefore, the two men who have the most to offer the nation—one as an engineer, the other a scholar—are largely able to manage their tasks because of the strength and support this woman has provided.

And of all the women in the story, Hideko is perhaps the best educated. She actively seeks knowledge. Hamako attends school, but her studies in piano and violin are worthless and her studies in English prove to be her undoing. Hideko, by contrast, values traditional Japanese learning while at the same time acquiring knowledge in additional (more Western and masculine) subjects by helping her brother with his lessons. Her acquisition of knowledge is therefore framed (and forgiven) by a maternal nurturing. She does not study for her own self-fulfillment (though she does seem fulfilled) but to benefit her brother. That he in turn grows up to be a successful engineer, contributing to the good of the nation, reflects on his sister—just as Napoleon's "reform of France" was believed to be the ultimate result of his mother's integrity (or so Namiko informs us in section six). Women aid men in the home so that men may aid the nation. Kaho's depiction of female success in this regard reflects the attitudes Iwamoto Yoshiharu expressed in *Jogaku zasshi*.

Nowhere does Kaho articulate dissatisfaction with traditional roles for women—roles, that is, that would have them confined to the house. Indeed, she seems to idealize marriage. But her narrative also reveals subtle, perhaps subliminal, strategic devices for challenging sexual and social conventions. The traditional woman—though the most "successful" in marriage—is also the most independent. She is resourceful, free of parental restraint, and intelligent. Kaho's championing of Hideko seems to be less a statement against the westernized, modern Hamako than it is a declaration in favor of female self-reliance and integrity. This type of strategic subliminal device is certainly not limited to Kaho. We note similar encoded readings in texts by Jane Austin and Charlotte Brontë, for example. Moira Monteith, in *Women's Writing*, observes that such ironies appear frequently in female-authored texts, almost of their own accord, as a reflection of the writer's own conflicted ambivalence and subconscious outrage—or at least confusion—at the contradictory and complex demands placed on women.[52]

Another such irony embedded in the text is Kaho's treatment of Count Shinohara. Not only does he represent the patriarchal family *(ie)* system, which uses daughters as commodities of exchange; he also signifies the Meiji government itself. Corrupt, egotistic, but mostly silly, Shinohara does far more harm than good. The daughter he has trained—for the sole purpose of using her to attract a sycophant son-in-law—fails to achieve his goal. More telling, the faithful wife he forced into denying her own desire for the simple

Japanese "pickle" triumphs in the end, and native traditions are restored. But the count's demise is not so much proof that native ways should reign supreme as it is a reaction on the part of the daughterly author. Kaho punishes the wayward father—and the system he represents—with death. The suffering wife is redeemed, and the marriage that follows is not the one the count intended but one initiated by individual (and unparented) choice. Even Hamako thwarts her father's intentions in the end by becoming a nun—the traditional escape route for women bent on resisting patriarchal authority (though Kaho tweaks tradition somewhat by substituting the Christian church for the Buddhist temple).

In keeping with contemporary attitudes, marriage is the only possible avenue to female success. Men work for success; women marry. The two female characters who elect not to marry are minor—and in any case, as the story concludes, the narrator holds out hope for them. Marriage, in *Warbler*, thus determines a woman's success as well as her character. Hamako, outwardly projecting an independent, modern character, rejects the marriage her parents have arranged for her. And though she marries out of personal choice, she does not marry for "love." Her match is hardly the "love union" represented by Protestant missionaries and advocated by such spokesmen as Iwamoto Yoshiharu. Hamako's motives are driven by a self-centered desire—a point made clear in the earlier tryst scene. A lustful woman who "loves love," Hamako differs from traditional portrayals of lustful women only in the clothing she wears. And like her traditional counterpart, Hamako's actions prove to be her undoing. Unable to fend for herself, she eventually enters a Christian convent, and in becoming a nun initiates a marriage of another kind.

Unlike Hamako, Hideko does marry "for love." Already self-sufficient and respectable, she is attracted to Tsutomu by mutual interests and the need for companionship. Orphaned, and thereby relieved of parental intervention, she is able to choose her future spouse freely. And she chooses wisely—good character that she is. The story, typical of marriage narratives worldwide, concludes with little indication of what becomes of Hideko and Tsutomu after the wedding. In many respects, for women like Hideko, the story ends with marriage. She has reached the pinnacle of her success in selecting a man like Tsutomu. Readers can assume that her life will therefore be happy ever after.

Contemporary Readings and Criticism

The critical reaction to *Warbler in the Grove* was mixed: generally positive but not without detractors. In many respects, Kaho was the perfect candidate for the title of "first woman writer in the Meiji period." Educated in the latest Western styles, she embodied the savvy persona of the Meiji New Woman; yet trained as well in the Japanese traditions, she lacked the "self-assertive, half-masculine" abrasiveness so often associated with the New Woman in the West. The fact that her debut was heralded both by Shōyō—the voice of literary modernity—and by Nakajima Utako—the renowned teacher of classical poetry—suggests the complicated nature of her early training and to most reviewers indicated the kind of privileged upbringing Kaho had enjoyed. It would have been unseemly for critics to treat such a well-bred lady too harshly. And many used this as an excuse, in a snidely underhanded way, to explain why they were not critiquing her work as severely as they would a man's. The implication, of course, was that if she had been a man, she would not have passed muster. Standards were necessarily (and generously) being lowered.

Though *Warbler in the Grove* was mentioned in most literary columns and journals, it received very little critical attention at first—save for the typically condescending remarks about the marvel of a woman writing. The anonymous critic who reviewed *Warbler* for *Jogaku zasshi*, for example, indicated that when he read section eight—in which Tsutomu launches into his theory of success and his anti-westernization tirade—he was so impressed with the incisiveness of the viewpoints that "it was hard to believe they were authored by a young lady in the flower of maidenhood."[53] The review, which Shioda Ryōhei suggests was written by Iwamoto Yoshiharu himself, was intended to be generous and encouraging. And appearing as it did in *Jogaku zasshi*—one of the premier literary journals at the time—it would have made a significant contribution to Kaho's reputation as a writer.[54]

But Ishibashi Ningetsu (1865–1926)—whom Donald Keene describes as the first professional literary critic in Japan and one quite pleased with his training in European literature—was not so enthusiastic.[55] His review, "*Yabu uguisu* no saihyō" (A Detailed Criticism of *Warbler in the Grove*), which appeared in the July 1888 issue of *Kokumin no tomo*, was the first to criticize Kaho's text in terms of its art. True to the title of his review, Ningetsu analyzes *Warbler* in clinical detail and bolsters his argument with esoteric references to the Greeks, Shakespeare, and Goethe. Before launching into his attack, however, Ningetsu castigates Shōyō and Fukuchi Gen'ichirō (contributors of the enthusiastically positive prefaces) for failing to see what he regarded as obvious and serious flaws: "I feel the story lacks the most essential ingredients for a novel. And I am baffled that critics as discerning as Fukuchi and Tsubouchi, who wrote such generous praise for the novel, would fail to see these huge gaping flaws right in front of their noses."[56] Apparently Ningetsu was not as baffled as he suggested, for he intimated that these critics were too enamored with the idea of a woman writer to see her text dispassionately. As unpopular as he may become for doing so, Ningetsu states, he has decided to set the record straight.

What were the essential ingredients the story lacked? A hero, for starters. Having presumably taken her lead from Tsubuochi Shōyō's *The Character of Modern-Day Students*, Kaho had also attempted to write "A Novel Without a Hero."[57] She presents readers with a large cast of characters but none among them captures the readers' sympathies or seems to dominate the author's. Just as earlier critics took Shōyō to task for this "flaw," so Ningetsu challenges Kaho. Second, he notes that Kaho's work lacks "peripetia" *(peripechii)*, or dramatic development. The author provides an exposition *(ekisupojishon)* and a catastrophe *(katasutoroofu)*—that is to say, an introduction and a conclusion—but she fails to present anything signficant in between. She offers no analysis of human fate, no explication of character. In short, she gives no "drama." Ningetsu refers readers to Aristotle and Plato by way of explanation. Third, Ningetsu observes that Kaho's characters are not well developed. She has made little effort to provide psychological portraits of them as individuals or even to distinguish one from another. Thus she has a cast of characters who are given different names but very little else to set one apart from the other. Finally, Ningetsu is annoyed that Kaho is not always consistent with certain speech markers for her characters. In one section the character will use the first-person pronoun *"watashi"* and in another section *"watai."* Similarly, she uses *"-gozaimasu"* here and *"-gozarimasu"* there. "These oversights are distracting and I urge the author to take more time to polish her work in the future."[58]

Ningetsu's critique is of course premised on an appreciation of Western theories of literature. Convinced that the "frivolous writings" *(gesaku)* tradition of the earlier period was shamefully lowbrow and in need of reform, Ningetsu could hardly countenance a work of literature that was anything but Aristotelian in structure and application. He compares a novel to a great river that twists and turns on its course to the sea. Like a river, the novel, too, should have depths and shoals—complications and development. Ningetsu's reading of fiction is incisive and intellectually grounded; but Kaho's training, naturally, had not prepared her to meet such expectations. Even Tsubouchi Shōyō, for all his experience with Shakespeare, had been unable to produce a modern novel that would live up to Ningetsu's criteria. Ningetsu's criticism of Kaho's work was more a rueful reflection on what she did not write than a careful evaluation of what she had actually accomplished.

Ningetsu's review was followed by that of another important critic of the time: Ishibashi Shian (1867–1927), whose essay *"Yabu uguisu no saihyō wo yomu"* (My Reading of "A Detailed Criticism of *Warbler*"), appeared in *Kokumin no tomo* that August. A member of the Ken'yūsha literary salon—known for its favorable regard of *gesaku*—Shian was therefore less inclined to embrace Western trends with Ningetsu's enthusiasm. He found it easier to read Kaho's work through the lens of tradition. This is not to imply that he read her work any more favorably. Tradition had taught Shian to expect women of Kaho's class to behave a certain way. When Kaho failed to conform to these expectations, she invited Shian's cynicism.

Just as Ningetsu used his review of *Warbler* as a soapbox upon which to preach his own theory of the novel (taking a few jabs at Shōyō as he did), Shian used his review as an opportunity to tangle with Ningetsu. As the title implies, his review is as much an evaluation of Ningetsu's "Detailed Criticism" as it is of *Warbler*. For all of Ningetsu's self-absorbed seriousness, Shian seems to have fun with his responsibilities as critic—at Kaho's expense. First he commends Kaho with a backhanded compliment: "I am most impressed that a young lady would have the boldness *(kenage)* to write a *shōsetsu*, and I have great hope for your future endeavors, so please let this criticism serve as your guide."[59] Next, Shian takes Ningetsu's points one by one. Although he agrees with most of Ningetsu's criticisms, he challenges his insistence on a "hero." Why, he asks, do novels need heroes? Before he can accept Ningetsu's argument, therefore, he exhorts his fellow critic to defend his idea more persuasively by explicating the definition of hero. Why can't novels be devoted to groups as well as individuals?[60]

Shian has no quibble with Ningetsu's other arguments; he simply rephrases them to meet his own interests. Shian recasts Ningetsu's "peripetia" complaint (or his irritation over the work's lack of dramatic substance), for example, in more indigenous terms: "Reading *Warbler in the Grove* is like dining on a cheap Western meal, like supping on *chazuke* and pickles. That is to say, it's light fare with no flavor and no 'meat' *(mi)*."[61] Shian then proceeds to indulge in characteristic wordplay *(kotoba asobi)* by punning on "*mi*" for "meat/substance" and *omoshiromi* (interest). His conclusion: "The work contains no substance/interest." With his next paragraph, however, Shian initiates a kind of criticism that would prove to be significant to the evaluation of women's writing. Whereas he has resorted to classical wordplay in his own text, he takes Kaho to task for embedding Edo-period wordplay in hers. To illustrate his point, he refers to the second section of *Warbler* and to the introduction of Yamanaka's mistress Osada. Here Kaho inserts an Edo period *senryū*, or caustic verse, into her description: "Done up fine, it draws criticism—the widow's coiffure" (p. 129). This one line, apparently, provoked Shian to the censure already referred to in Chapter One. Surely an innocent young maiden could not have written such:

> There are even some people who say that Miss Kaho is not the author of *Yabu no uguisu*. They say if a *tsūjin* (a man of the world) didn't write it, it must have been a *suikyaku* (a man about town) who revised it. I for one

earnestly desire that she transfer her enthusiasm from the vulgar conditions of the lower classes to that of the elegant manners of the upper classes. I hope that she will emulate the Murasaki Shikibu of old and not the Shikibu of the back alleys. I hope she will be like Sei Shonagon who preferred to dip [her brush] in pure streams rather than treat the vulgar conditions of men and women who live in muddied waters.[62]

It is unclear whether Shian's outburst was provoked by Kaho's familiarity with *senryū* itself—generally considered a "lowbrow" though nevertheless intellectual and thereby masculine verse form (which incidentally the Ken'yūsha members enjoyed composing)—or by the sexual innuendo inferred. A widow fusses over her hair for one reason and one reason only, and it was still unseemly in 1888 for widows to be so preoccupied. But it was even more unseemly for schoolgirls to be aware of this preoccupation, much less depict the kind of "poison woman" *(dokufu)* who would be likely to so indulge herself.

Unlike Ningetsu, who wished Kaho would write like a Westerner and not an Edo-period Japanese, Shian urged her to write like a "young lady" and not a "man." He prayed: "I hope that she will value her sweet innocence *(adonasa)*."[63] Kaho, of course, was a member of the upper class in a very class-conscious society. She was a sheltered young lady pampered by her parents and allowed to indulge in the elitist occupations of her age. Shian found it unseemly for such a young woman to bother with lower-class issues in her writing. Even though men in her social sphere—Tsubouchi Shōyō for one— wrote of women from the lower classes, it was unseemly for Kaho—a young woman carefully trained in the elegant *waka* tradition—to do the same. Rather she should emulate that great noblewoman of old, Murasaki Shikibu, who herself did not deign to peer beyond the curtains of the court. If the standards of Japanese literature were to be raised, then men may take the West as their model but women must keep to the classical past.

Just as Ningetsu's focus on "peripetia" blinded him to the carefully constructed narrative development Kaho employed in each section, Shian's allergy to a young lady penning conversations among the lowbrow deafened him to the playful variety in her narrative voices. In the space of a few pages, Kaho moves with seemingly no effort from a conversation between young ladies to that between the hired help and then on to a discussion among educated gentlemen. That she was able to maintain in each instance the mood and expression appropriate to her characters was in itself a remarkable feat.

This is not to suggest that she completely dispensed with the elegant flourish expected of a literary lady. She offers her share of literary allusions— a nod perhaps to her years of training at the Haginoya poetry academy. In section nine, for example, when Tsutomu is poised to cut his ties with Hamako, he is assailed momentarily with doubt and recalls their childhood together with warm nostalgia. Like the two children in *The Tales of Ise*, they had grown up side by side, measuring their heights at the well curb. And now Hamako "with her raven black hair and flowerlike face" will be hard to forget.[64]

The title of the work as well conjures forth the nuance of the poetry tradition. The warbler *(uguisu)* was a regular denizen of traditional *waka* diction and was associated with spring. The warbler in the plum blossoms was an early harbinger of spring and of all the human conditions associated with the season: love, youth, and rejuvenation. Perhaps the provocatively poetic title led critics such as Shian—expecting a classical love story—to be disappointed and annoyed when they found instead a tale of modern foibles. The poetic association the title conjures up is nevertheless appropriate for a story—set in the first flowering of the modern period—that describes the budding of social consciousness among a group of men and women in the bloom of their youth. The fact that the *uguisu* is in the *yabu* (bamboo thicket), and not on the plum, calls forth associations with the wild warblers of the field (or grove, *yase no uguisu*) as opposed to the domesticated warblers caged and raised at court. In many respects, Kaho's young warblers are "wild." Individuated and firmly resolved, they refuse simply to follow popular taste. Another connotation for the warbler in the wild *(yase no uguisu)* is that of an especially talented and gifted person trapped within the wilds of mediocrity. Again, a number of Kaho's characters fit this description.[65]

With the exception of the title and a few poetic allusions, Kaho's work is not heavily ornamented with rhetorical flourishes from the literary classics. In latter works, however, she seemed to heed Shian's advice as she began to pay greater attention to refining the *wabun*-style language of her narrative passages. And though she continued to feature girls from good homes who nevertheless had fallen on hard times, she was less likely to allow her narrative vision to drift into the teahouses and seedy back alleys. This did not mean that her reputation as a writer improved, however, or that the criticism which attended her works outgrew its preoccupation with who she was and how she came to write.

The Issue of Imitation: Tsubouchi Shōyō and the Student Novel

Indeed, in the reviews of *Warbler* the critic's voice so overwhelms the author's own that the criticism eventually displaced the text. Ningetsu and Shian, preoccupied with their own performance as critics, transformed Kaho's text into a stage upon which they strutted and fretted their "critic act." Ningetsu flaunts his impressive vocabulary; Shian trots out his clever wordplay. And while these two clamor for the spotlight, the woman and her work are pushed beyond the curtain. Readers today are left not with Kaho's text in its own right but with the critics' reinterpretations of it. Thus it is their performance that has made it into the literary histories, not Kaho's own. Most encapsulated expositions of Kaho's text are gleaned from this criticism and not from an actual reading of *Warbler*.

The greatest contributor in this disappearing act has been the criticism that damned Kaho's *Warbler in the Grove* as imitative. In Shōyō's letter to Kaho, published along with her story, he acknowledges that he made editorial changes to her text but suggests they were few and minor. Literary historian Shioda Ryōhei, however, has charged that the changes were so extensive the entire manuscript was crisscrossed with red correction marks.[66] Contradicting Shioda, Wada writes that he has seen the original manuscript and found that less than 18 percent bears Shōyō's marks.[67] Furthermore, Wada suggests that Shōyō's corrections had mostly to do with superficial matters of style. He did not tamper with the characterizations or plot but focused on phrasing, diction, and descriptive passages. He quibbled with choice of words—for example, he substituted "*ohanesan*" (vixen; minx) for "*otenba ojō*" (Miss Hussy; Miss Tomboy). He changed kana to kanji in some places, for instance, and kanji to kana in others. Moreover, he occasionally altered the way Kaho used kana to represent words. In one of the groom's speeches, for instance, Shōyō changed "*dotooshitanda*" (what happened?), written in katakana, to "*dooshitanoda*" (what happened?), rendered in hiragana.[68] These were minor changes, perhaps, but Shōyō was intent on making the dialogue more natural. For that reason, the bulk of his corrections involved conversations among the "common people"—primarily the dialogue in section seven between the rickshaw puller and the groom and the exchanges between Osada and Yamanaka in sections two and nine.

Tsubouchi Shōyō's "corrections" were not always improvements. In section seven, for example, Kaho has the men discussing the thirty sen that Hamako gave the rickshaw puller to buy his silence. Shōyō changed "*sanjū sen*" (thirty sen) to "*hansuke*"—a term used to belittle another (implying someone who is not fully a man) but with the secondary meaning of half a yen, or fifty sen. The editorial change makes for an amusing pun: "She gave me fifty sen/she belittled me." Yet by resorting to this kind of clever artifice, Shōyō diminishes the scene's authenticity.

Most critics, as we have seen, contend that Kaho's work was merely an imitation of Shōyō's. Critic and author Miyamoto Yuriko notes that because "the work follows so closely in the footsteps of *The Character of Modern-Day Students*, it is difficult to call *Warbler in the Grove* original."[69] Seki Ryōichi says that *Warbler* is so closely based on *The Character of Modern-Day Students* that it is little more than a female remake.[70] Criticism of this kind leads one to assume that Kaho merely transformed male characters in Shōyō's story into female characters in her own. If Shōyō wrote of male students *(shosei)*, then she would write of female students *(jogakusei)*. One wonders what exactly these critics read in reaching these conclusions. For Kaho's text is much more than a mere remake of Shōyō's. To appreciate the inappropriateness of this notion, let us turn briefly to an evaluation of Shōyō's story. As Marleigh Ryan in *The Development of Realism in the Fiction of Tsubouchi Shōyō* provides the most thorough summation in English of *Modern-Day Students*, there is no need to repeat the details here. Suffice it to say that Shōyō's work is long—well over four times the length of *Warbler*. The plot is complex and enlivened by subplots and intrigues. Ryan notes:

> Despite the title and the author's desire to write of student life as he knew it, the main plot actually concerns the origins of a geisha named Tanoji whose true parentage is not revealed to her or to the reader until the last chapter. . . . Her life is interwoven, directly and indirectly, with those of a considerable number of men and women, each of whom is in turn developed as a character in the novel.[71]

Ryan indicates that this attention to geisha and prostitutes in a novel purportedly about students should not be surprising, since a great deal of literature up to this point was devoted to detailing the activities of the licensed quarters:

> Looking back on the literature of the Tokugawa and early Meiji, it is as if virtually nothing interesting happened to women who did not reside in the few square miles encompassed by the licensed quarter of Japan's major cities. Merchants' daughters and even young women of the samurai class— provided they were immoral enough—occasionally received a writer's attention and there were, of course, those silently suffering wives of the young men who squandered all in pursuit of emotional satisfaction. But by and large the world of the imagination, both theatrical and fictional, was inhabited by women who were not bound by the restrictive conventions of normal Japanese life. Romance was a proper subject for fiction but had little to do with marriage or indeed with the lives of respectable young women at all.
>
> Tsubouchi's personal experience with women was almost exclusively in the licensed quarter. . . . Even if he had decided to break with convention and write about ordinary women, it is doubtful that Tsubouchi would have known what to say.[72]

As Peter Kornicki and others have pointed out, Tsubouchi Shōyō believed that an essential component of the novel was the depiction of *ninjō*, or human emotions. "Novels are principally concerned with *ninjō*," Shōyō declares in his preface to his 1885 *Imotosekagami* (A Mirror of Marriage). *"Ninjō,"* he continues, "is at its most acute in the emotion of love . . . and the emotion of love is at its most acute in [hetero]sexual love *(nanjo no renjō)*."[73] *Ninjō*, of course, has had a long history in Japanese literature from *The Tale of Genji* to *The Plum Calendar*. But generally the object of a hero's romantic impulses in fiction had been—as Ryan observes—the geisha or courtesan. "Romance" was colored by licentiousness and was therefore off limits to good girls. What took place in a marital union, or a socially sanctioned relationship, could hardly be considered "romance" and was thereby of little interest to writers. If romance *(ninjō)* was the essential element of the novel but "had little to do with marriage or indeed with the lives of respectable young women," then it would understandably be verboten for a proper young woman—such as Kaho—to write a novel. In other words, Kaho could not simply copy Shōyō's work because she could not write about the licensed quarters. Not only would it have been highly inappropriate for her to write about geisha and concubines (even so she was castigated for her perceived familiarity with women like Osada), but she would have had as little to say of such a romance as Ryan contends Shōyō had of relations with ordinary women.

Certainly Kaho knew that modern fiction needed to be based on modern life—if it were to be successful. With the exception of *gesaku* stories, kabuki dramas, and whatever whispered innuendos the servants dropped about her father, Kaho had little experience with the licensed quarters or with "poison women" like Osada. The only romance she knew was that of the dance halls or the entanglements young ladies had with their tutors and teachers, their brother's friends or friend's brothers. While Shōyō's students—enjoying the brief respite in their lives before the responsibilities of employment—were free to dally with prostitutes, Kaho's students—yet unencumbered with marriage and thus able to enjoy their position in a liminal space of temporary self-indulgence—were free to flirt and dream.

By the time Kaho set about writing *Warbler in the Grove*, the girl student *(jogakusei)* had become a popular object of curiosity, scorn, and infatuation in the public's imagination. With her fashion savvy and saucy attitudes, the *jogakusei* threatened to replace the geisha as the female sex object of choice in more and more stories, prints, and paintings.[74] Unlike the courtesan, who was often employed for her tragic as well as erotic potential, the girl student was usually the target of satire. In the October 1887 issue of *Garakuta bunko* (Rubbish Library), for example, Ozaki Kōyō published the first installment of what would have become the novel "Musume hakase" (The Girl Professor) had he not abandoned the project. The story opens on a satirical note as the narrator describes the Musashino Plain—once famed for its moonlight—now home to a gasworks. From here the reader's attention is directed to an imposing, white-washed Western-style building. Three girls linger before the gate bidding each other "adieu" *(achyu)* and "good-bye" *(guudo-bai)*. Two are dressed in kimonos, the other in Western attire. The two kimono-clad girls set off down the road speaking English to one another as they go. The narrator informs us that ever since they took their father's razor and whacked off their front bangs—without consulting the mirror—and thus abandoned their elaborate Shimada coiffures in favor of loosely flowing hair, their headaches have lessened considerably. The third girl, wearing a lavender dress and smartly displaying a rose in her jet-black hair, goes up to her room dangling her bookbag and whistling through her front teeth. Her room is fashionably Western with a flower-patterned carpet on the floor and green drapes at the window. She has a tiny desk alongside one wall and a glass-doored bookcase crammed full of Western-language books. The young lady goes immediately to the window, opens it, and then sits at the piano—the requisite symbol of modern feminine accomplishment at the time. When the maid enters, the girl requests a coffee. But soon the two begin to discuss the Rokumeikan and Western-style dancing. As the maid cannot quite imagine such an activity, the young lady teaches her a few steps before they are interrupted by visitors. And so the first and only section of the story draws to a close.[75]

Kornicki suggests that Kōyō's work may have been inspired by Yamada Bimyō's *Melody Played on a Mouth Harp (Fūkin shirabe no hitofushi)*, which he published in three installments in a newly founded women's magazine, *Iratsume*, from July to September 1887.[76] Bimyō's piece, written largely in a colloquial style, concerns two young maidens *(otome)* who are studying together at a women's school. Set primarily in their dormitory room, the narrative focuses on their dialogue (rendered in playscript style) as they discuss the infatuation one of them has with her male instructor. Despite the winsome quality of the colloquialisms and the frivolity of the subject, the authorial voice maintains a moralizing tone. The antics of the free-minded female student, for example, are clearly not to the narrator's liking.

It is difficult to ascertain whether or not Kaho was familiar with these stories. She may not have had access to *Garakuta bunko*, which was published privately and not widely disseminated before 1888. But *Iratsume*, primarily a poetry journal, was founded in 1887 with the specific goal of targeting young women of Kaho's age, background, and education. It is quite likely that she read *Iratsume* and therefore may have been familiar with Bimyō's work. Indeed, *Warbler in the Grove* bears perhaps more similarities with Bimyō's story (or for that matter with Kōyō's) than it does with Shōyō's *Modern-Day Students*. Both are set in a girls' dormitory and are advanced through conversations among the girls. Both concern romance; both are imbued with a moralistic tone. To suggest, therefore, that *Warbler* is a mere imitation of Shōyō's story assumes a singularity for Shōyō that is unwarranted. Moreover, it implies a singularly narrow reading practice on Kaho's part that is unreasonable.

This is not to imply that *Warbler* bears no likeness to *Modern-Day Students*. In the first place, the approach is similar. Both attempt to describe contemporary situations in a whimsical manner while at the same time investing their narrative with a moral message. In both works the use of language is similar. Like Shōyō, Kaho writes in a form of *gazoku setchū*—that is, she uses a primarily classical style in her narrative descriptions but resorts to the colloquial in her dialogue passages. Moreover, she intersperses these dialogues with English words—rendered in katakana. Both the colloquial and the katakana words give the dialogue a sense of freshness and modern immediacy. Finally, Kaho renders these dialogue passages in playscript style—as can be discerned from the sections translated here—much as Shōyō (and Kōyō) did. There are other similarities as well. Characters speak to one another for half a page or more before the narrator bothers to inform the reader of their identity, referring to them in neutral terms, such as woman or man, and then switching to a proper noun midstream. Additionally, much of the "plot" in the story is furthered through dialogue.

Shōyō, however, did not have a monopoly on this kind of narrative style. Kornicki notes that Shōyō's work bears much in common with the earlier *gesaku* fiction. In both *The Character of Modern-Day Students* and the *sharebon, kokkeibon,* and *ninjōbon* of the Tokugawa era, the plot is dominated and carried forward by dialogue, "so that there are long passages of conversation interrupted only by a brief indication of the speaker."[77] This dialogue and the occasional insertion of trivial and extraneous sounds bears "testimony to the influence of the theatre on Tokugawa prose literature."[78] Moreover, Shōyō's decision to fill his dialogue sequences with "colloquialisms, slang, fashionable words or exprssions, and corrupted or abbreviated speech" is not unique but "abound[s] in the works of writers from the late Tokugawa period."[79]

Nor did Shōyō invent the student-character novel. The genre of character sketches—or *katagi mono*—had been around for centuries. Being well read in *gesaku* fiction, Kaho was no doubt equally inspired by this earlier tradition. In fact, in her memoirs she indicates that when she was twelve years old she read Ihara Saikaku's *Five Women Who Loved Love* (*Kōshoku gonin onna,* 1686) and was so impressed that she tried her hand at a similar character sketch, writing five episodes about five of her school friends.[80] Since each friend kept the sketch that concerned her, we have no record of Kaho's *Five Women* today, other than what she has related in her essays.

Just as the genre of the character sketch was not Shōyō's invention, neither was the decision to focus on students. Kornicki reveals: "By 1885 the student and his world, and even the burgeoning female educational world, had already an established place in the fiction of the day."[81] Kanagaki Robun included a scene in his 1871 *Journey on Shank's Mare Around the West (Seiyō dōchū hizakurige)* in which students "conduct an inebriated conversation in a beef restaurant and introduce snippets of English into their conversation."[82] Other contemporary writers inserted school scenes or conversations between students in their works. Eventually a new genre devoted entirely to students and the problems they faced began to emerge. This genre was inaugurated in 1883 by Tanaka Ichirō with *New Comic Story—Amazing Students (Kokkei shinwa: shosei kimotsubushi)*, a lighthearted look at the scrapes and scandals in which students found themselves embroiled.

All the evidence, then, suggests that Kaho's work was not merely an imitation of Shōyō's earlier text but, rather, a product of its age influenced by a broad range of stimuli and trends. The insistence of certain critics in labeling Kaho's work a "copy" denies Kaho her own agency and forces her into a submissive role. She becomes the receptor, rather than the instigator, even of her own creativity. Yet studies in intertextuality have shown that no author is entitled to the name of "originator" and no text is an "original." Julia Kristeva observes, for example, that "the writer is first a reader of cultural texts; writing is always re-writing in the ceaseless construction of 'history and society's' intersecting textual surfaces."[83] And Roland Barthes insists that "a text is not a line of words releasing a single 'theological' meaning (the 'message' of the Author-God) but a multi-dimensional space in which a variety of writings, none of them original, blend and clash. The text is a tissue of quotations drawn from the innumerable centers of culture."[84] That being the case, Tsubouchi Shōyō's *Character of Modern-Day Students* is a rewriting—a tissue of Takizawa Bakin, *katagi mono*, kabuki, and so forth. Kaho's *Warbler in the Grove* is, in turn, a rewriting of Shōyō's rewriting and then some.

What is significant, however, is Kaho's motivation in claiming Shōyō as her model. On the one hand, her claim operates as a polite performance. After all, it was Shōyō who had originally encouraged Kaho by offering to provide her publication with his imprint. Without this kind of patronage, it would have been difficult for Kaho to have published so easily, despite her father's connections. But on the other hand, Kaho's alleged imitation is in itself a form of appropriation. By laying claim to Shōyō, the great male mentor, Kaho divests him of his authority. Her imitation allows a subtle inversion of power in that the imitator "masters" the master's text—much as a translator does—by laying bare its secrets and reproducing it in a new form. The imitator displaces the author and ensconces herself in his stead.

The subversive nature of imitation is manifest in the very fact that it is so easily overlooked. In Kaho's case, the critics' charge of "imitation" minimized the inventiveness and independence of Kaho's creation. Surely much of the reluctance to admit Kaho's agency in her own creation has to do with her distinction as a "first." Since she was hardly confronted with competition at the time from other women writers, it was as difficult for critics to ignore her as it was for them to give her a fair reading. She had no modern precedent—no group under which she could be subsumed. Placing her in Shōyō's shadow, therefore, helped to situate Kaho: it gave her a context that made her manageable. It also silenced her. For Kaho could not escape the derogatory label of imitator—just a silly schoolgirl dabbling in creative writing for no other reason than to entertain herself.

A cursory glance at Kaho's works after *Warbler in the Grove*, however, does not support the suggestion of frivolity.[85] Although Kaho never significantly advanced her characterizations beyond the idealizations she employed in *Warbler*, she nonetheless wrote thoughtfully and single-mindedly, imbuing her works with provocative and sensitive social content. By no means are these works the careless scribblings of a spoiled rich girl. Kaho uses her position as writer to air her own views on a number of controversial social issues. In "A Single Reed Stalk" (Ashi no hito fushi, 1890), for example, she deals with alcoholism. In *The Eightfold Cherry Blossom* (*Yaezakura*, 1890) and a number of subsequent works, she treats the evils of concubinage. In "Memories of Dew" (Tsuyu no yosuga, 1895), she considers the inequity of judging women on the basis of their physical beauty.

Although some of her works tend toward melodrama, most are brightened by devastatingly sharp cynicism—especially in her portrayals of superficially modernized or educated aristocrats. "Utabito" (The Poetasters, 1892), in a slightly different vein, takes on the pompous presumptuousness of the contemporary *waka* circles by detailing a poetry meeting with such a scathingly critical eye it is a wonder she was not slapped with a libel suit.

Kaho attempted a variety of plots and narrative strategies, but she could never quite break from the grip of "character sketches." She experimented with narrative voice, writing some stories in the first person, others in an epistolary style. One of her later works, "The Telegram" (Denpō, 1896), which Wada Shigejirō singles out for praise,[86] describes the Miyake family's reaction when a telegram informs them that Setsurei's older brother has died in the Sino-Japanese War. Derived from lived experience, the work offers a foretaste of the *shi-shōsetsu* (I-novel) genre that in the 1910s would become the staple of Japanese narrative.

Kaho wrote seriously, regardless of her claims to the contrary, and she wrote often—five or six stories a year until 1896, when her writing pace

slowed considerably but did not stop completely. Shioda Ryōhei and others
have charged that she did not have a passion for writing and thus let it slip.[87]
Perhaps she simply did not have the time. By 1896 she was teaching *waka* as
Nakajima Utako's disciple.[88] Additionally, she had young children and a husband who, by all accounts, was somewhat of a child himself—at least as far as
taking care of his day-to-day needs. That she even managed to write at all during this time is something of a miracle. Shioda Ryōhei, in regard to Yanagida
Izumi's statement that marrying Setsurei was the culmination of her career,
indicates that it was indeed the culmination—it was the finishing blow.[89]
Miyamoto Yuriko furthers this idea by suggesting that for a woman of Kaho's
age and upbringing, marriage was the ultimate destination. It was in marriage
that her energy and passion were expected to be spent.[90] Faced with a choice
between art and marriage, Kaho would inevitably select marriage.

Ironically, Kaho's choice was castigated by a contemporary critic. In a
brief essay for the journal *Bunko*, December 25, 1900, an anonymous critic
surveying the contemporary literary scene and regretting the sudden paucity
of writing women takes Kaho to task for relinquishing her career: "You say
you are now enmeshed in the joys of homemaking and are too busy to write.
But what does this suggest of your attitude toward writing? Is it merely a
hobby to turn to in your spare time?"[91] The implication seemed to be that
writers should put their craft before all else—even family obligations. Such
devotion may have been possible for a male writer in the Meiji period. But
regardless of this critic's charge, it was not an option for women.

From good daughter to good wife and mother, Kaho would forever be
defined by her relationships to men. No matter what she wrote, therefore, she
would always be a daughter and wife first. She could never be a "serious"
writer and still be devoted to family demands. An exemplar as a woman, she
was nevertheless exemplarily imitative—as all women are—and exemplarily
modest. Like the women she depicted in *Warbler in the Grove*, she would find
her success through the men with whom she affiliated.

Chapter Three

Behind the Veil

Wakamatsu Shizuko and the Freedom of Translation

Composing original works encourages publicity; translating invites true merit. The former calls for arrogance; the latter, humility. The former touches on fantasy; the latter on sobriety. This is why translation is, as I have said, a task for women.

—Kunikida Doppo, 1898

A child, who was wandering the fields with her mother, spied a tree that was curiously misshapen and bent. Pointing to the tree, the child said, "Mother, when that tree was small, someone must have stepped on it."

—Wakamatsu Shizuko, 1891

Wakamatsu Shizuko, perhaps more than any of her peers, embodies the early Meiji ideal of the woman writer. Born of the tumult that attended the Meiji Restoration, she was left at a very young age to fend for herself. By a stroke of fortune she received a Western-style education. Intellectually gifted, she learned English alongside the Japanese classics and devoted herself assiduously to the improvement of the female condition in Japan—all the while serving faithfully as wife and mother. Weakened by her early years of poverty, successive childbirths, and constant overwork, she died a few weeks shy of her thirty-second birthday but not before leaving behind an outstanding record of accomplishments: Japanese essays on education for women and on "home science"; English essays on Japanese literature and culture; prose fiction; poetry in both English and Japanese; and, most notably, a series of translations from English into Japanese.

Although Shizuko translated Longfellow, Tennyson, and sections of Dickens, it is for her translation of Frances Hodgson Burnett's *Little Lord Fauntleroy* (1885) that she is most remembered. Amidst the many possible candidates for translation at the time—Louisa May Alcott's *Little Women* (1868), Harriet Beecher Stowe's *Uncle Tom's Cabin* (1852), or Mark Twain's *Tom Sawyer* (1875)—the choice of Burnett's piece catches one by surprise. Shizuko had very specific reasons for selecting this work, however, and her translation was not only well received but contributed to the contemporary literary scene in numerous ways. Shizuko's efforts, for example, challenged the current level of translation in Japan. Moreover, her selection of *Little Lord Fauntleroy* opened the door to the entirely new genre of children's literature. Furthermore, the language she crafted for her translation substantially advanced the campaign to invent a modern literary idiom. Given the significance of her work, it is difficult to explain why she is overlooked today. As Yamamoto Masahide points out, she is hardly mentioned at all in the many studies that treat early Meiji translations or experiments with *genbun itchi* ("unification of speech and prose"). In studies of children's literature she is given slightly more credit, but her works are removed from context and abridged so severely that they lose all value.[1] Like Miyake Kaho, Wakamatsu Shizuko has become a footnote in a history that does not include her.

This chapter restores Shizuko from the back pages of literary history to the body of the text. In the process we will discover how it was that a writer like Shizuko was originally excluded from that history. I am interested in exploring Shizuko's perception of her literary career. Since to a large extent her career choices are tied to the experiences she underwent as a child, we will start with her biography, her education, and her self-perceived mission before considering her development as a writer and a translator, focusing ultimately on *Little Lord Fauntleroy*. Finally, we will explore the ramifications of this translation, its impact on the literary climate at the time, and its contribution to the definition of "women's writing."

A Lost Childhood

> When the Fushimi Battles—proclaiming the Imperial Restoration—erupted, I was three years old, and though I was but a child, I remember a number of the terrifying events that attended the transfer of political power. We—my parents and I—met head on the anguish that was born of the revolution. . . . My father was a famous Aizu warrior, a hero in the Boshin Civil War.[2]

Shizuko was born March 1, 1864, in what is present-day Aizu-Wakamatsu city, Fukushima prefecture. Her father, Matsukawa Katsujirō, was a retainer to Matsudaira Katamori (1836–1893), the lord of Aizu and one of the most fervent backers of the Tokugawa shogunate. Because Aizu refused to surrender, even after the Tokugawa armies suffered defeat in the Toba-Fushimi battles, imperial troops marched on Aizu-Wakamatsu, October 8, 1868 (according to the Japanese calendar, the twenty-third day of the eighth month). When the Aizu lord stubbornly refused to yield, vicious fighting ensued. Volleys of gunfire filled the air, fires raged, the citizenry was caught in an avalanche of terror. Shizuko fled her home with her mother and grandmother. As her biographer Yamaguchi Reiko describes the scene, the three women—one too old to flee, the second too young, and the third heavily pregnant—were trapped in a horrible tableau of death.[3] Wounded people—many of them felled by gunfire—lay shrieking in the streets while others ran around or over them, unable or unwilling to stop for fear of their own lives. The streets were clogged with carts, baggage, and corpses. Shizuko recalls seeing headless bodies along the way and witnessing groups of mass suicide—as one family member beheaded the others before turning the blade on himself or herself. In many cases, it was a female member of the family who was the only one capable of performing the deed, since most able-bodied men had gone to join the fighting.

Shizuko's group managed to find its way to a shrine where shelter was sought for the night. All told, Yamaguchi states, more than four hundred and sixty Aizu warriors lost their lives in the battle and over two hundred and thirty family members followed their men to death in ritual suicide *(junshi)*. Scores of others died as they fled the fighting. Amidst this death, Shizuko's mother gave birth to a daughter in the shrine precinct where they had taken shelter. She named the baby Miya.[4]

Names, like lives and family bonds, were ephemeral gifts during these turbulent years. When Shizuko was born she was given the name "Kashi" in honor of the fact that she had been born on the "first calendar sign" *(ki'-noene)* in the sixty-cycle zodiac. She was the first child, and the name seemed to augur a bright future. With its additional meaning of "armor," the name was appropriate for the daughter of a samurai. Her family name was Matsukawa. Her father had been adopted into the Matsukawa household and had originally been a member of the Furukawa family. To complicate matters, Shizuko's father assumed a new identity in 1868 because of his activities in the Kyoto region as a spy for the Aizu clan. Hereafter he and his immediate family were registered under the name Shimada. Shizuko, therefore, spent the first five years of her life as Shimada Kashi. Her name would go through several permutations, however, before she emerged as Wakamatsu Shizuko, the name she would use professionally.

Following the defeat of the Aizu clan in November 1868, Shizuko's father escaped to Hokkaido with the shogunal navy. Here at Goryōkaku, the pentagon-shaped citadel in Hakodate, he joined others in a plot to launch a new campaign to overthrow the restorationists—all to no avail. Eventually he was captured and imprisoned, but none of this information reached

Shizuko's mother. She was soon lured out of her hiding place in the mountains and sent with her daughters and foster mother to a barren strip of land north of Aomori. Most of the former Aizu samurai and their family members, nearly twenty-five hundred in number, were deported to this camp and left to fend for themselves.[5] Conditions in the camp were deplorable. The land was poor—not that these samurai would have known the first thing about farming. The local people were not inclined to help their new neighbors, having only disdain for these vanquished people they referred to as "Aizu worms."[6] Many died of starvation. Others contracted fevers. Shizuko's mother, never fully recovered from her childbirth in the battlefield, grew weaker and weaker. She died in 1870 at the age of twenty-eight.

The remaining relatives were uncertain what to do with her daughters, as the whereabouts of Shizuko's father were still unknown. They decided that Shizuko's younger sister—then two years old—would stay with the family. But unable to attend to the needs of a six-year-old as well, they sent Shizuko in adoption to another family. Overnight she became Ōkawa Kashi.

Ōkawa Jinbei, Shizuko's adoptive father, was a silk thread merchant with the Yamashiroya dry goods company in Yokohama. It is unclear how he came upon Shizuko's family. According to Sōma Kokkō, Ōkawa conducted business in the Aizu area. While there, he once bought out the contracts of the three women who were charged with entertaining him. One of the women, Oroku (also known as Otori), was so grateful that she vowed never to leave his side. Although Oroku's devotion was surely motivated by the lack of alternative options, Ōkawa was nonetheless touched by her attentions. Desolate himself after the death of his first wife, he brought her back with him to Yokohama and married her. Unaccustomed to life in the bustling port city and unable to bear children of her own, Oroku complained of loneliness whenever Ōkawa left her on his many business trips. The next time Ōkawa ventured to Aizu, therefore, he broadcast his intentions to adopt a child. News of a wealthy merchant in search of a child must have seemed a godsend to many of the beleaguered former samurai in the vicinity. Shizuko's relatives contacted Ōkawa. And the next thing Shizuko knew, she was on a large sailing vessel bound for Yokohama.[7]

In the summer of 1870, when Shizuko's ship made port, Yokohama was the center of trade with the West. The city teemed with Americans, Europeans, Chinese, and other exotic creatures. The sight that met Shizuko's eyes, therefore, as she stumbled down the gangway of the ship, must have been terrifyingly strange. Here she had come from the prison camps and battlefields of yesterday into the hustle and bustle of a new world. Streets were crowded with horse-drawn carriages, the newly invented jinricksha, and a strange mélange of pedestrians dressed in all manner of costumes.

Although Shizuko would eventually think of Yokohama as home, this is not what she thought of the city in the summer of 1870. Home was Aizu-Wakamatsu, and that is where she wanted to be. Bereft of her father and still grieving for her mother, Shizuko was in no mood to be the adorable child the Ōkawas had thought to procure. She was miserable. And though she maintained the good grace of a samurai daughter, she did not warm to their ploys to draw her out. To compound her discomfort, Shizuko fell ill. The summer that year had been unseasonably hot and wet, and shortly after Shizuko's arrival, there had been an outbreak of smallpox. The Ōkawas had her vaccinated against the disease, but as a consequence she came down with a fever that lasted off and on for most of the summer. Concerned for her lack of nourishment, Mrs. Ōkawa fed Shizuko raw eggs every morning. And when the child refused to drink water, she had spring water brought in regularly for her, as she recalled her own distaste for the city water upon her arrival. Despite Mrs. Ōkawa's efforts, Shizuko did not grow stronger. She felt disoriented, confused, and completely abandoned. Shizuko's depression, sulkiness, and habitual ill health did not endear her to Mrs. Ōkawa, who soon began to regret her husband's selection. Likewise, Shizuko was none too pleased with her "new" mother and her regimen of raw eggs. There may have been a sense of class consciousness in Shizuko's resistance to her new parents as well. Although she was still very young, Shizuko had been instilled from an early age with a samurai pride. Particularly during her sojourn in the Aomori prison camp, she had been made to feel the pride of the vanquished. Ōkawa was of the merchant class, and Oroku was an uneducated former prostitute. Perhaps as a solution to the growing animosity between Oroku and her foster daughter, or perhaps in an attempt to join the ranks of the newly "enlightened," Mr. Ōkawa enrolled Shizuko in "Miss Kidder's School."

A Mission-School Education

Mary E. Kidder (1834–1910) had been sent to Japan by the Dutch Reformed Church of America in 1869. Here she joined forces with Dr. James C. Hepburn, a Presbyterian missionary and an eye doctor who had been in Japan since 1859. Hepburn is perhaps best known today for his work compiling the first Japanese-English dictionary and for the system of romanization that bears his name. At the time he was known for the compound he had established in Yokohama where he practiced medicine, taught a variety of subjects from English to theology, translated the Bible into classical Japanese, and conducted worship services. His wife had been teaching an English class for boys and girls on the compound since 1867. Just prior to Mary Kidder's arrival, however, she had been saddled with the care of an infant whose missionary parents had died. Miss Kidder, therefore, assumed Mrs. Hepburn's work with the English class. When the school year resumed after the summer holidays, Miss Kidder announced her intention to teach only girls. Thus was inaugurated Miss Kidder's School for Girls in 1871, which she conducted in a single six-mat upstairs room in the dispensary on the Hepburn compound. She described her school in a letter to her mission board director:

> My school, the School and its furniture (it deserves the name) now numbers nineteen girls and with no better accommodations than I have at present it is about all I can have. They sit at two tables which they have had made for themselves on seats without books which they procured for themselves. A friend here loaned me a small stove & the girls procure the wood for it so we are very happy and comfortable.[8]

Figure 9   Miss Mary E. Kidder as she would have looked around the time she first reached Japan in 1869. (Courtesy of the Ferris Women's College Archives)

Shizuko began attending classes in 1871. She had no more interest in Miss Kidder's lessons, or in Christianity, than she had had in Mrs. Ōkawa's mothering. But she went through the motions until the school moved in 1872.

With the assistance of the governor of Kanagawa, whose wife was one of her students, Miss Kidder moved her ever-expanding school to Nogeyama, in the "native town" where the highest government officials maintained their own residences. The move was an important one for Miss Kidder, as it allowed her to establish a school independent of the Hepburns and the Presbyterian mission. But Nogeyama was two miles from Shizuko's home in Motomachi. Miss Kidder and the other girls traveled to the school by jinricksha, but Shizuko's foster parents could not afford such luxury. In fact, Ōkawa's business had faltered badly. The Yamashiroya closed its Motomachi store, and in 1873 Ōkawa was forced to move the family to the Shitaya area of Tokyo, putting Miss Kidder's School impossibly beyond reach. If Shizuko

Figure 10
Mrs. Miller (formerly Miss Kidder) late in life. (Courtesy of the Ferris Women's College Archives)

was unhappy before, she was wretched now. She longed to return to Aizu, to find her father, to live with him. But she had no idea how to contact him and was not even certain that he was alive. All she could think was that some day he would come and rescue her.

Katsujirō did come. But the rescue he had planned did not accord with Shizuko's dreams. Katsujirō had remarried in 1872, though it is unclear if he was back in Fukushima prefecture at this time. Wherever he was, he eventually received word of Ōkawa's financial situation and began to worry about Shizuko. Although there was little he could do for her at the time, he managed to make his way to Tokyo in 1875 and appeared at the Ōkawa residence unannounced. Shizuko was thrilled. She hardly knew her father, not having seen him since she was three, yet she was certain that he was there to take her "home." This he was unable to do. But he knew he could not leave her in the Ōkawas' custody. He and Mr. Ōkawa agreed that Shizuko would return to Miss Kidder's School in Yokohama and would live there in the newly opened dormitory. It is unclear how this arrangement was accomplished or who paid for Shizuko's expenses. Nevertheless, the move offered Shizuko a sense of stability for the first time in her life.

After agonizing negotiations with the Japanese authorities, Miss Kidder was able to secure the land and the permission to build a boarding school. Following equally trying discussions with her own mission, whose small size prevented elaborate foreign outreach, she was able to win a pledge of $5,000 for the construction. Yokohama residents and Miss Kidder's husband contributed the remaining $500 to the building fund. The new facilities, sited on more than one acre of land on the Yamate Bluffs, were visible from both Tokyo Bay and the streets of Yokohama—a resplendent monument at the time to Western wealth and Christian regard for female education. The name of the institution was changed to Ferris Seminary in honor of Isaac Ferris, an important leader in the Dutch Reformed Church in America. When the dormitory opened on June 1, 1875, it housed fourteen students. By the end of the year, the number had swelled to forty. There were also ten students who commuted to the school. Monthly fees for dormitory students, which included room and board, tuition, and the other essentials of daily life (clothing, bedding, and books), came to three yen. The school provided a scholarship for three students; it is likely that Shizuko was included among them.[9]

Miss Kidder had married while Shizuko was in Tokyo and was now Mrs. Miller. Her husband was a Presbyterian missionary and minister. With no children of her own, Mrs. Miller doted on her students. She was particularly fond of Shizuko, inspiring the eleven-year-old with the will to succeed. Although Shizuko had earlier been only halfhearted about her studies, she now applied herself to her books with earnestness, realizing perhaps that survival at school was her only guarantee of future stability. Mrs. Miller took special care of Shizuko, inviting her into her home and giving her a taste of the maternal love the child had craved. Moreover, Christianity gave Shizuko a sense of familial fellowship and self-worth. In 1877, when Shizuko was thirteen, she was baptized by Mr. Miller in the Yokohama Kaigan Church.

Eugene S. Booth replaced Mrs. Miller as headmaster of Ferris Seminary in 1881. He quickly set about making changes, updating the buildings, and ensuring that each course of study—from elementary to secondary—was organized and uniformly implemented. Thanks to his curricular modifications, Ferris was able to produce its first graduating class in 1882—a class of one, Wakamatsu Shizuko its sole representative. Nevertheless, Mr. Booth held a proper ceremony and Shizuko, having prepared for two days, delivered an impressive address in English before an audience of students and invited guests.

Like his predecessor, Mr. Booth was very fond of Shizuko. He would later say of her:

> She was a striking figure. Slender, but erect, above the medium height, whose delicate shoulders bore a large head, with a full rounded brow and

Figure 11   Isaac Ferris Women's Seminary, June 1, 1875. (Courtesy of the Ferris Women's College Archives)

intelligent face; open, observant, though mild eyes, out of which a soul of
rare gifts seemed to look. A nervous temperament, yet having a masterly
self-control that lent a quiet dignity to all her movements. She possessed
quick mental activity and vivid emotions, without the offensive forwardness
so often seen in such temperaments.[10]

After her graduation, Booth kept Shizuko on at Ferris as an instructor.
From the following fall Shizuko changed the way she transcribed her name
"Kashi." Rather than the character for "first zodiac sign," she used a combination of characters that together expressed the notion of "joyful determination." She was determined now to pursue her goals, and her determination
brought joy. Her name was soon to change in other ways as well. Her father,
Katsujirō, moved to Tokyo in 1883 and established a residence in Azabu. He
restored Shizuko to the earlier Shimada registry and formally severed her
connection to the Ōkawa family.[11] Shizuko's younger sister, Miya, also listed
under the Shimada registry, joined her father in Azabu along with
Katsujirō's second wife Ei and their son Hajime.

Figure 12
Wakamatsu Shizuko
as a young woman.
(Courtesy of the
Ferris Women's
College Archives)

Once the school year began, Shizuko applied herself to her duties with "joyful determination." As part of the eighteen-member teaching staff, she was responsible for four subjects: physiology and health, home economics, Japanese composition, and English translation. In addition to teaching, she organized a literature circle known as the Jishūkai, or Society for Timely Reflection.[12] Interested members met regularly to read English sonnets and stories aloud and discuss their own literary efforts. Shizuko hoped to encourage her students and friends to participate more actively in society through literature:

> Now our motive is, in view of the demands of the age, . . . to review and put into practice, in a quiet and unassuming way, the knowledge that we acquire with the aid of our teachers in our class rooms and from school privileges in general. . . . What a powerful weapon may the pen become in the hand of a noble woman! With what influence to elevate and purify society can she wield it![13]

Shizuko also joined the English Drama Society at Ferris and was frequently asked to serve as an interpreter for foreign guests or to lecture pub-

Figure 13
Wakamatsu Shizuko
as a writer. (Courtesy
of the Ferris Women's
College Archives)

licly, and often in English, on such topics as "the current state of education for women in Japan." Shizuko was not only Ferris Seminary's first graduate, she was its pride and joy—the supreme example of a mission-school education. Mrs. Miller praised her: "She was the best educated Japanese woman in the country. Although many of her sister Japanese have studied abroad . . . she was more than their equal."[14]

The Jeweled Palanquin

Although Shizuko would eventually marry Iwamoto Yoshiharu, he was not the first to propose. In 1886 Shizuko became acquainted with Serada Akira, whose younger sister was a Ferris student. Serada, formerly of the samurai class, was an officer in the Imperial Navy whose work with the Japanese Embassy had taken him to the United States where he had lived for a number of years. He was therefore conversant with American customs and mores, a Christian, gifted in English, and apparently very handsome. The foreign instructors at Ferris found him absolutely charming. Mrs. Miller adored him and was instrumental in arranging that he and Shizuko become engaged to be married. Everyone was therefore mystified when Shizuko broke the

Figure 14   Wakamatsu Shizuko's three children with their late mother's photograph inset. (Courtesy of the Ferris Women's College Archives)

engagement in 1887. No amount of pleading on Mrs. Miller's part would make her change her mind.

As Shizuko's motivation for breaking the engagement was never made public, her biographers are left with only speculation. Fujita Yoshimi, for example, suggests that because Shizuko knew her health was deteriorating—she had begun coughing blood in 1887—she did not think it fair to saddle a man like Serada with an invalid wife.[15] Since Shizuko went ahead and saddled Iwamoto Yoshiharu with such a wife two years later, this explanation is not persuasive. Yamaguchi Reiko notes that Shizuko wrote a fairly testy essay titled "The Jeweled Palanquin" when she learned that other members of the Ferris community were criticizing her for her decision:[16]

> I find there is no proverb more harmful to women than the one lauding the orphan maiden who, marrying above her station, is "borne aloft in a jeweled palanquin." In our society, a poor woman may marry into the manor, and all will applaud her great fortune. When I hear such I feel my heart is being rent with a sword.[17]

Marriage for Shizuko was not to be a conveyance for female advancement. Nor were women to rush into matrimony at the cost of their own integrity. It seems likely, therefore, that though Shizuko admired and respected Serada, she did not love him. Perhaps she also felt intimidated by his splendor, his success and position, and sensed that his goals and desires would overwhelm hers should she accept his offer of marriage. Shizuko was not averse to submitting to a husband. She believed that marriage was, for a woman at least, an exercise in sacrifice. But this yielding of self should be made gladly and with love. Acutely sensitive to her own shortcomings and to her troubled upbringing, Shizuko was perhaps afraid that her sense of pride would interfere with her ability to submit joyfully to Serada's will. Whatever her reason, for a twenty-four-year-old woman to turn down a perfectly appropriate marriage proposal must have seemed childish, selfish, and irresponsible. Both of the systems that Shizuko had been raised to respect—Japanese and American—saw marriage as the center of a woman's life. Indeed, a woman's *real* life did not begin until she had married. Shizuko was no longer young by nineteenth-century standards—both Japanese and American—and there was little guarantee that she would have another opportunity to marry. In an era when women almost never voluntarily considered alternatives to marriage, therefore, Shizuko's behavior must have appeared reckless. Keenly sensitive to the charges that mission schools masculinized women, rendering them unfit for marriage, Shizuko would have been aware that her decision to reject a good match only gave the opposition more ammunition to oppose higher education for women. And not only was she rejecting a prominent man, she was denying a marriage that her benefactor, Mrs. Miller, had advocated. That Shizuko was willing to face the censure of those closest and dearest to her shows the strength of her convictions. It also reveals that Shizuko did not adhere to the Victorian ideal of the "Perfect Lady, the genteel ornament of feminine innocence," but was willing to assume the mantle of the "New Woman, the independent but still feminine being who hesitantly opened the door to the world outside of marriage."[18]

"Sumire," a short story Shizuko wrote two years after this incident, is believed to shed additional light on her attitudes toward matrimony, and most biographers turn to it for an explanation of her behavior. Although the story is not intentionally autobiographical, it depicts a romantic entanglement that closely resembles the one between Shizuko and Serada. Miss Sumire Mano, though orphaned at a young age, was raised by a gentle cousin for whom she seems to have a lingering attachment. He is now deceased and, at the age of twenty four, she lives quietly with her elderly aunt. A mission-educated Christian, Sumire is economically independent, supporting herself with both a generous inheritance and her own income as a writer. As the story opens, she is being courted ardently by the handsome, courteous, and dignified Mr. Sawabe, who has recently returned to Japan with a degree from a Berlin university. Inexplicably Sumire turns down his marriage proposal. Her aunt and associates are shocked—but none so shocked as Mr. Sawabe:

> She listened quietly to what he had to say. Then at last she spoke:
>
> "I am truly grateful to you for your offer. But, as I have said, I have but one answer to give. Please, let us not discuss it further."
>
> Gentleman: "Are you saying you intend to end our discussion here? Just like that? Why, why must we not continue? (His heart was racing.) Do you not enjoy my company? Have you not relied on me as a dear friend? I say this at the risk of being judged overly persistent, but I must state unequivocally that I consider you a friend among friends. Amidst all of *Womankind* you are _the_ *woman* I most ardently respect. Our friendship began so happily, and it is my fondest desire that we allow it to grow to even greater heights. Yet you will not even consider such. I do not understand why.
>
> I realize that you have received a Western-style education and that you count many Americans among your friends. But I cannot imagine that you would choose to hurt me with the coquetry at which these American women are so adept."
>
> The woman had fixed her gaze on the floor. But at this last comment she raised her face toward him. "My dear Mr. Sawabe, I hold you in such high esteem, I cannot even begin to express how very grateful I am that you

would even consider spending a lifetime with someone such as myself. When a man asks a woman to be his wife, he speaks from his heart, granting that woman the highest honor by placing her first before the world. How could I make light of such a proposal? . . . Indeed this relationship is most important to me, and that is why I must refuse your offer. I trust we can continue to enjoy one another's company, as we have until now. I shall be ever vigilant not to mar the happy friendship we have nurtured."

Gentleman (growing more and more solemn): "I simply do not understand. Of course, I do not have license to interrogate you on your reasons. But if I may say one more thing. As you may know, after I returned from my travels, the business in which I am engaged has prospered, and the people with whom I work trust my opinions. Unlike the situation attending the Restoration, there are now more and more talented men appearing every day. Yet I have heard it said that I manage to acquit myself admirably. While I was in America, I lived for a time in a *Christian home* that was remarkable in its perfect beauty. Having received the benefits thereof, I have been progressively distressed by the unsatisfactory home life that I have witnessed here upon my return. . . . I realize that the only one who can dispel this dissatisfaction, the only one who can encourage and support me in both my personal and professional worlds, is you. Only you can help me uphold the principles in which I believe; only you can propel me to victory on the battlefields of this world. And so it is that your ability to refuse my proposal so effortlessly has left me deeply saddened."[19]

Mr. Sawabe is the ideal Meiji man, not unlike the vision of male perfection that Kaho created one year earlier in Shinohara Tsutomu. Replete with the inverted "v" of a moustache, he bears all the accoutrements of his superior Western education. Intelligent, sophisticated, sensitive to female concerns, he is in quest of that ever-ephemeral "perfect home." As indicated in Chapter One, Meiji intellectuals like Iwamoto Yoshiharu were concerned that the traditional Japanese family *(ie)* failed to produce a true "home" because it venerated family hierarchy and history over the individual. A true "home" (written in katakana as *"hōmu"*) was warm and sweet and created by the voluntary union of a man and woman who turned to one another for companionship above all else. A woman of Sumire's education and inclinations, therefore, should have been overjoyed to have found a soul mate as perfect as Sawabe. That she refuses his offer is inexplicable. Yet in her heroine's resistance, Shizuko tries to create something pure and principled. Sumire will not marry merely for the sake of convention. In many respects, therefore, Sumire is Shizuko's female ideal. Or in Wada Shigejirō's words:

The woman here described is not the radical women's rights agitator, nor is she the childishly sweet maiden tucked protectively away in her room. This is a woman of superior intelligence who possesses great self-awareness. In short, she is an idealized woman. Indeed, in her we sense Shizuko herself— or rather a sanctification of her ideal self. I suppose there is a cloying touch of narcissism here, but we can also perceive in her portrayal an overwhelming sense of mission as an enlightened individual to advance her cause while clinging to her idealism. To have appeared as early as it did, in 1889, I feel this work is deserving of high praise.[20]

"Sumire" follows close on the heels of *Warbler in the Grove*. And though the tone of the story is very different, the playscript-style presentation is similar and the work is therefore similarly flawed. "Sumire" was not celebrated at the time as a successful piece of prose fiction. But the scenario Shizuko crafted of a man and woman speaking intelligently and as equals about such ethereal subjects as friendship and platonic love was, as Wada has implied, ahead of its time.

Fundamentally, both Shizuko and Kaho were concerned with the state of matrimony in the 1880s. Both advocated a marriage based on individual choice. But whereas Kaho was more interested in the social aspect of marriage as a reward for female virtue and an avenue for female success, Shizuko was more concerned with the spiritual covenant of matrimony. She found the socialization of marriage regrettable. Marriage was not to be a woman's "jeweled palanquin." Women should be able to find other means for establishing themselves, thus allowing marriage to serve as a pure union between two individuals informed by personal choice and not by public pressure.

The notion that the love between a man and woman could circumvent the purely physical and unfold on a spiritual level was indeed a novel idea in Japan at the time. Mori Ōgai, freshly returned from Germany, would create characters in 1890 who struggled with the spiritual aspects of love. Two years later, Kitamura Tōkoku would disseminate the notion even further with his essays celebrating the potential of heterosexual love to cleanse the hearts of those who experienced it. Although the regard of heterosexual love as an expression of morally pure emotion may have been commonplace in a Western context, it was both shocking and liberating for those Meiji men and women who encountered it for the first time in the nineteenth century. Takayuki Murakami-Yokota, in his comparative study of "love," observes:

> The idea that love is closely related to a moralistic judgment, by virtue of which a loving man can be elevated to fit the lofty image of a lady he loves, is part of a uniquely Western tradition that is absent from Eastern countries.

It originated with "courtly" love in eleventh-century Southern France and then spread to Western culture as a whole, constituting a fundamental view of love for Europeans. The aggregate of this ideology, at variance with the Japanese erotic tradition, can be encapsulated by the term *romantic love*.[21]

In "Sumire," Shizuko dresses her two characters in the garb of the Western courtly tradition. Mr. Sawabe speaks not of carnal passion but of friendship and spiritual devotion. He woos Sumire not with suggestions of desire but by informing her of his deep respect for her. Shizuko has her gentleman hero "disguise" his ardor with friendship, to borrow Murakami-Yokota's argument. Sexual desire is denounced while the edifying nature of platonic love is celebrated. Separating love into dichotomies of flesh and spirit is, as Murakami-Yokota argues, a Christian impulse whereby the spirit is believed to be superior to the flesh and humankind is taught to deny the urges of the body. Given Wakamatsu Shizuko's exposure to both Christianity and Western literature, it is hardly surprising that she would chose to depict characters who deny erotic desire in their courtship.

In this sense, Shizuko continues the discussion of love and marriage begun in Kaho's text. Kaho had separated her couples into those who married for lust—Osada/Yamanaka and Hamako/Yamanaka—and those who married for companionship—Hideko/Tsutomu and Namiko/Miyazaki. What is surprising about Shizuko's text is that it does not end in marriage. By concluding her tale with the denial of matrimony, Shizuko shifts the focus of the story away from marriage as the inevitable conclusion to a woman's life and onto Sumire as an individual. Sumire's reasons for declining Sawabe's proposal are never made crystal clear, perhaps purposely so. Shizuko's focus in the story, after all, is on "choice" and not on "motivation." Whatever her reason, Sumire said no. And it is her ability to do so that Shizuko celebrates. By saying no, by establishing her own volition, Sumire represents a new type of woman. In Sumire, Shizuko creates a woman who is feminine, virtuous, and pure, yet independent of men.

Independence—the ability to name oneself and to follow one's own principles—was a concern that had troubled Shizuko for some time. Ever since her travails as an "orphan," she had recognized her need to fend for herself and preserve the boundaries of her own identity. Amidst all the changes in her life, all the permutations in name and status, she had clung fiercely to her sense of place and self. When she first began to write essays and stories for *Jogaku zasshi*, therefore, she selected a pen name for herself. From 1886, she began calling herself Wakamatsu Shizu. Carefully chosen, the name had special implications for Shizuko. Wakamatsu, of course, was the land of her birth. Memory of this land had offered the young Shizuko a metaphorical grounding and a sense of solace in a life that for years had threatened disorientation and despair. Whereas Wakamatsu suggested the physical realm, Shizu provided for the spiritual. Ultimately meaning "God's servant," the Chinese character for *"shizu"* is the same used in the word for peasant/outcast *(senmin)*, humble *(iyashii)*, or woman of lowly birth *(shizu no me)*. Born to a samurai family, Shizuko had nevertheless fallen into poverty. A child of poverty, she was nevertheless proud. As Yamaguchi Reiko points out, the word she chose for her name is also related to a particular kind of woven cloth, *shizu-ori,* known for its chaotic blend of red and blue threads in a seemingly haphazard pattern.[22] Similarly, Shizuko's life resembled a random interweaving of various cultures, beliefs, classes, and circumstances. Japan formed the woof, America the warp. As crazy as her life might have seemed, it was not without its own pattern—the creation of which she trusted to God.

The Bridal Veil

Most who ponder Shizuko's reasons for rejecting Serada's marriage offer fail to consider the possibility that she was in love with someone else at the time—a possibility supported by her story "Sumire." Iwamoto Yoshiharu has stated unequivocally that when he met Shizuko he was unaware that she was affianced. He rejected suggestions that his relationship with her had any bearing on the dissolution of her engagement.[23] Since he and Shizuko did not make their relationship public until 1888, most biographers take him at his word. I believe that circumstances suggest otherwise. Though Shizuko and Iwamoto may not have been actively or even consciously pursuing a relationship with one another, they were conducting a romance, subtly and quietly, in the pages of *Jogaku zasshi.*

Iwamoto Yoshiharu first met Shizuko, or so it seems, when he attended one of her Jishūkai literary meetings in 1885.[24] Obviously impressed by her enthusiasm and spirit, he published her English-language address to the meeting in the January 1, 1886, issue of *Jogaku zasshi* and invited her to contribute more of her work. Shizuko responded with "Furuki miyako no tsuto" (Souvenir of the Old Capital), an essay in classical literary Japanese, which Iwamoto published in May 1886, shortly after she had become engaged to Serada. In September and October of that year, Iwamoto Yoshiharu serialized his biography of Kimura Tō, the cofounder of Meiji Women's School, who had died of cholera that August. It seems that Shizuko did not know Kimura personally. But she was so impressed by Iwamoto's description of her life and dedication to Christianity and education that soon after he published the second installment of his biography, Shizuko translated the first parts of his essay into a fifteen-stanza English poem. She sent the poem to Iwamoto by way of condolence, and he published it that October under the title "Kimura Tōko wo tomurau eishi" (An English Poem in Memory of Kimura Tōko).

This exchange marks the first "public" correspondence between Iwamoto and Shizuko. Of course, this correspondence was inspired by mutual admiration for a fellow Christian educator. And yet the tenor of the communication seems to make it more personal than that. Shizuko, after all, did not know Mrs. Kimura. She was responding less to Kimura's death than to Iwamoto's evocative portrayal of his grief over her loss. That is to say, Shizuko was responding to Iwamoto. Moreover, she was responding to him through the medium of poetry: the medium of love. She did not resort to *waka*, the choice of Heian lovers. Rather, she opted for the English verse of the Victorian lady. To cite a few of her stanzas:

1
Leave me here the papers, friends, nor
chide thy comrade thus withdrawn;
Leave me with the dead awhile—the
frail, frail tree of life to mourn.

9
Loved ones miss thee, wife and mother
in thy home congenial;
Thy pew's vacant, death removing
mother rare in Israel.

15
When I weary of life's bivouac
and the race at last is won,
Then thy wings shall waft me
yonder up to meet the Blessed One.[25]

Shizuko's poetry is not particularly notable. Yet the small selection presented here reveals not only her ease with English versification but her close familiarity with the tone of Christian diction. With phrases like "mother rare in Israel," her poem reads as a pastiche of lines from hymns, biblical scripture, and Victorian verse. Iwamoto's biography did not contain language clearly identifiable as "Christian." Yet Shizuko heard in his rendering a Christian hymn, an English poem, a wisp of scripture, and she retranscribed his message into the expressions that she had come to love from her upbringing in a mission school. Although Shizuko and Iwamoto were not communicating their thoughts and feelings for one another directly—or even perhaps consciously—through this exchange, they were speaking to each other nevertheless on a very private, spiritual level. For two people so keenly devoted to Christian faith, this was the most appropriate form of communication they could take.

As other biographers have speculated about Shizuko's reasons for refusing Serada's troth, I will offer my own theory here. Having exchanged thoughts and emotions with a man like Iwamoto, and on such a personal level, perhaps Shizuko realized that there should be more in the relationship between a man and woman than just polite attraction and jeweled palanquins. Iwamoto Yoshiharu, unlike Serada, was not a rich man, and his livelihood as an editor/educator was capricious.[26] But he had touched Shizuko. And surely it seemed to her that he was struggling to achieve the very aims that she too had set for herself. If a marriage grounded on spiritual attraction was truly possible, then it could most likely be found in union with a man like Iwamoto Yoshiharu. In the year following this exchange in *Jogaku zasshi*, Shizuko broke her engagement to Serada.

Shortly thereafter Shizuko and Iwamoto enjoyed another public exchange of prose and verse in the pages of *Jogaku zasshi*. In May 1888 Iwamoto published "Keijin no nageki" (A Lady's Lament). The prose poem was left anonymous, but critics are convinced it is Iwamoto's. Furthermore, although the work is narrated from a woman's perspective, critics conclude that it speaks for Iwamoto, revealing his thoughts and feelings for Wakamatsu Shizuko. As a lady strolls through her garden, she gazes over the flowers and reflects on their innocence and peace. These qualities stand in contrast to her own inner turmoil. "I knew not love until I met you. For you I was taught to love. I knew not pain until I loved you."[27] Shizuko apparently heard Iwamoto speaking to her through this thinly veiled essay, for again she "translated" his Japanese prose into English verse. His "Lady's Lament" became her "Complaint." Unlike the earlier poem in memory of Mrs. Kimura, Shizuko substituted Christian scriptural diction for the "language of flowers," the traditional Victorian metaphor for feminine sensuality:

4

"One by one, thou yielded
Thy petals willing but shy;
Far too tender to withstand the charm,
Potent strange—Oh why!"—
Her voice was impassioned, low,—
"Am I not like to thee?
Who taught me the mystic pain and love,
Whoever could but he!"[28]

I do not believe Shizuko's description of petal pulling is intended to suggest a "deflowering" in the current connotation of the word. But in a very provocative and sensual way she has turned Iwamoto's grief over the pains of love into her "complaint" of love's cruelty and capriciousness. As her poem ends, the lady dashes the poor flower to the ground in angry grief over being neglected.

These published exchanges between Iwamoto and Shizuko, platonic and proper on the surface, nevertheless suggest an undercurrent of mutual passion. The very act of translation—of taking another's words and reproducing them in one's own—demands an intimate commune. The text, like the flower in the poem, must yield itself to the translator's pen. The translator must open the text and try to come to some sort of sympathetic union with it. Shizuko's unsolicited translations/adaptations of Iwamoto's Japanese texts, therefore, evince a boldness in her character that she was not accustomed to revealing. They also suggest an effort on her part to offer an agreeable sense of union between herself and Iwamoto. They were like souls in faith and in love.

In both examples of this exchange, Shizuko perceived what she assumed was Iwamoto's grief and attempted to touch it and in turn to be touched by it. Having made his grief her own, she could then "respeak" it in her own words. It is curious that in both cases "her own words" are realized in English. At the time, apparently English was the language that Shizuko turned to most naturally to express matters of the heart. In these public displays for *Jogaku zasshi*, therefore, we find an intimate commingling of voice, language, gender, grief, and love.

In 1888 Shizuko agreed to marry Iwamoto. They married the following year at the Yokohama Kaigan Church where Shizuko had been baptized. The day after the wedding, Shizuko composed the following English poem for her bridegroom:

The Bridal Veil

1

We are married, they say, and you think you have won me,
Well, take this white veil and look on me;
Here's matter to vex you and matter to grieve you.
Here's doubt to distrust you and faith to believe you.
I am all, as you see, common earth, and common dew,
be weary to mould me to roses, not rue!
Ah! shake out the filmy thing, fold after fold,
And see if you have me to keep and to hold,

Look close on my heart, see the worst of its shining.
It's not yours to-day for the yesterday's winning,
The past is not mine. I am too proud to borrow.
You must grow to new heights if I love you to-morrow.

2

We're married! O, pray that our love do not fail!
I have wings flattened down, and hid under my veil,
They are subtle as light, you can undo them,
And swift in their flight, you can never pursue them.
And spite of all clasping, and spite of all bands,
I can slip like a shadow, a dream, from your hands.

3

Nay, call me not cruel and fear not to take me,
I am yours for my life-time to be what you make me,
To wear my white veil for a sign or a cover,
As you shall be proven my lord, or my lover;
A cover for peace that is dead, or a token,
Of bliss that can never be written or spoken.[29]

"The Bridal Veil" is illuminating for the way it reveals Shizuko's honest ambivalence toward marriage. Although she felt love for her groom, she also felt a vague uneasiness about their future life together. People she had loved in the past had "deserted" her, leaving her distrustful of emotional attachments. What if her husband should grow disillusioned with her? What if he should try to control her? And so from the very beginning of their marriage Shizuko had challenged Iwamoto to remove her veil: to look beyond the lace and loveliness of the romantic ideal and see her for who she was. She was not a dainty rose but common earth. She was not to be possessed but respected. The future lay with her groom, with the way he regarded and treated her. This poem was a remarkable statement for a Meiji woman—who, once married, had no rights. Through the medium of an English poem Shizuko was able to address her husband frankly and tell him that he could not own her. Iwamoto was apparently impressed. He had the poem published in the next issue of *Jogaku zasshi*.

Shizuko's health had begun deteriorating steadily since 1887 when she had first coughed blood. She found that she tired easily and often was unable to teach her classes. Rather than accept a generous salary for classes she could not teach properly, Shizuko resigned from Ferris Seminary and withdrew from the campus. It was the first time she had been away from the

Ferris community since 1875, and the departure was not easy. Nevertheless, it allowed Shizuko to embark on a new phase in her career.

Wild Flowers, Wild Words

Shizuko's earliest contributions to *Jogaku zasshi* were not limited to poems in English. Her submissions included essays in both Japanese and English. On February 25, 1888, for example, she published "The Condition of Woman in Japan," an English-language essay she had written in 1887 for presentation at an international conference at Vassar College. Although Shizuko's English prose was impressive, it would be in translating English works into Japanese that she would find her greatest achievement. In 1886 she published her translation of Longfellow's "A Psalm of Life" in *Jogaku zasshi*. Other translations of the poem by Inoue Tetsujirō and Toyama Masakazu had been published earlier in *Shintai shishō* (New Poetry). Shizuko's, however, unlike the earlier translations, was rendered in *shichi-go-chō*, the five–seven–five syllabic meter of traditional Japanese verse, and was almost exclusively hiragana. Moreover, the earlier translators, scholars but not poets, had only been able to appreciate the language of the poem literally. Shizuko tried to capture what she felt Longfellow meant. The resulting translation is therefore imbued with Shizuko's own interpretation. As Yoshiko Takita notes, Shizuko's predecessors had been concerned only with what they perceived as the poem's message of "rising in the world." Shizuko, however, tried to emphasize "instead spiritual or Christian morality in her translation."[30]

Shizuko's early experience with Longfellow's poem reveals the fundamental approach she would bring to her translations. She was not terribly interested in literalness, as she felt that words were mere vessels of meaning. A careful translator could change these vessels any number of times without significantly corrupting the original meaning. Shizuko's challenge, therefore, became the selection of the appropriate vessel to convey the meaning she perceived in the original text. To meet this challenge, she would attempt a number of experiments with language, narrative voice, and self-expression.

After her experiments with Longfellow, Shizuko elected to translate the works of the British poet Adelaide Anne Procter (1825–1864). Now mostly forgotten, Procter's poetry—with its messages of charity and feminine virtue—appealed to Shizuko. In 1887, she translated two of Procter's verses: "A Doubting Heart" and "A New Mother." Both translations were rendered in classical style (*gabuntai*) and like "A Psalm of Life" were mostly hiragana. The language that Shizuko employed, Shimada Tarō has observed, gave the poems a decidedly feminine quality that was more appropriate to Procter's text than it had been to Longfellow's.[31] Chafing at the limits she felt classical verse placed on her translations of Western poems, however, Shizuko began to search for alternatives. She tinkered briefly with a prose style more heavily laden with Chinese characters and more masculine in tone, as she admired Kōda Rohan's work.[32]

Shizuko was also writing original works of fiction at the time and experimenting as well with language and style. "Souvenir of the Old Capital," described as a "travel piece" *(kikōbun)*, was strictly classical *(gabuntai)*. But her next piece, "Nogiku" (Wild Chrysanthemum, 1889), was more inventive. In writing this dialogue between two female students, Shizuko took pains to capture the tone and diction of a student's speech—much as Kaho had before her. Unlike Kaho's portrayal of girl students, however, there is nothing lighthearted or whimsical about Shizuko's students. They are frightfully serious.

The dialogue begins when two young women spy an unusually large chrysanthemum. Beneath the heavy bloom are three smaller stalks still in bud. One of the women remarks that the flower reminds her of a loving mother hovering over her children. The other replies that to her it looks as if the larger flower is sucking the life out of the smaller three:

> "To me this flower looks like a hateful *tyrant* who fills his belly at the expense of the weak in the world. It resembles a cruel man who assumes a pose of greatness while causing his gentle wife and children to suffer. Think about it. In the world there are so many who are made to submit to those who are big and powerful like this flower. They are not allowed to grow freely—like these withered buds—and they all too easily lose the happiness life holds for them. That is why we must resolve to root out these oppressors with our acts of charity."[33]

Although Shizuko certainly had other issues in mind with her wild chrysanthemum metaphor—the old customs and attitudes that suppress women, for example—she might well have been referring to the "tyranny" that traditional Japanese rhetoric held over prose fiction. Modern stylists in early Meiji, who had been struggling to invent a new mode of expression that would appeal to the modern movement in literature, were nevertheless oppressed by the weight of tradition. According to Nanette Twine, there were four major literary styles by the start of the Meiji period, none of them anywhere near the modern spoken language.[34] Of these styles three—*kanbun*, *sōrōbun*, and *wakankonkōbun*—were more heavily indebted to Chinese than to Japanese and were therefore limited primarily to the educated (male) elite. The fourth, *wabun*, while strictly Japanese, was so far removed from contemporary language that it required an entirely different grammar system. The written language had for centuries been primarily the domain of the upper classes, and many in the Meiji period "clung stubbornly to the old aristocratic view of writing as something apart from the mainstream of everyday life."[35] Most were willing to see a standardized written script for such mundane functions as newspaper reportage and postal deliveries. But to remove belles lettres from the province of literary language was to most literati a threat to the very integrity of their art. Writing in the colloquial—or some approximation thereof—would produce only doggerel, they argued. It was not easy, therefore, to jettison centuries of preference and prejudice and create an entirely new prose style. Nevertheless, by 1887 it was clear to most innovative practitioners of the art that a modern literature would never be possible so long as the language of choice was tied to "the restrictions imposed by stereotyped, archaic rhetoric and inadequate classical vocabulary."[36]

The problem was greater, it would seem, for women like Shizuko who wanted to express a side of womanhood that had not been voiced for centuries. The written idiom then available could not accommodate expressions of female ambition, self-motivated desire, or marital love. *Wabun* was too self-consciously soft to incorporate the directness and intensity of the emotions she felt. The other styles were too heavily weighted with Chinese rhetoric. Hence Shizuko's decision to write "The Bridal Veil" in English and the difficulty in seeing it translated into Japanese.[37] "Shizuko longed for a language appropriate to her situation," Yamaguchi Reiko suggests, "and she struggled to find one. Neither a simplified *kanbun* nor the classical *wabun* met her needs. She began to grope for a new prose style, one that would approximate everyday speech."[38]

"The Wild Chrysanthemum" was a step in that direction. But using a colloquial style for dialogue was nothing new at the time. The problem lay with descriptive narrative passages. Tsubouchi Shōyō had advocated the use of *gazoku setchū* in "The Essence of the Novel." Descriptive passages, he felt, were best rendered in a literary language whereas dialogue ought to approximate contemporary speech. But even as Shōyō made this pronouncement, he held out hope that a more colloquial style for both narrative and dialogue would be standardized in the future. Along with Futabatei Shimei, Yamada Bimyō, and others, therefore, Shizuko was eager to find a colloquial style that would be suitable for narrative as well.

Shizuko was aware of Futabatei Shimei's experiment with *genbun itchi* in *Ukigumo* (Drifting Cloud, 1887). But even Futabatei admitted imitating Shikitei Sanba and Aeba Kōson, two *gesaku*-style writers, in his experimentation. As Karatani Kōjin has pointed out in *The Origins of Modern Japanese Literature*, merely changing classical sentence endings from -*nari* to the colloquial -*da* or -*desu* did not make for a new literary style: "*The Drifting Clouds* is permeated with stylistic elements drawn from the comic fiction of Shikitei

Samba, and despite its use of the verb-ending *da*, it cannot be considered a *genbun itchi* work."³⁹ *Genbun itchi*, in other words, was not just a matter of transcribing the spoken word. The "spoken word," after all, was not an absolute entity but existed in a mind-boggling array of forms and varieties attributable to differences in class, age, sex, and region. As Satō Michimasa has argued, the *genbun itchi* debate was not simply about reforming the stylistic surface of literature; it necessitated fundamental changes in content and attitudes toward literature as well.⁴⁰ So long as literature was guarded as the property of the learned elite, it would never modernize.

An Anglo-Saxon Perception

To an extent the experiments necessary for creating this new language came more naturally to Shizuko. Bilingual and biliterate, she implicitly understood that no language, no system of values, was absolute. Having been brought up with an Anglo-American appreciation of literature and its insistence on the discovery and display of individuality, she was not so thoroughly influenced by the Japanese system of discipline that demanded complete submission to a master tradition—and, therefore, not so firmly wedded to the Japanese classics as Tsubouchi Shōyō, Miyake Kaho, and other peers. Of course, she had studied the Japanese classics at school—as a subject matter—just as she had studied the Western classics. But she had not been exposed to the kind of intense training that Kaho and Ichiyō had received at the Haginoya in which the practice of *waka* was more a way of life than a discrete subject of study. She, therefore, felt no particular claim to classical *wabun*. Nor was she claimed by it. For once, her orphan's status served her well. It allowed Shizuko greater freedom to play with language—and all the cultural baggage that attended it. E. S. Booth noted of Shizuko's linguistic skill:

> She had not only mastered the idiom of the English language, but she possessed the exceedingly rare faculty of being able to view things from an Anglo-Saxon viewpoint, which made her . . . an excellent interpreter of Western thought and temperament. [And she managed this without significantly losing] her Japanese qualities or instincts in any degree. Her character as a Japanese woman was enlarged, enriched, and broadened, by the knowledge she had gained of the characteristics of her foreign sisters, both of those with whom she came in personal contact and of those whose acquaintance she made by reading.⁴¹

In the same issue of *Jogaku zasshi* that featured "Wild Chrysanthemum," Shizuko also offered the short story "Omukō no hanare." (Literally the title translates to "The Cottage in Back," but Shizuko rendered it as "Grandmother's Room" for *Jogaku*'s English table of contents). Since "Wild Chrysanthemum" is more a dialogue than a story with a well-conceived plot, most critics consider "Grandmother's Room" to be Shizuko's debut as a fiction writer. The story is brief and simple. The narrator, a young woman, tells how one day her aunt called a kimono-shop clerk to her house to display his fabrics. While her aunt and cousin unfurled the bolts and held them one against the other trying to decide which to match with what, the narrator's grandmother sat silently in the corner. Finally, encouraged by the lively scene, she ran her finger admiringly along the fabric used for kimono collars and announced that she would like a new collar.

> My aunt glanced back in our direction. "Oh you would, would you? Well, that won't be necessary. We have so many old ones we no longer use—I'll just give you one of those."[42]

Two weeks later the grandmother died.

> After grandmother died, no one moved into the cottage behind the house and everything remained just as it had when she was alive. One day, while walking past the cottage, I noticed that someone had opened the drawers to the kimono chest in grandmother's room. As I drew closer I heard crying. It was my aunt. She had pulled out my grandmother's kimono with its old collar and was crying into it for all she was worth. She put it away when she had cried her fill and tiptoed out—unaware that I was there.[43]

Structurally, the story is well crafted. The narrator reflects back on an incident that occurred when she was sixteen years old. The reminiscing style allows for a natural cohesion. Moreover, by selecting a first-person narrative, an unusual feature in Meiji fiction at the time,[44] Shizuko avoids the problems of tone and level of speech invited by third-person narratives. That is, she does not have to worry about whether to render her descriptive passages in a classical, literary style. She is free to invent an appropriately colloquial style throughout her work since, as a first-person narrative, it maintains a consistent oral quality. Having paticularized her narrative voice as upper-class female, the choice of what level of speech to employ was more or less automatic. Shizuko writes in the *-desu, -gozaimasu* form of one educated woman speaking to another, most likely younger woman (or women), about an incident in her past. In other words: with a careful manipulation of narrative setting, Shizuko was able to create a voice not unlike her own.

Shizuko was not able to end the story, however, without adding a moral —as if the story had not sufficiently imparted her message:

And so I say to all of you, there is no call for filial behavior after your parents have died. Don't be wrapping their tombstone in blankets or lavishing money on their funeral. Pleasing an old person does not take such great effort. They have raised us since we were babies, and now their arms are tired. Give them rest from their labors. They have loved us selflessly with no thought of reward. Now it is our turn to comfort them in their final days and return the love we have received.[45]

By the end of the tale the narrator has returned from her past reminiscences to her present self where she feels obliged to address her readers directly in an instructive tone. A late-twentieth-century reader would find that this coda mars the lovely simplicity of the story. But for Shizuko, the coda was the point of the story—its raison d'être. For as we will soon discover, writing was for Shizuko a worthwhile endeavor only so long as it proved instructive.

Shizuko was not entirely pleased with her accomplishment in "Grandmother's Room." She was afraid her expressions lacked sufficient "elegance" and would therefore be wrong for the kind of readership she hoped to reach. After an experimental foray into the wilds of colloquial expression, therefore, Shizuko slipped momentarily back into the familiar realm of the traditional. The narrative passages in her next work, "Sumire," as we have seen, were typical of the classical *gabuntai*. Frustrated by her inability to settle on a particular style and propelled by her impatience to find the idiom that met her demands, Shizuko eventually returned to translation and adaptation. Because the foreign tradition within which she was working was less fettered by Japanese literary expectations or personal implication, she found she was better able to manipulate language.[46]

In 1890, therefore, Shizuko once again turned to her old friend, Adelaide Anne Procter, this time translating her long narrative poem "The Sailor Boy." Because in her approach to translation Shizuko was more interested in capturing the spiritual content of the poem, rather than its rhythms or turns of phrase, she rendered Procter's verse in a *monogatari*-style narrative. Moreover, though she told the story Procter told, she adapted her presentation to a Japanese setting. Procter writes of a lad of twelve who, separated from his mother as an infant, now lives with an old kinsman, Walter, in the "blue mountains of the north." Walter is the groundskeeper of a castle owned by an earl who comes with his fair countess every year in late autumn to hunt in the surrounding hills. Everyone but the boy narrator seems to realize that the countess is actually his mother. An impoverished widow, she was beguiled by the earl to marry him on the condition that she leave her son behind. Although she never speaks to the boy of their true relationship, she does manage to see him once a year during the hunting season. The poem, therefore, teems with the mother's guilty anguish and the boy's innocent love for this woman who treats him with such tenderness. Procter's original begins:

My life you ask of? why, you know
Full soon my little Life is told;
It has had no great joy or woe,
For I am only twelve years old.
Ere long I hope I shall have been
On my first voyage, and wonders seen.
Some princess I may help to free
From pirates, on a far-off sea;
Or, on some desert isle be left,
Of friends and shipmates all bereft.[47]

Shizuko removes the poem from the English countryside and sets it in Aizu-Wakamatsu just after the Meiji Restoration. The lad, fourteen in her adaptation,[48] is protected by his kinsman Tokuzō, who keeps an ancient, though mostly ruined, castle for its wealthy owner who visits once a year from Tokyo to hunt. Shizuko translates the opening lines:

Anata boku no rireki wo hanase tte ossharu no ? Jikki hanasetchimaimasu yo, datte jūshi in shika naranai-n desu kara, betsudan taishita yorokobi mo kurō mo shita koto ga nai-n desu mono wo, dagane, moo sukoshi sugiru to boku wa funanori ni natte hajimete kōkai ni yuku-n desu, jitsu ni tanoshimi nan desu, donna mezurashii mono wo miru ka to omotte . . . , dandan umi e noridashite yukuuchi ni wa, Tametomo nanka no yoo ni, kaizoku wo tairagetari, toriko ni natteru ohimesama wo tasukeru yoo na koto ga aru ka mo shiremasenkara ne, sore kara, robinson, kuruusoo, mita yoo ni, nansen ni atte hitorikkiri, jinseki no taeta shima ni yogitsuku nankamo, zuibun omoshiroo to kangaeru-n desu.[49]

Back-translating into English reveals something of Shizuko's stylistics and approaches:

You say you wish me to speak of my past history? It can be told in an instant for I'm not but fourteen, you see. And I haven't experienced any great joy or sorrow. But before much longer I'm to become a sailor and set out to sea. I am looking forward to it. I wonder how many incredible sights I will see. And on my voyage on the seas I may—like Tametomo—battle pirates and rescue the princess they have taken hostage. Or I may meet with a shipwreck like Robinson Crusoe and swim to a deserted island where there is no one else but me. I think it will be great fun.

A sight comparison of the two texts alone reveals that Shizuko's is significantly longer, though this owes much to the fact that in "narrativizing" the poem she had to include sentence connectives not needed in verse—such as "*sore kara,*" "*datte,*" and "*dagane.*" Semantically these connectives carry little meaning, but they are needed to impart an oral fluency, to connect the flow of ideas in a smooth and seamless manner, and to suggest something of the boy's breathless excitement. Moreover, Shizuko adds ideas and phrases Procter did not invent. The reference to Tametomo is such an example. Minamoto no Tametomo (1139–1170) was a valiant warrior known for his prowess on the seas. Shizuko's reference to Robinson Crusoe is her invention as well. *Robinson Crusoe* was the first translation of a European novel in Japan.[50] By 1890 it would have been fairly well known, and presumably Shizuko thought that a judicious interpolation of this kind would help her readers appreciate why a boy might look forward to being shipwrecked on a deserted island.

Donald Keene notes that in the early Meiji period, translators of European poetry were more concerned with imparting "only such sentiments as could naturally be expressed in Japanese."[51] Moreover, fidelity to the original was less important than mining the original for whatever important "lessons" might be learned. Shizuko was ever interested in important lessons, but she was able to manage this conveyance with notably accurate translations. From the small segment presented here, we can see that Shizuko is generally faithful to the original. More important, she captures the innocence and excitement of Procter's young sailor in a "nativized" Japanese narrative that is equally natural and fluid. Again by using a first-person voice she is able to select a colloquial style that is appropriate to her narrator's age, sex, and class. Unlike her earlier attempts at writing in the colloquial, therefore, a momentary "vulgarism" here only adds to the characterization of the youth, who is after all of a lower class. Few such vulgarisms appear, however. For the most part Shizuko's translation is lyrical, simple, and deeply moving. Reviews of her efforts were generally positive. Ueda Bin noted, for example, that only a heartless wretch could read the translation without weeping.[52]

"The Sailor Boy" was an important exercise for Shizuko on another level as well. Through the conduit of a mid-nineteenth-century English poem, she was able to express a variety of emotions that she had not been able to manage in any other idiom. By setting the story in Aizu-Wakamatsu just after the Meiji Restoration, Shizuko added a personal layer to the translation. In many respects the orphaned boy is Shizuko's surrogate—telling the story of her own childhood loneliness and bereavement. But by retitling the story

"Wasuregatami" or "The Keepsake," rather than trying to approximate "Sailor Boy" in Japanese, Shizuko shifts the focus of Procter's poem onto the mother as well. With the boy as the "keepsake" that her first husband left behind—a keepsake the woman eventually denies—she must spend the rest of her days contemplating the "good fortune" her ride in the "jeweled palanquin" has brought. Yamaguchi Reiko suggests that the bifocal dimension Shizuko added to the translation allowed her not only to see—as she had seen for years—through the eyes of the abandoned orphan but also from the position of the mother and thereby to appreciate the suffering experienced by the abandoning parent.

"The Keepsake" was published in *Jogaku zasshi* 194, the "New Year's Issue" for 1890. New Year's issues of a journal were particularly important, as they were believed to set the stage for the year to come. Issue 194 was no exception. In addition to Shizuko's translation, there were contributions from Nakajima Shōen, Shimoda Utako, Miyake Kaho, and Atomi Kakei. Eighteen ninety would prove to be an important year for the women associated with *Jogaku zasshi*, as it was the year that Iwamoto Yoshiharu appointed eight to positions on his editorial staff. The year would also be of particular significance to Wakamatsu Shizuko, as it would mark her most fecund period as a translator and essayist.

Little Lord Fauntleroy

From January to March 1890, Shizuko serialized her translation of Tennyson's long narrative poem *Enoch Arden* under the title *Inakku Aaden monogatari*. She began serializing her translation of *Little Lord Fauntleroy*, under the title *Shōkōshi* (The Little Lord), in August. The translation covered forty-five installments and took a year and a half to complete. In the process, Shizuko gave birth to two children, a daughter in September 1890 and a son in December 1891. Owing to the stress that successive childbirths placed on her already delicate health, she had to withdraw from her translation work temporarily, and serialization was therefore suspended from November 1890. Shizuko resumed her work in May 1891, submitting the final installment of the translation in January 1892.

Many Western readers today are amused and often puzzled by the selections of early Meiji translators. Of these first translations Donald Keene suggests: "These books . . . may have been the ones from which Japanese students abroad learned their English or French in the absence of proper textbooks. Perhaps they were borrowed from friendly landladies who were about to throw away the books anyway."[53] This may have been the case with the translations of Lord Bulwer-Lytton's books. Oda [Niwa] Jun'ichirō (1851–1919), as Keene reports, read two of Bulwer-Lytton's novels on the long sea voyage back to Japan from England in the 1870s. Although Edward George Bulwer-Lytton (1803–1873) now has the dubious distinction of an annual prize named in his honor—an annual prize for the most turgid prose—he was a tremendously popular writer in the mid-nineteenth century and ranked alongside his contemporary Charles Dickens. Perhaps by 1870 friendly landladies were willing to part with their well-thumbed copies of his novels, thus inspiring Oda's translation, which was first published in 1878–1879 and reissued with modifications in 1883. Bulwer-Lytton's works were so well received in Japan (no doubt largely due to the efforts of translators to abridge and naturalize his "turgid" prose) that Oda's translation of *Ernest Maltravers* (1837) and the sequel *Alice* (1838), which he had condensed into one volume entitled *A Springtime Tale of Blossoms and Willows (Karyū shunwa)*, was soon followed

Figure 15 Front cover of *Shōkōshi* (*Little Lord Fauntleroy*). (Courtesy of the Ferris Women's College Archives)

by his translation of *The Last Days of Pompeii* (1834) in 1879–1880. Others joined the effort with translations of *Paul Clifford* (1830) in 1879–1880; *The Haunted and the Haunters* (1859) in 1880; *Rienzi, the Last of the Roman Tribunes* (1835) and *Kenelm Chillingly* (1873) in 1885; and finally in 1887 Nakajima Shōen offered her adaptation of *Eugene Aram* (1832). Contemporary translations were not limited to the offerings of Lord Bulwer-Lytton, however, or to English. William Shakespeare, Charles Dickens, Jules Verne, Victor Hugo, Hans Christian Andersen, Nathaniel Hawthorne, Edgar Allan Poe, Ivan Turgenev, Fyodor Dostoevski, and others found their way into Japanese, as well, due to the efforts of such established men of letters as Morita Shiken, Uchida Roan, Mori Ōgai, and Tsubouchi Shōyō.

Given this list of literary classics, *Little Lord Fauntleroy* stands out as another peculiar choice for translation. The story is hardly read today in the

Figure 16
Illustration for *Little Lord Fauntleroy* as it appeared in *Shōkōshi*. (Courtesy of Nihon Kindai Bungakkan)

United States and indeed—unlike Frances Hodgson Burnett's more critically acclaimed *The Secret Garden* (1911)—rarely even rates mention as an example of children's literature. If the work has been all but forgotten, the word "Fauntleroy" still lingers in our vocabulary as a term for a simpering sissy, earning the work a notoriety not unlike Bulwer-Lytton's. This distinction is unfortunate, and mostly undeserved, as the "little lord" of the story was not himself a sissy. Indeed, he is a robust little fellow who endears himself to all he meets with his honest integrity and affable humor. His sissified reputation, however, grew among those who had not read the story but had only seen the illustrations by Reginald Birch or the publicity photographs for the stage versions featuring Elsie Leslie and later Buster Keaton. Each depicted pretty boys in velvet breeches and satin sashes, with ringlets of curls falling over lace collars. Apparently British and American mothers found the image so beguiling that they forced their own little boys into lace, velvet, and curls—much to the chagrin of the boys and the horror of their fathers. And so it was that the word "Fauntleroy" became metonymic for all that had been sinisterly wrong with the effeminate Victorian past. And *Little Lord Fauntleroy* was pushed to the back of the library shelves by the stoutly masculine stories of the twentieth century.

Before earning this reputation, however, *Little Lord Fauntleroy* had been a tremendously popular novel and Frances Burnett one of the most successful novelists of the late nineteenth century. In 1883, for example, a *Century* article listed Burnett alongside William Dean Howells and Henry James as one of the foremost American writers.[54] When *Little Lord Fauntleroy* was published in book form in 1886, "it became one of the biggest sellers of all time, selling over a million copies in English alone, and being translated into more than a dozen languages."[55] Phyllis Bixler notes that "in 1893, *Little Lord Fauntleroy* appeared in more American libraries than any book except *Ben Hur*, and the book's popularity spawned a variety of related products such as Fauntleroy toys, playing cards, writing paper, chocolate, and the notorious dark velvet suits with lace collars."[56]

It is unclear how Shizuko came upon *Little Lord Fauntleroy*. She did not keep a diary, nor did she write about her efforts as a translator. Certainly she did not receive the book from a kindly landlady. But given the book's staggering popularity among Americans at the time, and given Shizuko's regular association with Americans at Ferris Seminary and elsewhere, it is very likely that someone introduced Shizuko either to the book or to a journal that carried a review of the book. However she came upon the novel, clearly there was much about the story and its author that appealed to Shizuko's sensibilities concerning literature, childhood, and morality. In many ways, *Little Lord Fauntleroy* was just the book she had been looking for.

Like Shizuko, Frances Burnett (1849–1924) had suffered the vagaries of fate but had survived with a generous amount of pride and talent. Born to a prosperous tradesman in Manchester, England, her father died when she was three, forcing her family to move from their elegant townhouse to the cluttered back alleys. Before long the family crossed the Atlantic and settled in rural Tennessee, where Frances entertained herself and her siblings with the fantasies and fairy stories that would eventually become the source of her fiction.

Little Lord Fauntleroy, her greatest success, is a rags-to-riches romance imbued with the magic of childhood innocence. Marghanita Laski notes: "It is, in fact, the best version of the Cinderella story in modern idiom that exists."[57] Little Lord Fauntleroy, or Cedric Errol, as he is known at first, is the son of an English father and an American mother. After his father dies, his mother raises him in modest comfort in the lower East Side of New York City, where his closest friends are Dick the shoeshine boy and Mr. Hobbs the grouchy greengrocer. Suddenly Mrs. Errol receives word that Cedric is next in line to inherit his grandfather's estate and title in England. Cedric's grandfather, the Earl of Dorincourt, is a particularly nasty man. He disinherited Cedric's father when he married an American woman, believing that all Americans were vulgar and mercenary. Since his older sons have died without heirs, the earl has no choice but to bring Cedric to England where he can hopefully repair whatever damage American life may have wrought. Cantankerous, hardhearted, and stingy, the old man refuses to allow Mrs. Errol, whom he has never met, into his palatial mansion and keeps her sequestered away in a cottage. Cedric is allowed to visit her only on occasion. To avoid upsetting her son, Mrs. Errol does not tell him why she is not staying at the castle. And Cedric, with his innate goodness and childish innocence, does not see the wickedness in his grandfather. Rather Cedric assumes goodness in everyone he encounters. He treats the earl with such honest respect and trust that before long the old man's icy heart begins to melt. Thanks to the beneficent effect of Cedric's moral purity, the grandfather mends his ways. He helps the poor, and he welcomes Mrs. Errol into his home. For it is, after all, the gentle love of the mother that is responsible for producing this fine young man.

This kind of rags-to-riches story would not have been unfamiliar to Japanese readers. Prince Genji, in a way, had lived a similarly fated life. Demoted to commoner status, exiled from court, he eventually rose to the highest position of power, and all on account of his superior looks and sensitivity. Perhaps eleventh-century *mono no aware* is as close as one can come to an equivalent for nineteenth-century "goodness." In both traditions, it seems, a character's shining beauty is an outward sign of his inner purity. In the seventeenth century, Ihara Saikaku introduced rags-to-riches stories of another variety. He depicted wily (and not generally beautiful) merchants who rise from impoverished obscurity to prominence and wealth—all thanks to their ingenious miserliness. More to the point, the early Meiji period had seen a number of translations that had emphasized ambition, motivation, and self-reliance. Particularly, Nakamura Masanao's translation of Samuel Smiles' *Self-Help* (1859), which appeared in 1870 under the Japanese title *Saikoku risshi hen* (Success Stories of the West), was notably popular, running through several editions and selling in the thousands.[58] As Donald Keene observes, it inspired readers "by the accounts of boys who had been born in poverty but managed by hard work and intelligence to become rich and famous."[59] At the outset of the Meiji period, when the old class system was abolished and education was made more widely available, it seemed that success could come to any who worked hard. Thus the notion of *risshin shusse*—self-establishment and public success—became the mainstay of early Meiji, bringing with it heady enthusiasm and ambition.

But Cedric's "success" is not to be found in his newly acquired wealth or his inheritance, as these are earned by happenstance. His success lies in his ability to improve every situation he encounters—and this he accomplishes through selflessness and sensitivity. Surely it was this aspect of *Little Lord Fauntleroy* that appealed to Shizuko. In an age when the first promise of the Meiji was fading and self-centered ambition was replacing patriotic sacrifice, perhaps Shizuko felt that a story of a boy's selfless goodness was in order. It is clear that Shizuko believed literature should be instructive and that writers had a duty to do what they could to improve society.

As we have seen in Chapter One, debates regarding the purpose and function of literature raged throughout the early years of the Meiji. In the midst of the fray, Tsubouchi Shōyō had claimed that the principal aim of the novel was the depiction of human emotions *(ninjō)*. In response Ozaki Kōyō, a member of the Ken'yūsha, or Friends of the Inkstone, which was known for its emphasis on the craftsmanship and entertainment value of the novel, announced in the afterword to his *Ninin bikuni iro zange* (Two Nuns' Confessions of Love, 1889) that "the principal aim of this novel is tears."[60] And quite a tearjerker the novel was. Ishibashi Ningetsu claimed that "in this work truly every word excites a tear."[61] According to Keene, even the author himself was moved with emotion as he labored over his work.[62] Iwamoto Yoshiharu, however, was not much impressed with this kind of blubbering. What was the point of tears if they did not cleanse a man's heart and lead him on the path to righteousness?

Men were not the only ones voicing their opinions on the issue. In 1890, Wakamatsu Shizuko, in response to a survey of prominent women writers *(keishū sakka)* conducted by Shimizu Shikin for *Jogaku zasshi*, offered the following:

Many respected scholars have already presented their opinions on the novel, and my own judgment in the issue is not something in which I have great confidence. However, I do feel the novel possesses value as a means to an end. Let me offer a familiar example. I think the novel is not unlike a child's toy. Many people will tell you that the wares offered in a toy store lack value—and I think some will make similar statements about the novel. But the fact of the matter is, toys do have value. They play an important role in a child's education, proving to be far more effective at instructing the child on how to make and use items than are textbooks and teachers. Novels, too, have a similar role to play in moral reform and education. They have a power to influence that far exceeds that of lessons, lectures, and sermons. As long as toys and novels are in demand, they will be produced. And as long as they are produced people will purchase them regardless of whether or not they have value. Therefore, we must endeavor to ensure that what is produced serves to improve our society. . . .

In our novels we should take care not only to distinguish the bad behavior of bad characters from the good behavior of good characters but to lead our readers to cherish the good while despising the bad. I believe that this effort is a writer's duty. If a novelist is not prepared to do at least this much and merely writes for his own entertainment, then I, for one, should not wish to be counted among his ranks. If a writer limits himself to the depiction of human emotions *(ninjō)* simply for the sake of entertainment, then I cannot condone his work. Nor am I inclined to follow a writer whose only interest is the display of skill.[63]

Shizuko does not specifically name Ozaki Kōyō with her charges, but it can be assumed that she had him in mind along with others of the Ken'yūsha. Kōyō had been placed in charge of the literary page of the *Yomiuri Shinbun* late in 1889, thus providing Ken'yūsha members with a well-publicized forum for their brand of fiction, which was growing in popularity. Although the Ken'yūsha were concerned with writing stories that beguiled and titillated, this is not to suggest that they did not respect artistic craftsmanship. Kōyō apparently labored over his work with great intensity. Thus his attitude toward literature only infuriated Shizuko all the more. Both her Japanese Confucianism and her American Puritanism had taught her that if one worked diligently on a project, one's labors ought to have a beneficent effect. Entertainment as an end in itself did not qualify:

> How I regret that in our world, where we have the opportunity of turning
> weapons of destruction into instruments of survival, novels that nurture a
> young person's spirit and cleanse the air of society are far outpaced by those
> that damage the youth's fair spirit and poison the air.[64]

Since the male writers in her immediate periphery did not seem to be as
interested in nurturing and cleaning as she was, Shizuko challenged other
women to do so:

> I think women—who are well disposed to literature in preference and prepa-
> ration—should apply themselves to writing novels. If they accept their
> responsibility for the education and moral reform of other women and chil-
> dren, then many will be able to prove themselves of great assistance to cre-
> ating a just and noble world by availing themselves of the public's demand
> for novels. Of this I am convinced.[65]

Lacking confidence in her own ability to write suitably high-minded
pieces, Shizuko searched for appropriate works in English to translate. In
Little Lord Fauntleroy she found an enjoyable yet instructive story—much
like a good toy. Shizuko wanted her translation of *Little Lord Fauntleroy* to be
of service to other women and help them to nurture in their own children the
goodness that Cedric revealed. A child, like the tree in the epigraph to this
chapter, could grow up straight or it could become twisted and warped. It all
depended on the hand that nurtured it. Convinced that she had a great mission to fulfill with her translation, Shizuko threw herself into it with dedication and passion. Her goal was not merely to turn out an adequate equivalent
of Burnett's work but to use her skills to provide a window that would allow
Japanese readers to peer into a new world—a foreign world but one not
beyond the imagination. She had to make this world real to her readers. She
had to make them see that a home warm with "Christian love," a home cen-
tered on women and children, was accessible and desirable. Quibbling over
word choice, agonizing over what she perceived as her own inadequacies in
Japanese prose, Shizuko's efforts were heroic and at times exhausting. That
she could have managed as much as she did between childbirths is amazing.

A Celebration of Childhood

Today the original story, as well as Shizuko's translation, are categorized as
"children's literature." But when Shizuko first began serializing her translation, *Shōkōshi* did not have this distinction. Indeed, at the time there was no
such category in Japan. Iwamoto announced the forthcoming serialization in
the journal as follows: "Beginning Next Issue—A New Translation of the

Novel *Shōkōshi* by Wakamatsu Shizu. A pure, wholesome love."[66] Shizuko's offering was thereby poised to challenge the less "wholesome love"—presumably sexual love—that was the mainstay of Japanese fiction. The serialization was first included under the literature column, and judging from the reviews it received, it was read by old and young, men and women alike, without any particular regard of it as a "child's story."

In America, *Little Lord Fauntleroy* was first introduced in the pages of *St. Nicholas*, a magazine for children. But Ann Thwaite questions whether it was ever really "a child's story." There is much subtlety in the rehabilitation of the grandfather and in the relationship between him and Mrs. Errol that escapes the notice of the younger reader. From contemporary reviews of the story, it seems Burnett's offering was enjoyed "by children of an older growth as much as, if not more than, by juveniles."[67] Moreover, as Thwaite notes, "Cedric . . . is always seen from the outside, from the adult point of view."[68] The appeal to adults is of course an equal requirement for children's books, since it is adults who must buy the books and read them to their children. "Mothers bought it perhaps for their children," Thwaite comments, "but they read it themselves and they loved Cedric. They longed for their own children to be like him."[69] And perhaps they imagined themselves to be like his angelic mother, Mrs. Errol.

Although Shizuko's translation was not at first directed toward children specifically, by the fifth installment she had created a "Children's Column" for *Jogaku zasshi* and *Shōkōshi* began to appear there. The purpose of the column was to provide mothers with information about raising children, as well as to offer stories that parents could read to their young. Magazines for children would soon follow, along with stories written specifically for the young reader. Nevertheless, Shizuko's column was one of the first outlets in Japan for the consideration of the child as audience. Earlier of course there had been the conflation of woman and child as a single reader, and books and articles were often described as being written in a simple manner so as to prove instructive to "women and children." The "red books" and "yellow books" of the Tokugawa period and the *otogi-zōshi* of the earlier era were generally considered appropriate for this kind of reader. Even so, works of this variety were directed more at the "childish woman" than at the child and were therefore read primarily by adults.

Satō Michimasa, in his study of the creation of children's literature in Japan, notes that a prerequisite for writing children's literature is the acceptance of the child: "A statement of this kind may seem so obvious as to be simple-minded nowadays when children are regarded as individual creatures and not just as appendages or subordinates to adults."[70] But in the not so distant past, Satō reminds us, children were the property of parents, women the property of men, and the lower classes subordinate to the upper. In such a hierarchy, where children were clearly at the bottom of the heap, it would be very unlikely for any author—himself a little closer to the top—to deign to write *from* the child's perspective. "Children's literature," as a separate category, Satō maintains, does not consist of stories and verses handed down to children from above but, rather, works that explore a child's world from a child's perspective. Before such works could be created, of course, "the child" had to be invented.

It is not clear when Shizuko began to think of targeting children as readers. Perhaps she became interested in children as a category of reader after she herself became a mother in 1890. Or perhaps having learned so painfully herself of a child's vulnerability in an adult world, Shizuko was more keenly attuned than most to a child's integrity and need for encouragement. It seems likely that Shizuko's regard for children and her appreciation of childhood were fostered by Mrs. Miller and the other missionaries who brought with them to Japan a nineteenth-century Western perspective on childhood as a precious estate, separate from adulthood, in need of protection and love. Exposure to this Western treatment of children, in turn, may have led Shizuko to the discovery that her own childhood had been lost in the turmoil of the Meiji Restoration. Her emphasis on childhood, therefore, may well have been motivated by an attempt to recover her own.

In 1882, while she was still a student at Ferris Seminary, Shizuko had helped Mrs. Miller publish a small Japanese newsletter aimed at women and children entitled "Yorokobi no Otodzure" (Glad Tidings). Mrs. Miller's goal had been to proselytize—to provide young Japanese mothers with suitable reading material for their children so that they too might learn the Gospel. In her letters home, Mrs. Miller had on several occasions expressed her dismay over the lack of adequate games and entertainment for Japanese children who were left with no choice but to resort to vulgar amusements (more appropriate for adults). Like her mentor, Shizuko was equally concerned with the creation of a wholesome environment for children. Moreover, she saw the presence of children as a prerequisite to a Christian "*hōmu*" and their training as a woman's most sacred mission. As far as her writing was concerned, she was surely influenced by the Western regard of children and the notion of women as appropriate writers for children. Louisa May Alcott, with whom Shizuko was familiar, considered writing for children "a peculiarly fitting and gracious task for women."[71] Whatever her motivation, Shizuko soon became concerned by the lack of appropriate "literary toys" for the young mind and also by the lack of adult appreciation for the sanctity of childhood. In her preface to the first publication of *Shōkōshi* in book form she notes:

There are heartless people who say that children are merely intolerable nuisances up until the time they have finally reached adulthood. . . . I think that a child is a lotus blooming amidst the filth of the world. He is an angel in the home. This tiny creature's mission on earth is not a frivolous matter—for he is there to stay his father's foot from the path of sin, to pull his mother's heart from the waves of despair and return her to her noble virtue. None but a darling child can be entrusted with such a sacred mission—and none but he can accomplish it.[72]

Cedric, the ideal "home angel," certainly fulfilled his "sacred mission"—time and again winning his mother back from the brink of despair and transforming his grandfather with his uncalculated innocence and mirth. Burnett had given Shizuko a glimpse of a childhood she had never known. She had created for Shizuko a vision of the perfect union of mother and child. Moreover, Burnett had shown Shizuko a female-centered world where women and feminized males (young boys and lower-class men) triumph over the selfish male prerogative by virtue of their own innate goodness and strength. This vision only confirmed Shizuko's conviction that every woman had a social responsibility; that she met this responsibility in marriage; that every marriage should be based on love; and that no marriage could be complete without "an angel in the home."

Rummaging for the Perfect Fit

In translating *Little Lord Fauntleroy* for a Japanese audience, Shizuko was faced with the task of creating a language that would not only capture the meaning of Burnett's prose but transport Japanese readers into her magic world. To fulfill her mission, moreover, the language had to be easily understood. Burnett was not herself a difficult writer, and this is what made her so appropriate for children. She wrote "naturally." Or as Ann Thwaite quotes an unnamed critic: "It is doubtful that Mrs Burnett ever consciously made a phrase. [Rather, she wrote] always in the most simple and straightforward words that she could find."[73] Burnett was more concerned, Thwaite suggests, to keep "her eye on the one thing she was writing about and not on the way she wrote."[74] As a translator, of course, Shizuko could not afford to be so "natural." Although her resulting prose reads with seemingly effortless simplicity, the process in reaching this end was not easy.

Much of the dialogue in *Little Lord Fauntleroy* included dialect—either that of New York's East Side or rural England. Moreover, the world Burnett evoked was peopled and detailed with creatures and habits not to be found in Meiji Japan. Shizuko's understanding of English was not the problem, as she was apparently quite fluent. Contemporary translator Morita Shiken noted of

Shizuko's translation: "I have the feeling that she reads English as easily as she would read a letter from her parents. Like the back of her hand she knows the idioms and set phrases that even we bearded men misread."[75] Iwamoto remarked that English had become so natural to Shizuko that she spoke it in her sleep.[76]

Shizuko's weakness was Japanese. Having been trained in an American school, she was not always able to snap up the appropriate Japanese word just when she wanted it. Despite Headmaster Booth's assurance that Shizuko had not lost "her Japanese qualities or instincts in any degree," Miyake Kaho notes that she was fairly awkward in Japanese social situations.[77] Sōma Kokkō observes of her translating style that she would first "quickly sketch out a rough draft and then she would go back over it spending an inordinate amount of time searching out each word one by one. As much of this work was conducted while she was sick in bed, the fatigue that it caused was apparently quite severe."[78] Iwamoto says of his wife's translating method that she did not actually write while in bed but would pull herself to her desk when she felt strong enough. There she would begin translating—writing quickly and easily. Iwamoto comments that since she seemed to be composing rather than translating, he came to understand that while she was lying in bed she was pondering over her word choice and translating the lines over and over in her head until she had what satisfied her.[79] Laborious though this effort must have been, the results were rewarding. Iwamoto writes that Shizuko once remarked: "Struggling to come up with the most appropriate word in translation is an agonizing process. But once you have found it the joyful satisfaction you feel is like to that of a woman who, rummaging through her dresser drawers, at last comes upon the very kimono collar whose design suits her perfectly."[80]

Not only was Shizuko rummaging through her dresser drawers for the very word that would suit Burnett's story, but she was also intent on creating a Japanese prose style that would be equivalent to the original and suitable for her audience. Once again she selected a *genbun itchi* style. Unlike her earlier experiments with *genbun itchi*, however, she was not employing a first-person narrative with its problem of how to handle the descriptive scenes. She might have chosen an authoritative-sounding *kanbun* style for these narrative passages—much as Oda had used for his first translations of Bulwer-Lytton. Although women did not ordinarily use this kind of diction, Nakajima Shōen had adopted it for her 1887 translation of Bulwer-Lytton. Or Shizuko might have preferred the distinctively elegant style that Kōyō had crafted for his novels. Mori Ōgai and his younger sister Koganei Kimiko were then publishing numerous translations from English and German in *Shigarami zōshi* (The Weir) in a similar style—to very good reviews.

Although any of these styles would have been possible, none would have been appropriate to the goals Shizuko had set for herself. She wanted to create a text that could be easily read by women—even those without a high-level education. She particularly wanted to create a text that a mother would feel confident reading aloud to her children. Burnett's original has a wonderful oral quality, and it seems the author recited her stories to her sons—during their "hair curling sessions"—before she ever committed them to paper.[81] Shizuko's ability to offer a text with an equivalent orality was masterful. Morita Shiken, then known as "the king of translation," said of Shizuko's accomplishment:

> Whenever I came to a particularly beautiful passage in her work, I would stop and read it aloud to the women at home. They would set down their sewing and their eyes would mist over as I read to them.[82]

Of particular note in Shizuko's translation, as well as in the original itself, is the clarity of the different characters' voices. As the critic Ishibashi Ningetsu has noted, Burnett excelled at a mix of extremes.[83] She paired small angelic Cedric with crusty old Dorincourt; the lovely Mrs. Errol with the lower-class Mary; and the grouchy greengrocer Mr. Hobbs with Mr. Havisham, Dorincourt's kindly solicitor. Burnett gives each character a distinct voice. Shizuko meets the challenge admirably in her translation.

The following selection from the original opening passage introduces readers to Cedric and his mother. Cedric is recalling how he came to understand his father had died:

> "Dearest," said Cedric—his papa had called her that always, and so the little boy had learned to say it—"Dearest, is my papa better?"
>
> He felt her arms tremble, and so he turned his curly head and looked in her face. There was something in it that made him feel that she was going to cry.
>
> "Dearest," he said, "is he well?"
>
> Then suddenly his loving little heart told him that he'd better put both his arms around her neck and kiss her again and again, and keep his soft cheek close to hers; and he did so, and she laid her face on his shoulder and cried bitterly, holding him as if she could never let him go again.
>
> "Yes, he is well," she sobbed. "He is quite, quite well, but we—we have no one left but each other. No one at all."[84]

And this is Shizuko's translation:

> Kaasama, Toosama wa **moo** yoku natte? to <u>Sedorikku</u> ga iimashitara, tsuka-matta Okkasan no ude ga fuemashita kara, **chijire**ke no kashira wo agete,

Okkasan no okao wo miru to, nandaka nakitai yoo na kokoromochi ga shite kimashita, sore kara mata,

Kaasama, Otoosama wa **moo** yoku onan nasutta no? to onaji koto wo itte miru to, doo iu wake ka, kyuu ni Okkasan no kubi ni ryoote wo mawashite, ikutabi mo ikutabi mo **kisu** wo shite, soshite Okkasan no hoo ni jibun no yawarakana hoo wo oshiatete agenakereba, naranaku narimashita kara, sono toorishite ageru to, Okkasan ga, **moo moo** keshite hanasanai to iu yoo ni, **shikkari** Sedorikku wo tsukamaete, Sedorikku no kata ni jibun no kao wo oshiate, koe wo oshimazu ni onaki nasai mashita.

Soo da yo, **moo** yoku onari nasutta yo, **moo su—sukkari** yoku onari nano da yo, **dagane,** omae to watashi wa, **moo** futari kiri ni natte shimatta no da yo, futari kiri de, **moo** hoka no dare mo inai no da yo to kumori koe ni iwarete. . . .[85]

Again, translating back into English reveals some of the peculiar features of Shizuko's text:

"Mama, is Papa all better?" When Cedric asked, he felt his mother's arms tremble around him, and so he turned his curly head up and gazed into her face, seeing as he did something there that made him feel he wanted to cry, and so again he asked just as before, "Mama, is Papa indeed all better now?" and for some reason he suddenly felt he must throw his arms around his mother's neck and kiss her again and again and press his own soft cheek into her cheek and when he did his mother clutched him tightly as if she would never let him go, and she pressed her face into his shoulder and cried without trying to stifle her voice.

"Yes, he is all better, he is qu—quite better. But now, you and I, we are all that's left. It is just the two of us. There is no one else."

Her voice was clouded with tears. . . .

A comparison of these passages reveals above all that Shizuko's translation is quite faithful to the original in both content and orality. Burnett's sentences, though balanced and well paced, seem to race along—one into the other. Shizuko's rendition is similar. As I have tried to show with my back-translation, the first two sections are actually one long sentence. They are broken here and there with appropriate "fillers" and "connectives" that allow pauses but do not break the flow of the sentence. Thus Shizuko's text, like Burnett's, reads with the light breeziness of speech. Yoshiko Takita notes that although Shizuko captures the childish sweetness in her translation, she tones down some of the saccharine stickiness in Burnett's prose that would nauseate later readers of the original.[86] Shizuko does not even attempt to translate "Dearest," and indeed one wonders what on earth she might have offered as an equivalent. Furthermore, she eliminates some of the more egregious displays of emotion. Shizuko's Cedric is compelled to hug his mother by a sudden something and not by a "loving little heart." Her Mrs. Errol does not sob, nor does she cry bitterly. She simply refuses to stifle her cries and speaks with a "cloudy" voice. In a country where heroes have been known to cry until their sleeves were soaked and their pillows float, one wonders why Shizuko felt inclined to soften Mrs. Errol's sobs. Perhaps she thought the overt display diverted readers' attention from the import of the scene. The point was not Mrs. Errol's grief over losing her romantic partner but rather the warm and wordless communication she enjoyed with her son. Shizuko captures this nicely in the way she renders Mrs. Errol's speech in a gentle, familiar style. Sentences end in *"-da,"* often punctuated by the emotive marker *"-yo."* The phrases in the sentence are uttered in short spurts, suggesting Mrs. Errol's own gasps and "cloud-filled" voice. Moreover, her utterances and Cedric's are transcribed with a generous use of hiragana, which enhances the aura of familiarity and softness.

Shimada Tarō suggests that the narrative style Shizuko creates throughout the story is evocative of the *"taoyameburi"* or delicate style of writing so prominent in women's writing of the tenth and eleventh centuries. This "feminine" quality is especially noticeable when one compares her text to Iwaya Sazanami's *Kogane-maru* (The Golden Dog), a child's story written one year later and in "a hale and hearty" literary style that makes ample use of Chinese characters.[87] Morita Shiken, comparing Shizuko's translation style to that of Uchida Roan in *Crime and Punishment*, says that "her technique is especially feminine, delicate, graceful, and rich with emotion."[88]

Shimada also notes that by translating "his papa" and "his mama" as *otossan* and *okkasan,* which conveys the nuance of "my father/my mother," Shizuko shifts the narrative view closer to Cedric's own.[89] Although the narrative perspective is never completely aligned with Cedric's in Japanese, the shift diminishes the sense that Cedric is seen only from the adult point of view. In Shizuko's text there is a closer affiliation between the boy and the narrative perspective, as if the narrative voice were speaking at a vantage somewhat nearer to Cedric's own small height. Consequently, the level of speech employed in the narrative passages is more consistently appropriate to this child's perspective. Mothers, grandfathers, and other exalted beings are referred to in respectful tones, as is illustrated in the phrase *"koe wo oshimazu ni o-naki nasai mashita."* In this way, Shizuko could leave the narrative passages colloquial without having to worry unduly over which level and tone of speech to employ.

Cedric's conversations with his grandfather, in contrast to those with his mother, are conducted with a different nuance. In the following passage,

Cedric has only just met his grandfather. The old man—expecting the boy to be a gold digger even at seven years of age—has tried to draw out his true avarice with offers of parties and ponies. But the nature he draws out is anything but avaricious. Cedric chatters amiably with his grandfather, feeling no reason to fear or suspect him. Suddenly he begins to broach the topic of the American Revolution but stops when he realizes where he is heading. As Burnett writes the exchange:

> "What is the matter?" demanded his grandfather. "Why don't you go on?"
>
> Lord Fauntleroy moved rather uneasily in his chair. . . . "I was just thinking that perhaps you mightn't like it," he replied. "Perhaps someone belonging to you might have been there. I forgot you were an Englishman."
>
> "You can go on," said my lord. "No one belonging to me was there. You forgot you were an Englishman too."
>
> "Oh, no!" said Cedric quickly. "I'm American!"
>
> "You are an Englishman," said the Earl grimly. "Your father was an Englishman."
>
> It amused him a little to say this, but it did not amuse Cedric. The lad had never thought of such a development as this. He felt himself grow quite hot up to the roots of his hair.
>
> "I was born in America," he protested. "You have to be an American if you are born in America. I beg your pardon"—with serious politeness and delicacy—"for contradicting you. Mr. Hobbs told me, if there were another war, you know, I should have to—to be an American."
>
> The Earl gave a grim half laugh—it was short and grim but it was a laugh.[90]

Nanigoto da? Naze sono saki wo moosanu no da? to ojiisama ga otogame ni narimashita.

Fuontoruroi wa isu no ue de **moji moji** shite orimashite. . . .

Boku wa ne, anata ga **hyotto** sono hanashi iya ka to omottan desu yo. Dareka anata no shinrui ka nanka ga, ano toki ni ita ka mo shiremasen kara ne, boku wa anata ga eikoku no hito datta no wasuretchimattan desu mono,

Nani ii, **zun zun** hanasu ga ii, ore no fuzuko no mono nado wa, sore ni kankei wa nai kara, **daga** kisama wa jibun mo eijin da to iu koto wo wasurete iru na.

Sedorikku wa kuchibaya ni,

Iie, boku wa amerikajin desu.

Rōkō wa niganigashii to iu okao de, Kisama wa yahari eijin da, kisama no chichi ga eijin ja mono.

Rōkō wa koo iinagara, kokoro no naka ni sukoshi okashiku kanjiraremashita ga, Sedorikku ni wa sukoshi mo okashii koto de wa arimasenkatta, koo iu koto ni naroo to wa mae motte omoi mo fukenu koto deshita kara, kami no ke no nemoto made atsuku natta yoo na ki ga shimashite,

Boku wa <u>amerika</u> de umaretan deshoo, <u>amerika</u> de umarereba, dare datte <u>amerikajin</u> ni naranakutcha ikenai ja arimasen ka, (kono toki issoo majime ni natte, kotoba teinei ni) doomo anata no ossyaru koto to hantai shimashite gomen nasai, **desu ga ne**, <u>Hobbusu </u>san ga kondo tatakai ga areba, boku wa <u>amerikajin</u> ni naranakutcha, ikenai tte iimashita mono.

Kono toki Rōkō wa niganigashii yoo na warai yoo wo nasaimashita. Mijikakutte, niganigashii yoo deshita ga, yahari warai wa warai deshita.[91]

Here is my back-translation:

"What? Why don't you continue?" His grandfather reprimanded him.

Fauntleroy squirmed in his chair. . . . "I—I thought you might find what I had to say unpleasant. Some of your relatives or someone might have been there, you see. I guess I completely forgot you were from England."

"Oh? Well, that's all right, speak on. No one connected to me had anything to do with it, you see. But you are forgetting that you are English, too."

Cedric blurted out, "No, I'm American."

The old lord looked at him bitterly, "You are English. Because your father was English."

As the old lord spoke he felt somewhat amused in his heart. But Cedric was not the least bit amused. This sort of business had not occurred to him before, and so he felt himself grow hot up to the very roots of his hair,

"I was born in America, wasn't I? If you were born in America, no matter who you are, you have to be an American, don't you? (and then with great seriousness and politeness) please forgive me for contradicting what you have said, but Mr. Hobbs said that if there were another war, I will have to be an American."

This time the old lord smiled a bitter smile. It was brief and it was bitter, but a smile is a smile.

The language that Shizuko assigns the old man also ends in the informal *"-da"* but carries none of the softness of Mrs. Errol's speech. The grandfather's utterances are short and clipped—in contrast to Cedric and his mother's meandering and interlocking sentences. As is appropriate to his character, he tends to ask questions—to demand and reprimand—rather than to converse. Furthermore, the speech markers he uses—*"ore"* (I) and *"kisama"* (you)—not only indicate the great distance between him and his little guest but hint at a tone of condescension. Cedric's responses are cordial and polite and inevitably end in the *"-desu/-masu"* speech style—revealing that the relationship he shares with this old relative is not as familiar as that with his mother. Even when Cedric grows indignant he manages to remain polite by using *"desugane"* rather than the more informal *"daga"* his grandfather has just used. And yet his little speech carries the fervor of his conviction.

Unlike Burnett, Shizuko has her Cedric responding to the grandfather's claim with suppositions and interrogatives: *deshoo; arimasenka.* This rhetorical device, stronger than a bald statement, is more natural to Japanese speech patterns and certainly more appropriate to the polite though adamant Cedric. Moreover, Shizuko's Cedric does not launch his argument with Burnett's logical development. Burnett's Cedric claims: "I was born in America. . . . You have to be an American if you are born in America." Shizuko's hero, however, asks: "I was born in America, wasn't I? If you are born in America, no matter who you are, you have to be an American, don't you?" His statement unfolds in fits and starts, stopping here and there to solicit his grandfather's understanding. In many ways Shizuko's Cedric is even more endearing than Burnett's. Not quite so precocious, not quite so polished, he comes across as more a real little boy and less a "Fauntleroy."

Shizuko increases the naturalness of her translation in other interesting ways. As in her adaptation of Procter's "The Sailor Boy," she incorporates "fillers," "connectives," and sentence-end markers that, though not in the original, are necessary in the translation to impart a feel of fluidity and orality. *Anoo, soo, sora,* and *maa* begin sentences, whereas *ne, no,* and *mono* end them. And in between we have *datte, dakedo, dagane.* Importantly, Shizuko avoids the use of English loanwords. Only proper nouns are rendered in katakana. Otherwise she reserves katakana to transcribe the words she uses for emphasis—particularly onomatopoeia. Despite the appearance of castles, dells, carriages, coronets, and footmen in livery, Shizuko manages to ⸜ concoct a Japanese equivalent for almost everything without significantly "naturalizing" the American or British landscapes as she had done with Procter's poem.

Shizuko also makes use of a wealth of *giseigo* and *gitaigo*—onomatopoetic and mimetic words: "Cedric squirmed *(mojimoji)* in his chair." His mother's gaze is *bon'yari*; her embrace is *shikkari.* Hearts pound *doki doki.* Hair glistens *kira kira.* Leaves rustle *kasa kasa.* The sun peeks through the trees *pika pika pika.* And the grandfather laughs *mufufufu.* These expressions add color to the narrative. Shizuko also enlivens the text by including repetitive words *(jōgo).* "[My mother] will be expecting me all the time" becomes *"Kaasan, boku ga* kuru ka kuru ka *to omotte."* When Cedric kisses his mother again and again, we have *"ikutabi mo ikutabi mo."* The grandfather smiles bitterly *(niganigashii.)* The boy's answer was friendly *(narenareshii.)* All these devices imbue the text with a bright, melodic, and natural rhythm.

Shizuko does not try to capture the thick dialects Burnett uses so skill-fully, but she does incorporate a touch of Aizu dialect in the utterances of members of the lower class. That is, instead of the standard *"ne"* or *"nee,"* Shizuko renders the sentence-end marker as *"nei"* or sometimes *"bee."* Moreover, she offers *"jikki"* to mean "right away" instead of the standard *"sugu."* Nevertheless, Morita Shiken comments on her efforts to transcribe the conversations of the lower class:

> As one might expect, a lady scholar *[jogakushi]* would not have had much contact with the language spoken by the lower classes and the poor. Despite her heroic efforts, therefore, I am afraid that this lady fails two times out of three in her attempts. Nevertheless, her skill in capturing Cedric's youthful voice more than atones for this flaw.[92]

Shizuko made a few other mistakes in her translation, largely attribut-able to her unfamilarity with England's geography and with certain idiomatic phrases. As Shimada points out, she fails to recognize Eton as a prominent boys' school and treats it as if it were a city or town instead. She also takes the expression "name calling" literally, and has the mother of the pretender to the earldom fly into a rage and call everyone by their name, rather than "calling them names."[93] But these are minor flaws and in no way mar the suc-cess of the translation. Furthermore, given the circumstances under which Shizuko worked, it is a wonder that she did not make more glaring mistakes.

　Surely the most distinguishing feature of Shizuko's translation is her use of *"-masenkatta"* rather than what is now the standard *"-masendeshita"* as the formal, negative, past-tense predicate. Although contemporary critics did not mention this usage in their reviews of *Shōkōshi*, present-day critics have spent much energy examining Shizuko's word choice and offering their pronounce-ments on it. It must be remembered that when Shizuko was crafting her trans-lation, *genbun itchi* was still in a state of flux—as was the contemporary spoken language. Without the standardizing medium of television, the print media, and the Ministry of Education, the spoken idiom flourished in far greater variety. Different forms of speech were preferred in different regions, in different cities, and sometimes in different sections of the same city. The early "unifiers of spoken and written language," therefore, had to decide not only how to write in a natural "speechlike" way, but what speech to write.

　In the transition between the Tokugawa and the Meiji eras, various forms of the formal, negative, past-tense predicate *"-masendeshita"* were popular. Yamamoto Masahide points to the use of *"-mase'nanda,"* *"-mashi'nanda,"* *"-masendatta,"* *"-masenu datta,"* *"-masende atta,"* and *"-masenkatta"* before preference gave way to *"-masendeshita."*[94] By 1885, when Tsubouchi Shōyō attempted colloquial dialogues in his novel *The Character of Modern-Day Students*, he opted for "*-masendeshita*" and subsequent writers followed suit. This did not mean, of course, that those using all the other varieties of speech immediately converted. For ten years or more the other varieties lingered. Some claim that the use of "*-masenkatta*" was particularly strong in the Yokohama area among the foreigners, who thought it gave even their informal utterances a touch of formality.[95] Given Shizuko's relationship with the missionaries in Yokohama, she would have been familiar with this usage and perhaps even preferred it herself.

We do not know why Shizuko opted to use this particular predicate. The fact that she chose to use it—and did so consciously—while others routinely selected "*-masendeshita*" reveals her keen interest in creating a special language for her text. Indeed, by using "*-masenkatta,*" the Japanese form preferred by her American "family," Shizuko stamped *Shōkōshi* as peculiarly hers. Much of the story itself—like "The Keepsake"—speaks for Shizuko. In the exchange between Cedric and his grandfather cited earlier, Cedric defiantly but rightly names himself. He refuses the paternity his grandfather assigns to him and chooses rather to be identified with his mother's country: America. Cedric's insistence on aligning himself with the mother is a direct affront to the venerable patriarch who has failed to vanquish the maternal element. In many ways, therefore, Cedric's self-declaration—his impassioned self-assertion—is a poignant reminder of Shizuko's own struggles as a child to determine her own voice. She had lost her name and place very early in life and had been left to search for a sense of authenticity and belonging—first as a samurai daughter among merchants and then as a Japanese girl among Americans. Like Cedric, she insisted on naming herself. And the name she chose, Wakamatsu Shizuko, identified her as an independent woman. Surely, therefore, there was much in Cedric's self-certainty that appealed to Shizuko. Here was a child who, bereft of father and separated from both his mother and motherland, never lost his own inner sense of security. In an age when the Japanese nation was clamoring to define itself against a Chinese past and a Western future, there was much to be learned from Cedric's bold innocence and courageous integrity. He had stood up to the Dorincourt patriarch—not with belligerence but polite honesty—and his childish goodness had triumphed over the earl's power, prestige, and wealth. As the story concludes, it is the feminine/feminized characters—the gentle mother, the boy child, the lower-class bootblack—who triumph. For Shizuko, this too must have been an important lesson. Women could work within the narrow margins of their status and still prove victorious—and they could do so without compromising (masculinizing) their innate nature.

That none of her contemporary critics singled out Shizuko's language for comment indicates that her signature usage of "*-masenkatta*" was not especially peculiar.[96] In fact, most contemporary critics had only the highest praise for her translation style and language. Morita Shiken, for example, ranked Shizuko's work alongside Futabatei Shimei's as an excellent example of *genbun itchi*. What he admired most about her style was that it was so natural and unforced: "Others try too hard and in their struggles succeed only in hacking away at the language with battle axes, marring its natural beauty. . . . But look here at her language. Here we have nothing but sincerity and truth without an ounce of grandstanding or ostentation. Nor can we detect even the slightest foppish affectation."[97] Shizuko was able to create a colloquial style that was anything but vulgar and yet not self-consciously elegant either. Present-day readers may find her language somewhat florid, but they would no doubt feel the same about Burnett's "natural and simple" style.

Reception and Implications

When Shizuko fell ill early in 1891 and was unable to work on her translation, her husband collected her first installments, had them bound by the *Jogaku zasshi* company, and distributed them for private sale at thirty-eight sen a copy. On November 10, he sent copies to Tsubouchi Shōyō, Ishibashi Ningetsu, Morita Shiken, Mori Ōgai, Iwaya Sazanami, Ozaki Kōyō, Saganoya Omuro, and others—covering all the influential writers, critics, and translators then active—in an effort to solicit their attention and reviews. Most of the critics obliged. Morita Shiken's review for the *Hōchi Shinbun* (November 30, 1891) is notable:

> Frankly speaking, I have never had much desire to read the works of contemporary Japanese women writers. Consequently, I was not seriously inclined to consider this work. But a friend had given it to me to read, and so I thought I might at least thumb through it while taking a smoke. I glanced over the first page, and after reading two or three lines I realized that I was not dealing with any ordinary text. I continued reading, and after two or three pages, I was all the more impressed. In fact, I was so intrigued that I searched out the original for comparison.
>
> I read a passage from the original, and then I turned to the translation. Again I read the original, again I compared. When I had finished the first chapter, I had other work to attend to, but I could not wait to get back to my reading. Armed with my books, I returned to my study, lit the lamp, and proceeded with my comparison. . . . When I finally crawled into bed, it was three in the morning.[98]

Having learned the folly of "judging a book by its author," Shiken concludes his review with the following exhortation: "Having read this work, my immediate reaction is to admonish you men out there: 'You must not belittle women simply because you are men!'"[99]

The other reviews were generally positive. Ishibashi Ningetsu criticized the characterizations and the plot. But as Takahashi Masatoshi notes, these faults were not the responsibility of the translator. Tsubouchi Shōyō thought Shizuko overused the honorific marker "*go/on*," "but not enough to irritate."[100] Some present-day critics have remarked that the positive nature of the reviews was perhaps due more to Iwamoto's clout than to Shizuko's success. Iwamoto certainly was active in ensuring that Shizuko's work was noticed. But if all the critics of the day were like Morita Shiken before his "conversion," uniformly ignoring works by women, then Iwamoto's mentoring was not only instrumental to Shizuko's success but mandatory. Takahashi Masatoshi, however, concludes that Shizuko's positive reviews were not empty flattery.[101]

Indeed, Shizuko's translation lived beyond the limits of the original and influenced contemporary Japanese letters. Jacques Derrida contends that a translation completes an original work by transforming it and allowing it to exceed its borders.[102] Shizuko's translation propelled Burnett's work beyond English and reconstituted it in Japan, where it became another thread in the moving fabric of Meiji literary development—enlarging itself while enriching a once separate tradition. Higuchi Ichiyō, for example, who to this point had written only in a classical style, experimented with the colloquial in "Kono ko" (This Child), which she published in January 1896. Because Ichiyō occasionally employed the now famous "-*masenkatta*" in this work, Takahashi and others contend that her interest in the colloquial was inspired by Shizuko.[103] Donald Keene suggests that Ichiyō's interest in a group of juveniles in "Takekurabe" (Growing Up, 1896) was also inspired by *Shōkōshi*.[104] Similarly, Izumi Kyōka's first foray into the colloquial style is credited to *Shōkōshi*. According to Sasabuchi Tomoichi, the expressions he used, the plot he employed, and the characters he created in "Kechō" (Ghost Bird) were directly inspired by Shizuko's translation.[105] Finally, Yoshiko Takita notes that Oshikawa Shunrō based the portrayal of his young hero in *Kaitei gunkan* (The Submarine, 1900) on Cedric. She quotes from the novel:

> Charming sweet boy of eight, his name was Hideo. . . . [F]air complexioned with tufty hair, [he had] a firm mouth like his father, and clear eyes like his mother. Then I happened to remember the hero of the novel *Little Lord Fauntleroy* which I had read the previous night in the train from Rome.[106]

The influence *Shōkōshi* exerted over later works speaks not only to the dynamism of Burnett's story but also to the skill of Shizuko's translation and her keen appreciation of both Burnett's milieu and her own literary environment. A translator is foremost a reader; and a good translator is inevitably a good reader. Shizuko was not only able to understand and transmit the "information" of the original; more important, she was able to appreciate that which fell between the lines of meaning. And she was able to reveal her appreciation by constructing a Japanese narrative that proved she had equally mastered the special mystery of her own idiom.

Shizuko was well aware of the trends in the contemporary literary world— its traditions and its modern directions—and as she rummaged in her dresser drawers for kimono collars, she managed to select the one that was most appropriate to her own needs and those of her contemporaries. Although Shizuko's contributions have largely been overlooked, she entered the *genbun itchi* movement just when it was losing ground. The two most important figures in the movement, Futabatei Shimei and Yamada Bimyō, had distanced themselves from prose fiction and were no longer involved in *genbun itchi*. The literary world was dominated by Ozaki Kōyō, with his carefully crafted classical style, and Mori Ōgai, with his elegant translations. Following suit, most writers returned to the familiar beauty of the traditional written styles. Nanette Twine notes that this resurgence of the classical was tied to the political climate at the time: "Just as the colloquial style seemed assured of acceptance, a wave of nationalism swept Japan. . . . It was as if the nation had been seized with panic at the prospect of the imminent disappearance of its own unique characteristics under the increasing craze for Westernization."[107] Shizuko's experiments in the midst of this political shift, therefore, are all the more impressive.

After *Shōkōshi* Shizuko continued her work as a translator and essayist. She translated Burnett's *Sara Crewe* (1887) in 1893, in addition to works by Dickens, Jean Ingelow, Harriet Beecher-Stowe, and others. None, however, received the attention of her earlier translations. As Shizuko's tuberculosis progressed, she curtailed her translating but not her writing. She still contributed regularly to *Jogaku zasshi*, writing primarily for the children's column she had created. These contributions consisted of essays to mothers as well as several stories for children. According to Yamaguchi Reiko, her illness often induced feverishly strange dreams, many of which she wrote into fairy stories, such as the "Tree That Grew Kimonos" (Kimono no naru ki, 1895).[108] In August 1894, just before the birth of her third child, she resigned from the *Jogaku zasshi* staff. From June of that year she had accepted editorial responsibility for the "Women's Department" in the English-language periodical *Japan Evangelist*. Shortly thereafter she also agreed to help the editor with the newly launched "Children's Department." Between 1894 and her death in 1896, Shizuko's literary attentions were almost exclusively given to this journal, though she did make occasional contributions to the children's magazine *Shōnen en* (Child's Garden) and to *Jogaku*.

Because the audience for *Japan Evangelist* consisted primarily of North Americans, Shizuko wrote in English. She was the first and only Japanese member of the editorial staff at the time—her unique literary talents qualifying her for a role few could fill. Some of her contributions were in the form of translations of Japanese literature. She translated (or more accurately "paraphrased") a short piece by Ihara Saikaku, for example, as well as haiku verses by Kaga no Chiyo. But mostly Shizuko wrote articles introducing Japanese customs and culture to Western readers. She wrote on marriage, the Japanese sense of duty, and the siege of Aizu castle, and she compiled or translated the biographies of a number of Japanese women. Her essays crowing over the Japanese war successes in China and championing the Japanese nation—such as "Our 'Dai Nippon' (Great Nation) for Christ" (1894)—are rather difficult to stomach today. Her essays exalting the imperial family, though equally repugnant, reveal the pride she felt in a country that cherished "a single succession imperial line." Shizuko was not unique in her nationalism. Many of her contemporaries worked hard at similar projects in an effort to overcome the stigma Christians then suffered as being "unpatriotic."

Due to the resurgence of national fervor, the mid-1890s were difficult years for Japanese Christians. Enrollments at Christian schools dwindled precipitously. The student body at Ferris declined from one hundred and twenty to thirty-eight. At Meiji Women's School, as well, enrollments fell by two-thirds. But the threat to Christian education, and to Japanese Christians in general, simply spurred Shizuko on. She believed that one reason Japanese Christians were so misunderstood was because a small but vocal minority of foreign missionaries offended the local population with their proselytizing. In one of her early essays for *The Japan Evangelist,* for example, she commended the foreign missionaries for the inordinate sacrifices they had made in spreading the gospel but implored them to respect Japanese culture:

> For instance, they would show the Japanese the superiority of Christian morality. They must not begin by offending them by looking upon them as heathens and consequently a subject to be given lessons in the first elements of morality. They need first to study and appreciate their cherished moral standard which has hitherto guided their lives.[109]

Just as earlier Shizuko had used her skills in translating English into Japanese as a means to enlighten Japanese men and women, she now used her skills to enlighten Westerners. She hoped to create for foreign missionaries and the American churches that supported them a conduit through which they could learn what they needed to know to appreciate Japanese culture. In the last year of her life, she wrote more than forty English essays for *Japan Evangelist*. For these essays she consistently used her "married" name, Mrs. Kashi Iwamoto, thus reserving her "Wakamatsu Shizuko" identity for her Japanese audience.

In a sense then, Shizuko reinvented herself as two writers in one body: Wakamatsu Shizuko, the famed translator and essayist; and Mrs. Kashi Iwamoto, noble wife and devoted Christian. It is impossible to conclude that one incarnation was closer to the true spirit of the writer than the other or that they stood in opposition. But it is safe to say that the voice Shizuko articulated in English was different from the one she produced in Japanese. Perhaps the difference is reflected as much in the mind of the reader as in the author herself. Certainly Mrs. Kashi Iwamoto's English essays seem light and lighthearted—even though she was undertaking the serious business of instructing American children as well as adults (primarily women) in an appreciation of Japanese culture. In tackling her assignment she displays as much evangelistic zeal as the missionary preaching to heathens. Nevertheless one finds a charm in her English prose that is not so apparent in her Japanese. From her Children's Department of February 1895, for example:

A little boy three years old got up one morning crying as hard as he could. His father gently took him in his arms and carrying him to the window said, "See the sun yonder? What a bright beautiful face! Let me see my boy just as bright and happy."

The boy stopped crying as the case always is when the father happens to be the consoler. A few days later as the sun was setting in all its splendor, the rays were seen spreading out on all sides. "See, papa," the boy said, "the sun's got whiskers now."[110]

Often she reveals a humorous side to herself not so easily discovered in her Japanese essays. In her English farewell address to her friends at Ferris, for example, certainly a solemn occasion, Shizuko describes her graduation from the same institution several years earlier: "The next year the school conferred a certificate on the sole survivor of a class whose fate must always be an argument against Darwin's favorite theory."[111]

In 1895 Shizuko became pregnant with her fourth child. Her doctor warned that she would not be able to survive another childbirth and urged her to abort the child. Shizuko would not hear of it. This "angel of the home" may be "the next Napoleon or Milton."[112] And so, on February 10, 1896, weakened by pregnancy and exhausted by the fire at the Meiji Women's

School that had forced her to evacuate her sickbed five days earlier, Shizuko's heart gave out. She died at one in the afternoon with her husband at her side.

> "Please, all I want on my grave stone is 'Shizuko.' And tell only those who were close to me. I don't want a public funeral, and I don't want you to write a biography or memorial to me. There is nothing I want to tell others. But if they ask, just say that I was grateful my whole life through for the blessings received from Christ."[113]

Shizuko's Masks

Although Wakamatsu Shizuko slipped quietly from the memory of contemporary Japanese literary history, she left an important legacy. Recent critics have recognized her contributions to *genbun itchi* and to the creation of children's literature. Indeed, Takahashi Masatoshi said that her achievements in modernizing Japanese narrative rank alongside those of Futabatei Shimei:

> It would not be overstatement to claim that she and Futabatei are the twin pillars upon which *genbun itchi* was built. Yet when we think of *genbun itchi* nowadays, Futabatei's name looms large while Wakamatsu Shizuko's does not, and this I find highly questionable. Shizuko's work in our literary world was epochal. Indeed, she was the single most important contributor to the revitalization of our literary prose. In light of her significance [and the fact that she has been forgotten nevertheless], I wonder if we ought not to reevaluate our own critical standards.[114]

Satō Michimasa too questions critical standards that would ignore a writer of Shizuko's standing. While acknowledging her contributions to *genbun itchi*, Satō suggests that she deserves greater credit for initiating a genre of literature for children: "She was the pioneer who first imparted to childhood in Japan a modern meaning."[115] And yet, as he notes, most histories of children's literature in Japan begin with Iwaya Sazanami (1870–1933), making no mention of Shizuko. Iwaya—a founding member of the Ken'yūsha—turned to children's literature, according to Satō, in order to contribute to "the building of a rich country and strong army." Just as Iwamoto Yoshiharu and other patriotic figures aspired to the creation of a literature for women, Iwaya aspired to a literature for youth. For both, the goal was the improvement of the nation—and improving it in a way that ultimately benefited their own aims and desires. Satō asks:

> Why has Shizuko not been considered? The most important reason is because the newly evolving nation was one that was contemptuous of

women. The national policy of "rich country and strong army" solidified a society that put men at its center and kept women on the periphery. It was very difficult for women to affirm a space of their own therein.[116]

And this brings us to what, for the purpose of this study, is Shizuko's greatest contribution. With her life's work, but particularly with her translation of *Little Lord Fauntleroy*, she opened a space in the literary world for the woman writer. More so than Miyake Kaho, who preceded her to the literary arena by one year, Shizuko showed how a woman could be a devoted wife and a serious writer—indeed, how she could write between the bedroom and the kitchen. Importantly, Shizuko had the support and understanding of a sympathetic husband.[117] In a sense her poor health also worked in her favor as it relieved her of most of the everyday chores of housekeeping. Frequently bedridden, Shizuko found that she could make the greatest contribution to her family through her writing. And because Shizuko equated the good of the family with the good of the nation, she was able to combine her public aspirations as a writer with her wifely duties at home—thus turning writing into a virtuous act and not merely a frivolous pastime.

Significantly, it was what she chose to write about—and to translate— that lent her activities an aura of high-mindedness and purity. Most other writers of her generation focused on romantic love. Kaho, in an effort to give her portrayal of the relations between the sexes a dignified tone, had felt inclined to write of the injustices implicit in a system that denies women the right to decide their own marital fates. But since writing of this kind led to didacticism and then to charges of masculine "preaching," Kaho camouflaged her messages with a properly elegant and old-fashioned literary style. The typical triteness of her language led in turn to charges of frivolity and mimicry. Kaho was not offering the literary world anything new, it was said: she was simply spinning out tales in poor imitation of her male mentor. Shizuko avoided these pitfalls first by writing primarily of parental love. If she did touch on love between the sexes, it was always a spiritual, platonic type of love. In other words, though Shizuko kept her eye on "human emotions" *(ninjō)*, she offered nothing that would even hint at impropriety. It may have been unseemly at the time for a proper woman to give herself over in passion to a man. But there was nothing more appropriate for a woman than an ardent love for her child.

Not only was Shizuko's choice of subject matter appropriate, but her methods and motivations were equally admirable. She was not writing simply to earn money or to entertain. She was writing from a genuine concern over the state of family life in Japan. As she believed that women were the key to creating a happy family, she felt duty bound for the good of other women and society to do what she could to awaken women to their responsibilities. The stories she wrote and translated—focusing as they did on the beauty and goodness of a warm family life—were calculated to meet these ends.

That Shizuko distinguished herself as a translator and not as a writer is also significant. The author Kunikida Doppo (1871–1908), in fact, argued that translating was more natural to women than creative writing. In a fit of misogynistic spleen, Doppo charged that women were not human but were monkeys mimicking humanity.[118] As they were much practiced in imitation, it therefore followed that they would excel at translation. Citing the success of Wakamatsu Shizuko and Koganei Kimiko as proof, he encouraged women to abandon notions of becoming writers and to translate instead:

> To become a writer one needs to be observant. One needs a wealth of personal experience, inspiration, and a continuous span of time. Occasionally one needs to travel. At times one needs to be alone. And of course, one needs natural talent. Most women cannot ever hope for any of these requirements. But in translation the circumstances are much different, the nature of composition much different. Because translating is mechanical, one can do it whenever one can steal a moment or two. Today one might translate one line, tomorrow a paragraph, and this will not have much impact on the final outcome of the work.[119]

Translation, Doppo continued, was an appropriate pastime for women because it was so automatic that it required little thought. A woman could attend to her children and to her husband—whom she could consult on difficult matters—and still translate successfully whenever she managed to wrest a little time for herself. Of course, translation required diligence, attention to detail, and faithfulness—but who better than a woman to meet these demands? Moreover, with translation she did not have to worry about losing her inspiration or train of thought.

Doppo's misogyny was excessive even by Meiji standards, but his comments illuminate the essential bias against women's writing (as well as an ignorance of translation). Writing required thought. It required not only a space between bedroom and kitchen but a mental space as well, where a woman could enter at will and indulge in her own ideas, and dreams, and passions. But indulgence of this kind threatened men like Doppo, because it required that women place their own creativity above their devotion to husbands and fathers. Women who thought for themselves, who were creative, who had trains of thought entered a realm that put them beyond the control of men like Doppo—thus disrupting the proper balance in the sexual hierarchy.

Shizuko, we know, labored over her translator's art, and her efforts far exceeded a mere selection of words. Even so, she did not draw attention to her labors. She made translating seem simple because she made it so natural. And the texts she created as a result were equally readable. In a sense, translation became a mask for Shizuko. By presenting herself as a mere translator, she avoided charges of immodesty, selfishness, and creativity. Unlike Kaho, she did not require boldness *(kenage)* to present her work—because the work she presented was not her own. She was merely the conduit, the machine, the helpmeet, the wife. Through translation, however, Shizuko found she could explore other realms—realms she could not reach in her own voice. She could write of seafaring men and golden-haired boys. More important, she could dare to be inventive. As a translator she could try out a variety of voices and styles. A ventriloquist for Burnett, Dickens, or Tennyson, she could write about the lower classes or experiment with colloquial language with impunity. When Kaho wrote from the point of view of stableboys and rickshaw pullers, for example, she was taken to task—not because her portrayals were inept but because they were so skillful. How could an innocent "schoolgirl" have written with such incisiveness? Shizuko, on the other hand, was not chastised for writing about bootblacks and scullery maids because, of course, she didn't. She did not invent these scenes and hence was exempt from criticism. That she was not particularly successful in capturing their vulgarity in Japanese only endeared her more to her critics. She retained her integrity as a "lady scholar" *(jogakushi)*.

With translation Shizuko could touch an emotional depth she could not quite reach with her own (Japanese) words. Wakamatsu Shizuko, standing before the world unveiled as Iwamoto Yoshiharu's wife—"the lady scholar"—was inclined like Miyake Kaho to offer moral tales. Her original works, therefore, were generally narrow and self-conscious and ended with lessons and warnings. But translating freed her from herself. Translations allowed her the space to play without being unduly aware of her "lady scholar" self. Certainly she sought out works that represented her own values and ideas, but she was free to imbue her renditions with an emotional intensity she could not impart to her original works. In the process she was also able to express something of herself.

Shizuko was not a feminist by today's standards or even by Meiji standards. Shioda Ryōhei notes: "She did not try to establish a new morality like Yosano Akiko and the later Seitō women. Nor did she cast a doubting eye on the existing moral system like the other women writers of her own generation. Rather, Shizuko worked within the system."[120] By working "within the system" and behind the veil of translation, Shizuko found the space she needed to accomplish what she desired. Critics did not try to silence her or change her or redirect her—as they had tried with Kaho—for there was no need to do so. She did not threaten. Rather, she presented herself as the ideal, the exemplary "new" woman. As E. S. Booth, the Ferris principal, observed: "A new woman undoubtedly she was, not in the sense, however, which has come to be attached to that term on account of the appearance of a few monstrosities in modern civilization, but a new woman in the highest and best sense. A regenerated woman directed by the forces of a new life."[121] As Mrs. Kashi Iwamoto, Shizuko used her education and talents for the good of the nation—preaching the gospel of the Japanese nation. As Wakamatsu Shizuko, she modestly translated—using her skills to help educate her fellow citizens.

Masks, of course, have a way of manipulating even their wearer. Shizuko's masks—her English voice and her translator's veil—allowed her to be creative but also compelled her to retain those signifiers that marked her as properly feminine. She was successful as a translator, it was believed, because she was so feminine—willing, as Doppo tells us, to forgo publicity, arrogance, and fantasy and thereby able to yield her own ego to that of a greater mind: an original author. And so it is that *Shōkōshi* remains—a well-loved children's story and an important forerunner to the modern narrative—but the name of its translator has lapsed from historical memory.

The modern woman writer Nogami Yaeko (1885–1995), looking back on her early days at Meiji Women's School, describes in her autobiographical novel *Mori* (The Forest, 1972) the excitement her alter ego Kane felt when she first learned that the headmaster's late wife was actually the famous *Shōkōshi* translator, "Tatsumatsu Shizuko." Because of the pen name, Kane had not connected Shizuko with the school or with Okuno (the name the author assigns to Iwamoto): "So Mrs. Okuno had not simply been a wife and the mother of three small children! . . . Now Kane could understand why everyone always said Headmaster Okuno's wife was such a remarkable person. She felt a new wave of respect wash over her heart. How lucky she was to have entered this school!"[122]

Later writers may have forgotten her name, may not even realize that she existed. Nevertheless, as a "working mother" herself, Shizuko stood as a significant model for women of her generation and generations to come: she showed them that a woman could enter the public arena and produce changes if she was willing to veil herself with femininity.

Chapter Four

Shimizu Shikin

From Broken Rings to Brokered Silence

> If Ichiyō is the last flower caught in the fetters of feudalism, then Shikin, standing to face the bracing wind at the dawn of a new age, is the first standard bearer for modernity.
>
> —Yamaguchi Reiko, 1977

Wakamatsu Shizuko may embody the ideal Meiji woman writer, but Shimizu Shikin represents the conflicting challenges and expectations that attended the woman writer's career. Shikin herself is something of an enigma. Raised in the sheltered comfort of a Kyoto bureaucrat's home, she became an outspoken defender of human rights who traveled with the Freedom and Popular Rights Movement. One of the first Meiji women writers to experiment with *genbun itchi*, she nevertheless abandoned the style in favor of the conventional five–seven–five metrical flourish of *gesaku*. The first professional female journalist in Japan, she advocated vociferously in her essays and articles for a woman's right to equality and self-governance. Yet she chose, inexplicably it would seem, to "break her writing brush" in favor of silence in marriage.

Writing had always been for Shimizu Shikin, as it had for Wakamatsu Shizuko, a means to an end. She turned to writing once the government prohibited women from lecturing at or even attending political rallies, and she used fiction and essays to convey her messages. As a result of Shikin's preoccupation with moral tales and her insistence on delivering her stories in a moribund narrative style, the majority of her fourteen or fifteen fictional works do not stand up to a comparison with the best works of Higuchi Ichiyō, Futabatei Shimei, and the like. Yet there are, within this collection, two works that, while not exceptional as literature per se, are extraordinary nonetheless as harbingers of new directions in Japanese literature and society. "Koware yubiwa" (The Broken Ring, 1891), the first of these and signif-

159

icantly Shikin's debut work, pioneers a path for future female writers. As Yamaguchi Reiko suggests, Shikin is the primogenitor of "a strain in writing—flourishing today—that differs fundamentally from the traditional women's literature represented by Higuchi Ichiyō and those who followed her."[1] The true heirs to "The Broken Ring," therefore, could be said to be writers like Miyamoto Yuriko, Sata Ineko, and Hirabashi Taiko. Yet ironically, it is unlikely that these writers ever read "The Broken Ring" or even knew of Shimizu Shikin—so buried had this author and her works become in the few decades following her retirement.

"Imin gakuen" (A School for Émigrés, 1899), the second of these two works and Shikin's final piece, falls into the category of social issue fiction—particularly fiction treating the prejudices and marginalization experienced by the *burakumin,* the so-called outcasts. Scholars suggest that "A School for Émigrés" influenced Shimazaki Tōson's *Hakai* (The Broken Commandment, 1906), which it preceded by seven years. Nevertheless, "A School for Émigrés"

Figure 17   Shimizu Shikin. (Courtesy of Nihon Kindai Bungakkan)

is not anthologized in any of the collections devoted to *burakumin* literature. And while *The Broken Commandment* is a standard entry on high school and college reading lists, few today are familiar with Shimizu Shikin.

Shikin, of course, is not the only writer omitted from standard histories of Meiji literature. These histories cannot, of course, mention everyone who lifted a pen or signed a name. Nevertheless, as Komashaku Kimi suggests, if men like Kitamura Tōkoku and Futabatei Shimei, whose works though significant were few and far between, "enjoy citizenship in the pages of literary histories,"[2] why not a writer like Shimizu Shikin, whose mediocre though dramatic career is framed by two exceptional works? This is not to imply that Shikin is ignored entirely in literary histories. She appears in the major Meiji collections. Yet curiously she is represented by works such as *Kokoro no oni* (Devil in the Heart, 1897) or *Shitayuku mizu* (The Downflow, 1898), which are the least representative of her talent and originality. Fortunately her son, the Marxist-affiliated philosopher Kozai Yoshishige, collected his mother's writings in celebration of the hundredth anniversary of her birth, which coincided incidentally with the birth of the modern Japanese nation. Unlike Wakamatsu Shizuko, Miyake Kaho, and most other Meiji-era women writers, all of Shikin's published works are available in a modern print edition.

The Early Years

In this chapter I present readings of "The Broken Ring" and "A School for Émigrés" within the context of Shikin's other works and the social and political climate in which she wrote. As in the case of Shizuko and Kaho, we have little information about Shikin's private life. She did not leave a diary, and she wrote no memoirs. Her children, like most children, never thought to ask her about her past. Her son relates that it was only after her death that he learned, from his father, that he had a stepbrother and that Shikin had been married before. Although he admits to curiosity, his father offered no further information and Yoshishige refrained from digging any deeper out of respect for his parents' privacy. Yamaguchi Reiko, who would also write the biography of Wakamatsu Shizuko, provides the most authoritative information on Shikin in her impeccably researched *Naite aisuru shimai ni tsugu—Kozai Shikin no shōgai* (To My Beloved Sisters with Tears—The Life of Kozai Shikin, 1977). And yet even her four-hundred-and-fifty-page tome is riddled with question marks. For most of these questions there will be no answers.

The Bureaucrat's Daughter

Shikin, like Kaho and Shizuko, was born during the upheaval wrought by the Meiji Restoration. Unlike her two peers, however, Shikin's father was not of the samurai class nor was he opposed to the restoration. Shimizu Sadamoto was of peasant stock. But his family was wealthy and politically powerful and lived more like local gentry than farmers. The family's wealth and leisure afforded Sadamoto a distinguished education. Still, opportunities under Tokugawa rule were limited for a man of Sadamoto's birth. Talk of restoring the emperor to power must have seemed attractive. After all, notions of imperial rule conjured visions of the former courtly culture, where scholarship and taste were valued—or so Sadamoto assumed. He was quick to join the call to "revere the emperor/expel the barbarians," and he encouraged others in his region to do the same.

When Shikin was born, therefore, her father's world was in a state of flux. Yet it was a state that augured hope. Sadamoto's activities on behalf of the restorationists had brought him into contact with members of the Chōshū forces, who would soon be instrumental in bringing down the Tokugawa shogunate. Perhaps due to connections he fostered there, Sadamoto was asked to fill a position in the Kyoto municipal government three years following the restoration. Leaving his country home to assume his post, he began work with an office responsible for "modernizing" the old capital. The position was an extremely fortituous one for a lowly "peasant" like Sadamoto as most bureaucrats at the time were former samurai. Indeed, he seemed to personify the very promise of the era: *"risshin shusse"* (self-establishment and public success) writ large. Early in the period, therefore, the future looked bright for the Shimizu family. Sadamoto saw that his two sons received an education that represented the new age of civilization with its emphasis on improved technology and culture: the eldest received an advanced degree in agricultural science; the second pursued Western-style painting. Sadamoto even encouraged his daughters in their schooling. But the Shimizu family could not hold onto their early windfall. Death took two of Sadamoto's daughters while they were still quite young, and in 1898 his eldest son was blinded in a laboratory explosion. The future of the Shimizu family fell unexpectedly on the shoulders of Sadamoto's fifth child, Shimizu Shikin.

Shikin was born January 11, 1868, in what is present-day Bizen city, Okayama prefecture. Her given name was Toyo. Although the family maintained its ancestral home in Okayama, Shikin's childhood was spent in Kyoto where she enjoyed all the advantages of a bureaucrat's daughter. She and her elder sister advanced to the newly established Kyoto Muncipal Women's Teacher Training School. Shikin most likely entered the program when she was nine. She spent three years in the regular course and two in the teacher's training component. Completing the elementary level of that component when she was fourteen, she graduated at a considerably younger age than most girls. At this point, her father decided that she had had substantial education and for the most part Shikin's schooling ended. Higuchi Ichiyō, by way of comparison, concluded her schooling at the age of eleven. She had clearly wanted to continue her studies, and when she was forced to resign, largely at her mother's insistence, wrote in her diary, "I would rather have died, of course. I felt so miserable."[3] It is assumed that Shikin, too, longed to pursue further study, though evidence for this assumption is limited largely to an autobiographical reading of her fictional story "The Broken Ring." Her son, however, in relating the following anecdote, concludes that his mother was bitterly disappointed when her formal education ended sooner than she would have liked:

> I remember once my mother asked me to go to the post office on an errand. When I refused she told me that when she was young she had wanted to study, but because she had not been allowed to do as she wished, she had made certain that I would have every opportunity to study to my heart's content. "And now you won't even go to the post office for me?" She began to cry. I was twenty-five or twenty-six at the time, so Mother must have been over sixty.[4]

For several years after her graduation, Shikin spent her days reading in her father's library. Because her father was responsible for overseeing modern development in the old capital, he had an impressive collection of Western works in translation, as well as the latest treatises by progressive Japanese intellectuals. In a later essay Shikin indicates that in addition to the training in the standard Japanese literary classics she received at school, she was able to read Rousseau, Spencer, Smiles, Mill, Shakespeare, Dickens, Defoe, and others in translation. As for original works in Japanese, she had access to pamphlets and books by Fukuzawa Yukichi and Nakae Chōmin (1847–1901). In addition to these Meiji "best-sellers," Shikin admits to being most taken at the time with the Japanese poet and parodist Shokusanjin (Ōta Nanpa, 1749–1823) and with *Nihon gaishi* (The Unofficial History of Japan) by Rai Sanyō (1780–1832). Shokusanjin's poetry, Rai Sanyō's history and many of the translations just mentioned were written in *kanbun*, a Chinese orthographic style of writing with which many women at the time were unfamiliar. As none of these texts would have been included on the reading lists in Shikin's school, Kozai Yoshishige maintains, with good reason, that his mother was largely self-taught.

A Bride of Popular Rights

Shikin married in 1885, when she was eighteen. Most likely the marriage was arranged by her family. It is uncertain whether or not Shikin accepted the arrangement without protest. The question, nevertheless, is moot. Despite her

reading of Mill and Fukuzawa, it is unlikely that Shikin would have thought
to challenge her father's authority on the matter. Most women in nineteenth-
century Japan accepted that their lot in life was to marry. Furthermore, a marriage at eighteen would not have been unusual. According to Yamaguchi
Reiko, marriage procedures might even begin when a girl was fifteen. It
should be remembered that Higuchi Ichiyō was affianced when she was seventeen and might have married shortly thereafter if her family fortune had
not plummeted. That Wakamatsu Shizuko married at twenty-four and Kaho
at twenty-five highlights how exceptional their life histories were. Shikin's
elder sister had been sent in marriage immediately after her graduation when
she was nineteen. When Shikin ended her schooling, she knew, as she sat
amidst her father's books, that her own marriage would not be far behind.

In her later story "The Broken Ring," Shikin would compare marriage to
drawing lots *(mikuji):* "It made no difference whether the lot you drew was
a lucky one or not, it was your lot in life and you had to accept it."[5] A man's
lot in marriage did not necessarily affect the rest of his life, as he was able to
exist outside the confines of matrimony. But for a woman, marriage became
her life, her fate. In Shikin's case, the lot she drew did indeed alter the course
of her life, but it would not determine it indefinitely. For by the time Shikin
reached a marriageable age, winds of change had begun to alter Meiji marriage practices. Women were being offered a glimpse of a new freedom and
were being encouraged to construct a new role for themselves in marriage. It
was largely through publications such as *Jogaku zasshi* and through the activities of the Freedom and Popular Rights Movement, the Tokyo Women's
Reform Society, and those of their sympathizers that much of this change was
disseminated. Ironically, it was through her marriage that Shikin came into
contact with these organizations.

The Freedom and Popular Rights Movement had been in full swing not
far from Shikin's home for several years. But she was such an obedient *hako-
iri musume* ("daughter in a box") that her biographer doubts she was much
aware of the world beyond her father's library. She might have heard reports
of Kishida Toshiko's activities. Toshiko (Nakajima Shōen) was a Kyoto native.
She and Shikin had attended the same school, though at different intervals,
and her activities in the Kansai region were then drawing much attention.
Whatever Shikin's prior understanding of the movement, it was not until her
marriage that she came into direct contact with its principal actors.

Little is known of Shikin's first marriage. Biographers are not even certain of the name of her husband. Most agree that his surname was Okazaki,
that he was involved with the Freedom and Popular Rights Movement in
some capacity—perhaps as a lawyer—and that he was acquainted with the
well-known activist Ueki Emori (1857–1892). There were, however, two

men named Okazaki who fit this profile. Both are mentioned in Ueki's diary, as is the woman "Okazaki Toyo," who accompanied Ueki on several expeditions and even participated in a number of rallies.

Fukuda Hideko (Kageyama Hideko), in her autobiography *Warawa no hanshōgai* (Half of My Life, 1904), has the following to say about Shikin (for whom she creates the psuedonym Izumi Tomiko):

> Here I will say a word about Izumi Tomiko (presently the wife of a certain professor of agriculture) and her past. She was born in Bizen. Her father was appointed to a certain municipal office but implicated in a crime was thrown in jail. Henceforth Tomiko married a lawyer named Okazaki and had him see to her father's case. Thus she found herself deeply indebted to Okazaki. When I was imprisoned I too relied on Okazaki, and he and his wife came to meet me and traveled with me to my home town. His wife and I became fast friends—like sisters.[6]

Hideko's account, as we shall see, is biased against Shikin and therefore hardly reliable.

There are no records of Shikin's father running afoul of the law, for example, so it is unlikely that Shikin married Okazaki for his legal expertise. It is true, however, that she and Hideko became good friends. Profoundly moved by the idealism of the movement, Shikin began to travel with Ueki and Hideko in the late 1880s, joining them on the lecture platform on at least five occasions. Concerned with human rights overall, Shikin's speeches specifically targeted the issue of monogamy—or rather the lack of it among Japanese males. She was also concerned with raising the level of women's education and with encouraging women to take responsibility for their own lives. Obviously impressed with Shikin's diligence and passion, Ueki invited her to contribute a preface to his monograph, *Tōyō no fujo* (Women of the Orient), which he published in 1888. Her contribution opened with the following statement: "The social question defining the nineteenth century is the question of women; the history of civilization in the nineteenth century is a history of the expansion of women's rights."[7] She then describes Japan's unsatisfactory response to the Woman Question:

> In our country the discussion of women's issues is shallow; the debates extremely superficial. . . . In the first place, those leading the movement are noncommittal, unable to declare unequivocally whether they are for or against equal rights between the sexes. Second, there are those manipulators who seek to educate woman not for the benefit of her own mind but for their own needs. . . . Third are hypocrites who stand before the government

and coolly declare their liberal yearnings. But once they are home they lord it over their wives and children. Finally, there are impostors in our midst who, knowing the justice of equal rights between the sexes, nevertheless, out of personal convenience, approve of measures that "revere men and despise women." Although Mr. Ueki was born into this same man's world, he is able to appreciate the woman's position, feeling sympathy for those mistreated. He has resolutely been appointed to the great mission of protecting womanhood.[8]

Shikin's disappointment with male involvement in the women's rights movement may have been inspired by her own domestic situation. Her husband, most scholars assume, was a bigamist. There is no evidence for this claim, other than Shikin's fictional account of a woman's divorce in "The Broken Ring," yet it was not unusual at the time for men to leave their families behind in the countryside while they went to the city for work. After establishing themselves, some failed to return to their families and often acquired a new one in the city. Since women had little recourse under the law, most had no choice but to acquiesce to the situation. What infuriated Shikin, however, was not simply that men were allowed to continue in this behavior, but that men who presented themselves as advocates of women's rights were not averse to exploiting women all the same. Even Ueki himself, whom Shikin clearly admired, was criticized for preaching against prostitution by day and dallying in the brothels by night. As Watanabe Sumiko would observe, Shikin despaired that Japanese men, even those supposedly sympathetic to women's rights, "were predisposed to despising women."[9]

Early in 1889 Shikin divorced Okazaki. From March of that year she began appearing on the lecture circuit as Shimizu Toyo. Fukuda Hideko describes the rationale for Shikin's divorce as follows:

> At the time Okazaki's finances were in disarray and Izumi found that very distressful. Coincidentally, Omoii's prospects had never been better, and Izumi, finding herself thus attracted to him, left her husband and benefactor, Okazaki, and ran off to Tokyo where she began to see Omoii—the result being that she stole his love from me.[10]

Hideko's account is based more on personal rancor than fact. Shikin (Izumi) did eventually have an affair with Ōi Kentarō (1843–1922), Hideko's former lover and here identified as Omoii. But she did not begin her association with him until after her divorce, when it seems she worked briefly for him in a secretarial capacity. By this time Ōi's ardor for Hideko had cooled. The way in which Hideko, who still had strong feelings for Ōi, discovered the affair may have contributed to the bitterness with which she regarded Shikin. In 1892 while Shikin was hospitalized in Tokyo for a nervous breakdown very likely abetted by her relationship with Ōi, which had resulted in a pregnancy, he sent her a letter inquiring after her health and reaffirming his love for her. At the same time he also sent a letter to Hideko, explaining once again that he wanted no more to do with her. Inexplicably, Hideko received the letter intended for Shikin. It was a cruel shock. Rather than venting her anger at Ōi, however, she reserved her fury for Shikin. They had been friends—"like sisters"—and Hideko felt betrayed. Her portrayal of Shikin, therefore, is vicious. By the time her autobiography was published, Shikin was married once again, to a prominent scholar. Or as Hideko would have it: "She disappeared for a time and then, like a magician, reemerged as the lady wife of some great professor of agriculture and is now living in the lap of luxury. Or so I hear."[11] Shikin did not try to set the record straight. According to her son, she never spoke of her past. But once, toward the end of her life, she sighed and said: "Kageyama-san [Fukuda Hideko] and I really had been good friends."[12]

From Woman Lecturer to Woman Journalist

After Shikin's divorce she traveled to Tokyo where she was given a position with *Jogaku zasshi*. Sasaki Toyosu (1853–1901) was most likely responsible for introducing Shikin to Iwamoto Yoshiharu and helping her secure employment with his journal. Toyosu was secretary of the Tokyo Women's Reform Society and heavily involved in the movement to end prostitution. She often campaigned with Ueki Emori, and it is probably through this association that Shikin met Toyosu. After traveling to Tokyo in 1890, Shikin stayed with the Sasakis while she established herself.

It is here that Sōma Kokkō first encountered Shikin. She describes her, rather breathlessly, as a striking beauty "as lovely as a flower . . . as fresh as water."[13] Since Kokkō—Miss Blacklight—was herself a very vivacious young woman, Shikin must have been striking indeed to have so captured her admiration. In a letter Shikin wrote on May 1, 1891, she says: "This month last year I came marching to Tokyo, my courageous heart brimming with hope and vigor!"[14] Divorce, it seems, had favored Shikin. At last she could become the kind of woman she had preached about: independent and in control of her own destiny, at least for a time.

Shikin's appearance in the *Jogaku zasshi* offices could not have been better timed. Uchida Roan (Fuchian) had just vacated his position there to join the staff of *Kokumin shinbun*, and Iwamoto needed a replacement. He was also keen to employ Shikin at Meiji Women's School where, in addition to auditing classes herself, she would eventually teach composition. Shikin's energy and enthusiasm quickly began to produce results for the journal, which was now facing stiff competition from *Kokumin no tomo* and similar publications. She initiated several new features. For example, she began a series of interviews with contemporaries who were active in women's education and interested in women's rights. Among those she interviewed were Nakamura Masanao (1832–1891), former Meiji Six member, educator, and translator; Atomi Kakei (1840–1926), founder of the Atomi School for Women; and Ogino Gin (1851–1913), Japan's first licensed female physician.

Shikin also began a question-and-answer survey featuring women who had made a name for themselves as *keishū sakka*. She was interested in learning why these women had decided to become writers, what kind of experiences they had had, what their goals and ideals were, and who among past and present writers they admired. Her survey featured Koganei Kimiko (1870–1956), Kimura Akebono (1872–1890), and Wakamatsu Shizuko. Miyake Kaho was expected to respond in issue 209 (April 19) but declined due to ill health. At this point Shikin's interests shifted to other matters. Not only did she record the opinions of others, but she was also busy writing her own articles and editorials and in fact was responsible for contributing well over a third of the material in the journal at this time. Many of her essays were drawn from her earlier speeches. Her concerns were addressed, therefore, to education for women and equality in marriage practices. But she also insisted that women must learn to take responsibility for their own causes. They could not expect men to do the work for them. She appealed to women to strive for an adequate education and, more important, to open their eyes to the reality of their situation. In her November 1890 essay "Tōkon jogakusei kakugo ikaga" (What Will Today's Women Students Resolve?), for example, she encouraged her young readers not to be blinded by romantic fantasies but to be pioneers in real social change:

> You young ladies now harbor a variety of desires regarding studies and careers. Most of you dream that upon graduation you will find a good husband and together you will create a happy home. . . . But, young ladies, is this good husband so easy to find? Is that happy home so simple to create? You who set out into this flower-strewn-world—your dreams and desires to fulfill—where is the man who ought to welcome you and indulge you with a pure love and a pure heart? The marital home is not paradise. . . . At times it is a paradise lost. . . . To turn it into paradise, to turn your unsatisfactory husband into an ideal gentleman—this, dear ladies, will require patience and extreme effort. . . . Marriage is like leading a sheep to the lions. . . . In order to avoid becoming prey, you must lose your sheeplike passivity.[15]

The Broken Ring

Inspired perhaps by her conversations with Wakamatsu Shizuko and other women writers, Shikin decided to try her hand at a work of fiction. The result was "The Broken Ring," which was published in the New Year's issue of *Jogaku zasshi* in 1891. This brief work, describing a woman's "awakening" and escape from an unhappy marriage, augured the emergence of a new female voice in Japanese literature. Miyake Kaho had entertained the literary world with a romantic account of the modern schoolgirl and her journey into matrimony. Kaho's story, culminating in a happy marriage, seemed to suggest that a woman's greatest success, indeed her very life, depended on marriage. Wakamatsu Shizuko, however, had thwarted any such expectations by allowing her "Sumire" to conclude with a rejection of "the happy marriage." Even so, the implication seemed to be not so much a condemnation of marriage as a challenge to women to turn to alternative means for establishing their self-fulfillment. Perhaps it was inevitable, therefore, that Shikin should follow up on this impulse by creating a woman whose story begins after the failure of her marriage.

Not all marriages, Shikin knew from experience, have happy endings or produce "home angels." Shikin also knew that not all unhappy marriages end in disaster—the conventional view in fiction at the time. Ozaki Kōyō, Tsubouchi Shōyō, Mori Ōgai—writers of every stripe and standard—seemed to capitalize on the theme of the unhappy marriage with such frequency that the miserable, all-suffering wife had become something of a stock Meiji character. For some, the bankrupt marriage system and its victimization of women had become a metaphor for the oppressive backwardness of the outdated Japanese state. Kuzume Yoshi, however, in a 1991 article on the images of Japanese women in the West, suggests that the creation of the beautiful wife who suffers sadly (but nobly) the cruel injustices of matrimony bears similarities to the Victorian code of wifely virtue—and may indeed have been tailored by Japanese men in the Meiji period to counter Western men's negative view of Japanese women as immoral concubines.[16] And yet the image of the nobly suffering wife is certainly not limited to the Meiji period or to male writers. The lyrical beauty of the suffering woman, particularly the abandoned wife, has been an important element in Japanese poetics for centuries.[17] The woman who endured the unendurable—and did so without complaint—became the feminine ideal. But Shikin—just as she warned her young audience not to accept the myth of happy marriages—similarly warns her readers not to believe the beauty of female suffering.[18] She deconstructs the feminine ideal in "The Broken Ring" by creating a woman who, in the end, refuses to suffer in silence. She survives to tell the story and, indeed, has a story to tell.

The significance and originality of Shikin's creation is best approached through a comparative analysis of other Meiji-era marriage narratives. Let us begin by considering the various "emancipatory strategies"—to borrow Marianne Hirsch's terminology—that Shikin employs in "The Broken Ring" against the "dominant patterns" found in Tsubouchi Shōyō's "Saikun" (The Wife, 1889) and Higuchi Ichiyō's "Jūsan'ya" (The Thirteenth Night, 1895). After examining the critical reactions to "The Broken Ring," I want to discuss Shikin's unexpected withdrawal from the modern direction in narrative that she had charted.

The Daughter as Commodity

Some critics consider Shōyō's "The Wife" to be the precursor to Shikin's "The Broken Ring," conferring upon him the paternity of yet another woman writer. Shōyō's story was published in the New Year's issue of *Kokumin no tomo*, a journal Shikin is likely to have read.[19] But as J. Scott Miller points out, Shōyō's work appeared in the same issue that contained a "provocative seminude illustration for a new story by Yamada Bimyō. Public and critical attention zoomed in on this illustration, and *Wife* went relatively unnoticed."[20] It is not certain, therefore, that Shikin ever read Shōyō's piece. Yet because his work is typical of the kind of marriage narratives then popular, I think the comparison is valid. Moreover, the same critics who pronounced Shōyō's "The Wife" as the forerunner to "The Broken Ring" also describe Shikin's work as the antecedent to Ichiyō's "The Thirteenth Night." Again, there is no evidence to suggest that Ichiyō read Shikin's work, though we do know that she was familiar with *Jogaku zasshi*. If we accept the notion that "any text is the absorption and transformation of another,"[21] then the circular interrelation between these texts warrants comparison.

The similarities between these three texts are striking. But equally notable are the dissimilarities and the fact that Shikin's work, though preceding Ichiyō's by some four years, reads more like the logical progression to the later story. All three stories relate the unhappiness involved when daughters are used as objects of exchange in marriages of convenience. In each account the marriage of the daughters improves the prospects of her family. Not surprisingly, all three are married to men of higher social and financial status. In "The Wife," Otane's marriage to Sadao promises her father comfortable support in his declining years. It also offers a source of income for Otane's dissolute stepbrother. We find a similar situation in Ichiyō's "The Thirteenth Night," where the happiness of Oseki's entire family (that is, the success of the only son) depends on her continued marriage to the prominent (and abusive) Harada Isamu. In Shikin's account the parents are eager to have their daughter's future "settled," and though her husband is clearly "a match of a lifetime, with an excellent career and education," there is less indication of financial urgency. Time is the factor here. At eighteen the daughter will be too old for a good match.

In each of the stories, marriage is a state that none of the women seeks; rather, it is thrust upon them by parental or social concerns. Shōyō's Otane is not eager for matrimony, yet she is ashamed of her unmarried state. At twenty-two she is late in marrying, and rumor has it that she will not make an adequate bride because she is encumbered with too great an education. When her parents receive an offer from Sadao, a young bureaucrat with a promising career, she is eager to accept—not because of any intrinsic interest in the man or the institution of marriage but because of the envy such a catch will arouse among her peers. Although in Ichiyō's story Oseki's reaction to her impending marriage is evoked only subtly and in retrospect, readers realize that she had been in love with another man from her own social class and was forced to deny her feelings for him out of respect for her parents. Whereas the other daughters are silent in their objections to marriage, Shikin's daughter states her reasons plainly:

> I bit my trembling lip and mustered all my courage. "But since my education is still incomplete, couldn't I have a brief reprieve?" But before I had finished half of what I was to say, Father burst in, glaring at me.
>
> "What? Your education is incomplete, you say? What kind of foolishness is this? Did you not receive a normal education? What is incomplete? Why must you be so disagreeable! You ingrate!"
>
> He raged and Mother glanced at me as if I had said something horrid. I wanted to explain that I had not meant to offend but somehow could not find the words. At last I continued: "I want to go to the Women's Teacher Training School in Tokyo, and . . ." And again Father interrupted:
>
> "What? Teacher's Training School? And then what? You'll become a primary school teacher and spend the rest of your life alone. Do you think it will be easy? Stop saying these . . . these idiotic things." [P. 17]

Despite the daughter's attempt to articulate her desires, she is silenced by her father at every turn. Her sentences are left fragmented, as incomplete as her dreams. Silenced by the father, abandoned by the mother, the daughter has no choice but to submit. Almost before our eyes we see the daughter reduced in size and robbed of will.

Mother and the Daughter's Education

Since education for women was the topic of such debate at the time, it is not surprising that the repercussions of that debate are found in these stories. Ichiyō's

Oseki has no formal education, and her husband despises her for it: "All he ever says is how boring I am, how worthless. He sneers and says he can never have a conversation with me because I don't understand anything."[22] But a formal education does not necessarily lead to happiness. In "The Wife," even though Otane has received an above-average education for a woman, she and Sadao hold no conversations. Her education is shown to be little more than an embell-ishment—and perfectly useless. If anything it is a detriment and an invitation for ridicule. Her stepmother scoffs at her. The maids regard her as hopelessly inadequate to the task of running a household. And the implied author seems to join his characters in their low regard of the heroine and her learning. After all, he provides evidence for the unhappiness that excessive education can bring women. But more important, as Watanabe Sumiko observes, he never allows Otane to "think."[23] It is ironic that Shikin's heroine aspires to just the sort of education that marks her predecessor for scorn and unhappiness. Yet the lack of such an education precludes marital happiness as well.

For Shikin's heroine, and for most women, real education takes place at home: home is where she is schooled in the rigors of self-denial. Shikin's fic-tional daughter, like most of Shikin's peers, received her lessons from the great Confucian classics such as the eighteenth-century treatise on female morality, *Onna daigaku* (Greater Learning for Women), and the Chinese biographies of female paragons. From the latter she learned of women who cut off their ears and noses, who literally whittled themselves away, in demonstrations of fidelity. Others allowed their mothers-in-law to abuse them to death rather than transgress the bonds of filiality: sacrificial lambs every one of them.

The Meiji woman, after all, does not grow up to become a wife: she must grow down to the role. She must, in fact, force herself to disappear into the role. And for Shikin's fictional daughter, as for most women in patriarchal societies, the greatest text for such a lesson is the mother. Shikin's heroine tells us that her mother made herself a living example of the *Onna daigaku*:

> She waited on Father hand and foot, never speaking to him, but treating him
> as some honored guest. . . . Mother regarded Father with such reserve that I
> grew up believing that a woman's lot in life was pathetic indeed. [P. 16]

In teaching by example, the lessons the mother imparts to the daughter are lessons in shame and obedience. Ishimoto Shidzué, in her autobiographical work *Facing Two Ways* (1935), describes the obedience lessons her mother passed along to her:

> Consciously or unconsciously, my mother taught her daughter to crush her
> desires and ambitions, and trained her to be ready to submerge her individu-

ality in her husband's personality and his family's united temper. Girls were to study first of all how to please their husband's parents with absolute obedience. . . . Marriage for the Japanese girl meant losing individual freedom.[24]

Similarly the lesson that Shikin's fictional daughter learns from her mother is, quite literally at times, one of disappearance:

> When I was a child I rarely met anyone other than school chums or family members. Occasionally when a guest came to visit my father, I would hover about the entry hall. But whenever Mother caught me, she would say, "Someone is coming. Quick hide!" It was her custom to lead me into the storeroom. [P. 18]

The Daughter's Betrayal

The lessons the mother passes along to her daughter thwart her early attempts at self-expression and self-determination and leave her feeling stunted, ashamed, and angry. As Adrienne Rich observes in *Of Woman Born*:

> A mother's victimization does not merely humiliate her, it mutilates the daughter who watches her for clues as to what it means to be a woman. Like the traditional foot-bound Chinese woman, she passes on her own affliction. The mother's self-hatred and low expectations are the binding rags for the psyche of the daughter.[25]

For most daughters the mother's "binding rags" are accompanied by a bitter sense of betrayal. In "The Broken Ring" the daughter believes that her mother will help her resist marriage. She trusts that her mother will nurture her desires for self-completion. For three years the mother does what she can to protect her.

> And then, in my fifteenth year, my parents began strongly to promote marriage. Not once, not twice, but again and again until it reached the point where I could not believe they had found another match. I refused and refused but even so they always came back with: "Well, how about this one?" or, "How about that one?" And I was advised here and there about my future. But I persisted in my denials: "No!" "No!" In the beginning my mother did not feel pressed by time and asked my father if we could not look just a bit more. But by the advent of my eighteenth year—"Enough already!"—even she refused to stand in my defense. [P. 16]

When at last her father has exhausted his patience, he blames his wife for their daughter's "selfishness." With the next marriage request he is adamant. The daughter turns to her mother for protection, but to no avail:

My mother was sitting at my side, and I believed she would speak up for me. Was it because she feared Father's authority? Or was it that she was already in agreement with him? She said nothing on my behalf but looked at me worriedly. "Hurry up and say yes!" her eyes implored. [P. 17]

In a "trembling, faltering voice" her mother reasons with her until the daughter relents: "If it had been now I would not have been so easily convinced. But I was an innocent girl. Still, I find it strange that I did not resist more forcefully. . . . I did not know what I should say, and so I simply responded yes" (p. 18). When the daughter discovers that even her mother has deserted her—the one on whom she had depended for protection—she is all the more devastated and thus rendered incapable of defending herself. She has been denied any model in life but submission.

In Shōyō's "The Wife," the mother's betrayal takes place prior to the narrative, for the mother is already dead. She has been removed from the narrative—into perpetual silence. Unable to protect her daughter, her place is usurped by a stepmother who, in her shrillness, denies the daughter a voice. When Otane returns to her natal home, determined to leave her philandering husband, it is the stepmother who sends her back and ensures that the father will not "hear" his daughter's complaints. In somewhat of a reversal, Oseki's mother in "The Thirteenth Night" is quick to voice her indignation at Isamu's unjust treatment of her daughter. She flies to her daughter's defense and is prepared to take her home. But her angry voice is quickly quieted by the father ("Now, Mother, don't say anything rash") and his "reasonable arguments."[26] In each story we find attempts by the daughter to speak—attempts that are either silenced by the paternal authority (in the case of "Broken Ring" and "Thirteenth Night") or else never really heard ("The Wife").

Unable to make herself heard by the paternal authority, abandoned by the mother, the woman is as good as mute. And Otane's story ends in mute defeat. She leaves her husband and has no more story. Her silence is tragically embodied by the maid who, as a "contributor" to Otane's failure, drowns herself in the well. The husband, we learn, soon marries his French mistress. Things do not end well for Oseki, either. When her mother's attempt to speak for her daughter is silenced, Oseki is remanded to a wordless world of living death. She personifies her mother's silence by living it: by living a life that has no voice: "If I could think of myself as already dead, that would solve everything. . . . From tonight I will consider myself dead."[27] Oseki's avowal seems to echo the eighteenth-century Shingaku scripture: "A bride must become like a dead person."[28] Oseki, we assume, will persevere as a wifely ideal: patient, self-sacrificing, and silent. But the price of her silence has been plainly spoken.

Shikin's heroine falls into the bonds of silence as well. Her attempts to express herself, as we have seen, are rendered incoherent. Stifled by her father and abandoned by her mother, she is forced into the confines of marriage, just as surely as she was forced earlier into the silent darkness of the storeroom. Dutiful daughter that she is, Shikin's heroine learns to deny her natural instincts. When her husband begins to spend nights with another woman, she does not protest. She simply endures: a paragon of fidelity, pure, patient, suffering nobly. She is a sheep.

In the other two stories the wives are equally humiliated by their husbands. Generally this humiliation stems from his infidelities and from the fact that the entire household is now privy to her "shortcomings." Unable to bear more abuse, the wife returns to her natal home—to the mother (or at least to her place)—where she attempts to unburden herself of her pain. But when Shikin's heroine returns to her mother, she does so in noble silence. She does not give voice to her frustrations. And yet her mother senses her pain:

> As a female parent, Mother was quick to guess the situation. Whenever I visited, which was infrequently, she would see my sunken cheeks, my poor color, and ask: "Are you troubled by something? Wait until your father returns and discuss it with him. I'm only your mother and can't be of much help."
>
> "What?" I would respond, "No, there's no need to worry." Even though such fine words flew out of my mouth, the tears coursing down my cheeks like a waterfall were more honest than I in relating the truth. Not wishing her to see, I would dab quickly at my eyes with a handkerchief. But when I turned with feigned indifference toward her, I noticed that the corners of her eyes were already red. [P. 21]

Checked by patriarchal demands of submission, the mother is divested of even her most basic maternal instincts. Reduced to an ideal, she has no authority to help her daughter. Nor can she avail herself of the potential potency of the mother/daughter bond. Moreover, speech itself has been placed beyond the mother's reach. Denied access to their own (female) language, mother and daughter have forgotten how to speak in any but the father tongue. And the father tongue precludes female self-expression. Reduced to a language of silence—a language mediated through tears and shared experience—the daughter is powerless to tell her story, and the story she does not tell is enough to kill her mother. Unable to act, deprived of a voice, the mother's only recourse is death. By dying she is able to express at last her deep remorse at her daughter's unhappiness. But death is, after all, a noncommunicative act—an act of profound silence. By all rights Shikin's story should end here in sad submission to the inevitable bleakness of female existence.

Death of the Mother, Birth of a Heroine

The mother's death marks the true beginning of the daughter's life. In fact, the daughter's story is dependent upon her death, as the daughter cannot construct a life beyond her mother's until she has been released from the "binding rags" that have held her in silence. So long as the mother is alive, the daughter is tied to her by bonds of loyalty and love: "In the beginning Mother wanted to settle my affairs quickly for assurance sake and I, knowing how she worried, wanted to give her peace of mind, so I agreed to this unwanted marriage" (p. 21). The mother is the end of that story. But once the mother is removed from the story, the daughter is liberated from the model the mother represents.

To quote Marianne Hirsch: "Mothers—the ones who are not singular, who did succumb to convention inasmuch as they are mothers—thereby become the targets of this process of disidentification and the primary negative models for the daughter."[29] The daughter must not become her mother. She must, in fact, not "mother"—for to do so would mean the end of her story. Implotted firmly in the patriarchal narrative, the mother can have no plot of her own. Ichiyō's Oseki is a poignant example of the closure that is motherhood. Had she not had the child, she might have found a way to leave her husband. But tied by the demands of motherhood, she has lost her power to create a person of her own. She has no voice and must harbor no anger. It is, indeed, as Hirsch concludes: "The active, angry, rebellious woman cannot be a mother; the mother can be neither active nor rebellious."[30]

"Motherlessness" in both senses of the word, then, means freedom for Shikin's heroine. It frees her from her mother as exemplar and allows her to seek alternatives. She abandons her mother's "Chinese paragons" for an "Occidental" ideal of emancipation. More important, motherlessness frees Shikin's heroine from the protective silence her mother love had imposed and allows, even authorizes, anger: "Then marriage became my enemy; and when I thought that it might have shortened my mother's life, my heart felt as if it would be torn asunder" (p. 21). Having been trapped in marriage by love for her mother, the heroine is now paradoxically freed from her bonds by that same love. For, as Wada Shigejirō intimates, following the mother's death, the husband, who was the catalyst for the worry that shortened her life, becomes a veritable murderer.[31] The heroine's desire to leave him is thus transformed from an unfilial reaction to a filial one.

While struggling to solidify her resolve, the heroine begins reading newly published books and magazines. Unlike Shōyō's heroine, who is educated but does not "think," Shikin's heroine cultivates her mind and suddenly becomes aware of a world far beyond her marital enclosure. It is just at this time that discussions of women's rights are gathering momentum, and the protagonist becomes engrossed in the debate:

> Misfortune and sorrow, it was argued, were not by any means a woman's inherent state. . . . Before long Occidental theories of the rights of women had penetrated my brain and I began to believe that Japanese women, too, ought to attain happiness. . . . Up to this point, I had obeyed a Chinese ethic of passive resignation whereby it was deemed best to put up with anything, to sacrifice happiness. But after this period, I could no longer countenance this approach. [P. 22]

Shikin's heroine will not become a woman like her mother. Rather, she tries to remonstrate with her husband—to change *him:*

> My husband was quite a few years older than I and had accumulated infinitely more experience in matters great and sundry. As a result, he found it difficult to accept anything I said. Whenever I began to broach the subject he would snort: "My! Such a learned speech from the likes of a woman!" With a word he would cancel out all that I had said. [Ibid.]

When her husband refuses to hear her, she decides on divorce. She does not will herself into a living death like Oseki; nor does she disappear from the narrative like Otane. Shikin's heroine rejects the romantic image of the unhappy wife. "Japanese women," she asserts, "must realize that they too can make full the happiness with which they have been naturally endowed" (ibid). Sorrow, she tells us, despite prevailing opinion, is not inherent to women. In describing a woman who rises above her unhappy domestic situation, therefore, Shikin's work runs counter to those by Shōyō, Ichiyō, and other contemporary writers of marriage narratives. By giving her heroine a voice, by allowing her to live beyond marriage, Shikin violates the patriarchal code of the wifely ideal and perpetrates a "feminist act."

Critical Reception

Readers of *Jogaku zasshi* were ready for a "feminist act." Copies of the New Year's issue of the journal sold out, and Iwamoto Yoshiharu had Shikin's story printed along with another in a separate volume that sold briskly at five sen a copy. Reviews of the work soon appeared in a variety of journals and papers. Overwhelmingly positive, they focused on three points: narrative voice, language, and theme.

Shikin had written "The Broken Ring" entirely in *genbun itchi,* and one might expect contemporary critics to fault her for it. After all, Miyake Kaho before her had been castigated for recording the speech of household servants in a narrative that was otherwise appropriately *wabun*. Wakamatsu Shizuko, however, had just one year earlier been successful in her creation of a *genbun itchi* style in "Wasuregatami" (The Keepsake), her translation of Adelaide Anne Proctor's "The Sailor Boy," thus establishing a precedent for Shikin's experiment. With the exception of a review by Mori Ōgai, however, Shikin's language was hardly noted.

Ōgai, who had experimented briefly with *genbun itchi* himself before abandoning it, observed that Shikin's "so-called *genbun itchi* style" did not have "the grammatical consistency of a Bimyō nor the polish of a Saganoya." He criticized her for mistakes in usage of kana and particles. "Even with *genbun itchi*," he cautioned, "one must not overlook grammatical structure."[32] Komashaku Kimi, in agreement with Ōgai, notes that Shikin's writing was rough and uneven,[33] though in a sense this lack of polish only enhanced the novelty and realism of her account. Ōgai was quick to admit that he did find her writing close to "the feel of natural speech."[34]

Most of the critics were more concerned with Shikin's use of the first-person voice and her portrayal of divorce than they were with her choice of language. Kōda Rohan, writing for the *Kokkai shinbun* (Parlimentary News), considered the story an allegory *(hiyu)* which "lambastes the foolish parents of the world who selfishly oppress [their children]. . . . It is a pity that the author sees the old customs [of marriage] as the basis of unhappiness, while failing to recognize that it is the new ideals that contribute to the unhappiness of [divorce]."[35]

Both Rohan and Taguchi Teiken, in a review for *Keizai zasshi* (Economic Journal), concur that Shikin would have done well to provide further examples of the husband's cruelty. As it was, they did not feel the reasons for the divorce were adequately explicated.[36] Ōgai, as well, refers to the "first wife" in the story *(saki no okusan)* as a "mistress," thus failing to read the husband as a bigamist. Even those who did refused to see bigamy as sufficient grounds for divorce. The practice of maintaining two wives, though illegal, was not particularly unusual at the time.

Ishibashi Ningetsu and Uchida Roan say that the work reads like an autobiography because of Shikin's unusual choice of a first-person narrator. Both, however, offer oblique apologies for suggesting that it might be. None of the critics knew of Shikin or her life story.[37] Not only might it be considered scandalous to link an accomplished female writer with a divorcée,[38] regardless of the circumstances for the divorce, but the very notion of female self-presentation was somehow suspect.

In 1992 Takada Chinami pointed out that Shikin was indebted to Wakamatsu Shizuko for the first-person narrative as well as for the *genbun itchi* style.[39] The opening sentence to "The Broken Ring" is structurally almost identical to that of "The Keepsake." The latter opens with the following question:

> *Anata boku no rireki wo hanase tte ossharu no?*
> (You say you wish me to speak of my past history?)

Whereas Shikin's narrative opens:

> *Anata wa watashi no kono yubiwa no tama ga nukete orimasuno ga o-ki-ni-kakaru no?*
> (You have noticed that my ring has lost its stone?)

Although the narrative is rendered in the first person and the situations are strikingly similar to events in Shikin's life, "The Broken Ring" is no more autobiography than is "The Keepsake." Yamaguchi Reiko has shown that Shikin keeps her account purposely vague and unspecified.[40] Her own father was a prominent Kyoto bureaucrat. But the father in her story is unnamed and unparticularized. He is everywoman's autocratic father; the mother is everywoman's submissive mother; the husband is everywoman's philandering husband; and the narrator herself, with her everywoman's education in the Confucian classics of the day, is the kind of *hako-iri musume* that everywoman (at least everywoman of this social class) could have identified with—and many did. Sōma Kokkō writes that she first read the work when she was fifteen:

> I loved literature at the time and the mere idea of a work by a woman writer made my heart pound. . . . The story told of a woman's suffering and did so without artifice or embellishment. And though I was yet a young girl unversed in the ways of passion, I sympathized deeply with the heroine.[41]

Whether "The Broken Ring" was read by contemporary critics as autobiography or not, it seems the import of the story was generally overlooked. Some critics, such as Uchida Roan, thought the husband was the story's true protagonist.[42] Rohan read the work as an allegory, Ōgai as lyrical *(jojōteki)* fiction, and others as a protest against the marriage system. Although these readings (perhaps with the exception of Roan's) are all valid, they seem to miss the point. The story is much more than a protest. It is even more than a celebration of a woman's awakening. The point of the story is the "broken ring" and all that it signifies for the narrator.

Symbols of Sacrifice

In her analysis of "The Broken Ring," Imai Yasuko presents statistics indicating that divorce in Japan was not uncommon during the Meiji era. In fact, between 1882 and 1921 the divorce rate there was much higher than that of the United States, Denmark, England, or Sweden.[43] But what Imai's figures do not reveal is the percentage of those divorces that were initiated by women or the effect that divorce had on the women involved. For Shōyō's heroine, divorce is a mark of shame—a shame made worse if it is the husband who divorces the wife. Otane is eager, therefore, to leave Sadao before he can leave her. Divorce for Otane is not so much a choice as an inevitability; it is a course of action she does not determine but accepts "for the sake of her family."

Even so, divorce at the time was hardly a recourse for women. Those who sought divorce on justifiable grounds were held up for rebuke. When Yajima Kajiko left her alcoholic and abusive husband and set out on her own, her nephews Tokutomi Sohō and Tokutomi Roka—supposedly liberal men— were highly critical. That Shikin's heroine not only seeks and obtains divorce of her own volition but advertises her divorced state for all to see was at the time a highly provocative act. Her broken ring, therefore, becomes a symbol of female rebellion:

> You have noticed that my ring has lost its stone? It is, just as you say, unsightly to wear—broken as it is. Perhaps I might exchange it for another? No, for me this ring, in its broken state, is a sign, and I cannot possibly exchange it. [P. 14]

The ring had been introduced into Meiji Japan as a symbol of perfect conjugal love—along with the Christian marital union as the marriage ideal. Articles concerning both notions had appeared frequently in the pages of *Jogaku zasshi*.[44] The ring in this story, however, was not a marriage token: "It was not what is known these days as a wedding ring. [My husband] just bought it for me for no particular reason" (p. 15). The heroine's ring, like her marriage, is devoid of meaning. And like the marriage, the ring is given meaning only when it is broken. When the couple divorces after three or four years of marriage, the heroine removes the gemstone. By destroying the ring, she renders it significant. And in the process she makes of it a complex and contradictory symbol:

> Every time I look at this ring, I feel greater pain than if my entrails were sliced in two. And this is why I cannot be parted from my ring, not even for a second. Why? Because this ring is my benefactor. And how is that?

Because thanks to the pain and sorrow this ring has given me, it has forced me to arouse the zeal I need to become a full-fledged human being. For me there can be no greater inspiration than this ring. It has called forth my spirit and multiplied my courage. . . . When others look at this ring, I suppose they see something unsightly. But to me it is priceless, not to be exchanged for a million dollars. . . . You don't yet know my life story, do

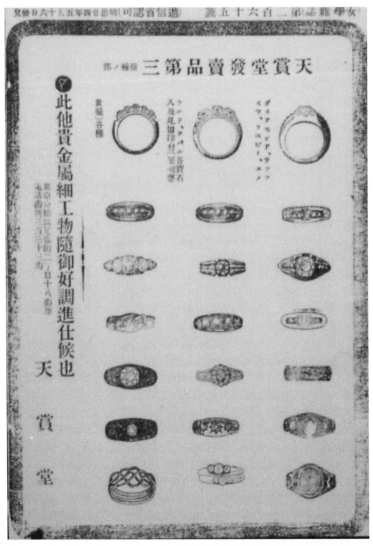

Figure 18   Advertisement for rings on the back cover of *Jogaku zasshi*, May 16, 1891.

you? Well, in fact, my life resembles this broken ring. . . . At one point I looked at this ring and cried tears of despair, believing that I was as pathetic as it. But I soon came to my senses. . . . This broken ring—alas, one hundred years from now will people finally come to understand the value this ring possesses? [Pp. 14–15]

Valueless as it may appear, the broken ring symbolizes the devaluation of women in divorce—and, more important, of women in marriage. But it also represents the woman's determination to seek her own value elsewhere: to mend her own broken state. As a child she had to break her dreams, her will, her pride, to make herself acceptable for marriage. The ring, then, reminds her of her broken dreams, her broken voice, and finally her broken silence, for now she will speak. Marriage might have forced her into hiding, but divorce allows her to remove her mask. The broken ring thus represents her freedom and self-establishment—qualities that can only be gained through the woman's willingness to deny social and financial comforts.

The narrator is no stranger to female self-denial, of course, and she is not averse to self-sacrifice. Indeed, she is willing to make a martyr of herself—but not for a worthless man. Shikin's heroine sacrifices herself for those pure jewellike maidens, "those countless pitiable young girls, so that they . . . will not fall into the trap as did I" (p. 23). She sacrifices herself for love.

Understanding this point illuminates the final statement in the story: "I have but one more wish, that the one who gave me this ring might make it new again. But at this late date, I wonder if . . ." (ibid). A narrative that began with a woman's voice breaking an ancient silence ends with a broken sentence as the woman's resolve trails off, or so it would seem. It is tempting to read the conclusion as a retraction of the narrator's earlier feminist stance. Just when the woman seemed certain of her own voice, that voice falters, and the story sighs into silence. Yamaguchi Reiko confesses: "The final lines of the story shock me. No matter how often I read them, they still wrest my heart away. I wonder, is it because this conclusion reveals the nakedness of the human condition? Is it because even within this whisper of a narrative there is a deeper truth?"[45]

Nagamatsu Fusako suggests that the final line is "camouflage"—a coy attempt to soften the threatening implication of the story's feminist message.[46] Sasabuchi Tomoichi lends credence to Nagamatsu's reading by noting that the closure reveals a very feminine grace in the heroine: "And yet, what has been done cannot be undone."[47] Perhaps the closure is an opening. The narrator remains open to love. She despaired of her marriage, not simply because her husband was insensitive, but because it had never been premised on love *(ai)*. She had not loved him nor he her: "When I see modern couples today [who can marry for love], I wonder why my husband had not loved me nor I him. And my broken ring gives evidence to my feelings" (p. 23). Thus "The Broken Ring" is not simply an allegory or a protest of contemporary marriage practices. Shikin's heroine is not opposed to these practices, per se, but to the result they invite: loveless marriages. Marriage, for this woman, is possible only through love. She is waiting to be fulfilled by love. She is willing to sacrifice herself for love.

To Marry for Love

"Love," of the profound, spiritual variety eventually to be known as *"ren'ai,"* was the single most discussed subject among the young male poets and female students in the 1880s and 1890s and largely the catalyst for the romantic movement in Japanese letters. Iwamoto Yoshiharu had sung the praises of "love" between the sexes, of the "Christian *hōmu,"* and of marriage based on mutual admiration and respect between two equals. Wakamatsu Shizuko had written of the spiritual purity of platonic love in her 1889 story "Sumire." In 1888 she and Iwamoto had engaged in an exchange of "love poems" in the pages of *Jogaku zasshi.* Portraying a love of more fleshy consequences, Mori Ōgai in "Maihime" (The Dancing Girl, 1890) and the subsequent "Utakata no ki" (Like Foam on the Waves, 1890) awakened Meiji youth to the beautiful anguish love wreaked. Young poets yearned for muse-like women to whom they might devote a worshipful solicitude. Young women in mission schools and Christian-founded private academies dreamed of sensitive husbands who would cherish them. In sensational cases some ran away or elected suicide over the marriages their parents had arranged for them, earning these schools reputations as training grounds for promiscuity. Many sought *ren'ai.* No one, it seems could secure it, thus imbuing the entire dialectic with a romantic fatalism.

Shikin, too, was drawn into contemporary discussions of love—both professionally and personally. Following her surprisingly successful debut, she busied herself with essays and editorials advocating greater freedom in marriage and did not produce another work of fiction for nearly two years.[48] Yamaguchi concludes that Shikin found her mission in her work for the journal and her campaigning for women's rights. Although she did not return immediately to the venue of fiction, therefore, she was nevertheless busy writing, working in this way to "protect the fate of the countless pitiable young girls" from loveless marriages.

Shikin was also preoccupied with personal matters at this time. Most biographers conclude that she was now enmeshed in her affair with Ōi Kentarō, an affair that most likely had begun in the fall of the previous year. Shikin had entered into a relationship with Ōi of her own choosing and with the mutual understanding that they were equals. Her relationship with him was thus quite unlike the one she had shared with her husband. Wada even goes so far as to suggest that Shikin's affair with Ōi inspired her to write "The Broken Ring." For having now tasted "love" for the first time, she was sharply aware of its absence in her first marriage.[49] Shortly after publishing "The Broken Ring," Shikin discovered that she was pregnant with Ōi's child. Their relationship grew strained. Although it seems Ōi was willing to take responsibility for the situation, Shikin was not interested in marriage. Perhaps allowing the relationship to evolve into a sexual affair had been a mistake. But for Shikin it was a mistake she had made of her own volition. She did not wish to compound the problem by marrying.

In April 1891 Shikin's father fell ill and she was required to return to Kyoto to nurse him. She had planned to leave her post in Tokyo for only a week or two. But once in Kyoto, she realized that given her own situation, it would be best for her to take a much longer leave of absence. She gave notice and was relieved of her duties on the jounal and at the school. That summer she and her father returned to their ancestral home in Okayama. She delivered her son there on November 26, 1891. The boy was adopted by her elder brother, and Shikin returned to Tokyo with her secret secure.[50] She fell ill shortly after her return, however, and had to be hospitalized from January to March. Apparently her illness was brought on by mental distress. The wages of defiance had taken their toll. For it seems the strain of nursing her father, giving birth to an illegitimate child, and enduring in silence what was most likely postpartum depression was just too much to bear. After struggling to regain her health and composure, she was released in late March and invited to stay once again with the Sasakis. Toyosu was planning to emigrate to Hokkaido and invited Shikin to join her. The offer was tempting. Shikin needed an escape at that point. She had just received the letter Ōi had intended for Fukuda Hideko—and, conversely, Hideko had received hers. Ōi was pressuring her to marry him. Hideko was accusing her of betrayal. Shikin suffered a relapse and was hospitalized once again in April.

Her elder brother had by this time become an assistant at the Tokyo School of Agriculture and, as he was living in Komaba, then on the outskirts of Tokyo, was able to visit Shikin regularly. At some point he brought with him Kozai Yoshinao, who was on the faculty of the Tokyo School of Agriculture and lived on the Komaba campus. Yoshinao began corresponding with Shikin. Clearly he was falling in love with her. In his letters he confessed that she was the first woman he had ever "looked up to" or "felt respect for." He urged her to open her heart to him: "Let us remove all barriers between our hearts."[51] Shikin was alarmed. She was a woman with a past, and Yoshinao was most definitely a man with a future. She feared that his continued association with her would damage his reputation. At a time when it was even unseemly for widows to remarry, a divorced woman's prospects were dismal. "Good women" simply did not take two husbands, and men concerned for their own reputation did not associate intimately with women who did. Against the fervent objections of her friends, who feared she would ruin herself socially, Shikin vowed to tell Yoshinao the truth about herself. "I have fallen to the deepest depths, stricken with despair. My body is damaged, my name soiled."[52] She imagined that he had already heard rumors, and she assumed that once he had learned all the details, he would have nothing more to do with her. But Shikin's plan backfired. When Yoshinao heard her confession, his respect and ardor for her multiplied. He found that he was all the more impressed with her purity, with her honesty and strength, and with the way she had borne her trials with integrity and grace. He countered her confession with a long letter of his own in which he described his marriage ideals. He intended her to be not just a marriage partner but a lifelong friend. He reminded her that he had fallen in love with the woman she was now. He was not interested in marrying whomever she might have been.

A Young Man's Surprising Reminiscences

Yoshinao's romantic pursuit inspired Shikin's next literary work, "Ichi seinen iyō no jukkai" (A Young Man's Surprising Reminiscences), which she published in the October 22, 1892, issue of *Jogaku zasshi*. Once again she used the pen name Tsuyuko, and once again she employed a first-person narration. But similarity to "The Broken Ring" ends here. The narrator of "A Young Man's Surprising Reminiscences" is a young man. And unlike the *genbun itchi* of "The Broken Ring," the narrative style of this piece appropriates the classical diction and syntax an educated man would employ in his journal or correspondence. And where the earlier story described a woman wrestling with the absence of love, this one portrays a man grappling with the presence of love. The reminiscence opens with a preface signed by "Tsuyuko":

> Most who write of love [*ren'ai*] have never experienced it themselves. They are like amateur pilots guiding their hapless readers along the channels and currents of their imagination. How much more true this is when a man writes of a woman's love, or a woman of a man's. If the pilot makes an error in guiding his ship it could result in the loss of life. If the writer makes a mistake, he earns the laughter of his readers. But I shall make bold and proceed all the same with my account. I do not propose to discourse on love in all its manifestations. I will offer what little I have discovered in my own experiences, and I will leave it to my readers to conclude whether I am right or wrong.[53]

After this humble disclaimer, Shikin allows her male narrator to take the stage and offer his reminiscences:

> Why is it that my heart is so completely captivated by her? It has been but days since first we met, and yet she is all I think about. . . . Up to this point, I had thought myself a stalwart man, yet in her presence I become a quivering maiden. I can only long for her to give me a command, for I would offer her my life. For her I would consign my character and conceit to the fires of destruction. [P. 25]

Most critics believe Kozai Yoshinao to be the model for this narrator—and, indeed, Shikin did cull her account from the letters he had sent her and, more significantly, from a short story he had penned for her shortly before she was released from the hospital.[54] Yet as Wada Shigejirō has shown, Shikin imbues this compilation with her own wishful longings, and her readings from Western romances, to create a lover ideal.

In his short story, Yoshinao describes a man who is experiencing love for the first time. Confused by the way love torments him, he struggles to understand its source and concludes that rather than the woman's external beauty, it is her spiritual beauty that has so disarmed him. Shikin's narrator, like Yoshinao's, enumerates his lady's attractions and similarly concludes that she harbors a spiritual beauty. Shikin goes much further than Yoshinao, however, in exploring this woman's spiritual purity and its effect on her paramour. Her narrator turns the woman into a virtual goddess and speaks of her with a Christian-inspired adoration: "Her person emits a radiant light. She purifies others, transforms them into gentle creatures" (p. 26). Before this paragon, Shikin's hero would gladly humble himself for life: "Indeed, worthless though I am, I feel I have already died and am now reborn, particle by particle, in her love. Because of her and her alone I am allowed to live" (ibid).

Yoshinao's narrator, though similarly devoted to the object of his affection, seems more interested in winning her than worshiping her. In his story we are told that when the woman deflects his advances, claiming that she is unworthy of his love, his ardor is inflamed and though his actions may prove an "offence against god," he tears through the "invisible iron wall" that had separated them.[55] Though Yoshinao writes again and again in his letters of his profound respect for Shikin, Wada notes that he also describes his feverish love *(netsujō)*.[56] His love may be pure but it is also physical. Shikin's hero, by contrast, manifests a love that supersedes the flesh. His goal is not so much to break through barriers and possess the woman as it is to commune with her on an elevated spiritual level—though not necessarily on an equal level. By transforming her lady into a goddess,

Shikin places her above and beyond the reach of the man. Thus she preserves her spiritual beauty indefinitely.

A number of months before Shikin wrote "Reminisences," and indeed during much of the time that Yoshinao was corresponding with her, the Meiji literary world was reeling from the appearance of several essays by Kitamura Tōkoku celebrating the purity and spiritual wonder of love. The first of these essays, "Ensei shika to josei" (The Pessimistic Poet and Women), appeared in *Jogaku zasshi* in two parts on February 6 and 20, 1892. While describing the irreconcilable conflicts that poets encounter between love and marriage, the essay positioned a profound love *(ren'ai)* between men and women as a spiritual ideal, thus legitimating a relationship between the sexes that exceeds the carnal. Tōkoku's championing of love as the pure and ultimate goal of humanity challenged earlier Confucian notions of self-effacement, filial duty, and emotional restraint. Yet his timing was right. For many of his generation, raised on the romanticism of the West, were hungry for a rationale that allowed a heterosexual love of a higher order. As Kinoshita Naoe wrote: "When I first read [Tōkoku's opening line] 'Love is the secret key to life,' I felt I'd been shot with a cannon. This was the first time in our country that love had been considered with such earnestness."[57]

This is not to suggest, of course, that love had never been a topic in Japanese literature. Indeed, as Tsubouchi Shōyō had declared, love *(ninjō)* was the basis of the novel. But the love Shōyō had imagined, as described in Chapter Two, was frequently tied to the brothels, and the object of the hero's desire was typically a courtesan, geisha, or mistress. Love, therefore, was conflated with sexuality, with the flesh, with the licentiousness of an earlier age, rendering "love stories" off limits to most women. Iwamoto Yoshiharu, in introducing Shizuko's translation of *Little Lord Fauntleroy* as a "love story," had invented a literary space for love that precluded the sexual. This space was shortly assigned, however, to the Children's Column. Tōkoku's bold equation of love and spirituality (rather than sensuality) freed heterosexual love from the confines of the brothel and made it a literary topic accessible to women.

Tōkoku followed this essay with "Wa ga rōgoku" (My Prison), also published in *Jogaku zasshi*. In first-person narrative form, Tōkoku describes a prisoner of love:

> I will make a confession. When she and I first exchanged glances I lost half my soul; it entered her, and half her soul, broken off from the rest, entered me. I possess half of her, and half of myself; she possesses half of me and half of herself. . . . Until our two severed souls are joined together neither she nor I can be said to possess a complete soul.[58]

Shikin's creation of an ideal love has much in common, therefore, with the dialogue on love and spirituality begun by Iwamoto and Shizuko and popularized by Tōkoku. Shikin's creation of an ideal male lover borrows as much from Tōkoku as from Yoshinao. Her lady is not unlike Shizuko's Sumire Mano, who similarly held herself above and beyond the reach of her male suitor and thus maintained her purity. Tōkoku would later write of the purity of the virginal woman, however, and this is where he and Shikin part company. Shikin's heroine's purity is divorced from her physicality. Indeed, the more wounded she is in the flesh, the purer she is in the eyes of her admirer. The basis of love for both participants in the story is their willingness to sacrifice for the other. The lady/goddess sacrifices by pronouncing herself unworthy of the man's love and exposing her sordid past, opening herself to humiliation and rejection. The man in turn sacrifices by refusing to adhere to social expectations. Rather than repudiating the woman, he deifies her.

In her creation of a hero who adores his love all the more for qualities that others would despise, Shikin absolves herself of her past. Like Wakamatsu Shizuko before her, she uses *Jogaku zasshi* as a forum for the presentation of her own intimate confession. Just as Shizuko had taken Iwamoto's words and made them hers through translation in "The Complaint," Shikin takes Yoshinao's profession of love and makes it her own. By revealing herself to Yoshinao as a woman worthy of love, indeed a woman worthy of worship, she also shows herself to be a woman capable of love. As Yoshinao's story was not published in *Jogaku zasshi* and presumably not available to a public readership, Shikin's incorporation of this private document in her own public literary creation suggests a personal declaration of love, the true import of which would have been known only to Yoshinao and perhaps their small circle of intimates.

The reminiscence was "surprising," therefore, on a number of levels. It was surprising that a man would feel such devotion to a woman in an era when "revere men/despise women" was still very much the norm. His confession of this devotion, therefore, was equal to the woman's confession in "The Broken Ring" of her divorce. Both were shocking admissions. It was also surprising that Shikin would take Yoshinao's confession and restructure it to present her own sense of self-worth and purity while at the same time covertly revealing her past for an audience that—knowing her from "The Broken Ring" (that is, knowing "Tsuyuko")—was vaguely aware of her divorce.

Despite dissimilarities between "Reminiscences" and "The Broken Ring," therefore, the former is the logical sequel to the earlier story. When "The Broken Ring" concludes, the narrator is despairing of ever knowing "love." Indeed, the entire story is a discourse on the brokenness of a loveless marriage and the emptiness of the traditional marital system.

"Reminiscences," however, makes true the promise of the ring by restoring to it the gemstone of love.

Nevertheless, Wada and other critics have read "Reminiscences" as a step backward for Shikin because the language she employed was "old-fashioned." True, she did hark back to a form of *gabuntai* or classical prose. But her prose is enriched by both *kanbun* (Chinese) and Western expressions to form a style known as "*wakan'yō gabuntai*." Phrases such as "I would gladly humble myself before her" are clearly derivative of Western translations, for example, while those like "my eyes swam, my lips trembled, my ears rang" are structurally Chinese. Mori Ōgai had employed a similar style in his "Dancing Girl," as had Tōkoku in his essays on love. The style was by no means Shikin's creation. But as Yasuyuki Ogikubo has pointed out, it was unusual for a woman to adopt this style and, moreover, to do so with such finesse.[59] It should be remembered that Shikin had had plenty of experience as a girl with both *kanbun* and Western translations. In a sense, then, Shikin's use of this particular type of *gabuntai* was just as innovative as her earlier use of *genbun itchi*. Both were, after all, styles normally off limits to female writers.

Seeking the Modern Murasaki

With Iwamoto Yoshiharu and Wakamatsu Shizuko standing by as witnesses, Shikin married Kozai Yoshinao shortly after the publication of "A Young Man's Surprising Reminiscences." They set up housekeeping on the Komaba campus and welcomed their first son on September 17, 1893. By this time, *Jogaku zasshi* had undergone its division into Red and White issues and Shikin had assumed responsibility for Red Covers. Writing primarily under the pen name Shōno Fumiko, she devoted herself to the household column, which offered information on childcare, childbirth, nursing, food and clothing, bookkeeping, market prices, and economics. Writing from experience, we can assume, Shikin contributed articles on "How to Select a Wet Nurse," "Tips for Nursing a Baby," "Communicating with Mother-in-Law," "Delicious Sweet Potatoes," "Laws for Household Governance," and "How to Manage Servants."

It might seem a regression for a woman who had spoken so ardently for equal rights to now be penning a column on a woman's domestic duties. But perhaps rather than regression, Shikin's efforts exemplify her awareness of reality. By 1893 the Japanese national state *(kokutai)* was firmly in place and Shikin's shift from *jokenron* (advocation of equal rights) to *tenshokuron* (advocation of a woman's natural mission) was inevitable. Women in 1893 had little alternative but to comply with state policies, which would have them endeavoring to be "good wives and wise mothers."[60] Rather than complaining about the victimization of women, Shikin found it more constructive to help women gain a modicum of control over their lives. And she found that such gains could begin in the kitchen. She offered recipes for quick and easy dinners. Since cookbooks were not as ubiquitous as they are today, the advice she gave was intended to ease—if only slightly—a woman's daily toil. While trying to aid the frazzled housewife and make her feel proud of her duties, Shikin also managed, whenever possible, to slip in her own brand of humanism. In her article advising women on how to deal with household servants, for example, she reminds her readers that "servants are human, too."[61] Her statement may seem curiously obvious today. But as Yamaguchi points out, in an age when class barriers were still rigid her argument that servants should be treated with respect was hardly the norm.[62]

While in their third year of marriage, Yoshinao accepted a grant from the Ministry of Education to study in Europe. His contract was for three years. He left on March 22, 1895. Shikin took her small son and moved to Hanazono in Kyoto, where she lived with Yoshinao's mother. She continued to contribute to *Jogaku zasshi*, now as a freelance contributor rather than an editor. Her most significant work at this time was *Hanazono zuihitsu* (Essays from Hanazono), which she serialized sporadically from November 25, 1895, to April 10, 1899. This series of essays consisted primarily of recollections and revelations in her daily contact with her son. Unlike Shikin's earlier essays on marriage and equal rights, *Essays from Hanazono* is written with a graceful simplicity. In the following passage she describes one of the many walks she takes with her two-year-old son:

> "What's that?" "What's that?" the little one asks me over and over again as we take our stroll. On an earlier evening he had pointed out the moon, and I had answered, "That's the moon." Tonight the little one spied the quarter moon and asked, "What's that?" "That's the moon," I replied without thinking. He looked puzzled. "Then what about the other moon?" he asked. I thought for a minute trying to fathom what he meant. Then I realized that the last time he had asked about the moon it had been full. He found it peculiar that the full moon and the quarter moon should share the same name.[63]

In the summer of 1896 Shikin returned to fiction. She began to publish with some regularity, almost every other month, and in journals other than *Jogaku zasshi*. More important, she began to use the pen name Shikin. Why this sudden flurry of literary activity? Some speculate that she may have found herself with more time on her hands now that her husband was away and she was no longer writing regularly for *Jogaku zasshi*. Others suggest that she needed the extra income. As can be gauged from Natsume Sōseki's experience as a grantee of the Japanese government in England, the funds for life abroad were far from sufficient. Now with a son to provide for, it is likely that Shikin and her husband found their finances strained.

Yamaguchi Reiko, however, offers another explanation. Women's writing in the early Meiji had reached a crescendo in 1896. *Bungei kurabu* had published its highly successful *keishū* issue in the winter of 1895. Kitada Usurai and Tazawa Inafune, two of Shikin's literary peers, were at their most fecund, publishing close to twenty works between them in 1895–1896 alone. Moreover, Higuchi Ichiyō was then at her peak and dazzling critics with "Takekurabe" (Growing Up), "The Thirteenth Night," and other works. But if 1896 represents the height of activity for women writers, it also suggests the beginning of its decline. Wakamatsu Shizuko died in February, Tazawa Inafune in September, Higuchi Ichiyō in November. Yamaguchi suggests that Shikin was profoundly moved by the strides these three had made in advancing the role of women in modern letters and thus felt obliged to fill the gap they had left.[64] "Where is the Modern Murasaki hiding? Where the Meiji Shōnagon?" she had asked in an 1890 *Jogaku zasshi* essay on the state of women's writing in Japan—and Shizuko, Ichiyō, and others had stepped forth to answer her challenge. Now that they had vanished from the literary arena, she offered herself in their stead and elected for her new penname, appropriately enough, "Shikin." The characters she chose were *"murasaki"* (purple) and *"koto"* (harp), words that virtually pulsate with classical nuance. But as Komashaku Kimi suggests, the *"kin"* of Shikin could also be read with the meaning of "now" or "modern" *(ima)*—as if Shikin indeed were declaring herself "the modern Murasaki."[65]

Shikin's presumed enthusiasm for establishing herself as "the Modern Murasaki" notwithstanding, her return to the medium of fiction was only moderately successful. Without the experimentation and training of Shizuko or Ichiyō, she was unable to pick up where they had left off. Rather, for the most part, her works read like a throwback to an earlier time. Lacking the novelty of her former pieces, her subsequent works return to the traditional marriage narrative, where women suffer unduly the vagaries of fate.

Shikin's most often cited works from this period are "Kokoro no oni" (Demon in the Heart, 1897) and "Shitayuku mizu" (The Downflow, 1898). Both works were published in the popular literary journal *Bungei kurabu*, and both are said to be studies of jealousy. The first concerns a man who is unduly jealous of his wife; the second concerns a wife who is unduly jealous of her husband's maid. Both are written in a highly elegant, almost self-consciously "feminine" *gabuntai* replete with five–seven–five *(shichi-go-chō)* metrical journey scenes *(michiyuki)*, elaborate puns *(kakekotoba)*, and other flourishes of the earlier traditions of both *waka* and *gesaku*. Even the dramatic action in the stories—a husband mad-as-a-hatter who imprisons his wife in the storage house and a beautiful maid who kills herself out of loyalty to her master—seems to be straight out of old romances, be they uta mono-gatari or ninjōbon. Yet just beneath the elegant fabric of the narrative, readers can detect a glimmer of the old Shikin.

The protagonist of "Demon in the Heart" is a merchant from the Nishijin area of Kyoto. As eccentric and miserly as a Saikaku townsman, he is terribly possessive of his wife Oito and warns her not to speak to another man in his absence. When she allows her stepfather to visit, her husband flies into a rage and begins locking Oito in the storehouse whenever he has to leave home. Once the stepfather learns of her plight, he tries to rescue her—only to find himself in a fistfight with her husband. Throughout the narrative, Oito does nothing to resist her fate. Raised on the Onna daigaku (Greater Learning for Women), she has no thought of leaving her husband. "A woman's lot in life is to marry," she says, "and to stay married until she dies. I plan to persevere. But if it is all the same, I'd rather die sooner than later."[66] Once her husband is confined to an asylum, Oito visits him dutifully.

Contemporary critics focused on the male protagonist. Had the author portrayed him successfully? Was this kind of jealousy really possible in a man? None of them paid much attention to Oito, as she was merely the object of the protagonist's obsession. This emphasis on the jealousy in the story, however, elides the more interesting aspects of Shikin's creation. The story is not about jealousy after all. Jealousy is merely the conduit for Shikin's broader message, which is not only a discourse on male privilege and the oppression of women but also on the way women are complicit in their own victimization.

The husband in "Demon" is essentially no different than most fictional husbands. It is simply his jealousy that is extraordinary. By making the jealousy so extreme, she underscores the ludicrous nature of a society that would expect a woman (and would require this expectation in the woman herself) to submit to a lunatic. Furthermore, society rewards the woman for her submissiveness by honoring her with a "good name." Whose heart is it, then, that harbors a "demon?" And what is the demon in the heart? Is it the man's outrageous jealousy? Is it the woman's enforced sense of victimization? Or is it a society that would condone the kind of marriage that nurtures such demons? The overtones in "Demon in the Heart" seem to reverberate with Shikin's pleas from her earlier addresses to young women—such as "What Will Today's Women Students Resolve?" in which she petitions women not to cling to unrealistic fantasies about marriage but to take responsibility for their own fate.

Shikin continues to explore the demonic nature of society in her subsequent work "The Downflow." Of the two, this is by far the superior and reveals an improvement in Shikin's art overall. Although her narrative style still depends on wordplay, classical allusion, and kabuki-style stage setting, she pays more attention to the psychological dimension of her main characters than in her earlier works. The plot of the story is convoluted. Essentially it concerns the budding love between the maid Osono and her employer Fukai Sumasu, who was also Osono's mother's nursling. Sumasu is the perfect Meiji gentleman, not unlike Kaho's Tsutomu. Educated in the West, enlightened, he even sports an inverted "v" of a moustache. Unlike Tsutomu, however, Sumasu was unlucky in marriage. His wife, into whose family he is adopted, resembles Kaho's Hamako in shrillness and selfishness, and surpasses her in homeliness. Osono, it might be expected, favors Hideko. She is intelligent, attractive, resourceful, demure, and noble. The similarity to Kaho's work ends with the rough outline of the characterizations, however.

There is nothing lighthearted about Shikin's work, with the exception of a few exchanges among the servants and scenes involving the shrewish wife. From page one of Shikin's work, we know tragedy is afoot. In short, the wife's misplaced jealousy forces Osono to leave the house. Concerned for her welfare, Sumasu sets her up in a little house, where it appears to the rest of the world that he is "keeping" her as a mistress. Try as she might to deny her feelings, Osono finds herself attracted to Sumasu and he to her. On the night when he proposes to leave his wife and presents her with a ring as a token of his troth, she resolves to commit suicide, as she knows that if she does not, Sumasu will be destroyed (if not by fate then by Osono's former husband). By dying, therefore, she reveals the depth of her love for Sumasu. As if to make this point clear, she dies with his diamond ring in her mouth.

Most who read "The Downflow," particularly those without any prior experience with Shikin, assume that it is yet another tale of female misfortune. Shioda Ryōhei says of Shikin's fiction:

> The women Shikin most often depicts are frail creatures who, while lamenting the fact that they are trapped between *giri* and *ninjō*, nevertheless manage to persevere with their chastity intact. Of these, the majority are of the pathetic sort seen in the feudal era who, without revealing the determination locked within them, love a man only to fade away quietly without ever allowing their ardor to burn too brightly.[67]

Yamaguchi Reiko suggests, however, that Shikin consciously creates these "frail creatures" and embeds their tale in a swirl of old-fashioned diction in an effort to camouflage the true import of her work. Beneath all the *gesaku* stage setting and the rhetorical flourish, "The Downflow," Yamaguchi contends, is not unlike "The Broken Ring." Both are accounts of a woman's struggle to assert her own personhood in the face of impossible odds. Osono, whose life is on the downward flow, hails from the lower reaches of society: she has no resources at her disposal and no way to escape the superficiality of existence. And yet she does not despise herself, nor is she to be despised. She is strong in principle, strong in will. Even while she submits obediently to the demands of a class-conscious and sexist society, she refuses to compromise her inner sense of integrity. Thus she displays an astonishing sense of self-awareness.[68] The tragedy of the story—and hence its point—is that hers is a selfhood that can only be realized in its destruction. To live beyond the constraints of a society that devalues women can very well mean death—social or physical.

If Yamaguchi's contention is to be accepted, however, we must ask why Shikin would feel the need to camouflage her message—especially when it had been so readily accepted in "The Broken Ring"? We can only speculate. Shikin might have been following the general trend in the literary world whereby the early experiments with *genbun itchi* were being temporarily abandoned in favor of a return to classical prose styles. Moreover, the *bundan*'s interest at the time for Saikaku had also revived the kind of *gesaku*-flavored characterizations we find in "Demon in the Heart" and "The Downflow," among other innovations. Given the nationalistic and conservative fervor gripping the Japanese state just before and after the Sino-Japanese War, perhaps Shikin felt—consciously or not—more comfortable delivering her message under the protective cover of an old-fashioned and exaggeratedly "feminine" style.

Nagamatsu Fusako explains the change in the author's style by relating it to Shikin's growing consciousness of herself as a writer. When Shikin published her first two stories, Nagamatsu contends, she did not visualize herself as a writer. Rather, she was a journalist writing not to be "literary" but informative. Hence the prose styles of her first two works—one in *genbun itchi*, the other *wakan'yō gabuntai*—appear more "natural." From 1896, when she renamed herself, Shikin grew conscious of her position as a writer and thus tried to write in a "writerly" way.[69]

Shikin's own regard of literature was fairly unsophisticated. Her 1890 essay "Why Are Women Writers So Slow to Emerge?" gives us her only statement on literature. From this essay it is clear that she, like Iwamoto Yoshiharu, evaluated women's literary efforts through a utilitarian lens:

> When the moon is on the water, it appears all the brighter; when the flower is by the willow, it appears all the redder; and when feminine vitality is added to the present literary world, it produces even greater interest

(shūmi). Thus that which was parched will be revived; and that which was soiled will be purified. . . .

My own period of study was brief, and I have no credentials to be giving you women advice on this, or urging you to do that. And yet, as a woman myself, I cannot but regret that our literary world is without female authors and that it is one into which no woman is poised to emerge. Moreover, I cannot help assuming that this is one of the reasons why the Meiji literary world is today so dry and tasteless.[70]

Like her colleague Wakamatsu Shizuko, Shikin believed women were responsible for cleaning up the literary world with their "own pure hands." She also believed that women writers should offer the literary world "beauty." Female-authored works should be instructive, but they should also be tasteful, elegant, and graceful—lending color to the desiccated world of male authorship. If such indeed was Shikin's approach to her writing, then it is not surprising that once she named herself "the Modern Murasaki" she felt compelled to provide literary beauty. For Shikin this literary excellence must have been flavored by her own early lessons in the classics and by her later independent study of *gesaku*. Presumably she thought, therefore, that to be literary—and just as important to be feminine—one should embroider one's works with classical allusions, clever wordplay, and tried-and-true characterizations and dramatic situations.

She was not alone in this regard of women's role in literature. Most critics, as we have seen, expected women's writing to demonstrate "female essence" *(josui)*—that is to say, a woman's *gabuntai* prose was to be scented with the elegance of the past. In an 1896 essay for *Jogaku zasshi*, a male literary critic had urged women writers to "make their hearts over in the mold of the ancients [presumably Murasaki Shikibu].[71] Successful women writers were praised for creating a prose that was at once elegantly beautiful *(yūbi)* as well as modest *(odayakana)*. In other words, women were expected to incorporate into their works those markers that signaled the classical style—wordplay, allusions, and five–seven–five meter—but they were to do so in a manner that was unobtrusive and seemingly effortless *(kushin no konseki mo miezu)*. In effect their prose was to be graceful, suggestive, and meandering without being bold *(daitan)* or direct. Higuchi Ichiyō was able to use the feminine literary past without allowing it to overwhelm her texts. Shikin was not.

If in fact Shikin's writing style was a cover-up, as Yamaguchi suggests, and not the naive choice of a writer trying desperately to be "artistic," it appears that the camouflage was too successful. With the exception of discerning readers like Yamaguchi, most contemporary critics failed to read beyond Shikin's *gesaku*-esque verbiage.

"A School for Émigrés"

Shikin continued her exploration of the lower reaches of society in "A School for Émigrés" (Imin gakuen, 1899), in which she portrays a woman of *buraku-min* or outcast origin. The Meiji government had redefined the former class system and in so doing had abolished the legal discrimination against members of the so-called *buraku*. Rather than continuing to refer to these former outcasts by the highly offensive term *"eta"* (literally "full of filth") and excluding them from the legal rights and guarantees enjoyed by other Japanese citizens, the government had the *burakumin* incorporated into the *"heimin"* or commoner/plebian class and distinguished as *"shin heimin,"* or "new commoner." The gap between legal incorporation and social acceptance was of course tremendous. A "new" common citizen was still not a citizen, and most *burakumin* continued to live in desperate conditions—economically deprived and socially reviled.

Shikin was not the first in the Meiji *bundan* to turn to the topic of the *burakumin*. Indeed, from 1856, when playwright Kawatake Mokuami (1816–1893) crafted a play on the subject, the theme of the *"eta* maiden and the *hatamoto* samurai" became something of a stock element in contemporary drama and fiction. Although Mokuami's play had a comic element—and all is well that ends well—others began to employ the theme for its political implication. In a story published in 1888, a young *burakumin* boy from Nagano performs so well in school that a kindly benefactor sends him to Kyoto where he continues to distinguish himself—earning tours to New York and London. Eventually the young man opens a shop in Yokohama, takes a "lady" for a wife, and becomes a representative in the legislature—thus emerging as the quintessential image of *"risshin shusse"* (self-establishment and public success). The moral of the story: Japan is now such a civilized place that all men have opportunity—regardless of background. With a little education and a lot of effort, even a *burakumin* can succeed in this new nation.

But not all *burakumin* stories ended happily. Kōtoku Shūsui (1871–1911), an outspoken advocate of a socialist agenda, published "Okoso zukin" (Woman in the Okoso Scarf, 1894) in the *Jiyū shinbun* (Freedom News). In this story a young man on the brink of marriage learns that he is of *burakumin* heritage. His father, a non-*burakumin*, was injured during the battles preceding the Meiji Restoration and was rescued by a *hinin* (a non-human or outcast). While being nursed back to health, he fell in love with the daughter of this individual and she bore him a son. Ashamed of her background, the young woman fled to Kyushu where she was able to hide her identity. Thus relieved of her past, her lover is able to join her there. When the son discovers the truth of his parentage, he is neither appalled nor ashamed: "Aristocrat or New Citizen—who is high? Who is low? I do not mind being a New Citizen, and I am determined to wear my identity proudly."[72] Shūsui's story exposes the duplicity of a society that claims equality while clinging to feudal distinctions.

Tokuda Shūsei (1871–1943) had incorporated the subject of the *burakumin* in his 1896 work "Yabu kōji" (Spearflower), and in the following month Oguri Fūyō (1875–1926) offered *Neoshiroi* (Bedtime Makeup). Unlike Kōtoku Shūsui, who was concerned with the ethical and political ramifications of social classification, Shūsei and Fūyō—both associated with the newly evolving "naturalist school"—were responding to a recent trend in literary circles to focus on the way issues of heredity and environment influenced the formation of a person's character: Shūsei writes of a woman who is driven insane by the circumstances of her life; Fūyō considers the implications of incest. Whatever the poignancy of these topics, Sasabuchi Tomoichi notes that most authors at this time treated their *burakumin* subjects like sideshow curiosities, hardly as human beings.[73] They were intrigued by the more salacious aspects of the *burakumin*'s existence. In Fūyō's *Bedtime Makeup*, for instance, which was banned upon publication, a brother and sister who are the sole remaining unmarried members of a *buraku* are obliged to engage in an incestuous relationship because social discrimination has thwarted their attempts to marry outside the *buraku*. Rather than delving into the tortured psychology of these individuals, or even the horrific social context, Fūyō was more concerned it seems with the sensational aspects of incest. As a result, he failed to make the story believable and certainly failed to develop sympathy for the characters.

Shikin, though clearly influenced by Kōtoku Shūsui's earlier work, does not grapple with the concept of *burakumin* as a social phenomenon in her story either. Rather, she uses the image of marginalization metaphorically, as we shall see, to suggest her own position as a "new woman" in Meiji Japan and her resistance to blindly following the status quo. The subject of "A School for Émigrés" might have appeared trendy at the time, but the narrative style was painfully old-fashioned. Similar to "The Downflow" and "Demon," it is lush with tortuous wordplay and other elegant flourishes. Nevertheless, the kabuki-style presentation in which the narrative unfolds is interesting. Scenes shift abruptly. And as different players take the stage in often seemingly unrelated sequences, the audience is slowly informed of the developing drama. All the while the narrative maintains a tone of suspense. As the story opens, we are met with a *gidayū*-style narrative prologue in which the central actor introduces herself and intimates her dilemma:

> I am not of the class to be draped in silk brocades and hidden deep within jeweled palaces. Yet when my husband's name is announced, all nod with

recognition. We dine on polished rice twice a day and are of such status that we might wash a whole year's worth down the drain and never notice. I am invited here and there by those who wish to curry favor and though I would prefer to shun all social intercourse, I am inevitably offered the seat of honor. All applaud me as the wife of Mr. Imao. Such is the source of my misfortune.

In the spring, the blossoms; in the autumn, the moon. My husband rarely leaves my side. Whether it is off to Ueno or over to Sumida, we are constantly together. He is so terribly busy now with worldly affairs that he rarely has time to relax. Still, he will not delight in our garden cherry if not in my presence, and he will turn his back on the moonlight glittering through the window if I am not at his side. His tears he hides from me; but his laughter he shares. Kind to all, he always seeks to please me. How might it be that I would feel misfortune?

My husband excels in scholarship; he is superior in statesmanship; and never was there a more chivalrous gentleman. . . . If this is misery, then what pray tell might happiness be?[74]

The narrator, we eventually learn, is Imao Kiyoko. She is, in a sense, the character that the heroine of "The Broken Ring" had aspired to be. Allowed to pursue her education until she was twenty, she worked for a time as a schoolteacher until finally marrying Imao Harue, a member of the newly inaugurated parliament. Not only is Harue a champion of human rights and a self-professed advocate of democracy *(heiminshugi)*, he is a remarkably kind and considerate man at home as well—unlike the hypocrites Shikin had berated in her earlier preface to Ueki Emori's *Women of the Orient*. Hence readers are confronted at the outset with a mystery. A woman who ought to be counting her blessings is nonetheless miserable. And she herself seems baffled by her emotions. After pondering the notion that fortune is never to be found without misfortune, the narrative voice shifts once again and a bevy of gossiping society ladies takes the stage.

The conversation between the women resonates with *gesaku* overtones, and once again Shikin proves herself adept at caustic sketches. The harpies might be society matrons, but they gossip like fishwives. Today they are in a snit because Mrs. Imao is the talk of town—beautiful, educated, wealthy, and married to a man who obviously adores her—but nevertheless wears a sad expression wherever she goes. The women interpret her drawn look as dissatisfaction: "She is certainly pleased as punch with herself but not wishing a happy face to betray her as common, she marches about with that scowl" (p. 212). Once started on the topic, each wife takes a turn venting her displeasure with Kiyoko. In the following passage the wife's jealousy is provoked by her husband's admiration for Kiyoko:

"Well, my husband insulted me by making fun of my 'fat face,' as if the nose I've had all my life had suddenly gone flat. . . . There's nothing more unfair in life than being born a woman. But what can we do but persevere?"

"This Mrs. Imao we've been discussing, she's a woman, is she not? Then why is she so lucky? I tell you, I despise my parents for giving birth to me. It was they who made me so ugly."

"I feel the same way, of course, but consider this: When the moon is full it's beautiful. And when it wanes it is less than perfect. Even so, the moon is still the moon. And it is the same with our noses. High bridges are beautiful, we hear. But even a flat nose is still a nose—and the proof is in the nostrils! They are all that's needed. These beautiful women with noses so perfect that they look as though they've been molded by hand had best take care. Whether they mean to or not, they soon earn a name for themselves as long-nosed wizards [Tengu] for taking pride in their fine profiles—and so they invite the scorn of others. Beauty, my dears, is a woman's enemy. Just take Mrs. Imao as an example. She is beautiful. She is educated. She is this and she is that and all our husbands are head over heels for her, wishing they could have her as a wife. Even my husband sings her praises, going to such lengths he might as well have pushed me into a corner. But you know, my dears, excessive praise is the seed of censure. With everyone so obsessed with her, there's bound to be someone who takes a mind to investigating her background. We all know of her present life. Yes, her flowery face may be lovely indeed. But what of its roots?"

"Well, I hear she was brought up by the Akitas, though just for appearances. They are not her real parents. Her real father was a moneylender who started with a little capital and loaned at inflated rates. He had no wife. And either because he was too eccentric or too pressed for money, he hired no maid but raised his daughter on his own, cooking rice with one hand and managing his business with the other. Gradually his profits grew—which he spent all on you-know-who, sending her away to girls' school where she stayed until her graduation at the age of twenty. She then became a teacher at the very same school. She might have been a modern girl, but she was a pampered daughter all the same. Protected in her glass box, her beauty was luminous. With her long hair wound in coils around her head, her graceful figure, soon she caught the eye of Mr. Imao, and through the intercession of another party, he married Miss Akita—their wedding a grand affair. . . . All's well that ends well, but then her father up and disappeared. Rumors went round that he had moved away, his whereabouts unknown. . . . Some say Mr. Imao had hidden him. [Pp. 213–214]

As the gossips continue to speculate about Mrs. Imao, readers add a few more pieces to the puzzle she has posed. She has a secret to hide, and it concerns her father. With each successive section to the story, each shift in scene and voice, Shikin pulls readers deeper into the mystery in a way that is suggestive of detective fiction.

In the next section, the focus turns to Imao Harue and the narrative shifts to third person. Now readers are given a glimpse of the domestic life in the Imao household:

> "You must be tired," his wife says as she greets him, kneeling at a discreet distance. She attends to him with cool breezes from her hand-held fan and warm smiles. Can this be the wife of the gossip? Her hair has been freshly done up in a rich chignon, her downcast eyes glitter. Her gossamer-thin summer kimono drapes softly over her shoulders. Though only cotton, she wears it elegantly. Could this lovely wife ever have been a schoolteacher? Her face overflows with smiles.
>
> "Look at the water dripping off the green leaves. It is a man-made rain shower, as Sanzō has been busy sprinkling the leaves. See how the water glitters like fireflies flitting among the garden hillocks. It is so lovely. Shall we compose poems on the theme 'the moon over the government mansion'?"
>
> "Hana, bring the hot water," she calls, and then with her own lovely hand she prepares her husband a bowl of fine tea. . . . How could such as she have earned a name for a scowling face? [Pp. 215–216]

The scene that unfolds is one of wedded bliss. Yet it is an artificial bliss. For readers are aware that the wife is forcing herself to smile while her heart is in turmoil. The source of her distress, we come to learn, is a letter her father sent her just before he disappeared:

> Owing to certain circumstances I have gone into hiding. You must think of me as no longer a person of this world and devote all your attention to your husband. I am by nature a stubborn man and do not enjoy the company of others, and yet I willed myself to face the indignities of the cold city. For whom have I thus sacrificed?
>
> For you, so that you might marry the best of the world's best. Now you are Imao Harue's wife, and you are no longer my daughter. . . . Serve your husband. Serve him well. And whenever you find yourself assailed by a desire to find me, turn your attentions to your husband doublefold—no triplefold. Serve him for all eternity—and when you die, enter his grave. Once you have done this, I will meet you again in the world of spirits, and I will tell you my reasons. Until then, comfort yourself in knowing that I have done nothing to be ashamed of before heaven. Still, there is shame in human society and so I must hide my secret from this world. . . . If for some mis-

guided reason you think you must search for me out of loyalty, don't. To do so will wound me, for you will expose my shame to the public. . . . You must not be unfilial to me or unfaithful to your husband. [P. 216]

Kiyoko worries about her father, yet she cannot reveal the source of her concern to her husband. In keeping secrets from her husband, however, she feels she is betraying him, as she wishes to be open with him on every score. This is the source of her sad expression. Her husband realizes that she is distressed and tries to draw her out, forcing her to put forth an even braver front. Shikin portrays the tension between them as they courteously tiptoe around each other's feelings and pretend nothing is bothering them:

> Harue gazes at his wife's thin hand on the handle of the fan. "What is the matter, Kiyoko? Of late your color has not been good. I fear you have taken ill. You know you must take special care in the summer. It would be best to consult a doctor as soon as possible."
>
> When she heard this Kiyoko struggled to respond brightly, "Ha, ha, ha! It's just a summer spell. It's my nature to lose weight in the summer. But I'll fatten up again, you'll see. For those who lose weight in summer, a glass of milk is better medicine than a doctor! And then turning plump in the fall— this is just a woman's misfortune. Quite funny, don't you think? Rather than worrying over me, I am quite concerned for you. I fear you are much too busy these days."
>
> "Ha, ha, ha! Me? I'm not of such a delicate constitution!" [P. 217]

Harue proceeds to deflect his wife's concern for him by describing his work, all the while probing gently for what is really bothering her. And so readers are made to see the tenderness and the mutual consideration these characters share—a consideration that infringes upon their abilities to communicate directly with one another. Yet despite their reluctance to speak openly, their feelings betray them. Like the mother and daughter in "The Broken Ring," this couple is so sensitively attuned one to another that they can intuit the other's emotions.

Much of "A School for Émigrés" concerns the conflict between outward appearance and inner turmoil. Each of the three main characters—father, daughter, and husband—tries to protect the other even if to do so means self-sacrifice. It is this self-denial that drives the narrative movement. Ironically, it is an act of conscious communication that breaks this impasse and spurs the narrative on to its climax. As the middle section comes to a close, Kiyoko receives a letter in an unfamiliar hand with her father's name on the envelope. Stealing a moment away from her husband's adoring gaze, she reads it.

In perhaps the most dramatic scene in the story, the next section opens with Kiyoko in Kyoto. Although we are not told why she has traveled there, we must assume the mysterious letter is the catalyst. With careful attention to detail, the narrator describes the press of people at the Kyoto station. Among them are revelers of all kinds: "Kyoto is the nation's amusement park. People travel here from all across the country. In spring there are those who come to view the blossoms, in autumn the leaves, and in summer they come for the cool evening breezes along the riverbanks" (p. 221). Amidst this throng of humanity is one delicate lady with a modest chignon. The rickshaw pullers clamor for her business. Through the intercession of a teashop proprietress, Kiyoko (for we know this is Kiyoko) hires a rickshaw to take her to Zeniza-mura in Yanagihara-shō.[75] The proprietress is taken aback by her destination and asks her a second time to be sure. This subtle hestitation prepares readers for the scene that soon confronts the heroine:

> To the left and right of the street are small houses, each with the toe straps of sandals spread out along the rooftops to dry. Children with scabby faces run barefoot along the muddy road. Covered head to toe in dirt, they are excited by the unexpected visitor and surround the rickshaw with great shouts. After they have gone a few blocks into the village, Kiyoko is assailed by a foul odor. It provokes within her an indescribable feeling of wretchedness. She notices that wilted onion tips, dead rats, and all manner of refuse are strewn along the street and the ditch at its side is an open pit piled high with garbage. Occasionally she will spy a house that looks cleaner than the rest, and then she notices that there are animal skins stretched out in front to dry. Suddenly uncertain of her surroundings she asks the rickshaw puller where he has brought her.
>   "This is an *eta* village," he replies. [Ibid.]

Kiyoko cannot imagine why she should have been taken to such a place, and she continues to question the rickshaw puller, assuming that perhaps there is more than one Zeniza-mura. But when the rickshaw puller locates a woman who knows Kiyoko's father, and leads her to him, Kiyoko knows there is no mistake. She is somehow connected to this horrible place. "Although it was a summer afternoon, she felt her skin pucker into gooseflesh and she shivered in spite of herself" (p. 222).

As the scene shifts she is in a shabby room speaking to an old man who is lying on a thin mattress, his face to the wall. She addresses him as "father" and apologizes for not visiting him sooner. She would not have known where to find him if it had not been for the letter she received. As she draws close to his bedside and begins to massage his shoulder, the man rebukes her and says she is mistaken. He is not her father. The letter was surely a hoax:

Judging from your dress and the way you carry yourself, I can tell you are a
fine lady. It's highly unlikely that a "new commoner" like me would have
such a daughter. There's been a mistake. Now hurry off before you ruin your
good name. [Ibid.]

Perhaps readers in 1899 were temporarily baffled by these developments and
imagined that there really had been a mistake. But the longer the old man
speaks, the clearer his identity becomes. In the following passage he seems to
address his daughter directly before once again lapsing into his pretense:

"Yes, yes, I do recall that I once had a daughter. But owing to various circumstances we severed our relations and she ought to have received a letter
to that effect. No matter how upset she might be, she would never be so foolish as to visit her old father in a place like this. So you see, there's been a
misunderstanding. . . . Hurry and leave. Please go. I may have severed ties
with my own daughter, but I still know what it means to be a parent. So even
though I don't know you, I will worry about you. If you are mistaken for the
daughter of a new commoner, it will ruin you. It will ruin your husband.
And that was your father's greatest fear, wasn't it? [Pp. 222–223]

As her father, Taichi, tries unsuccessfully to persuade her to leave, his
friend Kahei appears and confesses to having written the letter. With the
next section of the story, Taichi tells Kiyoko of her parentage and his past. He
was the son of a physician, but unable to get along with his stepmother he
became dissolute and was eventually disowned. One evening when he was
completely down on his luck, a kind man befriended him and took him home
and treated him with generosity, though he was not permitted to leave the
house. Disillusioned with the world outside the house anyway, Taichi fell in
love with the man's daughter and they married. At this point Taichi discovered that he was staying in a *buraku* and that his wife was in fact a *burakumin*. Rather than running away in horror, Taichi elected to stay on with his
new family, finding them much more charitable than his old. His wife, however, grew ill after the birth of their daughter. On her deathbed she implored
him to "wash clean the filth from this baby's blood" (p. 228). For his daughter's sake, therefore, Taichi moved to Tokyo, bought a new name, and placed
his daughter in a boarding school. He shunned social intercourse and did
what he could to erase any ties to his background. When Kiyoko (whose
name after all means "purity") married a man with a marvelous future,
Taichi felt he had indeed "washed clean the filth" from her blood. To avoid
damaging her relationship with her husband, he disappeared, hopefully to
bury the secret of her parentage with his death.

Kiyoko is shocked by her father's admission. Like the character Kōtoku Shūsui invented, she is not ashamed of her status. Yet she does feel guilt for having implicated her husband in a marriage that will ruin his career. She does not wish to damage his career. Thus she faces a choice: she may confess to Harue and accept his decision—should he wish to divorce her she will return to her father's side—or she may remain with her father and choose not to return to her husband's home, thus sparing him humiliation. After a great deal of worry and discussion with her father, she returns home. And with the next scene we learn the outcome of her decision:

> In no time at all the rumors had spread that Minister Imao had resigned his post. All who heard were shocked. There was now no hiding the fact that his wife was a new commoner. And because Imao was of a status that allowed him to stand in attendance on the emperor, well, it just wouldn't do—at least this is the childish, reactionary sort of thing people were saying. . . . The government system may have been the product of enlightment, but the people to be found in it were still beasts at heart, casting about in a whirlpool of competition. . . . Well, let them laugh and call him cowardly. Imao decided, for the sake of humankind, to try his hand at teaching. . . . He collected his capital and moved to Hokkaido, where he gathered all the little children throughout the nation who had been abandoned for various reasons and housed them in a school called the School for Émigrés. He will raise them to be citizens with hearts as fresh as the land of Hokkaido is new. "I will redeem these children of new commoners with my own strength. I am your father. Kiyoko is your mother," he tells them with a laugh.
>
> When the family left from Ueno Station, it is said that only two or three noble souls gathered to see them off. [Pp. 231–232]

Of Love and Broken Commandments

Most modern reviewers of "A School for Émigrés" compare the work to Shimazaki Tōson's *The Broken Commandment (Hakai)*. In a sense the two works are hardly comparable. Tōson's is a full novel that many have heralded as the first truly modern novel in Japanese letters. Shikin's story, by contrast, is a mere twenty-two pages, and most would relate it to the last glimmer of the *gesaku* tradition. Yet from the foregoing synopsis it is clear that the salient features in Shikin's story are also to be found in Tōson's (and in Shūsui's). Both describe a motherless child who leaves with the father for another region where no one will know of their heritage. The child is sent to school, away from the father's care, and the father retreats from the world into a solitary life. The father makes the child pledge not to mention its heritage, but the child cannot keep the promise. And so the child leaves, at the end of the story, for an entirely new territory.

Sasabuchi contends that the similarities between the two are too great for coincidence.[76] He also suggests that the weakest points in Tōson's work—such as the hero's flight to Texas—result from Tōson's appropriating the closure from the earlier story without incorporating it into the dramatic logic of his story. In "A School for Émigrés," the final flight to Hokkaido does not resonate with the implausibility that we find in Tōson's flight to Texas. As Sasabuchi observes, the trajectory of Shikin's narrative had been aimed at this goal from the very start. Moreover, Hokkaido was at the time a land of opportunity. Many "pioneers," such as Shikin's friend Sasaki Toyosu, had left Tokyo to seek new opportunities and solace in Hokkaido. For Shikin's protagonists, Hokkaido represented an untouched wilderness that was spared the taint of prejudice that had poisoned the main islands of Japan. In Hokkaido the couple can start afresh without the "new commoner" stigma that had haunted them in old Japan. The conclusion offers a utopian vision, but it does not stretch the limits of disbelief.

That Imao Harue would sacrifice his post and position for his wife does, however, tax one's imagination. According to Yamaguchi Reiko, intermarriage between *burakumin* and non-*burakumin* was not tolerated—even in recent times. If intermarriage took place out of ignorance, however, and the participants discovered the truth later, divorce would be inevitable, regardless of the couples' desire to remain wed.[77] Social pressure would not allow otherwise. In permitting her characters to remain married—in the face of popular opinion (only two or three people saw the couple off)—Shikin once again reveals her penchant for defiance. Imao Harue flaunts his marriage to a *burakumin* woman as certainly as the heroine of "The Broken Ring" flaunts her divorce. Yet by portraying this act as a defiant gesture that did not earn the respect of the general public—who preferred to view the Imaos as disgraceful failures—Shikin saves the closure from appearing too idealistic.

This brings us to what is the most significant distinction between *The Broken Commandment* and "A School for Émigrés." The former is, as Sasabuchi observes, a story of "passivity"—of being pushed and cornered by circumstances into "breaking the commandment." In "A School for Émigrés," by contrast, we have a story of "independence" *(shutaisei)*—of personal choice and determination. All three characters in the story—father, daughter, and husband—take responsibility for the fate they are dealt and act accordingly: the father strikes out for Tokyo to spare his daughter; the daughter races to Kyoto to comfort her father; the husband moves to Hokkaido to protect his wife. Most important, each action is motivated by love. Thus while *The Broken Commandment* focuses on the "breaking of the commandment" and the psychological pressures that precede it, the focus in "A School for Émigrés" is on the love between the characters—a love so great that each character would willingly sacrifice anything to preserve it. The father is willing to relinquish his relationship to his only child, and indeed to the rest of the world, in an effort to secure her happiness and fulfill the last wishes of his wife. The daughter is willing to jettison her wifely status in order to protect her husband. And the husband in turn gladly abandons his government post for his wife. This, the story seems to imply, is true *risshin shusse*, but it is a success that few can appreciate.

Almost all the early stories about *burakumin* concern marriage. The *burakumin*—man or woman—is inevitably described as wanting to marry outside the *buraku,* either intentionally or inadvertently, in order to escape his or her predicament. In the earliest works it is impossible to leave the *buraku* and often impossible to marry. Once the truth of the marriage partner's parentage is revealed, the marriage is broken and the *burakumin* is chased back into the *buraku*—to insanity or to incest. Marriage thus becomes the fundamental mechanism in these stories for social integration and self-betterment. It is equally important for male as well as female characters—though curiously it is the female who is generally described as the original *burakumin* and thereby the source of the male's misfortune. Marriage thus becomes metonymic of acceptance within the larger family of the nation. In almost all instances, the *burakumin* is exposed as an interloper and sent back down to the low life of the *buraku*—the world of his or her mother. But Shikin, and Kōtoku Shūsui before her, question just how low the *buraku* actually is. Its people may live in filth and squalor, but it is the world of the upper classes (the father's world) that proves to be corrupt and uninhabitable. Because the upper classes are so immoral, the pure *buraku* characters are chased back into their native realm—where they find not misery but human compassion and love.

The celebration of love in "A School for Émigrés" ties the story to Shikin's "A Young Man's Surprising Reminiscences." Kiyoko, the "pure" woman vilified for reasons beyond her control, is not unlike the "fallen" woman the young man idolizes in the earlier story. For that matter, she is not unlike the author herself. Shikin too had been the focus of gossip for reasons she surely found unfair and illogical. A woman should not be disparaged for divorce, for self-preservation, for love. Nor should a people be discriminated against because of their ancestry. Shikin had borne the brunt of prejudice—not as a "new commoner" but as a "new woman" in an age when women were commended for self-abnegation yet were reviled for self-reliance.

For this reason, perhaps, Shikin's portrait of Kiyoko incorporates all the standard characteristics of the "new woman" while at the same time revealing her to be pristinely feminine. Kiyoko has had an education and a career as a schoolteacher—both hallmarks of the quintessential "new woman." We recall Miyake Kaho's character in *Warbler in the Grove* who declares that a schoolteacher will bend her knee to no man. Female schoolteachers were portrayed as a particularly dangerous lot in Meiji Japan. They were believed to be willful, arrogant, needlessly schooled in unpractical matters, and mannishly self-sufficient. Although the female schoolteacher was the worst of her kind, the "new woman" in general, whatever her occupation or credentials, was depicted negatively in the press and literature at the time. She was masculine (Futabatei's Osei),[78] silly and superficial (Kaho's Hamako), or miserably unfit for contemporary life (Shōyō's Otane). Although largely imagined as the companion to the enlightened Meiji man, the "new woman" was not herself enlightened. Rather, she tried on Western ideas and modern notions like a new wardrobe—more for the pleasure of her mate than for her own comfort.

Shikin's "new women" were different. Shikin had herself been a schoolteacher; she had been a journalist and a writer and a public lecturer; and she was a divorcée. Even if she had not had all the education she wanted, she still possessed the prerequisites for a "new woman." Moreover, she had associated with women who had likewise been reviled in the press and in gossip circles for their self-assured and liberal behavior—women like Sasaki Toyosu, Yajima Kajiko, and Fukuda Hideko. Although Shikin did not seem to resist the appellation, she did resist the stigma. In "The Broken Ring," her "new woman" is brave and outspoken. Hardly concerned with the latest Western garments and finery (her ring is broken after all), she is more interested in dressing herself in the raiments of self-confidence and independence. In "A School for Émigrés," Kiyoko, though no less brave, is identified as the perfect wife and daughter. She combines modern defiance with traditional grace and modesty—thus creating a "new woman"—not unlike Wakamatsu Shizuko, who was able to span the divide between femininity and self-development. Faulting a woman for characteristics that distinguished her as "new," therefore, was certainly as foolhardy as faulting her for the circumstances of her birth. In either regard, Kiyoko emerges as a "pure" woman.

Brokered Silence

Shikin published "A School for Émigrés" in August 1899, several months after Yoshinao had returned to Japan from his five-year stay in Europe. Originally he had intended a three-year sojourn but had extended the stay an additional two years to enable him to complete his doctorate in agricultural science. Wada suggests that Shikin's portrait of a couple deeply devoted to one another was the synthesis of her five years of loving Yoshinao from afar. During the time they were separated, she idealized him and their relationship, Wada speculates, until she produced the utopian image of a modern marriage that we find in "A School for Émigrés." Kiyoko Imao reflects on her marriage to Harue:

> It has only been two years since first we married. Yet we are not like other couples who, trusting their union to the god of Izumo, were led into marriage knowing not the kind of person to whom they would be betrothed. Some among them were coerced to marry against their emotions. We were not strangers to one another when we married but had come to know each other in time and thus drawn together we pledged our troth and have been together ever since. Our love is not just of the flesh but in the spirit as well. Therefore, we are not like those wedded couples who are more like ceremonial dolls than husband and wife. They sit next to one another year in and year out without knowing the first thing about the other's heart. No, we are not like them. [P. 230]

The wedded bliss portrayed in "A School for Émigrés" contrasts sharply, however, with the image of married life we find between Shikin and Yoshinao after 1899. Neither husband nor wife left a record of their marriage, of course, so the image that emerges is a patchwork of speculation and innuendo created by current scholars and by Shikin's contemporaries. Because Shikin retired from the literary world shortly after Yoshinao's return, most believe that she was bullied into silence by a tyrannical husband. The notion that Shikin "broke her brush" under duress comes from three primary sources: Sōma Kokkō's biography of Shikin in which she states that Yoshinao made his wife promise upon marriage that she would desist from writing;[79] Tokutomi Roka's autobiographical novel *Fuji* (1925) in which he relates anecdotes told to him by a former maid of the Kozais to the effect that "the master detested his wife's past, and was not pleased that she wrote fiction;"[80] and an article in the journal *Bunko* from which it is assumed the earlier two accounts stem. The article in the December 25, 1900, issue of *Bunko* takes the form of an anonymous directive to Shikin beseeching her to return to her former literary activity:

> Dear Shikin:
> In placing you on par with Ichiyō, critics have tended to exaggerate your talents. Even so, you exhibit a superior skill—quite substantial enough to give the bearded writers pause—and so it is no wonder that you are rated highly. Of late I have heard that you have married and are now leading a very miserable life. . . . Such is the gap between dreams and reality. . . . You once wrote in *Jogaku zasshi* of the inner turmoil in a woman's heart when she is

made to endure such misery. With a cool visage and severe eye you cursed the insensitivity and inconstancy of the men in this world. . . .

My dear Shikin, I beseech you. Let your tears rain down on your ink-stone, grip your thin red brush between your white teeth. The fingers that hold the brush may be small, but the force of your anger is great. Your breast may be frail, but the bitterness that burns there against the injustice of this world is bright. Please, lift your song again to the god of literature.[81]

Yamaguchi Reiko takes issue with the claims by Kokkō and Roka that Yoshinao "forbade" Shikin to write. In fact, she wrote for the first seven years of their marriage. In the maid's statement that Yoshinao "detested his wife's past," Yamaguchi finds a contradiction. Yoshinao's own love letters to Shikin reveal that he loved and respected her all the more for her past. Did Yoshinao, nevertheless, badger Shikin into "breaking her brush"? One glance at Shikin's biography reveals that the question is moot.

The impulse in Meiji Japan, even among the most enlightened, was to separate women's duties from men's. Women, as we have seen, were charged with overseeing the home. This was their "heavenly mission," their duty, their *privilege*. While Yoshinao was in Europe, Shikin was expected to step into the void he had left in the household, thus giving her a breadth and freedom most wives did not enjoy. She had the time and, more important, the inclination to write. Once he returned, however, everything changed. Her sphere suddenly shrank while her duties within it multiplied.

Shikin had been, as she is described in the *Bunko* article, an outspoken advocate for women. It is difficult to reconcile the image we have of Shikin before 1900 with the later image. Even a glance at her photographs suggests the incongruence. In the portrait of Shikin sitting with Ueki Emori in 1884 or thereabouts, she appears tiny yet full of vitality. In the photograph later in life she seems haunted, wan, unhappy. How could this exuberant champion of women's rights have become such a haggard, frightened woman? The temptation is to blame Yoshinao. Indeed, he offers himself up as a very convenient target. Shikin's son, Kozai Yoshishige, takes aim at this target by recording the following exchange between his parents:

"What if I resumed my work as a writer here at home, and . . . ?" my mother would plead. But my father would answer, "Ha! The woman genius [*tensai*] is now a stupid wife [*gusai*]!" My father's words were cruel. At those times my child's heart went out to my mother.[82]

Kozai Yoshinao's "*tensai/gusai*" retort eerily echoes the husband's response to the wife's plea in "The Broken Ring" for recognition and respect: "such learned words from the likes of a woman." For this reason, perhaps, Yoshinao is depicted in Shikin biographies as a cavalier lover who, having wooed and won the lady of his choice, loses all interest in her. The higher his star climbs, the lower she must drag her own. Kozai Yoshinao ended his days as president of Tokyo Imperial University. Shikin ended hers in anonymity. Perhaps it is not worth mentioning that they died within five months of each other—she in January, he in June.

Whatever kind of villain Yoshinao might have been, the fact remains that once he returned to Japan, whether intentionally or not, Shikin lost the leisure that she had once enjoyed and perhaps as well the inclination to write. Between 1901, when she published her final story "Natsuko no mono omoi" (Natsuko Remembers), and 1904 she gave birth to three children. She would give birth to her fifth child in 1911 at the age of forty-four. Shikin, like most

Figure 19   Shimizu Shikin (seated on right) with Ueki Emori (standing), ca. 1888. (Courtesy of Kusa no ne Shuppankai)

women in the Meiji period, saw childrearing as her primary duty. As she notes in an 1896 essay for *Jogaku zasshi*, "Fujin no eisei" (A Woman's Immortality), for a woman to impart something of herself to her children was a way of gaining immortality. It was also a way of trying to bring about change in the world. Fittingly, Shikin's own "immortality" was largely abetted by her son, Kozai Yoshishige, and his determination to make her collected works available to a modern audience.

Much of Shikin's married life, however, was wrought with successive heartbreak. In October 1904, shortly before Shikin gave birth to a daughter, Fukuda Hideko published her autobiography, in which she portrayed Shikin in a very unfavorable light. In February 1905 Shikin's third son died, not yet two years old. His death was immediately followed by the death of her infant daughter. During much of this time Yoshinao was traveling internationally.

Figure 20   Shikin late in life. (Courtesy of Kusa no ne Shuppankai)

In 1903 he attended a study tour in the Philippines, Java, and Sumatra. In 1906 he spent three months in Korea. Between 1908 and 1909 he was in Europe and the United States. Unlike Yoshinao's earlier study trip to Europe, however, Shikin now had two sons to attend to and less time to herself. Furthermore, as Yoshinao's career accelerated—he became president of the Tokyo Imperial University School of Agriculture in 1911—so too did Shikin's responsibilities as his wife. Like Kaho before her, Shikin would find there was not enough time between the bedroom and the kitchen to write.

With the exception of a woman like Wakamatsu Shizuko, therefore, to be a wife in Meiji Japan almost by definition precluded one from being a writer. The lack of space and time was certainly a consideration. In the 1908 article for the journal *Shinchō* authored by five male writers, for example, we have the following explanation for why women are not successful writers:

> The number of women aspiring to become writers has increased dramatically, but the reason they cannot become great successes like men is dependent on their circumstances. When women are maidens they have time to read and plenty of time to write. . . . But once they have their own family, they lose this time. Compared to men, women have a far greater need of making a family and are far more tied to family matters. Once she has a house, it is her business, rather than the man's, to worry about housekeeping. . . . And then when she has children, it is impossible to read or write. I don't know how it is in wealthy households, but in the middle-income family the wife hardly spends a minute not worrying about her housekeeping. Even when she manages to find time to write on the side, she cannot write exceptional works and thus falls into the category of the mediocre. This is why women are not successful.[83]

But if lack of time were the only hindrance, surely some less than meticulous housewives would have cut corners here and there in an effort to write. More than a lack of time, it was the lack of social acceptance and critical regard for "writing mothers" that infringed upon a married woman's ability to write. Thus even if the problem of time were alleviated by maids and other household help, the Meiji literary world was not yet willing to regard the writings of "housewives" in a serious light. To return to the *Shinchō* article:

> Women, they say, make careful and detailed observations. But from what I have seen up to now, no one is as slipshod as a woman when it comes to writing. True, she may well be as careful as she can be when she's at her sewing or counting up the loose change at home. But when it comes to art,

a woman simply does not possess the wherewithal for scrupulous preparation. The way things are these days, women writers would be better advised
to close up shop. Japan has its premier woman writer in Higuchi Ichiyō and
that's enough. If a woman today has enough time to write, she ought to
spend it worrying about fixing her husband something nice to eat.

Really, these stories women write while they're dashing about with their
presents and treats are just no good. Men write to live. . . . Unlike women,
they do not write out of some shallow desire for fame.[84]

Women who persisted in writing, even after marriage, were caught in a
dilemma. If they endeavored to write seriously, they were scorned as women
who put on airs. A married woman could not be a serious writer because she
was not writing to live: she was only writing to entertain herself or, worse, draw
attention to herself. If the woman then catered to this prejudice and wrote
with less diligence, she was spurned for being a mere "wifely writer" *(okusama
sakka)* and was not dealt with seriously (if she were dealt with at all).

Shikin could ill afford negative attention of either kind. Married to a
man whose career, like Imao Harue's, was on the rise, Shikin could not allow
herself to remain in the public arena if to do so invited undue publicity—and
at the time, almost any publicity a woman received soon spiraled into criticism. As the gossips in "A School for Émigrés" affirm, "beauty [public atten-
tion] is a woman's enemy." And "excessive praise is the seed for censure."
Moreover, most contemporary observers of Shikin's marriage would have felt
(had they known the details of her background) that she had been extremely
fortunate to marry Yoshinao. Indeed, one such observer calls Yoshinao "mag-
nanimous" for his "selfless act" of marrying a woman with a past. To repay
her husband's generosity by continuing with her former activities and thus
inviting public scorn would have been unconscionable. Out of respect and
gratitude, Shikin "broke her brush," or so some have interpreted her silence.

To become a Modern Murasaki, it would seem, was thus a contradiction
in terms. "Modern," at the time, was associated with the West, with the male-
authored "new woman" (who was masculine, fickle, and superficial), and
with a reform of those values largely indentified with "feminine virtues"—
passivity, modesty, and inarticulateness. "Murasaki," by contrast, signified
all that was elegant and pure in Japanese womanhood and literary activity.
To be a proper Murasaki, one could hardly be modern.

Shikin tried to balance the contradiction inherent to her dual callings of
proper wife and woman writer. For a time, she returned her writing to the
elegant folds of feminine narrative, sublimating her own creative frustration
within the identities of heroines who suffer nobly to protect their chastity in

the face of immoral male desire and illogical social censure. But the pressure to write of modern issues through the medium of an antiquated past, along with the demands of domesticity and the blows to her already delicate psyche, were too daunting. For Shikin, the only solution was silence. Having inaugurated her career with a story describing a woman's refusal to endure her broken dreams, Shikin ends her career by breaking her own.

Conclusion

In the Shade of the Single Leaf

Someday, when I am older, will I be able to get rid of this impulse, this wanting to be a "good wife," without feeling lost? Would I then be able to write
my own story? I don't wish not to be a woman, but I'd certainly like to be a
woman whose sense of purpose comes from within.
                                        —Uno Chiyo, "A Genius of Imitation," 1936

The December 10, 1895, special issue of the newly established literary journal *Bungei kurabu* (Literary Arts Club) opened, as had all its previous issues,
with a sumptuously colored print. This one, by Watanabe Seitei
(1851–1918), depicted a woman in a languid position reading a little book,
her tiny mouth parted seductively as she stares intently at the volume in her
hand. Illustrations of women were not unusual in the *Bungei kurabu* frontispiece, not even of women reading.[1] But the contents of this particular issue
were surprising. Instead of the standard fare by Kōda Rohan, Yamada Bimyō,
and Izumi Kyōka, this special issue was devoted exclusively to the works of
keishū sakka (talented ladies of the inner chambers). Following Seitei's print
and the table of contents were photographs of three of the women represented in the volume: Koganei Kimiko, Wakamatsu Shizuko, and Higuchi
Ichiyō. Their portraits were placed in a triangular montage over a photograph
of a large and rather inelegant bird. Photographs of four other *keishū sakka*
were found on the next page arranged in similar fashion alongside a slightly
more delicate white bird. Then came examples of the calligraphy and ink
paintings of several more women writers, followed by a foldout page, also in
montage format, with snapshots of Kamakura and various animals. After
this, the literary works began: "Hagi kikyō" (Bush Clover and the Chinese
Bellflower) by Miyake Kaho; Wakamatsu Shizuko's "Wasuregatami" (The

Keepsake); and Higuchi Ichiyō's "Jūsan'ya" (The Thirteenth Night). The order of presentation denoted each woman's current standing in the literary world. Contributions by Koganei Kimiko, Kitada Usurai, Tazawa Inafune, and six others completed the volume.[2]

Selling at fifteen sen a copy, the *Bungei kurabu* special issue was a staggering success. As Robert Danly notes, the thirty thousand copies of its first printing were sold out immediately and the journal "had to go to press a second time to meet the unprecedented demand."[3] Not only did the issue provoke a tremendous increase in sales for the journal, it also drew an increase in critical attention. This publication of a special issue devoted to women's writing was feted in most of the literary journals of the day: *Taiyō*, *Jogaku zasshi*, *Teikoku bungaku*, *Kokumin no tomo*, *Seinen bun*, *Bungakukai*, and oth-

Figure 21   Front cover of the *keishū sakka* special issue of *Bungei kurabu*, December 10, 1895.

ers. Literary historians, reflecting on the success of this issue, have called 1895–1896 "the year of the *keishū sakka*."[4]

The Male Voyeur and the Female Celebrity

Critical reaction to the special issue was conflicted. Some reviewers thought that works such as Inafune's "Shirobara" (White Rose) went too far in the depiction of salacious sexual activity (in this case, a choloroform-induced rape). Other critics, however, said the works were too similar in their portrayal of marital relationships and offered readers nothing new. If Meiji critics agreed on anything it was that the women's contributions were worthwhile nevertheless because they allowed a rare "glimpse into the . . . interior of a woman's life"—a sphere that was as off limits to men as the domestic space of the kitchen.[5] It was this glimpse that gave the *keishū shōsetsu* value. Ironically, as we have seen, even when a woman writer did give her male reader a glimpse inside her life, she revealed largely what he wanted to see—presenting herself as she had been constructed by centuries of male creative writing and

Figure 22   Frontispiece to the *keishū sakka* special issue. Illustration by Watanabe Seitei. (Courtesy of Nihon Kindai Bungakkan)

performance. The window her writing offered, therefore, was little more than a mirror reflecting her readers' own biases, desires, and expectations. Women who refused to reinscribe their fiction with male-crafted versions of femininity were criticized as being imitative of men. What they were imitating, however, was the male prerogative to take control (authorship) of their own self-representation.[6]

The voyeurism implicit in the male regard of the woman writer did not limit itself to the assumed interiority of the woman's literary contribution. The *keishū sakka* herself, as a literary concept, became the object of the critics' scrutiny and admiration. Review after review of the *keishū* special issue described the authors as flowers, beauties, bright splashes of color. Because *Bungei kurabu* released the *keishū* issue on December 10, most of the reviews began to appear in early January. Inevitably the critics spoke of the special issue as a New Year's diversion: "Between games of battledore and poem

Figure 23   Photographs of the authors represented in the special issue. Wakamatsu Shizuko *(upper left),* Koganei Kimiko *(right),* Higuchi Ichiyō *(lower left).* (Courtesy of Nihon Kindai Bungakkan)

cards, I perused this *keishū* collection, a superlative book one might recommend to the proper and pampered ladies of the world."[7]

That the journal's editors had included photographs of the women created a sensation. This kind of publicity was unprecedented.[8] For women brought up in an environment that discouraged them from circulating indiscriminately among male company, this exposure must have been discomforting. Marianne Harrison notes that the reluctance among many aspiring women writers to take up the brush was perhaps due in large measure to the fact that it was still a sign of respectability among proper families to dissuade their daughters from reading newspapers or novels, holding up this refusal as a mark of their daughters' virtue and integrity.[9] If the very act of reading novels was frowned on, how much more damaging would it be for these daughters to appear in print—and not just as names (for names could be disguised) but as faces as well. The implications were great. One reviewer commended these women for their

Figure 24   Tazawa Inafune *(upper right)* and Kitada Usurai *(lower left)*. (Courtesy of Nihon Kindai Bungakkan)

courage: "So many women have shown such boldness *(kenage)* in bringing their works out in public. But how many more must still be unknown."[10]

Not all readers, however, were pleased with the women's "boldness." A reporter for the *Yomiuri* sent Ichiyō an indignant letter rebuking her for allowing her photograph to be printed. His ire was all the sharper because Kaho had "so nobly" refused to participate in such impropriety. Apparently Ichiyō had been tricked into submitting her photograph by *Bungei kurabu* editors who told her that Kaho had already sent hers. Ever competitive, Ichiyō did the same. But Kaho had sent a "ladylike" sample of her calligraphy, not a photograph.[11] At least one critic took a facetious view of the photographic display:

> Apparently the photographs of the beauties that have been appearing in every issue of this journal up to now have not been enough to entice the more intellectual fellow. And so now we have this special issue on women writers. . . . From Kaho and Ichiyō to Inafune and Usurai, the photographs selected easily meet the demands of the market. But what if, by the rarest of chances, you should have a woman writer who is not of even average good looks? In that case, you might consider this strategy: Announce the upcoming issue with flyers and posters enticing people to take a peek. But when you sell the issue, do so in a covered wrapper. This way, people will buy just for a look inside. Now isn't that a clever trick?[12]

This critic refers to *Bungei kurabu*'s practice of opening each issue with photographs of local beauties *(bijin)*. Almost all the young women depicted were denizens of select licensed quarters—"Kiyoko of Yoshiwara," for example, or "Shinbashi's Okin." Usually these pages were followed by photographs of scenic sites—Hakone or Kamakura, perhaps—or of new buildings or unusual animals. The *bijin*, therefore, were presented as little more than pleasant scenery *(fūkei)* to be viewed and enjoyed for its intrinsic beauty.[13] They were a selling point, and added to the somewhat titillating aura *Bungei kurabu* seemed to wish to project. It was, after all, unlike its contemporary *Shōnen sekai* (Youth's World), a literary journal for adults. From its first issues it had featured sumptuous prints by well-known illustrators. The *bijin* began to make their appearance from around the fourth issue, an innovation that prompted the journal *Seinen bun* to chide *Bungei kurabu*: "When we have the playboys *(suijin)* of *Bungei kurabu* running photographs of local *bijin*, it is no wonder there are claims that literature is to the pleasure quarters what lips are to teeth."[14]

Yet comments such as these, more teasing than critical, would hardly have persuaded the *Bungei kurabu* editors to discontinue a successful sales strategy. Like the showcasing of *bijin*, the *keishū* special issue was a commercial ploy—and one that anticipated a similar clientele. Although *Bungei kurabu* had been publishing *keishū shōsetsu* since the third issue, and doing so without drawing attention to the fact that the authors were female, this was the first time a mainstream journal had devoted an entire issue to women writers alone. The ploy was a success.

The merchandising nature of the venture was transparent. Less obvious was the eroticization of the woman writer that occurred in the process. The montage of the *keishū* photographs was similar to that of the *bijin* in previous issues. Moreover, in the issue immediately after the *keishū* special, the editors recycled the same layout by arranging the *bijin* around the photograph of a bird in much the same way that the earlier *keishū* had been displayed. In a sly, almost condescending way, the editors seemed to be implying, as Usurai's anonymous critic had similarly implied in the pages of the journal but a few months earlier, that a woman who sells her fiction is little more than a woman for sale. This sort of innuendo about women writers was hardly rare. Indeed, the very language that Meiji critics used to analyze women's works— or, more precisely, to compare the features of one author with those of another—almost arrived at the levity of the prostitutes critique *(hyōbanki)*. Although sexual attributes were certainly not being described, the vocabulary was nonetheless corporal and hinted at the carnal. Here a critic for *Seinen bun* compares Kaho with Ichiyō:

> *Jūsan'ya*: This is Ichiyō's work, and I cannot find words enough to praise it. Her writing is ripe and her use of dialogue skillful. . . . Personally I think that as a *shōsetsuka* she is a step ahead of Kaho. Kaho's works are elegant and beautiful, but they are limp, her prose flabby *(shimari naki)*. I don't suppose this is a good analogy, but in a way you can compare Kaho's works to a Kyoto harlot *(jorō)*. Both are beautiful as beauty goes, but they lack verve *(iki)*.
>
> Now when it comes to Ichiyō's works, there isn't even a suggestion of limpness, not a drop of listlessness. Her works are firm through and through, and tight without a single fissure. She is like the Tokyo courtesan *(gi)*, the very height of style *(iki)*.[15]

The impurity associated with literature at the time affected male writers as well, of course, but it threatened women in a way that was fundamentally more devastating because its implications were sexual. Even when guarded and couched in terms of "female essence" and "femininity," the criticism was there in the very presentation of the woman writer as a brave and bold creature who, unlike her modest sisters, allowed herself to become a public commodity. "Fame was not for women," Ann Rosalind Jones observes of Renaissance gender ideology:

The proper woman is an absence: legally, she vanishes under the name and authority of her father and her husband; as daughter and wife, she is enclosed in the private household. She is silent and invisible: she does not speak, and she is not spoken about.[16]

Similarly, a woman who spoke in Meiji Japan became a woman spoken about. Almost all the *keishū* writers were exposed to nearly unbearable scrutiny and often contradictory expectations. Shikin's debut is a case in point. When "Koware yubiwa" appeared in the January 1891 *Jogaku zasshi*, the issue was quick to sell out and had to go into a second printing. Shikin was soon to be feted in most of the major journals and by many of the major critics. It is unlikely that an unknown male writer would have received such attention.

Figure 25 Notable Tokyo Beauties *(bijin)* from the November 20, 1895, issue of *Bungei kurabu: upper right,* Shinbashi's Okin; *lower right,* Yoshiwara's Yakko; *upper left,* Yanagibashi's Yoshiko; *lower left,* Yoshiwara's Kiyoko; *center,* Shinbashi's Koi. (Courtesy of Nihon Kindai Bungakkan)

Nevertheless, the celebrity conferred on the woman writer of the early Meiji period generally harmed more than it helped her artistic development. For one thing, unlike many of her male counterparts, she was not allowed to labor within the protective folds of relative obscurity while she perfected her craft. For another, seldom was criticism based solely on the merits of her work; rather, it usually involved the reviewer's impressions of her character or physical appearance as a woman.[17] Adverse criticism sometimes verged on personal attack. Chūgai, in his review of Inafune's "Shirobara" (White Rose), after finding fault with the author's portrayal of the heroine Mitsuko as a flapper *(hasuha musume)* instead of a submissive woman, remarked that it was "not clear where the portrait of Mitsuko ended and the author's began."[18] Similarly Ōgai, in his brief assessment of Inafune's work, indicated

Figure 26 Notable Beauties from Nagasaki, Nagoya, Osaka, and Hiroshima as they appeared in the December 20, 1895, issue of *Bungei kurabu.* (Courtesy of Nihon Kindai Bungakkan)

that the author's heavily made-up face (a reference to her photograph in *Bungei kurabu*) was an integral component of his reading of the work.[19]

Like the *bijin* captured as photographic images for the entertainment of male readers, so the *keishū* writer was the product of male consumerism. Brought to the public eye through the largesse of a male mentor, she was packaged to please a male readership by savvy editors. As much as the prostitute is a creation of male desire, so the woman writer found herself compelled to conform to male assumptions. Confined by these constructions of her sex as object, how was the woman writer to give voice to her self as subject?

For Inafune the attempt ended in failure, as she soon lost control of the literary persona she had struggled to craft. When, mortally ill, she returned to Yamagata after her brief marriage to Bimyō, the media had a field day describing the rift. A month before she died, a Tōhoku newspaper reported that she had committed suicide. Somewhat later the paper printed a retraction, but not before the "news" had reached Tokyo. When Inafune finally did succumb on September 10, 1896, papers vied with one another in sensationalizing her death. None, it seemed, could settle for the fact that she had simply expired as a result of a long illness. They would have had her commit suicide out of desperation over her failed marriage. Even years after her death, the speculation continued—some claiming that she had swallowed a sleeping potion, others that she had stabbed herself in grief before her mother's grave.

By the end of the Meiji period, the woman writer was losing her status as an "unsullied" *keishū*—distinguished, prominent, and elegant—and was becoming more and more the object of scandal. The *keishū sakka* were young, most of them; because they were dependent on male mentors, it was not long before the relationships between these young women and their mentors seemed other than literary. The scandal inherent in the woman writer became so pronounced that more than one aspiring author chose silence over potential humiliation.[20] By 1914 it could be said: "If she's a woman involved in literature, the rumors go round that she's a menace to society. In this respect, female authors are celebrities known to all."[21]

Granted men too were the victims of unwarranted notoriety and the subjects of sensational journalism. Bimyō's failed marriage with Inafune cost him his seat in the *bundan*. His ouster, though, was due less to sexual misconduct than to his presumed coldness in the relationship. A man's actual involvement in sexual affairs did not detract greatly from his standing in society; indeed, if he were a writer, a "sensitivity" to love may have added to his perceived purity.[22] For a woman, however, her very status as noble and good was so tied to her sexual fidelity that even the suggestion of impropriety could destroy her. And to the extent that a male writer found himself pushed to the fringes of society because of the notoriety of his calling, he could seek solace and companionship in the fraternal shelter of the *bundan* and in the literary coteries it comprised. By contrast, the woman writer of this same period lacked a sorority that might have provided the sustenance she needed to nurture her style. More important, she lacked access to print through her own agency.[23]

To a certain extent, the women writers were allocated among the various *bundan* groups. The Ken'yūsha had Usurai; Bimyō, Inafune; Ōgai, his sister Kimiko. Shizuko was loyal to *Jogaku zasshi* and the early romantics, and to a lesser extent so was Kaho. It was Kaho who introduced Ichiyō to the *Bungakukai* members. Because Ichiyō did not owe any particular loyalty to the *Bungakukai,* not being related to any of the members or connected to them through family, her affiliation within the *bundan* was more or less up for grabs. In the last year of her life, the Ōgai camp fought the *Bungakukai* faction for possession of this single leaf.[24] Still, regardless of their affiliations, these women were not bona fide members of the coteries that "possessed" them. Like the *bijin* to whom the editors of the *Bungei kurabu* subtly compared them, they remained featured attractions, never members of the club. If these women belonged to any group at all, they were *keishū sakka.* Grouped together by virtue of gender, authors with social backgrounds and literary interests as diverse as Kaho and Ichiyō were expected to answer to identical programs, to share similar experiences and compatible visions, to write as one: "like women."

The tendency of the male *bundan* to fuse the *keishū sakka* together did not merely deny the women's artistic integrity. It invited comparisons to the brothel system itself. A *Jogaku zasshi* reviewer, for example, described the *keishū* as "an assemblage of famous flowers all in one hall."[25] Similarly, *Jogaku zasshi*'s announcement for the *keishū* issue stated: "Here the Murasakis and the Seis of Meiji meet under one roof and wage a contest of skills, a battle of wits."[26] These descriptions hint at the jealous sort of rivalry that ensues when women are forced to compete for the attention of a coveted male—as in the Heian court or in the Yoshiwara brothels. Thus even though thrust together under the rubric of *keishū sakka*, women writers ironically were kept apart from one another and forced to compete for the honor of "foremost woman writer."

One Single Leaf

In addition to exhorting women writers to be chaste and feminine, critics beseeched them to work hard at "maturing" their craft. Of all the irreconcilable demands imposed on the Meiji woman writer, this was perhaps the most impossible to satisfy. The *keishū sakka* was not allowed to grow up. If one equates "growing up" with marrying—as was generally the case in the Meiji period—then "grown women" were rarely on the roster of writing women. Inafune and Usurai were seventeen when they made their debut. Kaho and Ichiyō had not yet turned twenty. Shikin was twenty-three and Shizuko twenty-five. All were unmarried. All stopped writing within a decade of their debuts. There were two causes for the stoppage: marriage and death.

For a Meiji woman to be respectable, she needed to be respectably married. To acquit herself as a proper wife, she could hardly remain a serious, publishing author. To be sexually faithful, she had to remove herself from literature and its unchaste reputation. And to be selflessly devoted, she had to subjugate her own ambitions to those of the family.

The woman who put her commitment to art above her commitment to family was a woman of questionable virtue. The man who placed art before family, by contrast, was an artist of purest virtue. According to George Bernard Shaw: "The true artist will let his wife starve, his children go barefoot, and his mother drudge for a living at seventy, sooner than work at anything but his art."[27] One can only be reminded of Shimazaki Tōson, whose sacrifice of family for the sake of art, though earning him temporary censure from some critics, hardly diminished his literary reputation overall. One wonders, however, what the reaction would have been had Ichiyō sacrificed children or even neglected a husband to produce her work.

Ichiyō never had to juxtapose her role as writer against that of wife. Most of the other *keishū sakka* did. Shikin stopped publishing once married life became too demanding. Others, while not abandoning their craft altogether, altered the content of their stories to accommodate their new status as wives and mothers. Both Usurai and Shizuko turned to children's stories. Kaho grew noticeably more conservative after her marriage to a nationalist. She continued to write prose fiction in the early years of her marriage, but once her husband was financially stable she quit. Inafune was one of the few whose craft continued unaltered after marriage—no doubt because she was married to Bimyō. But her marriage barely lasted three months, and Inafune died before she could assert control over the literary persona she had created for herself.

Ichiyō was the only truly professional woman writer. Unlike her contemporaries, she was hardly from an elite background. She was the only *keishū sakka* not supported and protected by a father, brother, or husband. Legally the family head, she assumed the role of family caretaker. Whereas other female authors were criticized for investing too much of themselves in their craft, Ichiyō appeared all the more admirable and tragic for her dedication to writing. In this sense, Ichiyō was an aberration. Her rather humble beginnings and her premature death helped solidify her hold over a captivated *bundan*. By dying at twenty-four, unmarried, Ichiyō would ever remain a favored daughter. Maidenly, courageous, she would be forever denied the opportunity to perfect the promise not only of her debut as an artist but also her role as a woman—an incompletion that endears her to a reading audience long enamored with the "nobility of failure." Of course, Ichiyō was not the only *keishū* writer to die prematurely. Of the women discussed in this study, only Kaho, Shikin, and Kimiko lived beyond the Meiji era. Inafune died at twenty-three; Usurai at twenty-five; and Shizuko at thirty-two. The fragility of Meiji writing women did not go unnoticed:

> With pale faces and deep-set eyes, they struggle away, coughing all the while, "hack! hack!" Blowing their life out to warm the hardened tips of their brushes, their brush strokes thinner than a willow stem, thinner even are they. How can we praise them for throwing their lives away? And yet, without these innumerable sacrifices, we should never be able to produce a great writer.[28]

It was almost as if the pressure under which they labored and the sheer tenacity required to present themselves as public commodities were enough to exhaust the lives of these frail creatures.

And so ended the first era of women writers in modern Japan. It was an era characterized by hopes and contradictions. The very concept of *keishū sakka* was to become a paradox, for the talented lady of the inner chambers lost those qualities that distinguished her once she was exposed to the outer world. To compensate for charges of impropriety, the *keishū* writer resorted to elegant diction and hackneyed tropes, strategies that invited claims of narrowness and lack of creativity. Yet those who experimented with subject matter were accused of being imitative. At each turn the Meiji woman writer found her voice stifled, her sphere squeezed smaller. Expected to sacrifice her art for marriage, she was criticized for the shallowness of her commitment to writing when she did—and was despised for her selfishness when she did not.

But perhaps the cruelest blow came later. When this first wave passed, when the "era of the *keishū sakka*" drew to a close, most of the women who had struggled and experimented and sacrificed were forgotten. Their works were not collected and reprinted in easily accessible volumes; their stories were not retold.[29] In a 1925 *Waseda bungaku* article purportedly on "The *Keishū* Writers of the Meiji Period," the author Baba Kochō could speak with authority about only one of his subjects: Ichiyō, whom he had known personally and adored. About the other women, he could present only a few wisps of unsubstantiated hearsay. After summarily introducing those others by virtue of their relationships to the literary men in their lives, he spent the bulk of the article discussing Ichiyō. Three decades after their debut, the *keishū sakka* had disappeared beneath the identities of men. The only writer not to have been associated with a man remained to represent them all, though she was the one who was least representative of the collective *keishū* experience.

Ironically, the terms within which Ichiyō was evaluated in the *bundan* removed her from the *keishū* tradition—as if her true success as a writer could be established only by distancing her from the gender-coded program within which she had worked. Contemporary critics praised Ichiyō's stories in language that Margaret Atwood has called the "She-Writes-Like-a-Man" syndrome: "If you showed this story to someone, concealing the author's name, he would probably never guess it was written by a woman."[30] Despite the critics' insistence that women of Ichiyō's generation should "write like women," they reserved their highest accolades for the one who, they believed, "transcended her sex."

In a literary environment that was beginning to privilege the Writerly Image over the written product, Ichiyō appealed to the sympathies of an increasingly nationalistic readership. Seemingly spared the westernization of her "*jogakusei*" contemporaries, Ichiyō represented intrinsic Japanese values.[31] She was the "last woman of Edo" and the "personification of sorrow."[32] In Ichiyō readers found a repository of all that had been innocent, noble, and beautiful in Japanese womanhood before the waves of westernization had washed in.

This is not to denigrate Ichiyō's achievements. For all the delicacy and beauty of her prose—a trait she shared with other women writers of the period—her works evince a gutsiness and spunk not to be found in Kaho or Shizuko. Ichiyō's closeness to the impoverished conditions of the "low city" denizens imbues her works with a sensitivity and an immediacy that Shikin, despite her keen sympathy for the downtrodden, could not approximate. But according to some critics, even Ichiyō is not entitled to the appellation of "great writer"—for her position in the literary world today is based on the reception of a few slim volumes.[33] Therefore the question remains: Why has Ichiyō's canonization required the erasure of all the others? In opening the *bundan* to female inductees, did the "canon makers" determine that one was enough? Does the very process of female inclusion in a male-dominated arena require singularity? In allowing only one, does not the *bundan* further marginalize the marginal writer by presenting her as an anomaly? Rewriting a literary history to suggest there was only one woman writer breeds the assumption that there *can be* only one.

Positioning Ichiyō as a lone figure on the brink of modernity has enhanced her vulnerability and romanticized her. Adding other female voices would have ruined the solo. But by presenting Ichiyō as the *only* writing woman of the early Meiji period, literary historians elevated her to a status that made her inaccessible as a model to later women writers. The notion that Ichiyō's achievements occurred in a vacuum of female activity suggested that literary success was possible only for anomalous women. It erased those qualities that Ichiyō's peers had shared but she had lacked: the privilege, the education, the progressiveness, and, most important, the married status. It made of Ichiyō, like Murasaki and Sei before her, a romanticized ideal whose very idolization became a burden rather than birthright for successors.

Given the pressures on women to marry and devote themselves to household duties, lionizing a "favored daughter" at the expense of the "grown woman" hindered the maturation of women writers and contributed to the uneasy relationship that would ensue between writing women and marriage and between writing women and class privilege. In subsequent years, women writers came to be associated more and more with impropriety and scandal. Tamura Toshiko, Uno Chiyo, Sata Ineko, and Hayashi Fumiko were all poor or divorced or both. The trend became so noticeable that Setouchi Harumi would suggest in a 1962 essay, "Joryū sakka ni naru jōken" (Qualifications for Becoming a Woman Writer), that an inability to be a good wife and the courage to "strip in public" were among the essential requirements for a woman writer.[34]

Subsequent generations of women writers, therefore, would continue to wrestle with the association of publication and promiscuity. They would continue to struggle, as well, against male constructions of femininity—self-belittling battles that might not have been so stultifying had these women been more familiar with the dignity and strength of their *keishū* foremothers.[35] But having been denied access to the inspiration these earlier women might have offered as alternative models, women had to reinvent themselves as writers with each new generation—as if they were the first to arrive on the scene. Whatever ground had been gained by earlier generations was lost as each new wave of women writers labored to carve out a space for themselves between gender-based expectation and authentic self-expression. Women would toil for years, decades even, before a mature writer could emerge from the shade of that one slender leaf.

Notes

Introduction

1. Higuchi Ichiyō has been well represented in Japanese-language studies. The most extensive study in English is Robert Danly's *In the Shade of Spring Leaves: The Writings of Higuchi Ichiyō, a Woman of Letters in Meiji Japan* (New Haven: Yale University Press, 1981).

2. See, for example, Arthur Waley, *The Pillow Book of Sei Shōnagon* (London: Allen & Unwin, 1928), pp. 92–93.

3. "Ichiyō" means "one leaf." Danly, in *Shade of Spring Leaves,* describes its implication for the author as follows: " 'One leaf' referred to the legendary boat consisting of a single reed upon which Bodhidharma, the Zen patriarch, was said to have crossed the Yangtze River after a disastrous interview with Emperor Wu-ti (502–550). Tradition has it that he disembarked from his miraculous vessel and seated himself before a wall in the monastery of Shao-lin-ssŭ, where he remained without moving for nine years. . . . [B]y the time the nine-year stint was up, both of Bodhidharma's legs had atrophied. . . . It so happened that the expression 'to have no legs' *(oashi ga nai)* also meant to have no money. Natsuko, in her own way proud of her hardships and wanting to distinguish herself from 'lady writers,' decided to flaunt her humble circumstances. Like Bodhidharma, then, in a manner of speaking she had no legs, and so she adopted his single-leaf skiff as her literary sobriquet" (p. 51).

4. As quoted in Donald Keene, "Higuchi Ichiyō," in *Dawn to the West—Fiction* (New York: Holt, 1984), p. 178.

5. See Danly, *Shade of Spring Leaves,* p. 154.

6. The situation in Japanese scholarship is somewhat different. Studies by Wada Shigejirō as well as by Shioda Ryōhei discuss a number of Meiji women writers as *"keishū sakka"* (see note 9) but make little attempt to analyze the rationale underlying their separation from the literary mainstream. Since the late 1980s, several studies by Japanese feminist critics have emerged that reassess the writing by Meiji women. Among these are book-length biographies of Shimizu Shikin, Kitada Usurai, and Wakamatsu Shizuko. Yet the feminist "rereadings" *(yominaosu)* of Higuchi Ichiyō far outnumber the "recovery" of forgotten Meiji women writers. In English there is Marianne Harrison's dissertation, "The Rise

of the Woman Novelist in Meiji Japan" (University of Chicago, 1991). In this groundbreaking study, Harrison contextualizes women's writing by defining the dominant attitudes toward women, writing, and femininity in the Meiji era.

7. Margaret J. M. Ezell, in *Writing Women's Literary History* (Baltimore: Johns Hopkins University Press, 1993), pp. 41–42, cautions against the penchant for selecting "firsts," as such appellations inevitably deny the existence of possible predecessors. Although most scholars point to 1888 and Miyake Kaho's *Yabu no uguisu* (Warbler in the Grove) as the start of literary activity by women in the Meiji period, a few designate Nakajima Shōen (Kishida Toshiko) and her 1887 "Zen'aku no chimata" (The Crossroads of Good and Evil). But the selection of Shōen as a "first" is problematic since "Zen'aku no chimata" is a translation/adaptation of Bulwer-Lytton's *Eugene Aram* (1832). Some might suggest that Kaho's work, considered the "female version" of Tsubouchi Shōyō's *Tōsei shosei katagi* (Characters of Modern-Day Students), is also something of an adaptation. Any naming of a "first," therefore, is arbitrary and threatens to erase whatever strides had been made in the traditional and hence more private enclaves of women's writing, such as the *waka* circles, during the centuries between the Heian and Meiji eras.

8. See, for example, Margaret Mitsutani's characterization of Kaho as imitative and lacking artistic passion and dedication in "Higuchi Ichiyō: A Literature of Her Own," *Comparative Literature Studies* 22 (1985):54–55.

9. "*Keishū*" was a term derived from China, where it had denoted talented women of the "inner chamber." See Dorothy Ko's *Teachers of the Inner Chambers: Women and Culture in Seventeenth-Century China* (Stanford: Stanford University Press, 1994).

10. The first extensive study of modern Japanese women writers in English was Victoria V. Vernon, *Daughters of the Moon: Wish, Will, and Social Constraint in Fiction by Modern Japanese Women* (Berkeley: Institute of East Asian Studies, University of California, 1988). More recently Paul Schalow and Janet Walker have edited a first-of-its-kind collection of critical essays on Japanese women writers in English: *The Woman's Hand: Gender and Theory in Japanese Women's Writing* (Stanford: Stanford University Press, 1996). Anthologies of translations include: *This Kind of Woman: Ten Stories by Japanese Women Writers*, ed. Elizabeth Hansen and Yukiko Tanaka (Stanford: Stanford University Press, 1982); Phyllis Birnbaum's *Rabbits, Crabs, Etc.: Stories by Japanese Women Writers* (Honolulu: University of Hawai'i Press, 1983); *Stories by Contemporary Japanese Women Writers*, ed. Noriko Mizuta Lippit and Kyoko Selden (New York: M. E. Sharpe, 1983); Yukiko Tanaka, ed., *To Live and to Write: Selections by Japanese Women Writers 1913–1938* (Seattle: Seal Press, 1987) and *Unmapped Territories: New Women's Fiction from Japan* (Seattle: Women in Translation, 1991). Among the biographies are Danly, *Shade of Spring Leaves;* Rebecca Copeland, *The Sound of the Wind: The Life and Works of Uno Chiyo* (Honolulu: University of Hawai'i Press, 1992); Alan

Tansman, *The Writings of Kōda Aya, a Japanese Literary Daughter* (New Haven: Yale University Press, 1993); Joan Ericson, *Be a Woman: Hayashi Fumiko and Modern Japanese Women's Literature* (Honolulu: University of Hawai'i Press, 1997); and Ann Sherif, *Mirror: The Fiction and Essays of Kōda Aya* (Honolulu: University of Hawai'i Press, 1999). Additionally, translations have been made of Enchi Fumiko, Ariyoshi Sawako, Kurahashi Yumiko, Tsushima Yūko, and many others. A number of critical studies, moreover, are pending publication.

Chapter One: Educating the Modern Murasaki

1. The "completeness" of this silence over the centuries between the Heian and the Meiji is, of course, debatable. Women continued to write in the traditional (and thereby more acceptable) genres of poety—such as *waka* and haiku. They also composed in classical Chinese. There are a number of collections of female-authored works during this period, such as the two-volume *Joryū bungaku shi* (History of Women's Literature) edited by Kobayashi Jinsaku in 1901. For more on women's writing between the Heian and Meiji eras see Joan Ericson, "The Origins of the Concept of 'Women's Literature,' " in *The Woman's Hand: Gender and Theory in Japanese Women's Writing,* ed. Paul Gordon Schalow and Janet A. Walker (Stanford: Stanford University Press, 1996), pp. 74–115.

2. These figures are from Wada Shigejirō, *Meiji zenki joryū sakuhinron—Higuchi Ichiyō to sono zengo* (Ōfūsha, 1989), pp. 620–621. It should be noted that Ichiyō did not begin writing prose fiction until 1892.

3. See literary historians Wada Shigejirō and Shioda Ryōhei, for example.

4. Nor is it necessary to incorporate all the issues related to Meiji-era women, for numerous historians have already covered this ground in English. See particularly Sharon Sievers, *Flowers in Salt: The Beginnings of Feminist Consciousness in Modern Japan* (Stanford: Stanford University Press, 1983), for a thorough discussion of the political and social climate for women in Meiji Japan. Margit Maria Nagy provides an incisive overview of the family institution in her Ph.D. dissertation, "How Shall We Live?: Social Change, the Family Institution, and Feminism in Prewar Japan" (University of Washington, 1981). Although addressed to a slightly later period, Helen Hopper's biography of Katō Shidzue similarly provides background to the social and political aspects influencing women in Meiji Japan: see *A New Woman of Japan: A Political Biography of Katō Shidzue* (Boulder: Westview, 1996); see also Shidzué's autobiography, *Facing Two Ways: The Story of My Life* (Stanford: Stanford University Press, 1984). Barbara Rose discusses early attitudes toward education for women in *Tsuda Umeko and Women's Education in Japan* (New Haven: Yale University Press, 1992), as does Yoshiko Furuhi in *The White Plum—A Biography of Ume Tsuda: Pioneer in the Higher Education of Japanese Women* (New York: Weatherhill, 1991). Finally,

selections from the following edited volumes illuminate many aspects of Meiji womanhood: Gail Lee Bernstein, ed., *Recreating Japanese Women, 1600–1945* (Berkeley: University of California Press, 1991); Janet Hunter, ed., *Japanese Women Working* (New York: Routledge, 1993); Kumiko Fujimura-Fanselow and Atsuko Kameda, eds., *Japanese Women: New Feminist Perspectives on the Past, Present, and Future* (New York: Feminist Press, 1995); and Marius B. Jansen and Gilbert Rozman, eds., *Japan in Transition from Tokugawa to Meiji* (Princeton: Princeton University Press, 1986).

5.   Donald Keene has termed 1885 "the year of miracles for modern Japanese literature." The year saw the emergence of the Ken'yūsha, or "Friends of the Inkstone," and the serialization of Tsubouchi Shōyō's (1859–1935) seminal essay on the state of Japanese prose fiction, *Shōsetsu shinzui* (The Essence of the Novel), thought to herald the beginning of modern literature in Japan. See Donald Keene, *Dawn to the West—Fiction* (New York: Holt, 1984), p. 119. In the political arena, the year 1885 saw the trial of several members of the Freedom and Popular Rights Movement (Jiyū minken undō)—among them the women's rights activist Kageyama (Fukuda) Hideko—who had been implicated in a plot to launch a military expedition in Korea. In education, 1885 marked the founding of the Ministry of Education (Mombushō) and the naming of Mori Arinori (1847–1889) as its first minister. The year also realized a number of developments central to the women's movement in addition to the founding of *Jogaku zasshi*. The first female doctor of medicine, Ogino Gin (1851–1913), opened her own practice; Japanese Christians founded Meiji Jogakkō (Meiji Women's School) in Tokyo; and Fukuzawa Yukichi (1835–1901) serialized his essay "Nippon fujin ron" (On Japanese Women) in *Jiji shinpō*. Most of the year's highlights seem singularly unrelated. But in a curious way they are all linked, some more tightly than others, and all affected the emergence of women's writing in Meiji Japan, some more obviously than others. In describing the forces that led to a renewal of Japanese women's writing, most literary historians point to the work of Christians, both Japanese and foreign, who focused on education for women and on improving women's social welfare. Some cite the efforts of male and female activists to advance women politically; others credit the renewed interest in literature overall, both Western and domestic.

6.   Sōma Kokkō, *Mokui—Meiji, Taishō bungakushi kaisō* (Hōsei Daigaku shuppankyoku, 1961), p. 62. Sōma Kokkō is typical of the "enlightened" Meiji woman because she is so unlike other Meiji women. Born Hoshi Ryō to a samurai family in Sendai, she was raised between the cusps of traditional Confucian thought and newly imported Western ideas. Schooled by a variety of American missionaries, she struck out for Tokyo as an "ambitious girl." There she eventually gained admittance to Meiji Women's School. Iwamoto gave her the nickname Kokkō, or "black light," because of the way her dark eyes danced with excite-

ment. Kokkō failed to become a "woman writer," her original goal, and married a young entrepreneur. In 1901 she opened a bakery in Shinjuku, where she served Western-style breads and Russian cakes and conducted a literary salon for bohemian spirits of all nationalities. After meeting Indian émigrés, she began to serve curry, a dish that has become a mainstay in Japan today. Her bakery as well, the Nakamura-ya, continues to thrive.

7. Meiji Women's School was founded by Kimura Kumaji (1845–1927), a Christian minister, and his wife, Kimura Tō (1848–1886). Recently returned from studies in the United States, Kimura was embarrassed by the meager education available to Japanese women. His wife began a "Fujinkai" or Women's Circle in their church, and this eventually evolved into Meiji Women's School in 1885. Subjects covered in the school included English, geography, history, physiology, physics, chemistry, plant and animal science, mineralogy, mathematics, ethics, and classical Chinese. In addition to Mr. and Mrs. Kimura, other instructors at the school during the early period were Iwamoto Yoshiharu and Tsuda Umeko (1867–1929). Eventually the writers Wakamatsu Shizuko and Shimizu Shikin taught there, as did fellow writers Hoshino Tenchi (1862–1950), Shimazaki Tōson (1872–1943), and Kitamura Tōkoku (1868–1894). Among some of the more notable students were Sōma Kokkō, the journalist and educator Hani Motoko (1873–1957), and the writers Miyake Kaho (1868–1943), Ōtsuka Kusuko (1875–1910), and Nogami Yaeko (1885–1985). Although Kimura was headmaster of the school for the first few years, he left most of the work to his wife. When she died of cholera at the age of thirty-eight, Iwamoto, who had been assisting her from the start, took over her responsibilities, eventually becoming headmaster in 1892. The school closed in 1908.

8. The obvious exception is Michael Brownstein's "*Jogaku Zasshi* and the Founding of Bungakukai," *Monumenta Nipponica* 35(3) (1980): 319–336, which provides the most thorough information on the journal to date. See also Chieko Mulhern's chapter on Hani Motoko in *Heroic with Grace* (New York: Sharpe, 1991), pp. 208–264. Sharon Sievers' *Flowers in Salt: The Beginnings of Feminist Consciousness in Modern Japan* (Stanford: Stanford University Press, 1983), though it does not discuss the journal directly, provides the historical and political context for *Jogaku zasshi* and the women who contributed to it.

9. Inoue Teruko, "Iwamoto Yoshiharu no bungakuron," *Bungaku* 37 (October 1969):97. Some scholars erroneously believe that *Jogaku zasshi* became *Bungakukai*—a notion that Brownstein refutes.

10. The members of the Ken'yūsha, for example, were all affiliated with Tokyo Imperial University. Women were not admitted to this institution until 1913, and even then few attended. As for the importance of belonging to a particular coterie and associating with a particular journal, see Marvin Marcus, *Paragons of the*

Ordinary: The Biographical Literature of Mori Ōgai (Honolulu: University of Hawai'i Press, 1993), pp. 30–58. Marcus terms the Meiji literary institution "a journalistic fiefdom, with aspiring writers having to apprentice themselves to an influential sensei in order to get into print and establish a career" (p. 36).

11. Ōba Sōkichi is listed as one of the founders in the *Kōdansha Encyclopedia of Japan*, vol. 4. Little mention is made of him otherwise, however, and it seems his contribution to the journal, once it was established, was minimal.

12. Sievers, *Flowers in Salt*, p. 16. To characterize this "silliness" it should be noted that much ink was expended at the time in arguing the pros and cons of the "ladies first" customs observed in Western countries. In the thirty-first issue of *Meiroku zasshi* (March 1875), for example, Katō Hiroyuki fusses angrily over the notion that females should be treated with respect and delicacy. He misunderstands chivalry as veneration and cannot fathom why men should "humble" themselves before women. He is particularly incensed by Western men's practice of refraining from smoking in a woman's presence. Apparently his anger was piqued by an incident in which he was rebuked, by a foreign guest, for smoking: "Even though I of course knew the custom that forbids smoking in the presence of Western ladies, I dared not to follow it since it is completely unreasonable. . . . [I]t is my free right to smoke since I enjoy tobacco. If ladies do not like smoking, they may themselves leave their seats. It can never be right for them to obstruct a man's freedom for the reason that they themselves disapprove. . . . Furthermore, if the habit violated morals or if it injured another's health, then I too, naturally, would not smoke." See *Meiroku zasshi*, translated by William Reynolds Braisted, assisted by Adachi Yasushi and Kikuchi Yūji (Cambridge, Mass.: Harvard University Press, 1976), pp. 376–379.

13. As noted in Ann Harrington, "Women and Higher Education in the Japanese Empire (1885–1945)," *Journal of Asian History* 21 (1987):170.

14. Ibid.

15. Sievers, *Flowers in Salt*, p. 10.

16. Mulhern, *Heroic with Grace*, p. 214. We must distinguish, however, between elementary school and "higher" school for both girls and boys. Compulsory education eventually covered six years of schooling and was coeducational up to grade 3. Male students could advance to middle school *(chūgakkō)* for grades 7–11 and then to either high school *(kōtō gakkō)*, generally four years, where they took courses prepatory to university, or to a similarly advanced but terminal three-year school. According to Harrington, girls advanced directly from compulsory schooling to girls' "higher" school *(kōtō jogakkō)*, which included grades 7–11 and thus was equivalent to a boy's middle school "in years but not in quality" (p. 172). In 1884, the first Higher Normal School for Women was opened in Tokyo: known as the Tokyo Joshi Kōtōshihan Gakkō, or Tokyo Women's Higher

Normal School, it was "the only educational institution for women above the high school level" (p. 174). Harrington notes that only two more "higher" high schools for women were established in Japan between this time and the end of World War II. For the most part, women were expected to find contentment in the numerous private high schools, such as the Meiji Women's School.

17. Miss Mary Kidder (1834–1910) was the first single woman missionary in Japan. Sent under the auspices of the Dutch Reformed Church of America, her goal was to educate Japanese women and win them to her faith. To that end she opened a school for women in 1870. In 1875 the school became known as Ferris Seminary, in honor of Isaac Ferris, former general secretary of the Dutch Reformed Church Mission. Ferris Seminary survives today under the name Ferris Women's College. More information on this institution will be given in Chapter Three on Wakamatsu Shizuko, who in 1882 was the first graduate of Ferris Seminary.

18. Edwin Luther Copeland, "The Crisis of Protestant Missions to Japan, 1889–1900" (Ph.D. dissertation, Yale University, 1947), p. 37.

19. Ibid., p. 35.

20. Sōma, *Mokui,* p. 11.

21. Carol Gluck, *Japan's Modern Myths: Ideology in the Late Meiji Period* (Princeton: Princeton University Press, 1985), p. 110.

22. As cited in Harrington, "Women and Higher Education," p. 173.

23. Cited in Fujita Yoshimi, *Meiji jogakkō no sekai* (Seieisha, 1984), p. 243.

24. Ibid., pp. 242–243.

25. Ibid. Fujita also notes that Iwamoto resented the "high-collar" approach to education that the mission schools provided: "For a student accustomed to Ferris Seminary, the school buildings and dormitories at Meiji Women's School would have seemed abysmal. The desks and chairs were rickety, there were no modern facilities, and the level of English was low" (p. 171).

26. Sōma, *Mokui,* pp. 53–54.

27. A member of the influential Meiroku (Meiji Six) Society, Nakamura Masanao is most remembered today for his translations of Samuel Smiles' *Self Help* and John Stuart Mill's *On Liberty.* Dōninsha, now defunct, was then on a par with Fukuzawa Yukichi's private academy Keio Gijuku (now Keio University). Tsuda Sen, an educator in his own right, is perhaps best remembered today as the father of Tsuda Umeko (1864–1929), who was sent as a child to study in the United States and returned to found Tsuda Juku Women's University. See Rose, *Tsuda Umeko.*

28. John D. Pierson, *Tokutomi Sohō, 1863–1957: A Journalist for Modern Japan* (Princeton: Princeton University Press, 1980), p. 154.

29. James Huffman, *Politics of the Meiji Press: The Life of Fukuchi Gen'ichiro* (Honolulu: University of Hawai'i Press, 1980), p. 85.

30. As cited in Yanagida Izumi, "*Jogaku zasshi*," *Bungaku* (January 1955):30.

31. Mulhern, *Heroic with Grace*, p. 214.

32. As cited in Otis Cary, *A History of Christianity in Japan: Protestant Missions* (New York: Revell, 1909), p. 188.

33. Art historian Elizabeth Lillehoj suggests that illustrations of Empress Jingū grew in popularity in the early Meiji period, perhaps because certain factions inside and outside the government were advocating military campaigns in Korea. For similar illustrations of Jingū preparing for battle in Korea, see Lillehoj's *Woman in the Eyes of Man: Images of Women in Japanese Art from the Field Museum* (Chicago: DePaul University Publications, 1995), pp. 72–73.

34. From Lady Ise and Izumi Shikibu of the Heian era (794–1185) to Yosano Akiko (1878–1942), hair has been used as a poetic metaphor for female sexuality. Moreover, a woman's hairstyle signified her social and sexual standing by identifying her as belonging to the city or the country and by marking her as married or as a member of the demimonde or the religious orders.

35. Sievers, *Flowers in Salt*, p. 15.

36. *Hako iri musume* ("daughters kept in boxes") gained currency after people's rights activist Kishida Toshiko (later known as Nakajima Shōen) used it in the title of a lecture she delivered on October 12, 1883. When Kishida's speech attacked a family system that physically and mentally "boxed" its daughters, she was interrupted by police and arrested. See Sievers, *Flowers in Salt*, pp. 34–41.

37. The categories offered were: hair, face, eyes, nose, perspiration, food, manners, language, and so on. Under "hair," for example, we have "Western women: short, blonde, and curly; Japanese women: long, black, and straight." "Nose" gives us "Western women: large, long, starting beneath the brow; Japanese women: small, short, starting beneath the eyes." And under "urination/defecation" we have "Western women: both functions performed separately; Japanese women: simultaneously."

38. G. B. Sansom, *The Western World and Japan: A Study in the Interaction of European and Asiatic Cultures* (Tokyo: Tuttle, 1950), pp. 370–371. See also Donald H. Shively, "Japanization of the Middle Meiji," in Donald H. Shively, ed., *Tradition and Modernization in Japanese Culture* (Princeton: Princeton University Press, 1971), pp. 94–96.

39. The journal was banned twice more. Issue 466 (May 25, 1898) ran afoul of government officials because it included an editorial critical of parliamentary behavior. Issue 508 (March 25, 1900) carried an editorial by Iwamoto titled "Kōdoku bungaku" (Literature of Copper Poisoning), which criticized the Ashio mining

incident. For each infraction the journal received a two-month ban. See Ōta Saburō, "*Jogaku zasshi* kenkyū, 1," *Shomotsu tenbō* (May 1950):25.

40. Not all admired Kajiko's actions, of course. Her own nephews, Tokutomi Sohō, editor of *Kokumin no tomo*, and Tokutomi Roka (1868–1927), a popular author, were highly critical (Sievers, *Flowers in Salt*, pp. 89–93). After her divorce Yajima took a position with Joshi Gakuin, a Christian women's school, where she served as head administrator from 1889 to 1914. She also represented Japan at temperance conferences in Boston (1906) and London (1920). See Mulhern, *Heroic with Grace*, pp. 210–211.

41. Kathleen Uno, "One Day at a Time: Work and Domestic Activities of Urban Lower-Class Women in Early Twentieth-Century Japan," in Janet Hunter, ed., *Japanese Women Working*, (New York: Routledge, 1993), p. 39.

42. Ibid.; see also the sources cited therein.

43. Wakamatsu Shizuko, "The Condition of Woman in Japan," an insert in *Jogaku zasshi* 98 (February 2, 1888):4. The insert is the text of an 1887 report Shizuko wrote in English for a conference on women held at Vassar College.

44. First a daughter, then a wife, and finally a mother, a woman had no identity and thereby no real "home" of her own. The proverb is: "Onna sangai ni ie nashi" (Woman has no home in three worlds).

45. See Brownstein, *"Jogaku Zasshi,"* p. 321.

46. Titles for featured articles such as these were routinely rendered in English in the table of contents, occasionally to humorous (though unintentional) effect.

47. For a general discussion of literature as a tool for educating women, see Peter Kornicki, *The Reform of Fiction in the Meiji Period* (London: Ithaca Press, 1982), pp. 16–19. Tomi Suzuki, in *Narrating the Self: Fictions of Japanese Modernity* (Stanford: Stanford University Press, 1996), p. 17, quotes Shikitei Sanba (1776–1822) on the subject of using fiction to educate women and children: "To educate and raise children, we use both bitter medicine and sweet candy. When it comes to books, the three Chinese classical histories and the five Confucian classics are bitter medicine, while narrative fiction [*haikan-yashi*, "unorthodox, vulgar history"] is sweet candy. Although there are many manuals for the education of women, such books as *Onna daigaku* and *Imagawa* are so bitter that women and girls can hardly appreciate them. This *shōsetsu* about a bathhouse for women [*Ukiyo burō*] may appear to be no more than light entertainment, but it is as easy to appreciate as sweet candy and the ways of good, evil, and righteousness can be learned without effort." For more on Iwamoto Yoshiharu's regard of literature as an educational implement see Inoue Teruko, "Iwamoto Yoshiharu no bungakuron," *Bungaku* 37 (October 1969):97–110.

48. As quoted in "*Bungei kurabu* dai shichi hen," *Seinen bun* 2 (August 1895):12.

49. Brownstein, *"Jogaku Zasshi,"* p. 324, discusses Iwamoto's critique of these earlier *gesaku* works.

50. Kornicki, *Reform of Fiction*, p. 12.

51. According to Buddhist belief, language itself is the product of the illusory world and may prove destructive because it deludes people into falsely placing trust in the power and efficacy of words. The four Buddhist sins of the word are false-hood, equivocation, slander, and frivolous talk. Fictional narratives, it was believed in the medieval period, construct illusory worlds that lure the gullible away from the truth. The only proper way to employ fiction is as an expedient *(hōben)* to enlightenment. Buddhist parables fit this description. Similarly, tradi-tional Confucian views of prose narrative held that value and merit were found only in that which performed a service to the state. History was acceptable because it rectified wrongs and cultivated correct moral behavior. Fiction did not do so and hence was disdained.

52. Kornicki, *Reform of Fiction*, p. 13.

53. Inoue, "Iwamoto Yoshiharu," p. 103.

54. As cited in Ōta, *"Jogaku zasshi* kenkyū 1," p. 23.

55. "Truth," of course, is an ambiguous term. Here I am using the word as Tomi Suzuki has defined it in *Narrating the Self: Fictions of Japanese Modernity.* Traditionally the idea of *"shōsetsu"* in Japan had been associated with vulgar, dis-torted accounts of "history." In an effort to overcome this negative connotation, Meiji-period defenders of the *shōsetsu* tried to align it with "realism" and "truth." Suzuki quotes from an 1886 essay by Tsubouchi Shōyō: "What matters is the power of writing to depict human truth [*ningen no shinri*]. . . . A *shōsetsu* should depict the formless, invisible truth [*shinri*] and give it life." See Suzuki, *Narrating the Self,* p. 22.

56. James A. Fujii, *Complicit Fictions: The Subject in the Modern Japanese Prose Narrative* (Berkeley: University of California Press, 1993), pp. 11–12.

57. See Sharon H. Nolte and Sally Ann Hastings, "The Meiji State's Policy toward Women, 1890–1910," in Bernstein, *Recreating Japanese Women,* pp. 151–174.

58. Iwamoto indicated that Item 7 of these regulations limited editorship to men. For more on government censorship of the press see Huffman, *Politics of the Meiji Press;* see also Gregory Kasza, *The State and the Mass Media in Japan: 1918–1945* (Berkeley: University of California Press, 1988); Richard H. Mitchell, *Censorship in Imperial Japan* (Princeton: Princeton University Press, 1983); and Jay Rubin, *Injurious to Public Morals: Writers and the Meiji State* (Seattle: University of Washington Press, 1984).

59. Brett de Bary, "Introduction to Special Issue: Gender and Imperialism," *U.S.-Japan Women's Journal, English Supplement* 12 (1997):3.

60. The *furigana* accompanying the title reads *"Joshi to shōsetsu"* for the first install-
    ment. But successive installments are *"nyoshi."*

61. Fujii, *Complicit Fictions,* p. 14.

62. Marleigh Grayer Ryan, *The Development of Realism in the Fiction of Tsubouchi Shōyō*
    (Seattle: University of Washington Press, 1975), p. 23. It was not until 1890 that
    the complete *Tale of Genji* was available in a movable-type reprint. Prior to this,
    complete copies were not easily accessible. For more on the impact of this and other
    Genji reprints on a Meiji readership, see G. G. Rowley, "Literary Canon and
    National Identity: *The Tale of Genji* in Meiji Japan," *Japan Forum* 9(1) (1997):1–15.

63. Harrison, "Rise of the Woman Novelist," p. 99.

64. Ibid., p. 101.

65. Sociologist Ueno Chizuko suggests that "the Japanese" (male as well as female)
    have been gendered female by the matrix of Orientalism in which the West is
    posited male and the East female. This metaphor poses a problem for modern
    Japanese feminists: "On the one hand, if feminists ask for equal rights, they are
    accused of being anti-Japanese; on the other hand, if they stress feminine virtues,
    men think it over and say, 'Look, in contrast to Western men we are already fem-
    inine enough. Why do we have to become more feminine?'" See "Ueno
    Chizuko," in Sandra Buckley, ed., *Broken Silence: Voices of Japanese Feminism*
    (Berkeley: University of California Press, 1997), p. 297. See also Ueno Chizuko,
    "In the Feminine Guise: A Trap of Reverse Orientalism," *U.S.-Japan Women's
    Journal, English Supplement* 13 (1997):3–25.

66. Ann Ardis, *New Women, New Novels: Feminism and Early Modernism* (New
    Brunswick: Rutgers University Press, 1990), p. 90.

67. See Carol T. Christ, " 'The Hero as Man of Letters': Masculinity and Victorian
    Nonfiction Prose," in Thais E. Morgan, ed., *Victorian Sages and Cultural
    Discourse: Renegotiating Gender and Power* (New Brunswick: Rutgers University
    Press, 1990), pp. 19–31. I am indebted to Michael Brownstein for bringing this
    idea as well as this study to my attention.

68. Ryan, *Fiction of Tsubouchi Shōyō ,* p. 62.

69. As cited and translated in Suzuki, *Narrating the Self,* p. 24.

70. Harrison, "Rise of the Woman Novelist," p. 120.

71. Ibid., p. 110.

72. Wada, *Meiji zenki joryū sakuhinron,* p. 18.

73. Ibid., p. 23.

74. Harrison, "Rise of the Woman Novelist," p. 92.

75. As cited in Todoroki Eiko, *Kitada Usurai kenkyū* (Sōbunsha, 1984), p. 38. The
    allusion to Usurai's friendship with her inkstone and brush *(hikken no yū)* may

have been a pun, as she was a disciple of Ozaki Kōyō and his Ken'yūsha (Friends of the Inkstone).

76. Wakamatsu Shizuko, "Keishū shōsetsuka tō, dai san: Wakamatsu Shizuko," in *Jogaku zasshi* 207 (April 5, 1890):188.

77. In Japanese, the word *"kei"* also denotes bedroom *(neya)*. But when used in combination with *"shū"* the (hetero)sexual connotation of "bedroom" is replaced by the single-sex sanctum of a woman's separate sphere: the "inner chambers" of the Chinese derivation.

78. For a discussion of *"joryū"* see Joan Ericson's essay in *The Woman's Hand*.

79. As translated in Harrison, "Rise of the Woman Novelist," pp. 93–94.

80. Sandra Gilbert and Susan Gubar, "Tradition and the Female Talent," in Nancy K. Miller, ed., *The Poetics of Gender* (New York: Columbia University Press, 1986), p. 201.

81. "Keishū shōsetsuka tō: dai ichi—Koganei Kimi joshi," *Jogaku zasshi* 205 (March 22, 1890):127–128.

82. Shimizu Shikin, "Koware yubiwa," in Imai Yasuko et al., eds., *Tanpen josei bungaku kindai* (Ōfūsha, 1987), pp. 13–14. For more on Shikin's work see Chapter Four.

83. Wakamatsu, "Keishū shōsetsu ka tō dai san: Wakamatsu Shizuko," p. 188. Shizuko was responding to a questionnaire designed by Shikin for *Jogaku zasshi* and circulated in 1890 among the prominent women writers of the day, including Kimiko and Kaho. Shizuko, like Kimiko before her, limited her responses to women's writing, judging it inappropriate to address writing by her male counterparts.

84. Kitada Usurai, "Asamashi no sugata," *Bungei kurabu* (March 1895):230–231.

85. " 'Asamashi no sugata' wo yomite," *Bungei kurabu* (April 1895):212–213.

86. Ibid.

87. As quoted in Joanna Russ, *How to Suppress Women's Writing* (Austin: University of Texas Press, 1983), p. 28.

88. In 1898, with Kōyō as her go-between, Usurai married Kajita Hanko (1870–1917), an illustrator who worked with Kōyō on the *Yomiuri* and who also illustrated many of Kōyō's books, including *Konjiki yasha* (The Demon Gold).

89. Oguri Fūyō et al., "Joryū sakka ron," *Shinchō* (May 1908):10. Among the five authors were Ikuta Chōkō (1882–1936), the "benefactor" of *Seitō* (1911–1916).

90. Iwamoto, "Joshi to bunpitsu no gyō, dai ni: shinbun, zasshi onna kisha no koto," *Jogaku zasshi* 80 (October 15, 1887):181–184. Presumably Iwamoto was referring to Bodhidharma's nine-year meditation marathon.

91. Oguri et al., "Joryū sakka ron," p. 7.

92. "Shōsetsuka toshite no josei," *Teikoku bungaku* 2(2) (1896):91–92.

93. Kimura Akebono, denied a chance to study overseas, created a surrogate heroine who sailed to England and the United States. Akebono writes of Harlem, Cambridge, and other sites in a most imaginative way. Like many Meiji women writers, she died before fulfilling her potential.

94. After a decade devoted to improvements in women's education and an emphasis on women's rights, newly enacted Meiji state policy put a halt to further advancement and began to erode whatever ground had been gained. When the Constitution was proposed in 1889, for example, women were dismayed to find that they had been completely excluded. Specific note was made of the fact that women were to be denied the throne (a tacit custom up to this point), but otherwise women were not mentioned in the Constitution and therefore not legally entitled. Moreover, Article 5 of the Police Security Regulations was revised in 1890 to deny women the right to public assembly or participation in politics on any level. In conjunction, women were not allowed in the Diet, not even as observers. Simultaneously, the Imperial Rescript on Education, issued in October 1890, emphasized a return to traditional virtues and sought to make the classroom a training ground for patriarchal values. See Nolte and Hastings, "The Meiji State's Policy Toward Women," pp. 151–174; and Sievers, *Flowers in Salt.*

95. Harrison, "Rise of the Woman Novelist," p. 120.

96. Akiyama Shun, "Ima joryū bungaku to wa nani ka: sengo shi to no kanren de," *Kokubungaku: kaishaku to kyōzai no kenkyū* 15 (December 1980):124–127; as cited and translated in Ericson, "Women's Literature," p. 81.

97. As quoted in Seki Reiko, *Ane no chikara: Higuchi Ichiyō* (Chikuma raiburarii, 1993), p. 141.

98. See, for example, Richard Torrance's study of Tokuda Shūsei, and the difficulties he had early in his career conforming to Ozaki Kōyō's mentoring, in *The Fiction of Tokuda Shūsei and the Emergence of Japan's New Middle Class* (Seattle: University of Washington Press, 1994).

99. As quoted in Seki, *Ane no chikara,* p. 247.

100. Tazawa Inafune, "Godaidō," in *Meiji joryū bungakushū,* pt. 1, *Meiji bungaku zenshū* 81 (Chikuma shobō, 1966), p. 263.

101. *Bungei kurabu, Taiyō,* and the youth-targeted *Shōnen sekai* were all founded by a large commercial publisher, Hakubunkan.

102. Okonogi Hideno (Shin'ichirō), "Keishū shōsetsu wo yomu," *Jogaku zasshi* 418 (January 25, 1896):10.

103. Shimizu Shikin, "Jobungakusha nanzo ideru to no osokiya," *Jogaku zasshi* 241 (November 29, 1890):222.

104. Brownstein, *"Jogaku Zasshi,"* p. 336.

105. Ōta Saburō, "*Jogaku zasshi* kenkyū 2," *Shomotsu tenbō* 17 (August 1950):18–19.

106. In the winter of 1890 he had named eight women to the staff, placed them in charge of a variety of columns, and encouraged submissions from them. Wakamatsu Shizuko and Miyake Kaho oversaw literary articles; Nakajima Shōen, the current affairs and political column; Ogino Gin, the health column; Yoshida Nobuko, a recent graduate of the Tokyo Higher Normal School for Women, was responsible for the science column; Andō Tane, who had studied shorthand *(sokkibon)* at Meiji Women's School, transcribed speeches and sermons for the journal; and Kojima Kiyoko oversaw the household affairs column. While Iwamoto retained control over the editorials, Shimizu Shikin assumed responsibility for the entire operation. See Fujita, *Meiji jogakkō no sekai*, pp. 55–56. It was not until Fukuda Hideko began her *Sekai Fujin* (Universal Women) in 1907, and Hani Motoko her *Fujin no tomo* (Woman's Friend) the following year, that a woman took charge of a magazine. In 1890 the best a woman could hope for was for a man to allow her the chance to speak for herself by giving her access to print. And this is what Iwamoto intended with *Jogaku zasshi*. Wakamatsu Shizuko's biographer, Yamaguchi Reiko, suggests that Iwamoto's decision to place women in positions of authority was a direct reaction to the recent promulgation of the Constitution, the opening of the new parliament, and the first general election—developments that not only excluded women from any form of political involvement but eroded whatever gains had been made up to this point. Critic Noehiji Kiyoe takes the the argument one step further by suggesting that Iwamoto meant singlehandedly to "foster a woman's movement." See Noheiji Kiyoe, "*Jogakusei* hakuhyō *Jogaku zasshi* ron no nagare no naka ni mita," *Bungaku* 47 (April 1979):20; and Yamaguchi Reiko, *Tokuto ware wo mitamae* (Shinchōsha, 1980), pp. 146–147.

107. Hani Motoko (1873–1957) was eventually given the task of adding the *furigana*. Often described as the first female journalist, due to her employment with *Hōchi Shinbun*, which began in 1897, Motoko pleaded with Iwamoto to allow her to attend Meiji Women's School. As she had no source of income, Iwamoto admitted her and housed her on campus, provided that she worked on the journal. For more on Hani Motoko's career see Mulhern, "Hani Motoko," pp. 208–235.

108. For more on the characteristics of *sōgō zasshi*, or composite magazines, see Pierson, *Tokutomi Sohō*, p. 165; see also Nishida Taketoshi, *Meiji jidai no shinbun to zasshi* (Shinbundo, 1966), pp. 219–220.

109. The legacy he left to women would take years to fade, however. Even today bookstores market female-authored books with pink bindings.

110. The separation of groups into teams of red and white can be seen in accounts ranging from twelfth-century battles between the victorious Genji (white) and the effeminate Heike (red) to twentieth-century singing contests televised every

New Year between male (white) and female (red) talents. As a literary collorary, refer to Tsuruta Kin'ya's discussions of red and white imagery in Mishima Yukio's "Onnagata" and Kawabata Yasunari's *Nemureru bijo* (House of Sleeping Beauties); see Tsuruta, "Onnagata no bunseki," in *Akutagawa, Kawabata, Mishima, Abe—gendai Nihon bungaku sakuhinron* (Ōfūsha, 1973), and "Nemureru bijo," in *Kawabata Yasunari no geijutsu* (Meiji shoin, 1981).

111. For further discussion of *Bungakukai*'s emergence from *Jogaku zasshi*, see Brownstein, *"Jogaku Zasshi,"* and Noheiji, *"Jogakusei."*

112. Yamaguchi, *Tokuto ware wo mitamae,* pp. 188.

113. Ibid., pp. 178 and 190.

114. Sievers, *Flowers in the Salt,* p. 104.

115. Brownstein, *"Jogaku Zasshi,"* p. 336.

116. Sievers, *Flowers in the Salt,* p. 111.

117. Ibid.

118. Shikin, "Jobungakusha nanzo ideru to no osokiya," in *Shikin zenshū,* p. 222.

Chapter Two: Through Thickets of Imitation

1. Joanna Russ, *How to Suppress Women's Writing* (Austin: University of Texas Press, 1983), p. 76.

2. Miyake Kaho, "Watashi no ayunde kita michi—omoide no hitobito," *Fujin kōron* (April 1939):106.

3. Ibid.

4. See Wada Shigejirō, "Miyake Kaho," in *Meiji zenki joryū sakuhinron* (Ōfūsha, 1989), pp. 174–175.

5. Miyake, "Omoide no hitobito," p. 106.

6. Ibid., p. 108.

7. Ibid., p. 111.

8. Ibid. Kaho began using this pen name in 1890. While writing for *Jogaku zasshi* she also used the pen names Hidago Joshi and Mushakusha-chachako.

9. Ibid., p. 108.

10. Wada, "Miyake Kaho," p. 169.

11. Miyake, "Omoide no hitobito," p. 108.

12. Haginoya, or Bush Clover Cottage, was the foremost school for *waka* training at the time, and Nakajima Utako was one of the most prominent *waka* instructors. According to Kaho, lessons were conducted every Saturday. Mrs. Nakajima assigned the students a topic, and they were expected to write a *waka* poem on the

spot. After they had copied the poems over in a clean hand and given them to their instructor, she would mark them and return them to the girls on the following Saturday. In addition, the girls were given composition topics to take home. On the ninth of every month, Mrs. Nakajima would hold a special poetry session for invited guests and former students. There would also be large poetry meetings and contests on New Year's Day and other holidays. Moreover, Mrs. Nakajima conducted special lectures on the Japanese classics. The school thus provided its students with a firm grounding in the literary tradition. For more on the Haginoya see Miyake, "Omoide no hitobito," pp. 117–118. See also Robert Danly, *In the Shade of Spring Leaves* (New Haven: Yale University Press, 1981), pp. 15–21.

13. Yajima Kajiko, as described in the previous chapter, became the head administrator of Sakurai Jogakkō (Joshi Gakuen) from 1889 to 1914. She was also the founder of the Tokyo Women's Reform Society and the Japanese representative to several international temperance conferences.

14. Miyake, "Omoide no hitobito," p. 112.

15. Ibid.

16. Ibid.

17. Ibid., p. 113.

18. Ibid., p. 109.

19. Ibid., p. 114.

20. For more on the Rokumeikan building and the age it represented, see Edward Seidensticker, *Low City, High City: Tokyo from Edo to the Earthquake* (New York: Knopf, 1983); and Donald H. Shively, "Japanization of the Middle Meiji," in *Tradition and Modernization in Japanese Culture,* ed. Donald H. Shively (Princeton: Princeton University Press, 1971), pp. 94–96.

21. Miyake, "Omoide no hitobito," p. 114.

22. Ibid., p. 115.

23. An interview with Miyake Kaho recorded by Katada Fujio in *"Yabu no uguisu,* Ichiyō, Tōsui," *Kokugo to kokubungaku* (August 1934):258.

24. Marleigh Grayer Ryan, *The Development of Realism in the Fiction of Tsubouchi Shōyō* (Seattle: University of Washington Press, 1975), p. 32.

25. Miyake, "Omoide no hitobito," p. 116.

26. Ibid.

27. Though she was a student of Iwamoto's only briefly, Kaho was no doubt familiar with his opinions on literature and with his essays in *Jogaku zasshi.* In *Yabu no uguisu,* for example, she includes a scene where Hamako, the westernized heroine, is reading a copy of *Jogaku zasshi.*

28. Wada Shigejirō, "*Yabu no uguisu* no shiron," *Ronkyū Nihon bungaku* (June 1959):2.

29. Wada, "Miyake Kaho," p. 165.

30. Miyake, "Omoide no hitobito," p. 116.

31. Shioda Ryōhei, "Miyake Kaho," in *Shintei Meiji joryū sakka ron* (Bunsendō shuppan, 1983), pp. 97–98.

32. Miyamoto Yuriko, in her essay on *Yabu no uguisu*, cites this figure as the average salary at the time; see *Gendai Nihon bungaku taikei*, vol. 5 (Chikuma shobō, 1972), p. 455. By way of comparison, Shioda Ryōhei notes that Kōda Rohan, then a relatively unknown writer, received 100 yen from Kinkōdō Publishers for a book at approximately the same time. See Shioda, "Miyake Kaho," p. 122. Shioda defends the discrepancy in earnings by indicating that Rohan's work had previously been published in *Miyako no hana*, the Kinkōdō journal, with good reviews.

33. Wada, "Miyake Kaho," pp. 160–163.

34. From Katada Fujio's interview with Kaho; see Katada, *"Yabu no uguisu,"* p. 259.

35. Ibid.

36. For example, in the prominent literary series *Gendai Nihon bungaku taikei*, vol. 5, published by Chikuma shobō in 1972, we find the following statement describing the writing of *Warbler* in Kaho's line-item biography: "When the student-apprentice Saihachi showed her *The Character of Modern-Day Students*, she determined that she too could write a novel. This was her immediate inspiration. But she was also motivated to raise money for a first anniversary service in honor of her elder brother who had recently passed away" (p. 481).

37. Katada, *"Yabu no uguisu,"* p. 259.

38. Wada, in "Miyake Kaho," pp. 178–179, cites her grandson saying as much.

39. Shioda, "Miyake Kaho," p. 97.

40. Miyake Kaho, *Yabu no uguisu*, in *Gendai Nihon bungaku taikei*, vol. 5, p. 125. The italicized words in the translation are written in katakana in the original text.

41. Kaho uses a playscript-style presentation in her dialogues: she indicates speakers by name if they have been previously introduced or by a general descriptive marker, such as Woman A or Woman B *(kōjo* and *otsujo)*. Once a name or marker has been introduced, Kaho uses a shortened version of the name for successive entries in the dialogue. Thus Shinohara becomes "Shino" and Woman B *(otsujo)* becomes "B" *(otsu)*. In section four, where there is dialogue between a group of minor characters, she identifies speakers by geometric symbols such as a triangle or a square. English words, as noted, are transcribed in katakana. In the case of "wallflower," however, the Japanese definition *"kabe no hana"* is given parenthetically within the body of the text. Kaho offers no such definition of other English words.

42. In the chambermaid's speech there is a pun on the word *"takuwan."* If the Chinese characters are read *"takuwan,"* they refer to a pickled radish—a common accompaniment to a Japanese meal. If they are read *"takuan,"* another possibility, they refer to a Buddhist priest of the Rinzai sect who lived from 1573 to 1645. The houseboy misinterprets—perhaps deliberately—the mistress's desire for a priest and not a pickle. The punning only adds to the silliness of the situation.

43. Shimoda Utako (1854–1936) was a prominent educator at the time. She had served for several years as a tutor in the imperial court. In 1881 she opened a small school for young women in her home, where she taught primarily the aristocratic elite in the Chinese and Japanese classics, poetry, calligraphy, history, moral ethics, embroidery, and such. That Kaho's fictional character attended this school indicates that she was a member of an aristocratic family before her father's fortunes fell. Some critics were distressed by Kaho's decision to use the name of an actual person in her story. But Ishibashi Ningetsu defended Kaho's choice by stating that such practices were common in the West and gave the work a touch of realism.

44. As cited in Miyamoto, *"Yabu no uguisu,"* p. 456.

45. Incidentally, "H" (which is given the *furigana* pronunciation *"etchi"*) is the girls' code word for "husband." It is not used with the connotation of "lewd" or "indecent" that the word *"etchi"* now has.

46. Wada, "Miyake Kaho," p. 193.

47. Gluck, *Japan's Modern Myths,* p. 19.

48. Miyake, "Omoide no hitobito," p. 109.

49. See John Pierson, *Tokutomi Sohō, 1863–1957: A Journalist for Modern Japan* (Princeton: Princeton University Press, 1980), p. 154.

50. As cited in Wada, *"Yabu no uguisu no shiron,"* p. 5. In fact, Kaho received a lot of fan mail from men after the publication of *Warbler*. Some of the letters contained marriage proposals.

51. Ibid., pp. 4–5.

52. Moira Monteith, *Women's Writing: A Challenge to Theory* (New York: St. Martin's Press, 1986), p. 154.

53. *"Yabu no uguisu,"* *Jogaku zasshi* 115 (June 23, 1888):10.

54. Shioda, "Miyake Kaho," p. 99.

55. Donald Keene, "The Meiji Period (1868–1912)," *in Dawn to the West—Poetry, Drama, Criticism* (New York: Holt, 1984), pp. 512–513. It should be recalled that Ningetsu termed Iwamoto's regard of literature "mistaken."

56. Ishibashi Ningetsu, *"Yabu uguisu no saihyō,"* *Kokumin no tomo* (August 1888):23.

57. This is the label Takada Sanae appended to Shōyō's text in his critical review of *Tōsei shosei katagi* in April 1886. Ningetsu was indebted to this review.

58. Ningetsu, "*Yabu uguisu* no saihyō," p. 26.

59. Ishibashi Shian, "*Yabu uguisu* no saihyō wo yomu," *Kokumin no tomo* (August 1888):36.

60. Ibid. Wada Shigejirō too challenges Ningetsu's insistence on a single hero. Carefully he shows how Kaho created three distinct *groups* of characters who are intertwined by complicated but believable relationships. Considering the story as an exposition of groups or character types, rather than individual protagonists, frees the reader from dependence on a single hero or heroine. Wada's point is interesting, but his analysis grows tedious. After surveying each section in the story, he discovers that Hamako appears (or is mentioned) in eleven of the twelve sections, Tsutomu in eight, Namiko and Hideko in four. In a statement that undercuts his previous argument, Wada says this proves that Hamako is the protagonist and her dilemma is the heart of the story. See Wada, *Meiji zenki joryū sakuhinron*, pp. 197–198.

61. Shian's point is that Kaho's work lacks substance. But he belabors the message with a clever pun on the word "*mi*" and a reference to an anecdote from the poetic tradition.

62. Shian, "*Yabu uguisu* no saihyō wo yomu," p. 37; translation from Harrison, "Rise of the Woman Novelist," pp. 93–94.

63. Shian, "*Yabu uguisu* no saihyō wo yomu," p. 37.

64. Kaho's reference to *The Tales of Ise* episode and to Hamako's raven locks *(midori no kurokami)* may have inspired Ichiyō's "Takekurabe" (Growing Up, 1896). But *The Tales of Ise* was an oft-cited classic at the time and one of the texts the students would have studied at the Haginoya.

65. I am grateful to Professor Sumiko Shinozuka of Kyōritsu Women's University for bringing these associations to my attention.

66. Wada, "Miyake Kaho," p. 180.

67. Ibid.

68. Wada provides textual comparisons in "Miyake Kaho," pp. 181–185.

69. Miyamoto, "*Yabu no uguisu*," p. 455. This criticism is ironic coming from Miyamoto Yuriko. According to Shioda, her debut work, which was also brought out under Shōyō's auspices, was equally described as being more his authorship than hers. See Shioda, "Miyake Kaho," pp. 99–100.

70. Seki Ryōichi, "*Yabu no uguisu*," *Kokubungaku* 13(5) (1968):17–20.

71. Ryan, *Development of Realism*, p. 32.

72. Ibid., pp. 36–37.

73. As quoted and translated in Peter F. Kornicki, *The Reform of Fiction in Meiji Japan* (London: Ithaca Press, 1982), p. 28.

74. Although concerned with a later time period, Mariko Inoue explores the use of the *jogakusei* image in Taishō and early Shōwa art. See her essay "Kiyokata's *Asazusa*: The Emergence of the *Jogakusei* Image," *Monumenta Nipponica* 51(4) (1997):431–460.

75. Ozaki Kōyō, "Musume hakase," in *Kōyō zenshū*, vol. 1 (Iwanami shoten, 1994), pp. 446–452. Kornicki provides a summary of this story on p. 65.

76. Kornicki, *Reform of Fiction*, p. 67.

77. Ibid., p. 45.

78. Ibid.

79. Ibid., pp. 45–46.

80. Miyake, "Omoide no hitobito," p. 115. Shioda doubts that Kaho's alleged *Five Women* was modeled on an actual reading of Ihara Saikaku's work. It is unlikely that Kaho would have been familiar with Saikaku at this time, 1879, since the "Saikaku Revival," largely initiated by Kōyō and Rohan, did not begin until 1894 following the publication of the first complete edition of his work. Furthermore, Kaho credits Sasaki Nobutsuna with introducing her to Saikaku. But Nobutsuna did not move to Tokyo until 1882—two or three years after Kaho claims to have written her version of *Five Women*. See Shioda, "Miyake Kaho," p. 96.

81. Kornicki, *Reform of Fiction*, p. 44.

82. Ibid.

83. Kristeva as paraphrased by Susan Stanford Friedman, "Weavings: Intertextuality and the (Re)Birth of the Author," in *Influence and Intertextuality in Literary History* ed. Jay Clayton and Eric Rothstein (Madison: University of Wisconsin Press, 1991), p. 147. I am grateful to Eleanor Hogan for bringing this essay to my attention.

84. Roland Barthes, "The Death of the Author," in *Image Music Text*, trans. Stephen Heath (New York: Hill & Wang, 1977), p. 146.

85. A cursory glance is all that is possible. Not only does the context of this study preclude further elaboration on Kaho's career beyond *Warbler* but, more important, Kaho's works are largely inaccessible. She is represented in various literary series by only three or four of her thirty to forty works and never in a volume to herself. Volume 5 of the *Gendai Nihon bungaku taikei* series (Chikuma shobō, 1972), for example, includes *Yabu no uguisu* along with fourteen works by Higuchi Ichiyō, "representative" works by seven other Meiji-era women writers, and twelve selections from the oeuvre of Izumi Kyōka. Volume 81 of the *Meiji bungaku zenshū* series (Chikuma shobō, 1966) is devoted to women writers of the

early Meiji period and contains three works by Kaho: *Yaezakura* (The Eightfold Cherry Blossom, 1890), "Utabito" (The Poetasters, 1892), and "Hagi kikyō" (Bush Clover and the Chinese Bellflower, 1896), in addition to a selection of works by twelve other women writers. Readers interested in other works by Kaho will have to turn to the original publications in journals, many of which are not easily available.

86. Wada, "Miyake Kaho," p. 265.

87. Shioda, "Miyake Kaho," p. 101.

88. Actually, Kaho had been teaching *waka* with Nakajima Utako's informal consent *(naidaku)* since 1889. She received her formal permission in 1894. See Shioda, "Miyake Kaho," p. 106.

89. Ibid.

90. Miyamoto, *"Yabu no uguisu,"* p. 460.

91. As cited in Yamaguchi Reiko, *Naite aisuru shimai ni tsugu: Kozai Shikin no shōgai* (Sōdō bunka, 1977), pp. 329–330.

Chapter Three: Behind the Veil

1. Yamamoto Masahide, "Wakamatsu Shizuko no hon'yaku shōsetsu genbun itchi bun no shiteki igi," *Senshū kokubun* 14 (September 1973):23–25.

2. As cited in Yamaguchi Reiko, *Tokuto ware wo mitamae: Wakamatsu Shizuko no shōgai* (Shinchōsha, 1980), p. 13.

3. This description of Shizuko's flight is culled from Yamaguchi's biography, which is to date the most authoritative study of Wakamatsu Shizuko; ibid., pp. 13–19.

4. Ibid., p. 19; "Miya" means "shrine."

5. Ibid., p. 26.

6. Ibid., p. 27. The term the local people used was *"Aizu no gedaga,"* which was dialect for *kemushi* or caterpillar.

7. Ibid., p. 44.

8. Letter from M. E. Kidder to J. M. Ferris, general secretary of the Board of Foreign Missions of the Reformed Church in America, January 22, 1872; from the Ferris Women's College archives.

9. Yamaguchi, *Tokuto ware wo mitamae,* p. 62.

10. E. S. Booth, "Foreword," in *In Memory of Mrs. Kashi Iwamoto* (Ryūkei shosha, 1981; first published by Yokohama seishi bunsha, 1896), pp. iii–iv.

11. Shizuko had not lived with the Ōkawas since she was eleven, so emotionally her relationship with the couple had been severed years ago. Even so, Shizuko did not relinquish all her ties to the family. After Mr. Ōkawa died and her former fos-

ter mother's fortunes declined, Shizuko sent her money as often as she could. At the time, Shizuko was also the sole support for her younger sister and her father's second wife and son.

12. In her English essay, "Bungakukai jo," *Jogaku zasshi* 242 (1890):11, Shizuko explains that the term "timely reflection" *(jishū)* is derived from one of Confucius' sayings. Her society adopted the term out of their "desire to form a habit of not slighting anything because it is old, and to keep fresh whatever has value."

13. Ibid.

14. Mrs. E. R. Miller cited by Booth, *In Memory of Mrs. Kashi Iwamoto*, pp. iv–v.

15. Fujita Yoshimi, *Meiji jogakkō no sekai* (Seieisha, 1984), p. 35.

16. Yamaguchi, *Tokuto ware wo mitamae*, p. 95.

17. Wakamatsu Shizuko, "Tama no koshi," *Jogaku zasshi* 195 (January 11, 1890):556.

18. Susan Rubinow Gorsky, *Femininity to Feminism: Women and Literature in the Nineteenth Century* (New York: Twayne, 1992), p. 19.

19. Wakamatsu Shizuko, "Sumire," *Jogaku zasshi* 183 (October 19, 1889):215–216. Words italicized in the translation are rendered in English in the original. Underlining of the word "the" is also in the original.

20. Wada Shigejirō, "Wakamatsu Shizuko," in *Meiji zenki joryū sakuhinron* (Ōfūsha, 1989), p. 278.

21. Takayuki Murakami-Yokota, "Lovers in Disguise: A Feature of Romantic Love in Meiji Literature," *Comparative Literature Studies* 28(3) (1991):216. See also Takayuki Murakami-Yokota, *Don Juan East and West* (New York: SUNY Press, 1998).

22. Yamaguchi, *Tokuto ware wo mitamae*, p. 10.

23. See Isozaki Yoshiji, "Wakamatsu Shizuko to Iwamoto Yoshiharu," in *Wakamatsu Shizuko: Fumetsu no shōgai* (Kyōeisha, 1977), p. 60.

24. It is difficult to be certain of anything in the relationship between Iwamoto and Shizuko. In the first place, Shizuko asked her husband not to write her biography. As E. S. Booth reports in his foreword to her collection of English works: "'I have nothing in my life to be talked of,' she said, 'except the fact that I knew the grace of God to the last' " (p. xxii). It seems, however, that Iwamoto did manage to collect a few materials for the purpose of writing memoirs. But whenever he would amass his notes, he would fall victim to some kind of conflagration and all his work would be burnt. His residences were destroyed by fire at least twice in his lifetime.

25. As reprinted in Suzuki Fumio, "Wakamatsu Shizuko to '*Jogaku zasshi*,' " pt. 2, *Ferris ronsō* 9 (April 1964):1.

26. Yamaguchi Reiko says that Iwamoto was furious when a reporter suggested that Shizuko married him for his name: "When we married, I was nothing more than a poor schoolboy!" he growled. See Yamaguchi, *Tokuto ware wo mitamae*, p. 119.

27. As cited in Isozaki, "Wakamatsu Shizuko to Iwamoto Yoshiharu," p. 56.

28. Ibid., p. 65.

29. Wakamatsu Shizuko, "The Bridal Veil," *Jogaku zasshi* 172 (July 28, 1889):401.

30. Yoshiko Takita, "Wakamatsu Shizuko and *Little Lord Fauntleroy*," *Comparative Literature Studies* 22 (1985):2.

31. Shimada Tarō, "Wakamatsu Shizuko yaku *Shōkōshi* no seiritsu," in *Kindai Nihon no hon'yaku bunka*, ed. Kamei Shunsuke (Chūō kōronsha, 1994), p. 243.

32. Ibid., p. 244.

33. Wakamatsu Shizuko, "Nogiku," *Jogaku zasshi* 183 (October 5, 1889):183.

34. Nanette Twine, "The Genbunitchi Movement: Its Origin, Development, and Conclusion," *Monumenta Nipponica* 33(3) (1978):334.

35. Ibid., p. 346.

36. Ibid., p. 350.

37. According to Satō Michimasa, the poem was not easy to translate. Thus it was not until 1984, when Norisugi Tatsu tackled the problem, that a Japanese translation was made available. See Satō, "Wakamatsu Shizuko," in *Nihon jidō bungaku no seiritsu josetsu* (Yamato shobō, 1985), p. 69.

38. Yamaguchi, *Tokuto ware wo mitamae*, p. 132.

39. Karatani Kōjin, "The Discovery of Interiority," in *Origins of Modern Japanese Literature*, ed. Brett de Bary (Durham: Duke University Press, 1993), p. 51.

40. Satō, "Wakamatsu Shizuko," p. 81.

41. Booth, "Foreword," p. v.

42. Wakamatsu Shizuko, "Omukō no hanare," *Jogaku zasshi* 182 (October 5, 1889):188. This text is also found in *Gendai Nihon bungaku taikei*, vol. 5 (Chikuma shobō, 1972), pp. 145–147.

43. Ibid., pp. 188–189.

44. Most cite Mori Ōgai's *"Maihime"* (Dancing Girl, 1890) as the first instance of a first-person narrative in Meiji Japan.

45. Shizuko, "Omukō no hanare," p. 189.

46. Similarly, Futabatei Shimei's experiences translating Russian literature had a direct effect on his experiments with *genbun itchi*.

47. Adelaide Anne Procter, "The Sailor Boy," in *Legends and Lyrics Together with a Chaplet of Verses* (London: Oxford University Press, 1914), p. 100.

48. Honda Hayao suggests that Shizuko raised the boy's age to fourteen in consideration of the Japanese system of counting ages. See Honda, "Wakamatsu Shizuko no 'Wasuregatami' kangai," *Fukushima jogakkō tanki daigaku kenkyū kiyō* 17 (1988):4.

49. Wakamatsu Shizuko, "Wasuregatami," *Jogaku zasshi* 194 (January 1, 1890):12.

50. Keene, *Dawn to the West: Fiction*, p. 160.

51. Ibid.

52. As cited in Yamaguchi, *Tokuto ware wo mitamae*, p. 138.

53. Keene, *Dawn to the West: Fiction*, p. 63.

54. Phyllis Bixler, *Frances Hodgson Burnett* (Boston: Twayne, 1984), p. 7.

55. Ann Thwaite, *Waiting for the Party: The Life of Frances Hodgson Burnett 1849–1924* (London: Secker & Warburg, 1974), p. 94.

56. Bixler, *Burnett*, p. 9.

57. Marghanita Laski, *Mrs. Ewing, Mrs. Molesworth, and Mrs. Hodgson Burnett* (London: Arthur Barker, 1950), p. 83.

58. Keene, *Dawn to the West: Fiction*, p. 61.

59. Ibid.

60. Ibid.

61. As cited and translated by Keene, *Dawn to the West: Fiction*, p. 130.

62. Ibid., p. 131.

63. Wakamatsu Shizuko, "Keishū shōsetsu ka tō dai san," *Jogaku zasshi*, 207 (April 5, 1890):188–189.

64. Ibid.

65. Ibid.

66. As cited in Satō, "Wakamatsu Shizuko," p. 87.

67. As cited in Thwaite, *Waiting for the Party*, p. 94.

68. Ibid., p. 93.

69. Ibid.

70. Satō, "Wakamatsu Shizuko," p. 50.

71. As cited in Thwaite, *Waiting for the Party*, p. 94.

72. Wakamatsu Shizuko, "*Shōkōshi* no jo," *Jogaku zasshi* 288 (October 24, 1891):329.

73. Thwaite, *Waiting for the Party*, p. 93.

74. Ibid.

75. As cited in Yamamoto, "Wakamatsu Shizuko," p. 40.

76. As cited in Takahashi Masatoshi, "*Shōkōshi* no hyōka—'Shizuko' no risō to bun-shō hyōgen wo chūshin ni," in *Jidō bungaku* (Yūseidō, 1977), p. 94. This essay was originally published in *Nihon bungaku kenkyū* 9 (1969).

77. Miyake Kaho, "Yukishi san saien no tomo: Akebono joshi, Wakamatsu Shizuko joshi, Ichiyō joshi," in *Ichiyō no omoide*, ed. Yoshida Seiichi (Nihon tosho sentā, 1984), pp. 126–128. Kaho describes visiting the Iwamoto house on *Jogaku zasshi* business. She was not familiar with Shizuko at the time and found her direct form of speech and abrupt movements offensive. She states that Shizuko was not ladylike in a Japanese way, but neither was she completely westernized. She had her own unique style.

78. As cited in Yamaguchi, *Tokuto ware wo mitamae*, p. 166.

79. As cited by Suzuki Fumio, "*Shōkōshi* ni tsuite," in *Wakamatsu Shizuko: fumetsu no shōgai*, pp. 19–20.

80. Ibid.

81. Bixler, *Burnett*, p. 51.

82. Morita Shiken, "*Shōkōshi* wo yomu," *Jogaku zasshi* 292 (November 21, 1891), cited in Takahashi, "*Shōkōshi* no hyōka," p. 90.

83. Ishibashi Ningetsu, *Kokumin no tomo* 142 (January 13, 1892); cited in Satō, "Wakamatsu Shizuko," p. 78.

84. Frances Hodgson Burnett, *Little Lord Fauntleroy* (New York: Dell, 1990), p. 12.

85. Wakamatsu Shizuko, *Shōkōshi*, in *Meiji bungaku zenshū* 32 (Chikuma shobō, 1973), p. 41. The underlined words in this excerpt are underlined in Shizuko's text and distinguish English words (proper nouns) rendered in katakana. The words that I have put in boldface are not English loanwords but are rendered in katakana in Shizuko's text, presumably for emphasis.

86. Takita, "Shizuko and *Fauntleroy*," p. 6.

87. Shimada, "Wakamatsu Shizuko," p. 253.

88. As cited in Yamamoto, "Wakamatsu Shizuko," p. 25.

89. Shimada, "Wakamatsu Shizuko," p. 252.

90. Burnett, *Fauntleroy*, pp. 87–88.

91. Shizuko, *Shōkōshi*, p. 75.

92. From Morita Shiken, "*Shōkōshi* wo yomu"; cited in Takahashi, "*Shōkōshi* no hyōka," p. 91.

93. Shimada, "Wakamatsu Shizuko," p. 255.

94. Yamamoto, "Wakamatsu Shizuko," p. 33.

95. Ibid., pp. 34–35.

96. Yamamoto notes that the expression was used when transcriptions of San'yūtei Enchō's oral narrations were published; Yamamoto, "Wakamatsu Shizuko," p. 35. Shimada suggests that when the Japanese speeches of foreigners were transcribed in journals like *Jogaku zasshi*, the expression would have been recorded, since so many foreigners allegedly used "*-masenkatta*"; Shimada, "Wakamatsu Shizuko," p. 248. Shizuko first began using the expression in her translation of *Enoch Arden*.

97. As cited in Yamamoto, "Wakamatsu Shizuko," p. 41.

98. As cited in Takahashi, "*Shōkōshi* no hyōka," p. 81.

99. Ibid.

100. Ibid., p. 91.

101. Ibid., p. 92.

102. Jacques Derrida, "Des Tours de Babel," in *Difference in Translation,* ed. Joseph F. Graham (Ithaca: Cornell University Press, 1985), p. 188.

103. Takahashi, "*Shōkōshi* no hyōka," p. 85; Yamamoto, "Wakamatsu Shizuko," p. 51.

104. See Keene, *Dawn to the West: Fiction,* p. 179.

105. Suda Chisato, "Kodomogatari—Meiji Nijū nen dai ichininshō shōsetsu ippan," *Bungaku* 9(2) (1998):51–53; Yamamoto, "Wakamatsu Shizuko," p. 51.

106. Takita, "Shizuko and *Fauntleroy*," p. 7.

107. Twine, "Genbunitchi Movement," p. 351.

108. Yamaguchi, *Tokuto ware wo mitamae,* p. 218.

109. Iwamoto Kashi, "Woman's Department," *Japan Evangelist* 1(6) (1895):330.

110. Iwamoto Kashi, "Children's Department," *Japan Evangelist* 2(3) (1895):170.

111. Wakamatsu Shizuko, "Yesterday and Tomorrow," in *In Memory of Mrs. Kashi Iwamoto,* ed. Iwamoto Yoshiharu (Ryūkei shosha, 1981), p. 167.

112. Yamaguchi, *Tokuto ware wo mitamae,* p. 193.

113. Ibid., p. 231.

114. Takahashi, "*Shōkōshi* no hyōka," p. 89.

115. Satō, "Wakamatsu Shizuko," p. 53.

116. Ibid., p. 54.

117. Takahashi believes that Iwamoto proofread Shizuko's work before publishing it in *Jogaku zasshi.* Although Takahashi has no basis for this statement, we do know that Iwamoto provided the title "Shōkōshi" and that he took proud interest in Shizuko's endeavors. See Takahashi, "*Shōkōshi* no hyōka," p. 92.

118. Doppo's statement is cited in Oguri Fūyō et al., "Joryū sakka ron," *Shinchō* (May 1908):8–9.

119. Kunikida Doppo, "Joshi to hon'yaku no koto," in *Kunikida Doppo zenshū*, vol. 1 (Gakushū kenyūsha, 1965), p. 364. This essay was originally published in *Katei zasshi* 2(23) (February 15, 1898).

120. Shioda Ryōhei, "Wakamatsu Shizuko," in *Shintei Meiji joryū sakka ron*, p. 176.

121. Booth, "Foreword," p. xi.

122. Nogami Yaeko, *Mori*, in *Nogami Yaeko zenshū, dai ni ki*, vol. 28 (Iwanami shoten, 1991), pp. 158–161.

Chapter Four: Shimizu Shikin

1. Yamaguchi Reiko, *Naite aisuru shimai ni tsugu: Kozai Shikin no shōgai* (Sōdō bunka, 1977), p. 5.

2. Komashaku Kimi, "Shikin shōron—josei gaku tekina apurōchi," in *Shikin zenshū*, ed. Kozai Yoshishige (Sōdō bunka, 1983), p. 584; hereafter cited as *SZ.*

3. Danly, *Shade of Spring Leaves*, p. 14.

4. As cited in Yamaguchi, *Naite aisuru shimai ni tsugu*, p. 24.

5. Shimizu Shikin, "Koware yubiwa," in *SZ*, p. 16. Although these translations are my own, readers may find a complete translation of "The Broken Ring" in Harrison's dissertation, "The Rise of the Woman Novelist in Meiji Japan" (University of Chicago, 1991).

6. As cited in Yamaguchi, *Naite aisuru shimai ni tsugu*, pp. 64–65.

7. *SZ*, p. 240.

8. Ibid., pp. 240–241.

9. Watanabe Sumiko, "Shimizu Shikin *Koware yubiwa*," *Nihon bungaku* (March 1980):79.

10. Yamaguchi, *Naite aisuru shimai ni tsugu*, pp. 64–65.

11. As quoted in Kozai Yoshishige, "Meiji no onna—Shimizu Shikin no koto," *SZ*, p. 556.

12. Ibid., p. 555.

13. As cited in Yamaguchi, *Naite aisuru shimai ni tsugu*, p. 7.

14. Ibid., p. 106.

15. *SZ*, pp. 287–288.

16. Kuzume Yoshi, "Images of Japanese Women in U.S. Writings and Scholarly Works, 1860–1990: Formation and Transformation of Stereotypes," *U.S.-Japan Women's Journal, English Supplement* 1 (1991):3–47.

17. Consider Episode 23 of *The Tales of Ise*. The wife who waits patiently while her husband courts another woman is "rewarded" for her suffering (eventually), whereas the wives who concentrate on their own happiness—even on their own

survival—are made to suffer horrible fates in Episodes 24, 60, and 62. The lonely wives of the *Man'yōshū*, the languishing wives of the imperial poetry collections, *The Tale of Genji*'s Akashi Lady are but a few more examples on a very long list.

18. Shikin's work followed fictional forays in *Jogaku zasshi* by Nakajima Shōen and Wakamatsu Shizuko, both outspoken advocates of women's rights, who believed that literature for women should maintain an "instructive" tone. For more about the journal and its influence on Shikin see Takada Chinami, "'Koware yubiwa' to 'Kono ko,'" *Nihon kindai bungaku* 47 (October 1992):13–28. For more on the impact of the women's rights movement on the development of women's literature see Kitada Sachie, "Joken to bungaku no aida—Kozai Shikin ron," *Hoppō bungei* (August 1984):8–27.

19. Marleigh Ryan provides a summary of "The Wife" in *The Development of Realism in the Fiction of Tsubouchi Shōyō* (Seattle: University of Washington Press, 1975), pp. 102–120.

20. J. Scott Miller, "Tsubouchi Shōyō (1859–1935)," in *Japanese Fiction Writers, 1868–1945*, ed. Van C. Gessel, *Dictionary of Literary Biography*, vol. 180 (Detroit: Gale Research, 1997), p. 243.

21. Julia Kristeva as cited by Susan Stanford Friedman, "Weavings: Intertextuality and the (Re)Birth of the Author," in *Influence and Intertextuality in Literary History*, ed. Jay Clayton and Eric Rothstein (Madison: University of Wisconsin Press, 1991), p. 147.

22. Higuchi Ichiyō, "The Thirteenth Night," in *Shade of Spring Leaves*, p. 245.

23. Watanabe Sumiko, "Shimizu Shikin ron—Meiji nijūnendai zenki shōsetsu 'Koware yubiwa' no imi," *Shinshū shirakaba* (April 1983):317.

24. Shidzué Ishimoto, *Facing Two Ways: The Story of My Life* (New York: Farrar & Rinehart, 1935), p. 78.

25. Adrienne Rich, *Of Woman Born: Motherhood as Experience and Institution* (New York: Norton, 1986), p. 34. For a somewhat similar discussion of the mother/daughter relationship in the works of other Japanese women writers, see Rebecca Copeland, "Motherhood as Institution," *Japan Quarterly* (January–March 1992):101–110.

26. Ichiyō, "Thirteenth Night," p. 247.

27. Ibid., p. 249.

28. See Jennifer Robertson, "The Shingaku Woman: Straight from the Heart," in *Recreating Japanese Women, 1600–1945*, ed. Gail Lee Bernstein (Berkeley: University of California Press, 1991), p. 97.

29. Marianne Hirsch, *The Mother/Daughter Plot: Narrative, Psychoanalysis, Feminism* (Bloomington: Indiana University Press, 1989), p. 11.

30. Ibid., p. 38.

31. Wada Shigejirō, "Shimizu Shikin," in *Meiji zenki joryū sakuhinron*, p. 293.

32. As cited in Yamaguchi, *Naite aisuru shimai ni tsugu*, p. 137.

33. Komashaku, "Shiki koron," p. 587.

34. As cited in Yamaguchi, *Naite aisuru shimai ni tsugu*, p. 187.

35. Ibid., p. 137.

36. As cited in Yamaguchi, *Naite aisuru shimai ni tsugu*, pp. 134–135.

37. Shikin had published the story under the name "Tsuyuko."

38. Even if critics did not know Shikin's identity, they could assume that she was of a respectable social status if she had sufficient education, inclination, and connections to publish.

39. Apparently Shizuko initiated a momentary enthusiasm for first-person narratives among her female peers. Not only did Shikin adopt this approach in "Koware yubiwa," but so did Miyake Kaho in "Hakumei" (1890) and Higuchi Ichiyō in "Kono ko" (1896). For more on the narrative style of "Koware yubiwa" see Takada, "'Koware yubiwa' to 'Kono ko,'" pp. 13–28. For summaries of the critiques of "Koware yubiwa" by Ningetsu and Fuchian, see Yamaguchi, *Naite aisuru shimai ni tsugu*, pp. 136–137.

40. For more on "Koware yubiwa" as an "everywoman's tale," see Yamaguchi, *Naite aisuru shimai ni tsugu*, pp. 145–147.

41. Sōma Kokkō received copies of *Jogaku zasshi* from her aunt, Sasaki Toyosu. Eventually Kokkō found her way to Meiji Women's School where she met Shimizu Shikin. She recorded her impressions of Shikin, Wakamatsu Shizuko, and Nakajima Shōen in *Meiji shōki no sanjosei* (1940). Here I am citing from *Meiji joryū bungakushū*, 1, in *Meiji bungaku zenshū*, 81 (Chikuma shobō, 1966), p. 403.

42. See Uchida Fuchian, "'Koware yubiwa' wo yonde," *Jogaku zasshi* 249 (1891):652–653.

43. Imai Yasuko, "Shimizu Shikin 'Koware yubiwa,'" in *Tanpen josei bungaku kindai*, ed. Imai Yasuko et al. (Ōfūsha, 1987), pp. 16–17.

44. The practice of exchanging wedding rings did not become popular in Japan until the Taishō period. But *Jogaku zasshi* carried a series of articles on rings in the spring of 1888 explaining that the ring symbolized marital union and a broken ring meant a broken marriage.

45. Yamaguchi Reiko, "Kozai Shikin no koto," *Bungaku* 43 (September 1975): 119–120.

46. Nagamatsu Fusako, "Josei ni totte no Meiji—Shimizu Shikin no baai," *Hōsei daigakuin kiyō* 5 (1980):39–57.

47. Sasabuchi Tomoichi, "Shimizu Shikin ron," in *Meiji Taishō bungaku no bunseki* (Meiji shoinkan, 1970), p. 124.

48. Shikin's fans must have been disappointed to learn that she had temporarily withdrawn from writing fiction. Sōma Kokkō writes: "Every time I acquired a copy of *Jogaku zasshi*, I would hunt immediately for Tsuyuko's name. Surely this issue would carry another of her stories, I told myself. Unable to find her name anywhere, I felt myself overcome with a sense of loss." Kokkō was not aware that at the time Shikin was writing under the pen name "Fumiko." She reserved "Tsuyuko" for forays into fiction.

49. Wada, "Shimizu Shikin," p. 298.

50. This boy's childhood, however, was not uneventful. When his foster father—Shikin's elder brother—died in 1901, he was taken into the Kozai home. Shortly thereafter he was sent to live with his biological father, Ōi Kentarō. Complaining that Ōi's wife treated him little better than a servant, he ran back to his original home in Okayama and Shikin's father restored the boy to the Shimizu family registry. When he graduated from high school, he entered Keio University in Tokyo. Shikin's father paid the boy's tuition and Kozai Yoshinao assumed the responsibility upon the father's death. Upon graduation, he married, had children, and eventually joined the foreign service where he was dispatched to Czechoslovakia.

51. As cited in Yamaguchi, *Naite aisuru shimai ni tsugu*, p. 215.

52. See Takeda Kiyoko, "Shimizu Shikin no 'Imin gakuen': Kirisutokyō to jiyūminken to no aida," in *Dochaku to haikyō* (Shinkyō shuppansha, 1967), p. 189.

53. Shimizu Shikin, "Ichi seinen iyō no jukkai," *SZ*, p. 24.

54. The letters are collected in *SZ*, pp. 569–582; the short story, "Hitotsu no tanpen," appears in Yamaguchi, *Naite aisuru shimai ni tsugu*, pp. 217–219.

55. Yamaguchi, *Naite aisuru shimai ni tsugu*, p. 218.

56. Wada, "Shimizu Shikin," p. 303.

57. Cited in "Kitamura Tōkoku," in *Kindai bungaku kenkyū sōsho*, vol. 2 (Shōwa joshi daigaku kindai bunka kenkyū jō, 1979), p. 154.

58. As translated by Donald Keene in *Dawn to the West*, p. 194.

59. Conversations with Professor Yasuyuki Ogikubo of Kokugakuin University, Tokyo, on November 17, 1997.

60. Sharon Sievers comments on this tendency, even among the most vocal of feminists, to soften their rhetoric and aim for a "middle ground." See Sievers, *Flowers in the Salt*, p. 109.

61. As cited in Yamaguchi, *Naite aisuru shimai ni tsugu*, p. 238.

62. Ibid.

63. Shimizu Shikin, "Hanazono zuihitsu," *SZ*, p. 459.

64. Yamaguchi, *Naite aisuru shimai ni tsugu*, p. 275.

65. Komashaku, "Shikin shōron," p. 605.

66. As cited in Wada, "Shimizu Shikin," p. 316.

67. Shioda Ryōhei, "Shimizu Shikin," in *Shintei Meiji joryū sakka ron*, p. 201.

68. Yamaguchi, *Naite aisuru shimai ni tsugu*, p. 1.

69. Nagamatsu, "Josei ni totte no Meiji," p. 44.

70. Shimizu Shikin, "Nanzo jobungakusha deru no osokiya," *SZ*, pp. 294–295.

71. Okonogi Hideno, "Keishū shōsetsu wo yomu," *Jogaku zasshi* 418 (January 25, 1896):14.

72. As cited in Umezawa et al., eds., *Bungaku no naka no hisabetsu burakuzō, senzen hen* (Akashi shoten, 1980), p. 58.

73. Sasabuchi, "Shimizu Shikin ron," p. 128.

74. Shimizu Shikin, "Imin gakuen," in *SZ*, p. 211.

75. Zeniza-mura is an actual place and immediately recognizable as a *buraku* by those familiar with Kyoto. A reader from the Tokyo region, however, would probably not know this distinction and would make the discovery along with the heroine.

76. As cited in Yamaguchi, *Naite aisuru shimai ni tsugu*, p. 317.

77. Ibid., p. 312.

78. Ishibashi Ningetsu identifies Osei as "masculine" in a review of *Ukigumo* published in *Jogaku zasshi*. For a detailed analysis of this review see Marleigh Ryan, *Japan's First Modern Novel: "Ukigumo" of Futabatei Shimei* (Ann Arbor: University of Michigan Press, 1965), p. 12.

79. Sōma Kokkō, *Meiji shōki no san josei*, p. 294.

80. As cited in Wada, "Shimizu Shikin," p. 358.

81. As cited in Yamaguchi, *Naite aisuru shimai ni tsugu*, p. 329.

82. Kozai, "Meiji no onna," p. 563.

83. The authors of this article were Oguri Fūyō, Ikuta Chōkō, Maiyama Seika, Yanagawa Shun'yō, and Chikamatsu Shūko. Although Shūko, Seika, and Shun'yō were hardly notable for their interest in women's issues, Oguri Fūyō did encourage his wife's career as a writer. Ikuta Chōkō was the motivating force behind *Seitō*. Nevertheless, the negative attitude expressed in this article toward women writers was typical of the late Meiji period; see "Joryū sakka ron," *Shinchō* (May 1908):8.

84. Ibid., p. 10.

Conclusion

1. Among the other illustrators for the journal were Mizuno Toshikata (1866–1908) and Tomioka Eisen (1864–1905).

2. Ichiyō was represented under two different names. The author of *Yamiyo* was listed as Natsuko (as if she and Ichiyō were different writers). For most of Ichiyō's brief career, she was not distinguished from her female contemporaries. It was only in the last year of her life, when "Jūsan'ya" and "Takekurabe" (Growing Up) were published, that she was said to have surpassed Kaho in prominence.

3. Danly, *Shade of Spring Leaves,* p. 149.

4. See, for example, Shioda and Wada.

5. "Keishū shōsetsu wo yomite," *Kokumin no tomo* (January 11, 1896):34.

6. In her 1936 essay "Mohō no tensai" (A Genius of Imitation), Uno Chiyo (1897–1996) would complain of her inability to be anything but a "wife" in her career as a writer. That is, she felt unable to "husband" (author) her own works. Should a writer still have felt this tension in the 1930s, how much greater must the impact have been on writers in the late nineteenth century. See "A Genius of Imitation" in Yukiko Tanaka, ed., *To Live and to Write: Selections by Japanese Women Writers 1913–1938* (Seattle: Seal Press, 1987), pp. 181–196.

7. "Keishū shōsetsu," *Seinen bun* 2(6) (1896):19–20.

8. In 1897, two years after the first *Bungei kurabu* special issue, *Shin shōsetsu* (New Fiction) published a photo layout of male writers. Generally, however, photographs of male writers did not become a prominent feature of literary journalism until after 1905. See Nakayama Akihiro, "Sakka no shōzō no saihensei," *Bungaku* 4(3) (1993):37, and the sources cited therein.

9. Harrison, "Rise of the Woman Novelist," p. 81.

10. Okonogi, "Keishū shōsetsu wo yomu," *Jogaku zasshi* 418 (January 25, 1896):14.

11. Seki, *Ane no chikara,* pp. 199–200. Indeed, it would perhaps be inaccurate to regard published samples of calligraphy as "ladylike." A century earlier it had become popular to publish and distribute samples of courtesans' calligraphy— along with other personal statistics and details.

12. "*Bungei kurabu* no daisekkei," *Seinen bun* 2(4) (1895):15.

13. From around the eleventh issue, the journal began, in its announcement section, to solicit photographs of beauties *(bijin),* scenic sites *(sansui no keishoku),* and shrines and temples *(jinja bukkaku).* Occasionally the journal printed photographs of men: kabuki actors, boys with hunting rifles or fishing poles, but not writers.

14. "*Bungei kurabu* dai shichi hen," p. 12.

15. "Keishū shōsetsu," p. 20.

16. Ann Rosalind Jones, "Surprising Fame: Renaissance Gender Ideologies and Women's Lyric," in *The Poetics of Gender*, ed. Nancy K. Miller (New York: Columbia University Press, 1986), p. 74.

17. This tendency to critique the woman rather than the work—which Mary Ellman terms "phallic criticism"—is still very prevalent in Japanese literature today. Chieko Ariga discusses the "phallic criticism" of contemporary Japanese women writers in her essay, "Text Versus Commentary: Struggles Over the Cultural Meanings of 'Woman,'" in *The Woman's Hand: Gender and Theory in Japanese Women's Writing*, ed. Paul G. Schalow and Janet A. Walker (Stanford: Stanford University Press, 1986), pp. 352–381.

18. Gotō Chūgai, "Keishū shōsetsu wo yomu," *Waseda bungaku* (January 1896):31.

19. As quoted in Shioda, *Shintei Meiji joryūsakka ron*, p. 182.

20. Sōma Kokkō, for example, had resolutely withstood pressure to marry so that she could develop a writing career. But when her first published piece, too closely modeled on actual personages, provoked charges of slander, she forswore further literary activity, accepted a marriage to a silk farmer, and moved with her husband to Nagano—out of harm's way.

21. Ubukata Toshirō, "Joryū sakka no mure," *Bunshō sekai* (January 1914):294.

22. This certainly seems to have been the case for Kitamura Tōkoku, Hoshino Tenchi, and Shimazaki Tōson. Their affairs with their young students at Meiji Women's School, rather than diminishing their reputation as writers, seem to have added to their romantic image.

23. *Seitō* was the first female-edited journal to serve as a significant conduit for women's writing. But even *Seitō* was beholden, at least in its early years, to its male mentor, Ikuta Chōkō, and soon was diverted by political issues. Hence *Nyonin geijutsu*, inaugurated in 1929, probably should be viewed as the first fully female literary enterprise.

24. For a lively account of this tug-of-war see Danly, *Shade of Spring Leaves*, pp. 151–158.

25. Okonogi, "Keishū shōsetsu wo yomu," p. 10.

26. "Hakubun hatsuda, 'Keishū shōsetsu,'" *Jogaku zasshi* 417 (December 25, 1895):28–29.

27. Quoted in Dale Spender, *The Writing or the Sex? Or Why You Don't Have to Read Women's Writing to Know It's No Good* (New York: Teachers College Press, 1989), p. 121.

28. "Keishū shōsetsu," *Teikoku bungaku* 2(1) (1896):110.

29. The problem with the limited samplings offered by the standard collections, such as *Meiji bungaku zenshū*, is that the selection of "representative" works for these

women skews their achievements or ignores works that, while not representative, clearly surpass those selected. Although the families of a few of the *keishū* writers have collected their works and published them in private volumes, these collections are neither well circulated nor easy to obtain.

30. As quoted in Keene, *Dawn to the West*, vol. 1, p. 178.

31. Nishikawa Yūko in a *taidan* with Ueno Chizuko, "Feminizumu hihyō to wa nani ka," *Gunzō* (January 1993):361.

32. Seki Reiko, *Ane no chikara: Higuchi Ichiyō* (Chikuma raiburarii, 1993), p. 141.

33. "Surely one or two of Ichiyō's works will remain for future generations as masterpieces of the Japanese literary tradition. But even so, she was not a 'great writer.'" See Shioda, *Shintei Meiji joryū sakka ron*, p. 37.

34. Setouchi Harumi, "Joryū sakka ni naru jōken," in *Kaku koto* (Kawade bunko, 1990), pp. 20–26.

35. For a reading of one modern woman writer's strategy to overcome the pressure of "femininity," see Rebecca Copeland, "The Made-Up Author: Writer as Woman in the Works of Uno Chiyo," *Journal of the Association of Teachers of Japanese* 29(1) (1995):3–25.

Bibliography

All Japanese-language texts were published in Tokyo unless indicated otherwise.

Akiyama Shun. "Ima joryū bungaku to wa nani ka: sengo shi to no kanren de." *Kokubungaku: kaishaku to kyōzai no kenkyū* 15 (December 1980):124–127.

Aoyama Nao, et al. *Jogaku zasshi shosakuin.* Keiō tsūshin, 1970.

Ardis, Ann. *New Women, New Novels: Feminism and Early Modernism.* New Brunswick: Rutgers University Press, 1990.

Ariga, Chieko. "Text Versus Commentary: Struggles Over the Cultural Meanings of 'Woman.'" In *The Woman's Hand: Gender and Theory in Japanese Women's Writing,* ed. Paul Gordon Schalow and Janet A. Walker. Stanford: Stanford University Press, 1996.

"'Asamashi no sugata' wo yomite." *Bungei kurabu* (April 1895):212–213.

Bacon, Alice Mabel. *Japanese Girls and Women.* Rev. ed. Boston: Houghton Mifflin, 1902.

Barthes, Roland. *Image Music Text.* Translated by Stephen Heath. New York: Hill & Wang, 1977.

Bernstein, Gail Lee, ed. *Recreating Japanese Women, 1600–1945.* Berkeley: University of California Press, 1991.

Birnbaum, Phyllis. *Rabbits, Crabs, Etc.: Stories by Japanese Women Writers.* Honolulu: University of Hawai'i Press, 1983.

Bixler, Phyllis. *Frances Hodgson Burnett.* Boston: Twayne, 1984.

Booth, Eugene S. "Foreword." In *In Memory of Mrs. Kashi Iwamoto,* ed. Iwamoto Yoshiharu. Ryūkei shosha, 1981. First published by Yokohama seishi bunsha in 1896.

Braisted, William Reynolds, trans. *Meiroku zasshi.* Assisted by Adachi Yasushi and Kikuchi Yūji. Cambridge, Mass.: Harvard University Press, 1976.

Brownstein, Michael. "*Jogaku Zasshi* and the Founding of Bungakukai." *Monumenta Nipponica* 35(3) (1980):319–336.

Buckley, Sandra, ed. *Broken Silence: Voices of Japanese Feminism.* Berkeley: University of California Press, 1997.

"*Bungei kurabu* no daisekkei." *Seinen bun* 2(4) (1895):15.

"*Bungei kurabu* no daishichi hen." *Seinen bun* 2(2) (1895):12–13.

Burnett, Frances Hodgson. *Little Lord Fauntleroy.* New York: Dell,1990.

Cary, Otis. *A History of Christianity in Japan: Protestant Missions.* New York: Revell, 1909.

Christ, Carol T. "'The Hero as Man of Letters': Masculinity and Victorian Nonfiction Prose." In *Victorian Sages and Cultural Discourse: Renegotiating Gender and Power,* ed. Thais E. Morgan. New Brunswick: Rutgers University Press, 1990.

Copeland, Edwin Luther. "The Crisis of Protestant Missions to Japan, 1889–1900." Ph.D. dissertation, Yale University, 1947.

Copeland, Rebecca. "Broken Rings and Broken Brushes: The Broken Dreams of a Modern Murasaki." *GA/ZOKU Dynamics in Japanese Literature: Proceedings of the Midwest Association for Japanese Literary Studies* 3 (1997):242–260.

———. "The Made-Up Author: Writer as Woman in the Works of Uno Chiyo." *Journal of the Association of Teachers of Japanese* 29(1) (1995):3–25.

———. "The Meiji Woman Writer 'Amidst a Forest of Beards.'" *Harvard Journal of Asiatic Studies* 57(2) (1997):383–418.

———. "Motherhood as Institution." *Japan Quarterly* (January–March 1992): 101–110.

———. "Shimizu Shikin's 'The Broken Ring': A Narrative of Female Awakening." *Review of Japanese Culture and Society* 6 (1994):38–47.

Danly, Robert. *In the Shade of Spring Leaves: The Writings of Higuchi Ichiyō, a Woman of Letters in Meiji Japan.* New Haven: Yale University Press, 1981.

de Bary, Brett. "Introduction to Special Issue: Gender and Imperialism." *U.S.-Japan Women's Journal, English Supplement* 12 (1997):3–16.

Derrida, Jacques. "Des Tours de Babel." Translated by Joseph F. Graham. In *Difference in Translation,* ed. Joseph F. Graham. Ithaca: Cornell University Press, 1985.

Ericson, Joan. "The Origins of the Concept of 'Women's Literature.'" In *The Woman's Hand: Gender and Theory in Japanese Women's Writing,* ed. Paul Gordon Schalow and Janet A. Walker. Stanford: Stanford University Press, 1996.

———. *Be a Woman: Hayashi Fumiko and Modern Japanese Women's Literature.* Honolulu: University of Hawai'i Press, 1997.

Ezell, Margaret J. M. *Writing Women's Literary History.* Baltimore: Johns Hopkins University Press, 1993.

Friedman, Susan Stanford. "Weavings: Intertextuality and the (Re)Birth of the Author." In *Influence and Intertextuality in Literary History,* ed. Jay Clayton and Eric Rothstein. Madison: University of Wisconsin Press, 1991.

Fujii, James A. *Complicit Fictions: The Subject in the Modern Japanese Prose Narrative.* Berkeley: University of California Press, 1993.

Fujimura-Fanselow, Kumiko, and Atsuko Kameda, eds. *Japanese Women: New Feminist Perspectives on the Past, Present, and Future.* New York: Feminist Press, 1995.

Fujita Yoshimi. *Meiji jogakkō no sekai.* Seieisha, 1984.

Furuhi, Yoshiko. *The White Plum—A Biography of Ume Tsuda: Pioneer in the Higher Education of Japanese Women.* New York: Weatherhill, 1991.

Gilbert, Sandra, and Susan Gubar. "Tradition and the Female Talent." In *The Poetics of Gender,* ed. Nancy K. Miller. New York: Columbia University Press, 1986.

Gluck, Carol. *Japan's Modern Myths: Ideology in the Late Meiji Period.* Princeton: Princeton University Press, 1985.

Gorsky, Susan Rubinow. *Femininity to Feminism: Women and Literature in the Nineteenth Century.* New York: Twayne, 1992.

Gotō Chūgai. "Keishū shōsetsu wo yomu." *Waseda bungaku* (January 1896):30–33.

"Hakubun hatsuda 'keishū shōsetsu.'" *Jogaku zasshi* 417 (December 25, 1895):28–29.

Harrington, Ann. "Women and Higher Education in the Japanese Empire (1885–1945)." *Journal of Asian History* 21 (1987):169–186.

Hansen, Elizabeth, and Yukiko Tanaka, eds. *This Kind of Woman: Ten Stories by Japanese Women Writers.* Stanford: Stanford University Press, 1982.

Harrison, Marianne. "The Rise of the Woman Novelist in Meiji Japan." Ph.D. dissertation, University of Chicago, 1991.

Hirsch, Marianne. *The Mother/Daughter Plot: Narrative, Psychoanalysis, Feminism.* Bloomington: Indiana University Press, 1989.

Honda Hayao. "Wakamatsu Shizuko no 'Wasuregatami' kangai." *Fukushima jogakkō tanki daigaku kenkyū kiyō* 17 (1988):1–9.

Hopper, Helen. *A New Woman of Japan: A Political Biography of Katō Shidzue.* Boulder: Westview, 1996.

Huffman, James. *Politics of the Meiji Press: The Life of Fukuchi Gen'ichiro.* Honolulu: University of Hawai'i Press, 1980.

Hunter, Janet, ed. *Japanese Women Working.* New York: Routledge, 1993.

Ikebukuro Kiyokaze. "Joshi no bungaku." *Jogaku zasshi* 158 (April 20, 1889):424–425.

———. "Joshi no bungaku (sono ni)." *Jogaku zasshi* 159 (April 27, 1889):447–449.

Imai Yasuko. "Shimizu Shikin *Koware yubiwa.*" In *Tanpen josei bungaku kindai,* ed. Imai Yasuko et al. Ōfūsha, 1987.

Inoue, Mariko. "Kiyokata's *Asazusa*: The Emergence of the *Jogakusei* Image." *Monumenta Nipponica* 51(4) (1997):431–460.

Inoue Teruko. "Iwamoto Yoshiharu no bungakuron." *Bungaku* 37 (October 1969):97–110.

Ishibashi Ningetsu. "*Yabu no uguisu* no saihyō." *Kokumin no tomo* (August 1888):34–36.

Ishibashi Shian. "*Yabu no uguisu* no saihyō wo yomu." *Kokumin no tomo* (August 1888):35–37.

Ishimoto, Shidzué. *Facing Two Ways: The Story of My Life*. New York: Farrar & Rinehart, 1935.

Isozaki Yoshiji. "Wakamatsu Shizuko to Iwamoto Yoshiharu." In *Wakamatsu Shizuko: Fumetsu no shōgai*. Kyōeisha, 1977.

Iwamoto Kashi. "Children's Department." *Japan Evangelist* 2(3) (1895):169–173.

———. "Women's Department." *Japan Evangelist* 1(6) (1895):329–334.

Iwamoto Yoshiharu. "Bunshō no risō." *Jogaku zasshi* 152 (March 9, 1889):243–248.

———. *In Memory of Mrs. Kashi Iwamoto*. Ryūkei shosha, 1981. First published by Yokohama seishi bunsha in 1896.

———. "Joryū shōsetsu no honshoku." *Jogaku zasshi* 153 (March 16, 1889):269–273.

———. "Joshi to bunpitsu no gyō, dai ichi." *Jogaku zasshi* 79 (October 8, 1887):161–163.

———. "Joshi to bunpitsu no gyō, dai ni: shinbun, zasshi onna kisha no koto." *Jogaku zasshi* 80 (October 15, 1887):181–184.

———. "Joshi to shōsetsu, dai ichi." *Jogaku zasshi* 27 (June 25, 1886):241–243.

———. "Kan'in no kūki." *Jogaku zasshi* 65 (May 21, 1887):81–83.

———. "Nihon no kazoku—dai shichi: ikkazoku no nyo ō." *Jogaku zasshi* 102 (March 24, 1888):23–27.

———. "Nyoshi to shōsetsu, dai ni." *Jogaku zasshi* 29 (July 15, 1886):274–275.

———. "Nyoshi to shōsetsu, dai san." *Jogaku zasshi* 32 (August 15, 1886):22–24.

Jansen, Marius B., and Gilbert Rozman, eds. *Japan in Transition from Tokugawa to Meiji*. Princeton: Princeton University Press, 1986.

Jones, Ann Rosalind. "Surprising Fame: Renaissance Gender Ideologies and Women's Lyric." In *The Poetics of Gender*, ed. Nancy K. Miller. New York: Columbia University Press, 1986.

Karatani Kōjin. "The Discovery of Interiority." Translated by Brett de Bary. In *Origins of Modern Japanese Literature*, ed. Brett de Bary. Durham: Duke University Press, 1993.

Kasza, Gregory. *The State and the Mass Media in Japan: 1918–1945*. Berkeley: University of California Press, 1988.

Katada Fujio. "*Yabu no uguisu*, Ichiyō, Tōsui." *Kokugo to kokubungaku* (August 1934): 258–261.

Keene, Donald. *Dawn to the West: Japanese Literature of the Modern Era—Fiction*. New York: Holt, 1984.

———. *Dawn to the West: Japanese Literature of the Modern Era—Poetry, Drama, Criticism*. New York: Holt, 1984.

"Keishū shōsetsu." *Seinen bun* 2(6) (1896):19–20.

"Keishū shōsetsu." *Teikoku bungaku* 2(1) (1896):110.

"Keishū shōsetsu wo yomite." *Kokumin no tomo* (January 11, 1896):34–36.

Kitada Sachie. "Joken to bungaku no aida—Kozai Shikin ron." *Hoppō bungei* (August 1984):8–27.

Kitada Usurai. "Asamashi no sugata." *Bungei kurabu* (March 1895):230–233.

"Kitamura Tōkoku." *Kindai bungaku kenkyū gyosho*, 2. Shōwa joshi daigaku kindai bunka kenkyū jō, 1979.

Ko, Dorothy. *Teachers of the Inner Chambers: Women and Culture in Seventeenth-Century China*. Stanford: Stanford University Press, 1994.

Koganei Kimiko. "Keishū shōsetsuka tō: dai ichi—Koganei Kimi joshi." *Jogaku zasshi* 205 (March 22, 1890):127–128.

Komashaku Kimi. "Shikin shōron—josei gaku tekina apurōchi." In *Shikin zenshū*, ed. Kozai Yoshishige. Sōdō bunka, 1983.

Kornicki, Peter. *The Reform of Fiction in Meiji Japan*. London: Ithaca Press, 1982.

Kosaka Masaaki. *Japanese Thought in the Meiji Era*. Tokyo: Pan Pacific Press, 1958.

Kozai Yoshishige. "Meiji no onna—Shimizu Shikin no koto." In *Shikin zenshū*, ed. Kozai Yoshishige. Sōdō bunka, 1977.

Kunikida Doppo. "Joshi to hon'yaku no koto." In *Kunikida Doppo zenshū* 1. Gakushū kenyūsha, 1965.

Kuzume, Yoshi. "Images of Japanese Women in U.S. Writings and Scholarly Works, 1860–1990: Formation and Transformation of Stereotypes." *U.S.-Japan Women's Journal, English Supplement* 1 (1991):3–47.

Laski, Marghanita. *Mrs. Ewing, Mrs. Molesworth, and Mrs. Hodgson Burnett*. London: Arthur Barker, 1950.

Lillehoj, Elizabeth. *Woman in the Eyes of Man: Images of Women in Japanese Art from the Field Museum*. Chicago: DePaul University Publications, 1995.

Lippit, Noriko Mizuta, and Kyoko Selden. *Stories by Contemporary Japanese Women Writers*. New York: Sharpe, 1983.

Marcus, Marvin. *Paragons of the Ordinary: The Biographical Literature of Mori Ōgai*. Honolulu: University of Hawai'i Press, 1993.

Miller, J. Scott. "Tsubouchi Shōyō (1859–1935)." In *Japanese Fiction Writers,*

1868–1945, ed. Van C. Gessel. *Dictionary of Literary Biography,* vol. 180. Detroit: Gale Research, 1997.

Mitchell, Richard H. *Censorship in Imperial Japan.* Princeton: Princeton University Press, 1983.

Mitsutani, Margaret. "Higuchi Ichiyō: A Literature of Her Own." *Comparative Literature Studies* 22 (1985):53–66.

———. "A Mirror for Womanhood." *The Magazine* 3(5) (1988):30–55.

Miyake Kaho. "Watashi no ayunde kita michi—omoide no hitobito." *Fujin kōron* (April 1939):106–122.

———. *Yabu no uguisu.* In *Gendai Nihon bungaku taikei* 5. Chikuma shobō, 1972.

———. "Yukishi san saien no tomo: Akebono joshi, Wakamatsu Shizuko joshi, Ichiyō joshi." In *Ichiyō no omoide,* ed. Yoshida Seiichi. Nihon tosho sentā, 1984.

Miyamoto Yuriko. *"Yabu no uguisu."* In *Gendai Nihon bungaku taikei* 5. Chikuma shobō, 1972.

Monteith, Moira. *Women's Writing: A Challenge to Theory.* New York: St. Martin's Press, 1986.

Morita Shiken. *"Shōkōshi* wo yomu." *Jogaku zasshi* 292 (1891): Supplement.

Mulhern, Chieko. "Hani Motoko." In *Heroic with Grace: Legendary Women of Japan,* ed. Chieko Mulhern. New York: Sharpe, 1991.

Murakami-Yokota, Takayuki. *Don Juan East and West.* New York: SUNY Press, 1998.

———. "Lovers in Disguise: A Feature of Romantic Love in Meiji Literature." *Comparative Literature Studies* 28(3) (1991):213–233.

Nagamatsu Fusako. "Josei ni totte no Meiji—Shimizu Shikin no baai." *Hōsei daigakuin kiyō* 5 (1980):39–57.

Nagy, Margit Maria. "'How Shall We Live?': Social Change, the Family Institution, and Feminism in Prewar Japan." Ph.D. dissertation, University of Washington, 1981.

Nakayama Akihiro. "Sakka no shōzō no saihensei." *Bungaku* 4(3) (1993):24–37.

Nishida Taketoshi. *Meiji jidai no shinbun to zasshi.* Shinbundō, 1966.

Nishikawa Yūko and Ueno Chizuko. "Feminizumu hihyō to wa nani ka." *Gunzō* (January 1993):357–379.

Nogami Yaeko. *Mori.* In *Nogami Yaeko zenshū, dai ni ki* 28. Iwanami shoten, 1991.

Noheiji Kiyoe. *"Jogakusei* hakuhyō *Jogaku zasshi* ron no nagare no naka ni mita." *Bungaku* 47 (April 1979):15–27.

Nolte, Sharon H., and Sally Ann Hastings. "The Meiji State's Policy toward Women, 1890–1910." In *Recreating Japanese Women, 1600–1945,* ed. Gail Lee Bernstein. Berkeley: University of California Press, 1991.

Oguri Fūyō, et al. "Joryū sakka ron." *Shinchō* (May 1908):6–11.

Okonogi Hideno (Shin'ichirō). "Keishū shōsetsu wo yomu." *Jogaku zasshi* 418 (January 25, 1896):10–14.

Ōta Saburō. "*Jogaku zasshi* kenkyū 1." *Shomotsu tenbō* 17 (1) (May 1950):21–27.

———. "*Jogaku zasshi* kenkyū 2." *Shomotsu tenbō* 17(2) (August 1950):14–19.

———. "*Jogaku zasshi* kenkyū 3." *Shomotsu tenbō* 18(1) (January 1951):11–16.

Ozaki Kōyō. "Musume hakase." In *Kōyō zenshū* 1. Iwanami shoten, 1994.

Pierson, John. *Tokutomi Sohō, 1863–1957: A Journalist for Modern Japan*. Princeton: Princeton University Press, 1980.

Procter, Adelaide Anne. "The Sailor Boy." In *Legends and Lyrics Together with a Chaplet of Verses*. London: Oxford University Press, 1914.

Rich, Adrienne. *Of Woman Born: Motherhood as Experience and Institution*. New York: Norton, 1986.

Robertson, Jennifer. "The Shingaku Woman: Straight from the Heart." In *Recreating Japanese Women, 1600–1945*, ed. Gail Lee Bernstein. Berkeley: University of California Press, 1991.

Rose, Barbara. *Tsuda Umeko and Women's Education in Japan*. New Haven: Yale University Press, 1992.

Rowley, G.G. "Literary Canon and National Identity: *The Tale of Genji* in Meiji Japan." *Japan Forum* 9(1) (1997):1–15.

Rubin, Jay. *Injurious to Public Morals: Writers and the Meiji State*. Seattle: University of Washington Press, 1984.

Russ, Joanna. *How to Suppress Women's Writing*. Austin: University of Texas Press, 1983.

Ryan, Marleigh Grayer. *The Development of Realism in the Fiction of Tsubouchi Shōyō*. Seattle: University of Washington Press, 1975.

———. *Japan's First Modern Novel: "Ukigumo" of Futabatei Shimei*. Ann Arbor: University of Michigan Press, 1965.

Sansom, George B. *The Western World and Japan: A Study in the Interaction of European and Asiatic Cultures*. Tokyo: Tuttle, 1950.

Sasabuchi Tomoichi. "Shimizu Shikin ron." In *Meiji Taishō bungaku no bunseki*. Meiji shoinkan, 1970.

Satō Michimasa. "Wakamatsu Shizuko." In *Nihon jidō bungaku no seiritsu josetsu*. Yamato shobō, 1985.

Schalow, Paul Gordon, and Janet A. Walker, eds. *The Woman's Hand: Gender and Theory in Japanese Women's Writing*. Stanford: Stanford University Press, 1996.

Seidensticker, Edward. *Low City, High City: Tokyo from Edo to the Earthquake.* New York: Knopf, 1983.

Seki Reiko. *Ane no chikara: Higuchi Ichiyō.* Chikuma raiburarii, 1993.

———. *Kataru onnatachi no jidai: Ichiyō to Meiji josei hyōgen.* Shin'yōsha, 1997.

Seki Ryōichi. "*Yabu no uguisu.*" *Kokubungaku* 13(5) (1968):17–20.

Setouchi Harumi. *Kaku koto.* Kawade bunko, 1990.

Sherif, Ann. *Mirror: The Fiction and Essays of Kōda Aya.* Honolulu: University of Hawai'i Press, 1999.

Shioda Ryōhei. *Shintei Meiji joryū sakka ron.* Bunsendō shuppan, 1983.

Shimada Tarō. "Wakamatsu Shizuko yaku *Shōkōshi* no seiritsu." In *Kindai Nihon no hon'yaku bunka,* ed. Kamei Shunsuke. Chūō kōronsha, 1994.

Shimizu Shikin. *Shikin zenshū,* ed. Kozai Yoshishige. Sōdō bunka, 1983.

Shively, Donald H. "Japanization of the Middle Meiji." In *Tradition and Modernization in Japanese Culture,* ed. Donald H. Shively. Princeton: Princeton University Press, 1971.

"Shōsetsuka toshite no josei." *Teikoku bungaku* 2(2) (1896):91–92.

Sievers, Sharon. *Flowers in the Salt: The Beginnings of Feminist Consciousness in Modern Japan.* Stanford: Stanford University Press, 1983.

Sōma Kokkō. *Meiji shōki no san josei.* Kosei kaku, 1940.

———. *Mokui—Meiji, Taishō bungakushi kaisō.* Hōsei Daigaku shuppankyoku, 1961.

Spender, Dale. *The Writing or the Sex? Or Why You Don't Have to Read Women's Writing to Know It's No Good.* New York: Teachers College Press, 1989.

Suda Chisato. "Kodomogatari—Meiji Nijūnendai ichininshō shōsetsu ippan." *Bungaku* 9(2) (1998):47–56.

Suzuki Fumio. "Wakamatsu Shizuko to *Jogaku zasshi* 2." *Ferris ronsō* 9 (April 1964):1–32.

Suzuki, Tomi. *Narrating the Self: Fictions of Japanese Modernity.* Stanford: Stanford University Press, 1996.

Takada Chinami. "'Koware yubiwa' to 'Kono ko.'" *Nihon kindai bungaku* 47 (October 1992):13–28.

Takahashi Masatoshi. "*Shōkōshi* no hyōka—'Shizuko' no risō to bunshō hyōgen wo chūshin ni." In *Jidō bungaku.* Yūseidō, 1977. First published in *Nihon bungaku kenkyū* 9 (1969).

Takeda Kiyoko. "Shimizu Shikin no *Imin gakuen*: Kirisutokyō to jiyūminken to no aida." In *Dochaku to Haikyō.* Shinkyō shuppansha, 1967.

Takita, Yoshiko. "Wakamatsu Shizuko and *Little Lord Fauntleroy.*" *Comparative Literature Studies* 22 (1985):1–8.

Tanaka, Yukiko, ed. *To Live and to Write: Selections by Japanese Women Writers 1913–1938.* Seattle: Seal Press, 1987.

Tanaka, Yukiko. *Unmapped Territories: New Women's Fiction from Japan.* Seattle: Women in Translation, 1991.

Tansman, Alan. *The Writings of Kōda Aya, a Japanese Literary Daughter.* New Haven: Yale University Press, 1993.

Tazawa Inafune. "Godaidō." In *Meiji joryū bungakushū,* pt. 1, *Meiji bungaku zenshū* 81. Chikuma shobō, 1966.

Thwaite, Ann. *Waiting for the Party: The Life of Frances Hodgson Burnett 1849–1924.* London: Secker & Warburg, 1974.

Todoroki Eiko. *Kitada Usurai kenkyū.* Sōbunsha, 1984.

Torrance, Richard. *The Fiction of Tokuda Shūsei and the Emergence of Japan's New Middle Class.* Seattle: University of Washington Press, 1994.

Tsuruta Kin'ya. *Akutagawa, Kawabata, Mishima, Abe—gendai Nihon bungaku sakuhinron.* Ōfūsha, 1973.

———. *Kawabata Yasunari no geijutsu.* Meiji shoin, 1981.

Twine, Nanette. "The Genbunitchi Movement: Its Origin, Development, and Conclusion." *Monumenta Nipponica* 33(3) (1978):333–356.

Ubukata Toshirō. "Joryū sakka no mure." *Bunshō sekai* (January 1914):294–301.

Uchida Fuchian (Roan). "'Koware yubiwa' wo yonde." *Jogaku zasshi* 249 (1891): 652–653.

Ueno Chizuko. "In the Feminine Guise: A Trap of Reverse Orientalism." In *U.S.-Japan Women's Journal, English Supplement* 13 (1997):3–25.

Umezawa Toshihiko. *Bungaku no naka no hisabetsu burakuzō, senzen hen.* Akashi shoten, 1980.

Uno, Kathleen. "One Day at a Time: Work and Domestic Activities of Urban Lower-Class Women in Early Twentieth-Century Japan." In *Japanese Women Working,* ed. Janet Hunter. New York: Routledge, 1993.

Vernon, Victoria V. *Daughters of the Moon: Wish, Will, and Social Constraint in Fiction by Modern Japanese Women.* Berkeley: Institute of East Asian Studies, University of California, 1988.

Wada Shigejirō. *Meiji zenki joryū sakuhinron—Higuchi Ichiyō to sono zengo.* Ōfūsha, 1989.

———. *"Yabu no uguisu* no shiron." *Ronkyū Nihon bungaku* (June 1959):1–8.

Wakamatsu Shizuko. "The Bridal Veil." *Jogaku zasshi* 172 (July 28, 1889):401.

———. "The Condition of Woman in Japan." *Jogaku zasshi* 98 (February 2, 1888): supplement.

————. "Keishū shōsetsu ka tō dai san: Wakamatsu Shizuko." *Jogaku zasshi* 207 (April 5, 1890):188–189.

————. "Nogiku." *Jogaku zasshi* 183 (October 5, 1889):182–183.

————. "Omukō no hanare." *Gendai Nihon bungaku taikei* 5. Chikuma shobō, 1972.

————. *Shōkōshi. Meiji bungaku zenshū* 32. Chikuma shobō, 1973.

————. "*Shōkōshi* no jo." *Jogaku zasshi* 288 (October 24, 1891):329–330.

————. "Sumire." *Jogaku zasshi* 183 (October 19, 1889):215–217; 184 (October 26, 1889):245–247; 186 (November 9, 1889):304–307; 187 (November 16, 1889): 335–338.

————. "Tama no koshi." *Jogaku zasshi* 195 (January 11, 1890):558.

————. "Wasuregatami." *Jogaku zasshi* 194 (January 1, 1890):12–18.

Waley, Arthur. *The Pillow Book of Sei Shōnagon*. London: Allen & Unwin, 1928.

Watanabe Naomi. *Nihon kindai bungaku to sabetsu*. Ota shuppan, 1994.

Watanabe Sumiko. "Shimizu Shikin 'Koware yubiwa.'" *Nihon bungaku* (March 1980): 74–80.

————. "Shimizu Shikin ron—Meiji nijūnendai zenki shōsetsu 'Koware yubiwa' no imi." *Shinshū shirakaba* (April 1983):306–321.

Yamaguchi Reiko. "Kozai Shikin no koto." *Bungaku* 43 (September 1975):116–122.

————. *Naite aisuru shimai ni tsugu: Kozai Shikin no shōgai*. Sōdō bunka, 1977.

————. *Tokuto ware wo mitamae: Wakamatsu Shizuko no shōgai*. Shinchōsha, 1980.

Yamamoto Masahide. "Wakamatsu Shizuko no hon'yaku shōsetsu genbun itchi bun no shiteki igi." *Senshū kokubun* 14 (September 1973):23–54.

Yanagida Izumi. "*Jogaku zasshi*." *Bungaku* (January 1955):28–32.

Yoshida Seiichi, ed. *Ichiyō no omoide*. Nihon tosho sentā, 1984.

Index

Page numbers in *italic* refer to illustrations.

About the Author

Rebecca L. Copeland is associate professor of Japanese Language and Literature at Washington University in St. Louis. Born to missionary parents in Fukuoka, Japan, she was raised in North Carolina. Dr. Copeland has a B.A. from St. Andrews College in Laurinburg, North Carolina, and a Ph.D. from Columbia University. She is the author of *The Sound of the Wind: The Life and Works of Uno Chiyo* as well as a variety of translations and essays on Japanese women writers. Currently she resides in University City, Missouri, with her husband and three German shepherds.